T0330487

TOURISM AND HOSPITALITY

Issues and Developments

TOURISM AND HOSPITALITY

Issues and Developments

Edited by
Jaime A. Seba

Apple Academic Press

TORONTO   NEW JERSEY

© 2012 by
Apple Academic Press Inc.
3333 Mistwell Crescent
Oakville, ON L6L 0A2
Canada

Apple Academic Press Inc.
9 Spinnaker Way
Waretown, NJ 08758
USA

First issued in paperback 2021

Exclusive worldwide distribution by CRC Press, a Taylor & Francis Group

ISBN 13: 978-1-77463-228-4 (pbk)
ISBN 13: 978-1-926692-91-3 (hbk)

Library and Archives Canada Cataloguing in Publication

Tourism and hospitality: issues and development/Jaime A. Seba, editor.

Includes index.
ISBN 978-1-926692-91-3
1. Tourism–Management. 2. Hospitality industry. I. Seba, Jaime

G155.A1T635 2011   338.4'791   C2011-905425-6

Apple Academic Press also publishes its books in a variety of electronic formats. Some content that appears in print may not be available in electronic format. For information about Apple Academic Press products, visit our website at **www.appleacademicpress.com**

Preface

All over the world, technological advances are being made at the speed of light, and the hospitality and tourism industry is growing and changing just as quickly. Customers can get a special rate when they follow a hotel on Twitter. They can book tour reservations online with a simple click. Cruise destinations around the world can be explored without leaving home, and bloggers on different continents share dining recommendations. Travelers can even plan a vacation that allows them to commune with nature while printing e-mails from their smartphones.

In order to stay competitive in an international market, businesses must adjust to these emerging social trends and respond to the ever-changing needs of their customers. The traditional focus on customer service and guest loyalty has become intertwined with rapidly progressing technological enhancements influencing all areas of the industry, including sales, marketing, human resources, and revenue and asset management. The result is a visitor experience personalized to each specific guest, through strategic data collection, market trend research, and the capabilities of integrated online self-service. This means knowing what matters most to consumers and recognizing emerging innovations that will be the next big thing for the next generation of customers.

One such movement is the worldwide recognition of the need for environmentally friendly "green" initiatives, which are becoming significantly reflected in the hospitality industry. There has been an increased interest in ecotourism and sustainable tourism, which provide travelers with destinations and activities that have a lower negative impact on the environment. This trend is evidenced by the growing prevalence of green conferences that attract everyone from hotel general managers and tour operators to the tourists themselves. Ecotourism, responsible tourism, jungle tourism, and sustainable development have become prevalent concepts since the late 1980s, and ecotourism has experienced arguably the fastest growth of all sub-sectors in the tourism industry. The popularity represents a change in tourist perceptions, increased environmental awareness, and a desire to explore natural environments.

Health issues are another growing concern within the hospitality and tourism industry How do local health concerns impact tourists to other countries? How do tourist sites impact local health? The answers to these two questions cannot be separated from one another, since they intertwine. Tourists must be protected from disease exposure, while local populations must be equally protected from the possible negative impacts on health created by a resort or other tourist destination.

We live in an interconnected world today, and this reality has enormous bearing on the hospitality and tourism industry. Considering these impact and meaningful trends, the future of the industry will depend on a skilled workforce that can react quickly to rapid changes at the forefront of global culture.

— **Jaime A. Seba**

List of Contributors

Eugene J. Aniah
Department of Geography and Regional Planning, University of Calabar, Calabar, Nigeria.

Doug Arbogast
Travel Green Appalachia, R. A. Hobbs, Ansted, WV, USA.

Abrisham Aref
Department of Social Science, Tehran Education, Ministry of Education, Iran.

Fariborz Aref
Department of Social and Development Sciences, Faculty of Human Ecology, Putra University, Malaysia.

Ian Bateman
CSERGE, School of Environmental Sciences, University of East Anglia, Norwich, Norfolk, NR4 7TJ, UK.

Maureen Y. Bender
Division of Forestry and Natural Resources, West Virginia University, Morgantown, WV 26506-6125, USA.

Dennis M. Brown
Regional Economist, Economic Research Service, U.S. Department of Agriculture, 1800 M St., N.W., Room N2187, Washington, DC 20036, USA.

Christina Cameron
Director General of the National Historic Sites Directorate, Parks Canada.

Matthew M. Chew
Department of Sociology, Hong Kong Baptist University, Kowloon Tong, Kowloon, Hong Kong SAR, China.

Jinyang Deng
West Virginia University, WV, USA.

E. I. Eja
Department of Geography and Regional Planning, University of Calabar, Calabar, Nigeria.

Fard Teimouri S.
Department of forestry, Faculty of Natural Resources, University of Mazandaran, 10 km Sari-Neka Rd, P.O. box 737, Sari, Iran.

Wei Fei
College of Resources and Environment Science, Hebei Normal University, Shijazhuang 050016, China.

Sarjit S. Gill
Department of Social and Development Sciences, Faculty of Human Ecology, Putra University, Malaysia.

Manuela Guerreiro
Faculty of Economics, University of Algarve, 9, Campus de Gambelas, 8005-139 Faro, Portugal.

Cheryl M. Hargrove
The HTC Group, from St. Simons Island, Georgia, USA.

R. A. Hobbs
Ansted, WV, USA.

Zulkifli Ibrahim
Faculty of Hotel and Tourism Management, Universiti Teknologi MARA Shah Alam, 40450, Selangor, Malaysia.

Li Jin
College of Tourism Management, Tianjin University of Commerce, P.R. China, 300134.

Andy Jones
CSERGE, School of Environmental Sciences, University of East Anglia, Norwich, Norfolk, NR4 7TJ, UK.

Kamaruzaman Jusoff
Yale University, Yale Tropical Resources Institute, School of Forestry and Environmental Studies 205, Prospect St., New Haven, CT 06511, USA.

Latifi H.
Faculty of Forest and Environmental Studies, University of Freiburg, Freiburg, Germany.

Shen Li
School of International Tourism and Hospitality Management, Dalian University of Foreign Languages, Dalian 116002, China.

Yana Liu
College of Resources and Environment Science, Hebei Normal University, Shijazhuang 050016, China.

Júlio Mendes
Faculty of Economics, University of Algarve, 9, Campus de Gambelas, 8005-139 Faro, Portugal.

Oladi D.
Department of forestry, Faculty of Natural Resources, University of Mazandaran, 10 km Sari-Neka Rd, P.O. box 737, Sari, Iran.

Zulhan Othman
Faculty of Hotel and Tourism Management, Universiti Teknologi MARA, Shah Alam, 40450, Selangor, Malaysia.

Judith E. Otu
Department of Sociology, University of Calabar, Calabar, Nigeria.

Ma'rof Redzuan
Department of Social and Development Sciences, Faculty of Human Ecology, Putra University, Malaysia.

Marije Schaafsma
Institute for Environmental Studies (IVM), VU University Amsterdam, De Boelelaan 1087, 1081 HV, Amsterdam, The Netherlands.

Steve Selin
West Virginia University, WV, USA.

Hejiang Shen
College of Resources and Environment Science, Hebei Normal University, Shijazhuang 050016, China.

Masood H. Siddiqui
Faculty-Decision Sciences, Jaipuria Institute of Management, Vineet Khand, Gomtinagar, Lucknow-226010, India.

João Albino Silva
Faculty of Economics, University of Algarve 9, Campus de Gambelas, 8005-139 Faro, Portugal.

Sohrabi Saraj B.
Department of Forestry, Faculty of Natural Resources, University of Mazandaran, 10 km Sari-Neka Rd, P.O. box 737, Sari, Iran.

Gail Vander Stoep
Michigan State University, Michigan, USA.

Maimunah Sulaiman
Faculty of Hotel and Tourism Management, Universiti Teknologi MARA, Shah Alam, 40450, Selangor, Malaysia.

Shalini N. Tripathi
Faculty-Marketing, Jaipuria Institute of Management, Vineet Khand, Gomtinagar, Lucknow-226010, India.

M. A. Ushie
Department of Sociology, University of Calabar, Calabar, Nigeria.

Patricia Oom do Valle
Faculty of Economics, University of Algarve 9, Campus de Gambelas, 8005-139 Faro, Portugal.

Bin Wang
School of Management, Dalian University of Technology, Dalian 116024, China.

Craig Wiles
Public Sector Consultants, 600 W. Saint Joseph St., Suite 10, Lansing, MI 48933, USA.

Jan Wright
CSERGE, School of Environmental Sciences, University of East Anglia, Norwich, Norfolk, NR4 7TJ, UK.

Yachkaschi A.
Department of Forestry, Faculty of Natural Resources, University of Mazandaran, 10 km Sari-Neka Rd, P.O. box 737, Sari, Iran.

Zhang Ying
College of Resources and Environment Science, Hebei Normal University, Shijazhuang 050016, China.

Limei Yuan
College of Resources and Environment Science, Hebei Normal University, Shijazhuang 050016, China.

Mohd Salehuddin Zahari
Faculty of Hotel and Tourism Management, Universiti Teknologi MARA, Shah Alam, 40450, Selangor, Malaysia.

Liming Zhao
School of Management, Tianjin University, P.R. China, 300134.

List of Abbreviations

CATPCA	Categorical principal components analysis
CCB	Community capacity building
CHRO	Cultural Heritage and Recreation organization
CITS	Chinese International Travel Service
CJA	Conjoint analysis
CPD	Central Postcode Directory
CVBs	Convention and visitors bureaus
CVM	Contingent valuation method
DMOs	Destination marketing organizations
FBI	Federal Bureau of Investigation
FGD	Focus group discussion
FTAs	Foreign tourist arrivals
GDP	Gross domestic product
GIS	Geographical information system
HAL	History, arts and libraries
HPM	Hedonic pricing method
NAICS	North American Industry Classification System
OLSs	Ordinary least squares
OMB	Office of Management and Budget
PCA	Principal component analysis
PRM	Participatory research method
RMSEA	Root mean square residual of approximation
RMSR	Root mean square residual
RNCA	Ramsey Canyon Reserve and the San Pedro National Conservation Area
SEM	Structural equation modeling
SPSS	Statistical Package for Social Science
TCM	Travel cost method
TIA	Travel Industry Association of America
TTRA	Travel and Tourism Research Association
UiTM	Universiti Teknologi MARA
USTDC	United States Travel Data Center
VFR	Visiting friends and relative
WLS	Weighted least squares
WTP	Willingness to pay
WTTC	World Travel and Tourism council

Contents

Chapter 1

Tourism

National Park Service

INTRODUCTION

Greenways, rivers, and trails which attract visitors from outside the local area can stimulate the local economy. This chapter begins with examples stressing the importance of natural and cultural areas for attracting visitors, followed by examples showing how rivers, trails, and greenways can contribute to the travel and tourism sectors. The last section demonstrates how corridor projects can increase tourism appeal and marketing potential of a local community.

THE TRAVEL INDUSTRY

Travel and tourism is the leading employer in several states and has been predicted to be the leading industry in the US and the world by the year 2000. Travel is also a leading industry and source of jobs within regions and local communities, and is increasing in relative economic importance. Expenditures for travel and tourism impact transportation, lodging, eating establishments, retail, and service businesses. These expenditures support jobs, personal income, and government tax revenues.

- Travel industry employment for 1989 increased by nearly 3 million jobs from 1988. This employment includes air transportation, intercity highway travel, eating and drinking establishments, hotels and motels, and amusement and recreation services. The travel industry has continually out-performed the overall economy in creating new jobs. (U.S. Travel Data Center, 1989, 1990).

- In 1992, travel-generated visitor expenditures in California reached approximately $52.8 billion. These expenditures generated $938 million in local taxes, $2 billion in state taxes, 668,000 jobs, and $11.5 billion in payroll expenditures.

For purposes of this section, "travel and tourism-related expenditures" refer to those visits that originate from beyond the boundaries of your local economy. Typically, these are trips from at least 50 miles away and any trips which may involve an overnight stay. Expenditure patterns for visitors are usually higher than for local users.

A greenway, which provides local opportunities and enhances tourist draw, can be an important asset to your community. Recent trend analyses show that weekend trips to nearby areas are on the increase, while the traditional 2-week summer vacation is on the decline for today's travelers. This is due to the job complications of 2-income families, limited time budgets, interest in more specialized recreation experiences, increased mixing of personal and business travel, and year round schools.

NATURAL/CULTURAL AREAS ATTRACT TRAVELERS

Outdoor recreation, natural, historical, and cultural resources are increasingly important attractions for travelers. Ecotourism is an environmentally responsible form of travel in which the focus is to experience the natural areas and culture of a region while promoting conservation and economically contributing to local communities (Adventure Travel Society, 1994). Ecotourism is one of the fastest growing areas of the travel industry. According to the *Travel Industry World Yearbook*, in 1992 ecotourism comprised 10–20% of all travel (Bangs, 1992).

- A poll commissioned by the President's Commission on Americans Outdoors found that natural beauty was the single most important criterion for tourists in selecting a site for outdoor recreation (Scenic America, 1987).

- In a recent report, the governors of five New England states officially recognized open space as a key element in the "quality of life" in their region. They credited "quality of life" as providing the foundation of a multi-billion dollar tourism industry and bringing rapid economic growth to the region (Governor's Committee on the Environment, 1988).

- Ramsey Canyon Reserve and the San Pedro National Conservation Area (RNCA) in southern Arizona attract a significant number of visitors from outside the local area. Approximately two-thirds of the visitors to these sites are from outside of Arizona and approximately 5% are from the US. These visitors bring economic activity not only to southeastern Arizona, but to the state as a whole. The typical non-resident visitor to Ramsey Canyon spends $55/day in Sierra Vista, while a non-resident visitor to the San Pedro RNCA spends $51/day in Sierra Vista. The total economic impact in the Sierra Vista area associated with nature-based visitors to Ramsey Canyon and the San Pedro RNCA is estimated at nearly $3 million/year (Crandall et al., 1992).

- Several kayak outfitters have teamed up with environmental groups working to protect and enhance the quality of the San Francisco Bay in northern California. This cooperative effort has resulted in naturalist-lead kayak tours of the bay which raise funds for the effort to improve the ecological integrity of the bay (Sunset Magazine, 1994).

In 1988, 75% of all travel was for pleasure. Outdoor recreation and entertainment are growing in importance and accounted for 41% of pleasure travel, while 34% was attributed to visiting family and friends. Business travel accounted for 17% of all travel in 1988, with the remaining 8% attributed to personal and other reasons.

Travelers are also increasingly attracted to educational-oriented experiences provided by cultural and historic sites. Along with recreation and beautiful natural sites, tourists cite cultural heritage as one of three major reasons they travel to specific locations (U.S. Travel Data Center, 1991).

One of the fastest growing areas of tourism includes cultural and historic community festivals, events, and competitions. This will be a boon to community-based tourism. Greenways and trails can provide a link between historic and cultural sites. For example, the Azalea Trail in Mobile, Alabama, serves as a city beautification project and attracts tourists. Because preservation of these historic sites serves as a stimulus for tourism, there can also be significant impacts to the local economy.

- A 1993 study by the Travel Industry of Association of America shows that 35% of 1500 respondents intended to visit an historic site while on vacation. A separate study notes that visitors stay a half-day longer and spend $62 more at historic sites than at other locations (Wall Street Journal, 1993).
- In less than a decade, the establishment of Lowell NHS in Massachusetts, spurred the economic renewal of a repressed economy. The city of Lowell is prosperous and vibrant today. Investment by the public sector has totaled $122.7 million (including $18.7 million from the National Park Service to establish the National Historic Site.) For every $1 of public investment there has been a total private investment/return of $7 (Cassandra Walter, Superintendent Lowell National Historic Park, 1989).

ATTRIBUTING EXPENDITURES TO RIVERS, TRAILS, AND GREENWAYS

Greenways, rivers, and trails can have varied levels of tourist draw. They can be travel destinations in themselves, encourage area visitors to extend their stay in the area or enhance business and pleasure visits. The "level of tourist draw" determines the appropriate proportion of the visitor's time and travel expenditures that can be attributed to the greenway. If visitors extend their trip an extra night to visit a greenway, the additional night's lodging and meals can be attributed to the greenway.

- San Antonio Riverwalk is considered the anchor of the tourism industry in San Antonio, Texas. Tourism is the second largest economic sector in the city, accounting for $1.2 billion annually. An auto survey concluded that the Riverwalk is the second most important tourist attraction in the state of Texas (Richard Hurd, SanAntonio Department of Parks and Recreation).
- In 1988, users of the Elroy-Sparta Trail in Wisconsin averaged expenditures of $25.14/day for trip-related expenses. Total 1988 trail user expenditures were over $1.2 million. Approximately 50% of the users were from out-of-state, and the typical user traveled 228 miles to get to the trail (Schwecke et al., 1989).
- In Montana, an estimated 75,000 visitors to the upper Missouri Wild and Scenic River, and Lewis and Clark National Historic Trail, contribute $750,000 annually to the economy of the area around the 149 mile river corridor (Bureau of Land Management, 1987).
- Once trail construction is complete along Sonoita Creek in Patagonia State Park, near Nogales, AZ, the trail is projected to bring $150,000 into the area from increased visitation. The Arizona State Parks Board purchased seven square miles of riparian habitat along Sonoita Creek from Rio Rico properties who planned to build homes on the site (University of Arizona Water Resources Center, 1994).
- •More than 600,000 Americans took a bicycle vacation in 1985. Touring cyclists, when traveling in a group, spent $17/day (camping), and $50/day (staying in motels). Cyclists traveling alone spent an average of $22/day (camping) and $60/day (motels) (Moran, Wilkinson, and Fremont, 1988).

- River recreation in Oregon is one of the activities that attracts people from other areas. In the Columbia Gorge region (consisting of the Hood River and Wasco Counties), revenues from transient lodging taxes grew just over 25% during 1992/93, following a similar increase of approximately 21.4% in the previous fiscal year (Oregon Tourism Division, Economic Development Department, 1994).
- Anchorage, Alaska hosted two US National X-Country Skiing Championships in 1991. It was estimated that the competitors and their companions, totaling approximately 1,000 people, in these two events spent almost $1,200,000 during the course of the competitions, both of which lasted just over one full week (Hill, 1991).
- The Gauley River is a high quality whitewater rafting and kayaking resource in West Virginia. It is growing in popularity and increasing its economic impact on the surrounding region. Dam releases provide whitewater opportunities on a 24 mile stretch of the Gauley for 10–25 days in the fall. The rafters, during this short season, generate almost $20 million in economic activity in the region. Every $1 spent per visitor day generated $2.27 of sales in the state. Each visitor day generated an average of 1.79 days of employment. Economic rationale was instrumental in precluding potential additional dam construction on the Gauley; it was recently designated a National Recreation Area (Logar et al., 1984).
- On North Carolina's Nantahala River, raft trip participants increased approximately 700% between 1972 and 1981. Rafters generated $1.8 million in expenditures in 1982. (Swain County Board of Commissioners, 1982).

Tour operators, outfitters, and guides are also important to local economies due to the expenditures their businesses generate, the fees they pay to operate, and their advertising and promotion of local resources. Some companies such as "A Day in Nature," based in San Francisco, which offers a day in nature complete with a gourmet picnic and door-to-door transportation, have capitalized on the demand for nature-oriented experiences.

- Backroads, a US travel outfitter, offering a range of trips from bicycling to hiking, competes with 200 other US travel outfitters. One of these other companies, All Adventure Travel, added 200 vacations to its catalog of 500 in 1993. Purchases of accessories for adventure travel can have impacts on companies like Coleman Co., which increased 1992 camping-goods sales by 21% to approximately $66 million in 1993 (San Francisco Examiner, July, 1994).
- The total economic impact of commercial river rafting in Colorado was estimated to be approximately $70 million in 1991. This estimate is based on 410,000 user days with an average expense of $65.80/day per user, using an economic multiplier of 2.56 (Colorado River Outfitters Association, 1992).
- An Oregon study of guides and packers indicates that in 1986, the outfitter/guide industry in Oregon (for, river, land, and marine activities) had a direct economic impact of $42.5 million. This resulted in a total economic impact of $300 million (Bureau of Land Management, 1987).
- For every $1 paid to canoeing outfitters, customers spent $5 for gas, groceries, restaurants, campgrounds, and other lodging. 70 canoe liveries in Florida generate $38.5 million/year (Stout, 1986).

"Volkssporting", "Volksmarching", and other similar types of activities may also be ideal for attracting tourists to local communities. Volkssporting, meaning "sport of the people", organizes non-competitive public events open to all ages. The events include walking, bicycling, swimming, and skiing. Many participants travel to events regionally.

- An issue of the *American Wanderer* advertised volkssport events on trails in the state of Washington. Sponsored by the Washington Bed and Breakfast Guild, trail maps and event information are available from the Guild and local inn owners. (American Volksspporting Association, 1989).

MARKETING POTENTIAL

Rivers, trails, and greenways provide unique resources which nearby travel and tourist-serving establishments, chambers of commerce, and local visitors bureaus can capitalize on and feature in their advertising. Because a greenway is a desired and profitable amenity for these businesses, they may also be willing to contribute to the funding and development of the greenway.

- As a condition for development, the Campbell Inn (Campbell, California) was required to provide an easement for the Los Gatos Trail. Upon realizing the marketing potential of the trail, developers constructed part of the trail, an additional spur, and now provide rental bicycles for hotel guests. They also promote the trail in their brochure: "For fitness and fun, The Campbell Inn offers a jogging/biking trail connecting to a full series par course which . . . runs along a scenic trail, passing through forests and alongside a stream and two beautiful lakes." Room rates at the Campbell Inn range from $80 to $275/night.
- Implementation of the Yakima Greenway spurred many business changes in the city of Yakima, Washington. The Rio Mirado motel credits their almost year-round occupancy to their proximity to the Greenway. Marti's restaurant built a patio adjacent to the Greenway and enjoys increased business from trail users and hotel guests. Svend's Mountain Sports, a mountain climbing and cross-country ski shop, now stocks mountain bikes and roller blades due to the opportunities created by the Greenway. Svend's would like to set up a rental concession on the Greenway during the summer season. Even nearby auto dealerships invite people to buy their next car at the "Greenway Auto Plaza" (Feasey, 1989).

HOW TO USE THESE RATIONALES IN YOUR COMMUNITY
Quote Examples
Choose relevant information from the examples provided to include in newsletters and presentations. Gather your own testimonies from lodging, restaurant owners, and travel agents in your community. Cite quotes from their promotional materials and advertisements.

Find Out Whether any Studies have been Done in Your Area
Contact local university departments of tourism, recreation, business, or economics, to see if anyone has done research or special projects related to the economic impacts

of tourism in your area. Discuss your greenway with them. Also contact federal, state, regional, and local agencies to see if there are any relevant studies. At the state level, try the agencies that govern commerce and tourism. At the regional and local levels, try local convention and visitors bureaus, chambers of commerce, marketing specialists, and major banks. There may be current reports on average tourism expenditures in your community.

Depending upon what studies you can acquire, and their focus, you may be able to adapt them to your needs. Consult the authors of those studies, or other specialists, before doing so.

Determine the Influence of Natural/Cultural Resources on Travel Trends

Determine how natural/cultural greenway-related resources play a part in determining travel preferences and trends in your area. Cite examples with which your audience will be familiar. Look at promotional materials in your area, including newspapers, brochures, magazines, and phone books to see how resource-based attractions are being promoted and featured in advertisements. Check with your local visitor information center.

Get to Know Your Visitors

Find out who your visitors are; where they come from; why they visited the greenway; how long they are staying in the area; what brought them there; and their expenditures while in the area. This can be accomplished in a variety of ways, ranging from casual conversations with visitors at the greenway, to intensive phone, mail, and/or visitor interviews at greenway entrances. It may be possible to do surveys of local overnight accommodations and businesses along the greenway. The appropriate method will depend upon the desired level of detail and reliability of results.

- A survey of visitors to the Northwood's area in Wisconsin found that almost 1.5 million non-residents visited this area in July and August of 1987. These non-resident guests spent almost $153 million in July and August of 1987, with an average daily expenditure of $14.66/person. Figure 1 was generated from this information. Many tourism expenditure studies focus upon guests staying in commercial lodging facilities. This study illustrates that those staying in camp grounds, or with friends and relatives, are also an important part of total visitor expenditures.

Lodging Type	Percent of Total Non-Resident Visitors	Percent of Total Non-resident Expenditures
Resorts	25.8%	39.7%
With Friends and Relatives	17.3	10.8
Second Homes	15.2	29.6
Motel/Hotel	8.6	7.1
Campgrounds	16.7	10.4
Day Trip	12.3	1.6
En Route Somewhere Else	3.9	0.8
	99.8%	**100.0%**

Source: Gray, Hamilton, and Mistele, 1987.

Figure 1. Northwoods non-resident visitors; type of lodging, and percent of total expenditures by type of lodging.

Determine the Level of Visitor Draw of Your Resource
Is it a destination in itself? If not, would visiting the greenway require people to spend more time, or the night, in your area? Would it encourage business and pleasure travelers to patronize businesses near your resource, or pay more to stay, dine, or shop near it?

Estimate Where Expenditures are Going
Your promotion will have more impact if you can state who benefits from tourism expenditures. This may include tax revenues, jobs, and payroll expenditures.

Estimate Corresponding Expenditures Attributable to Your Resource
The level of visitation to your project will determine the type and amount of expenditures that can be attributed it. If your greenway project is a separate destination in itself, the resource can be credited with all or most of the expenditures associated with the visit. If a greenway encourages staying another day in your area, figure the expenditures associated with spending one night and the following day, and credit the resource with that amount. If people will pay more to be near the greenway, find out how much, and credit the resource with that amount. Expenditures in your area can include transportation, food, lodging, entrance fees, outfitter/guide fees, and taxes.

- A survey of expenditures associated with recreational use of the St. Croix River (Maine and New Brunswick), found that anglers spent over six times as much per person, per day, in the local Maine economy as canoeists and over four times as much as general vacationers. In fact, anglers spent more in the local economy than all other recreationists combined (Miles, 1987).

Design your visitor surveys to determine what types of activities visitors participated in; how much each visitor spent per day for food, lodging, retail products; and other visitor-related services. The survey results would then provide an estimate of total annual expenditures.

If you cannot perform a site-specific survey, the expenditure information in Table 1 may be applicable. You should note the year the expenditures were calculated for Table 1 or any other study findings you may use. Remember the actual value of money changes each year. You should always be certain you work with expenditures calculated for the same year, or corrected for inflation.

Project impacts from changes in visitation. If travel trends and/or potential greenway management changes are expected to alter visitation to your greenway, you may be able to quantify the economic impacts of this change. To do this, you need to estimate the increase in expenditures and use relevant multipliers if available.

Estimate total impacts. If you have economic expertise on your staff or within your citizen group, you may be able to estimate total impacts. Visitor expenditures for your project can be estimated by conducting a survey. Once you have determined the expenditures, you can use appropriate multipliers to determine the total impacts. Multipliers for your city, county, or state may already be available.

Promote your resource to the tourism community. Develop a plan for marketing your greenway. Be careful the designated name of the project and any related brochures or information, accurately reflect the nature of the project and create the image you desire. Combine efforts with tourism promoters such as the local Chamber of Commerce, hotels, event planners, travel agents, convention and visitor bureaus, tour guides, and transportation operators to include promotion of the greenway in their literature/brochures. Assist in distributing this information to visitor centers, conference centers, and other traveler information locations.

SOURCES OF INFORMATION

The US Travel Data Center

The United States Travel Data Center (USTDC) is a national non-profit center for travel and tourism research. The Center publishes the following reports:

- Outlook for Travel and Tourism
- Economic Review of Travel in America
- National Travel Survey
- Survey of Business Travelers
- Annual Travel Outlook Forum

According to Center publications, USTDC maintains the only national economic model for estimating annual travel expenditure and their economic impact on cities, counties, and states (USTDC, 1989). The USTDC will perform research on the economic impact of tourism at various levels. To determine costs for these services, contact the USTDC in Washington, DC, at (202) 408–1832.

Table 1. Tourist expenditures, by activity.

Activity	Location	Expenditures	Year	Source
Sailboarding	Columbia Gorge (Oregon)	$47–85	1987	Povey, et al. '88
Long distance	Elroy-Sparta Trail (Wisconsin)	$25	1988	Schwecke, et al. 1989
Cross-country	Northwoods (Wisconsin)	$17	1978–79	Cooper, et al. '79
Bicycle touring	United States	$17–$50	1986	Moran, '86
River recreation	Upper Delaware	$20	1989	Cordell & Bergstrom, '89
Canoeing	St. Croix River (Maine)	$15		
Angling	St. Croix River (Maine)	$42		
River Rafting	Gauley River (West Virginia)	$60–$133	1989	Logar, et al. '84
	Colorado	$65	1991	Colorado River Outfitters Assoc., '92
Nature Conservation	Sierra Vista (Arizona)	$51	1991–92	Crandal, et al. '92

Note: The above table includes a column for the year these expenditures were calculated. Because the actual value of money changes each year, always be certain to work with expenditures calculated for the same year, or corrected for inflation.

Discover America: Tourism and the Environment
This publication, prepared by the USTDC and published by the Travel Industry Association of America, provides a survey of current environmental efforts, consumer attitudes toward those efforts, and business and government responses to emerging consumer attitudes. Contact the Travel Industry Association of America at (202) 408–8422 for this publication.

Impact of Travel on State Economies
This publication from the USTDC includes information concerning travel spending in each state, and the employment, payroll, income, and tax revenue generated. Reports are available for 1984, 1985, 1986, and 1987. The 1987 report, released in April 1989, is available from USTDC for $70.

Tourism USA
Published by the US Department of Commerce, *Tourism USA—Guidelines for Tourism Development* is a valuable resource for those interested in any of the following: appraising tourism potential, planning for tourism, assessing the product and market, marketing tourism, determining necessary visitor services, and obtaining assistance. It is targeted at local communities interested in initiating or developing tourism.

Rural Tourism Development Training Guide
This training guide, published by the University of Minnesota Tourism Center, is part of an education training package which includes a video highlighting case study communities of San Luis, Colorado; Dahlonega, Georgia; Sandpoint, Idaho; and the Villages of Van Buren, Iowa. Contact the Minnesota Extension Service Distribution Center at (612) 625–8173 for more information.

CONSIDERATIONS IN USING THESE RATIONALES
Use Existing Information
Make every effort to use available, existing information. Generating original economic impact information can be time consuming and expensive. When adapting existing information, list the assumptions and limitations of your analysis.

Use Good Survey Methods
Consult with someone experienced in designing and conducting surveys, and interpreting survey results. Someone on your staff may have these skills. If not, contact your local college or university. Be wary about using license plate tallies to determine visitor origin, since a high percentage of domestic and international tourists use rental cars to explore the countryside. If possible gather survey information that is comparable to locally published per person tourism expenditure data.

Be Careful in the Policy Implications of Your Results
Be careful in considering the implications of your analyses and the tradeoffs between tourism/economic development and resource protection. For example, development of

vacation homes or tourist attractions in the local area may bring dollars to the economy, but could also completely alter the community and its ecological character.

KEYWORDS

- **Ecotourism**
- **Gauley River**
- **Travel industry**
- **US Travel Data Center**

Chapter 2

Tourism Development in Local Communities

Fariborz Aref, Ma'rof Redzuan, Sarjit S. Gill, and Abrisham Aref

---

INTRODUCTION

This chapter attempts to summarize the findings of a study, which explored the levels of community capacity building (CCB) that contributed to tourism development in local communities. The study was carried out in Shiraz, Iran. The study focused on the level of CCB in local communities that involved in tourism activities. The research methodology of the study was based on qualitative and quantitative methods. Findings of the study show that the level of CCB in tourism development in the study area is generally low. Second, the CCB in the Old District of Shiraz was higher compared to the New District. The result also shows that the level of CCB is different according to types of tourism activities. The objective of the study also was to determine the relationship between the level of CCB and community leaders' perception of tourism impacts and their characteristics. The results from the multiple regression indicated that CCB can be predicted by community leaders' income, tourism income, extra activities, length of residence, educational level, and number of family members engaged in tourism activities.

Although CCB has been given only limited attention in the tourism literature, it has, however, been extensively discussed in other areas of development, especially health (George et al., 2007; Labonte and Laverack, 2001a; 2001b; Labonte et al., 2002; Maclellan-Wright et al., 2007; Raeburn et al., 2007; Seremba and Moore, 2005; Wickramage, 2006), education (Harris, 2001; Smyth, 2009), and agriculture (Dollahite et al., 2005). Lack of community capacity, coupled with limited understanding of tourism and its impacts, has been recognized as barriers to effective tourism development in third world countries (Moscardo, 2008). Capacity development in communities can be seen as the capacity of community residents to participate in tourism activities. One important aim of CCB is to verify whether individuals, organizations and communities have been building their capacity for development of tourism in their communities.

Tourism development in local communities cannot be successful without the participation of community leaders and community residents. In the case of tourism development in local communities cannot be successful without participation of community leaders and community residents. In the case of study area, Shiraz has a lot of prospects in building various forms of tourism activities. However, in the absence of community participation, tourism industry in Shiraz is not likely to improve (Aref and Ma'rof, 2008). The CCB is the key to tourism development. Understanding how CCB could develop tourism in local communities is fundamental to continued successful tourism development projects. Hence, assessing the level of CCB is an important step in developing community strategies for achieving community development (Marre and Weber, 2007).

LITERATURE REVIEW

Many local communities recognize the importance of tourism in stimulating change in social, cultural, environmental, and economic dimensions, where tourism activities have had a close connection with the local communities (Beeton, 2006; Richards and Hall, 2000). Tourism is a community development tool used by many local communities to promote community economic development. In relation to this, local community leaders play a vital role in addressing tourism issues. Meanwhile, tourism development and CCB programs have increasingly placed emphasis on community development. In pursuing this direction, the concept of community capacity has become of particular importance in identifying priorities and opportunities for community development (Hackett, 2004; Victurine, 2000). Moreover, CCB is a necessary condition for improving the process of tourism development and enhancing its benefits for local communities. There is an argument that CCB is necessary for community development and participatory processes at the community level (Reid and Gibb, 2004). The term community capacity is widely used among those who are concerned about community development or involved in social work and social service delivery (Marre and Weber, 2007). Community capacity in tourism development can be seen as the capacity of the people in communities to participate in tourism activities (Cupples, 2005), where tourism developers often have the tendency to invest in community training and CCB as a way of contributing to long-term community development. In relation to this, community development practitioners should regard the concept of CCB not as something new, but as a refinement of ideas found within literature (Gibbon et al., 2002). The CCB, like community development, describe a process that increases the assets and attributes that a community is able to draw upon in order to improve their lives (Labonte and Laverack, 2001a).

Balint (2006, p. 140) states that CCB as a level of competence ability and skill and knowledge, is necessary in order to achieve the community goals. It, therefore, concerns the development of skills and abilities that will enable local people to make decisions and actions for tourism development. The decisions and actions of the community are based on their desire to develop their community tourism. Thus, community capacity in tourism development is closely linked to community development. This study provides a portrait of applying an approach of the level of CCB in 175 local communities which involved in tourism development. While, there is a substantial body of literature on the definition and conceptualization of CCB (Chaskin, 2001; Clinch, 2004; Goodman et al., 1998; Laverack, 2001), however, CCB has proven difficult to measure (Ebbeseb et al., 2004), and also there is very little literature which discusses practical application of approaches that have been successfully used to measure CCB in tourism development. The CCB can be seen as the capacity of community residents to participate in tourism development activities, both as individuals and through groups and organizations. It is not primarily about their ability to act in their personal, family or employers' interest, which are catered for in other spheres.

However, many of the same skills are involved, and people who are active in the community invariably benefit in other ways as well (Cupples, 2005). Meanwhile, CCB is widely acknowledged as an important strategy for community development. It is recognized as an essential strategy to strengthen the wellbeing of individuals and local communities and underpins much of the work of government and non-government agencies (Fiona 2007). The CCB also is the ability to empower community residents to self-manage their community tourism through participation in the building and enactment of shared community vision.

METHODOLOGY

The study was carried out in local communities of Shiraz. Shiraz is a central area for Persian civilization and culture. It is situated in the south western region of Iran. Shiraz also is one of the most popular cultural tourism destinations in Iran with a long interesting history of the Roman Empire (Cultural Heritage News Agency, 2006). Throughout history, foreign visitors to Shiraz have praised the city's gardens, its site, its wines, and the charm of its people. Iranians themselves, however, have long treasured Shiraz as a city of Islam. Its traditional Iranian name is Dar al -Elm (Abode of Knowledge) (Aref and Ma'rof, 2009b; Limbert, 2004).

The research methodology of this study was based on qualitative and quantitative methods to evaluate building community capacity for tourism development. The geographical area of analysis is divided into two districts; the Old District and the New Districts. The Old District includes 84 communities, which are located on the central part of Shiraz, whereas the New District includes 91 communities which are modern (Aref et al., 2009d, 2009e). The research study uses questionnaire survey and focus group discussion (FGD).

The data for this study were collected from community leaders and local residents which engaged in tourism activities. Community leaders was identified as a key factor in developing tourism in local communities (Aref and Ma'rof, 2009a; Moscardo, 2008). According to Eyler et al. (1999), Thompson et al. (2000), and Von et al. (1992) community leaders are able to speak for the community because of their knowledge and their roles in the community. For this study, community leader is defined as those who can influence policy, or opinion, or action on community because of their roles and positions in the community (Aref et al., 2009). For the purpose of this survey, questionnaire was designed for data collection. Moutinho (2000) believed that questionnaire is the most commonly used in tourism marketing research. The items in the questionnaire for this survey were measured using Likert scale. The Likert scale is also commonly used in marketing research (Grover and Vriens, 2006).

In this study, CCB is a composite variable, consisting of eight domains, namely, participation (7 items), community leadership (6 items), community structure (5 items), skill and knowledge (5 items), community power (5 items), sense of community (7 items), resource mobilization (5 items), and external support (5 items). The study used Likert scale to measure every item. For measurement of the level of CCB in tourism development, as well as to determine the relationship between level of CCB and the leader characteristics and their perception towards tourism impacts, this study performed descriptive statistics, utilizing t-test, one-way Anova, correlation and multiple regression analysis. The sample population for questionnaire survey were community leaders. The respondents for FGD were residents who engaged in tourism activities.

FINDINGS OF THE STUDY

Level of CCB in Tourism Development and its Difference Based on Districts and Types of Tourism Activities

The result from questionnaire indicated that generally the level of CCB in tourism development is low, except for the sense of community. However, based on the findings of the measurement of the three levels of CCB, it shows that according to the scores of individual level of CCB, sense of community is higher than skill and knowledge. In the organizational level of CCB; it shows that the score of leadership in higher than external support and resources mobilization. At the community level of CCB, the level of participation scores higher than community structures and community power. Overall, the results which illustrate the skill and knowledge, community structure, external support and resource mobilization are given a low rating of 2.0, and have been identified as being weak. This is might be due to the failure of community leaders to provide resource and skills to other members of the community. Therefore, it can be deduced that the leaders had failed to develop community structures adequately. The findings also show that "sense of community" received a high rating of three (3). This is an indication that the overall level of CCB is weak, and that there is a need for the community to prioritize which domains they wish to strengthen. Hence, the findings imply that the community leaders were unable to develop CCB for tourism development. However, due to lack of technical assistance and other support from the government, community leaders could not be blamed as the main reason for the low level of CCB for tourism development. When comparing the three levels of CCB descriptively, the results show a high level of CCB in individual level for tourism development. By using the mean readings, it is found that generally, the individual level in tourism development is higher than organizational and community levels.

To support of the findings, the FGDs were also performed. Base on FGD, local people illustrated that community capacity in tourism development was weak. This finding emerged pursuant in 10 FGD sessions conducted in response to this objective. The findings support the researchers' argument that CCB needs to be developed further to enable local people to participate in tourism development processes. However, as it was mentioned earlier, one of the reasons of underdevelopment of tourism industry in Iran is the low level of collaboration between government sector and the local communities. In other words, the government has taken little initiative to improve tourism as a source of income for local communities. The role of government is important for tourism development in third world countries. In support with this argument, Cole (2007) believes that government can play an important role in mediating for tourism development in local communities. Some writers also believed technical assistance from government as the key element in building community capacity (Rural Voices for Conservation Coalition, 2007). This might also the reason why there was a little effort taken by the community leaders to building capacity in tourism development, even though there are many tourist attractions found in Shiraz. In relation to the above discussion, community leaders could not be blamed as the main reason for the lack of community capacity for tourism development.

According to the results of this study, individual level of capacity building has more effect in the process of CCB in tourism development. The findings illustrate a range of strengths and weaknesses of the level of building capacity in local communities for tourism development. Skill and knowledge, community structure, external support and resource mobilization were given a low rating of 2.0, and were identified as being weak because of the failure of community leaders to provide resources and skills to other members of the community. Therefore, the community leaders failed to develop the community structure for tourism development. In local communities of Shiraz, this situation had led to a reduction in the number of community meetings and low level of participation in tourism decision making among community residents. However, most research suggests that tourism is a community decision making, and tourism development is an effort that has community support (Luloff et al., 1994). But in some local communities of Shiraz, the respondents indicated that the decision making to develop tourism was not a community decision. This follows the paradigm that without community participation, it "is difficult to develop a tourism industry in the community" (Andereck and Vogt, 2000, p. 27). The interpretation of the findings gives "sense of community" a high rating of 3. Therefore, the hospitality of the local community is vital to the tourism development. Hence, tourism in the local communities should be developed according to sense of community (Andriotis, 2005). However, Chapman and Kirk (2001) state that skill and knowledge is vital to CCB, but the finding of this study shows that skill and knowledge is not that important. However, the result of analysis of the 392 case studies of tourism development indicated that the most barriers to effective tourism development were a lack of skill and knowledge. The lack of tourism knowledge is a critical barrier that not only directly limits the ability of local people to participate in tourism development but also contribute to the next barriers: a lack of local tourism leadership and domination of external agents (Moscardo, 2008).

To prove whether the differences are significant, t-test statistical analysis was used. According to the results, the Old Districts of Shiraz reported significantly higher level of CCB compared to the New District of Shiraz, with significant comparative levels of 0.000, $t = 9.465$, $p < 0.05$. Findings show that development of sense of community in the New District is lower than the Old District of Shiraz. This is because of community diversity in culture and ethics. This result also indicates that most people in this city are hospitable towards tourists. However, participation in the New District is lower than the Old District. This is due to fact that people in this district are closely related to each other. The findings of this study also illustrate the level of sense of community as a high when compared to other levels. This finding is consistent with Andriotis' finding (2005), which illustrated that hospitality of the local communities is vital to development of tourism industry. Meanwhile, Murphy (1985) agrees that tourism development depend not only on the natural and community resources but also on the sense of community. Thus the sense of community is essential for tourism development. Therefore, the communities that are antagonistic to tourists, no amount of attractions will compensate for the hospitality. The findings can be support by the Gemeinschaft theory. According to Tonneis's theory; the local communities in the Old District of Shiraz are a sample of Gemeinschaft and local communities in the New District are a sample of Gesellschaft. Based on Tonneis theory, in a Gemeinschaft society, the members live together and develop common experiences, interests, memories, and histories (Appelrouth and Edles, 2007).

To test the difference between the levels of CCB based on types of tourism activities One-way Anova was performed. The results show that the levels of CCB in medical services (Mean = 93.25) and culture tourism activities (Mean = 91.67) are higher than other types of tourism activities. These results show the variance between groups and the variance within groups. For CCB significant level =0.000 shows a significant difference of CCB between different types of tourism activities, $F_{(4,170)} = 9.014$, $P < 0.000$. The findings of comparison of CCB according to types of tourism activities illustrated that level of building capacity in cultural activities is the highest than others tourism activities. The findings are consistent with previous studies about cultural tourism (Aref and Ma'rof, 2009c). According to Moscardo (2008, p. 86) types of tourism activities identified which supposedly has the potential to involve and capacity development for tourism development. Therefore, these finding are consistent with the findings of Moscardo (2008) about the importance of cultural tourism activities. It is considered that the government has special vision and attention on cultural tourism activities. Also, Godfrey and Clarke (2000) stated that types of tourism activates do not have same effect and impacts on local communities. Therefore, level of development in each type of tourism activity is different. The finding of this study is also supported by Cole (2007) in which he believes that cultural tourism is one of the important types of tourism activities that brings community development. According to the Travel Industry Association of America (2005), the cultural tourism is more educational when compared with others types of tourism. Thus, cultural tourism, in addition to having more impacts on the level of community development, it has many potential for development. Among all findings, the work of Ivanovic (2009) is highly supporting the findings of this study. Ivanovic (2009) states that the cultural tourism has more resources than other types of tourism activities. This is because cultural tourism is dependent more on community cultural resources than on expensive infrastructures and accommodations. This characteristic gives cultural tourism activities the power to become the main tool of socio-cultural development through poverty alleviation and job creation among historically disadvantaged communities (Ivanovic, 2009, p. xx).

Community Leaders' Perception Towards Tourism Impacts and its Relation with Level of CCB

Descriptive statistics reveal that respondents from both districts of Shiraz rated high positive perception and lower negative perception towards tourism impacts in local communities. Based on the mean measures of impact items, the impact items related to economic impacts has the lowest scores. When comparing between the three aspects of tourism impacts descriptively, the findings reveal that the community leaders have positive perceptions towards these threes aspect of impacts. Meanwhile, differences among respondents were also observed. The size of the standard deviations of 20 statements also indicated a moderate spread around the theoretical mean of three (3). The study has also found that the community leaders perceived socio-cultural aspects of tourism impacts as more favorably than environmental and economic impacts (Aref et al., 2009d).

This study also recognized community residents' perception towards tourism impacts through FGDs. It indicates a certain level of harmony between residents' perception and community leaders' perception toward tourism impacts. Relationship between leaders' perception toward tourism impacts with the level of CCB was also measured. For an alpha level of 0.05, the correlation between socio-cultural impacts and level of CCB was found to be statistically significant, ($r = -0.092$, $N = 175$, $p < 0.224$), and the correlation between economic impacts and level of CCB was found to be statistically significant too, ($r = -0.252$, $N = 175$, $p = 0.001$). This indicates that environmental impacts, and level of CCB are correlated negatively significant ($r = -0.257$, $N = 175$, $p < 0.001$). The result also illustrated that leaders' perception towards total tourism impacts has no significance ($r = -0.075$, $N = 175$, $p < 0.325$). When comparing the socio-cultural, environmental, and economic impacts of tourism and total tourism impacts descriptively, only economic impacts show positive relationship with the level of CCB for tourism development (Aref, Ma'rof, and Sarjit, 2009). However, the perception of environmental impacts has a negative significant relationship with levels of CCB. As have been mentioned earlier, Moscardo (2008) believed that the lack of understanding of tourism impacts can be a factor for underdevelopment of tourism in third world countries. Therefore, the findings of community perception towards tourism impacts on local communities helps to understanding relationship between community perceptions of tourism impacts with community support for building capacity for tourism development.

Based on all results that have been indicated above, it could be concluded that community leaders' perception towards tourism impacts cannot be a factor for underdevelopment tourism industry in local communities of Shiraz. These findings are inconsistent with the findings of Hafeznia et al. (2007), in which they believed in local communities of Iran; many people have negative perceptions especially about external tourism. In addition, the findings provide an introduction for discussion about relationship between level of CCB in tourism development and community leaders' perception towards tourism impacts. Gursoy and Rutherfor (2004) suggested that tourism developers need to consider the perception of residents before they start investing resources in tourism development. Fisher (2005) also states on importance of leaders perception as an effective element in the processes of community economic development. The findings from this study supported the previous studies in terms of positive tourism impacts and their support for tourism development.

The finding which related to the perception towards economic impacts is consistent with the past studies that have been conducted by Ap (1992) and Yoon et al. (2001). Most of these studies evaluated community residents' perception and assessments of cost and economic benefits of tourism and their support for further tourism development in their communities. In relation to this, social exchange theory supports that community residents balance the costs and benefits of tourism development, and their support for tourism depends on the outcome of this cost-benefits equation (Andriotis, 2005). Thus, it is believed that the economic impacts of tourism are the most widely researched impacts of tourism on a destination (Mason, 2003). Studies done by Andereck and Vogt (2000) also support the findings of this study. According to their studies, there is a relationship between community residents' support for tourism development and their perception toward tourism impacts. However, it can be concluded that community leaders support for building community capacity in tourism development is positively related to their benefits from tourism development. Empirical findings from these studies have suggested that people will act to maximize benefits and minimize costs in different situations. They also weigh total benefits against total costs that effect their decision to participate in tourism decision making and tourism development planning (Kayat, 2002; Lawler, 2001; Yoon et al., 2001). Andriotis and Vaughan (2003) also found that when the exchange of the economic, social, and environmental resources is at least balanced for the local communities, only then tourism will be perceived positively by residents. However, they caution that the benefits of tourism may be experienced by only a handful of individuals in the community and only those who benefit will be more likely to support tourism development. Accordingly, in order to have tourism be supported by all community members, the benefits of tourism must be evenly distributed (Andriotis and Vaughan, 2003). Hence, social exchange theory helps us to build a clear relationship between perceived impacts and support for tourism development (Perdue et al., 1990).

Leaders' Characteristics and Level of CCB in Tourism Development

The result from the present study shows that there was a significant positive correlation between age and CCB ($r = 0.416$, $N = 175$, $p = 0.000$). Moreover, there is a significant positive correlation between duration of residence and CCB ($r = 0.402$, $N = 175$, $p = 0.001$). The result also shows there is a significant positive correlation between duration of position held and CCB ($r = 0.462$, $N = 175$, $p = 0.000$) and significant positive correlation between income and CCB ($r = 0.601$, $N = 175$, $p = 0.000$). A Spearman correlation also found that there is a significant positive correlation between education and CCB ($rs = 0.401$, $N = 175$, $p < 0.000$), income and CCB ($rs = 0.644$, $N = 175$, $p < 0.000$), extra activities and CCB ($rs = 0.214$, $N = 175$, $p < 0.004$), tourism jobs and CCB ($rs = 0.546$, $N = 149$, $p < 0.000$) and number of family engaged in tourism activities with CCB ($rs = 0.356$, $N = 175$, $p < 0.000$). The present findings are consistent with the findings of study by Fisher (2005) which stated that the characteristics of the leaders have successful effect in the context of community economic development. Meanwhile, Schultz (2004) also stated the importance of leaders characteristics in relations to community development effort. One of the key leaders' characteristic in this study is educational level. In relation this, Vaughan (2003) stated that people with high education have the tendency to support tourism development.

The finding also shows that educational level has a significant relationship with level of CCB. This consistent with the finding of the study Andriotis and Vaughan (2003), who found that the higher the level of education, the more likely residents were to express their apprehension to tourism development in their communities.

Meanwhile, age is also considered as a leaders' characteristic which has a significant relationship with the level of CCB. Consistent with this finding is the findings by Chen (2000) and Lawton (2005), who found that older residents also more likely to support tourism. Other key leaders' characteristic is income. A leaders' annual income is also found to have a significant relationship with the level of CCB. Chen (2001) also states that people with high income have more tendencies to get involve in tourism development. He stated that economic benefits of tourism have an effect on the support given by local people for the development of tourism. Income from tourism and the number of family members who engage in tourism activities also have a positive significant relationship with the level of CCB for tourism development. Moreover, social exchange theory also supports the findings of the study. Length of resident was significantly relation to level of CCB. These findings are also supported by the studies carried out by Green et al. (1986) and Lawton (2005). Green et al. (1986) state that permanent residents may be more supportive of tourism development than seasonal residents (Green et al., 1986). Lawton (2005) also finds that the duration of residence in the destination plays an important role when examining community residents' support for tourism development. The duration of the leaders' position is also considered to have a significant relationship with the level of CCB. Those community leaders who have lived in the community with the longer duration as leaders have a tendency to exert more effort for development of CCB for tourism development. However, the variable related to having activities related to tourism, has a negative significant relationship with the level of CCB for tourism development. The finding shows that community leaders who may not work directly in the tourism industry may have different effort in CCB for tourism development. Martin et al. (1998) conclude that those who do not receive real economic benefit from tourism do not have the tendency to seriously involve in the development of tourism industry.

Contributing Factors in Predicting the Level of CCB in Tourism Development

A multiple regression analysis was conducted to identify the factors that contributed to the level of CCB in tourism development. Twelve predictors were included. However, based on the interviews with the leaders, only six predictors (income, tourism income, extra activities from tourism, duration of residence, educational level, and family engaged in tourism activities) were considered in the regression modeling. In the first model, only income was adopted as a predictor. The R^2 value of 0.737 implies that the six variables explain around 74% of variance/variation in the CCB in tourism development in local communities of Shiraz. According to the model summary, about 74% of the variation in the criterion variable Y (level of CCB) can be explained by the regression model with the six predictors. The regression model with six predictors is significantly related to the criterion variable Y, $F (6,141) = 65.912$, $p < 0.05$. The finding shows that the largest beta coefficient is 0.350, which is for the tourism income. The beta value for "income" is the second highest (0.299). Thus, the model summary information reveals that the R^2 for this data set was 0.737. This indicates that 74% of CCB for tourism development by community leaders could be predicted by the independent variables of leaders' income, tourism income, extra activities, length of residence, educational level, and family engaged in tourism industry.

Since the findings of the present study shows that the important predictors for CCB in tourism development are income and income from tourism activities, therefore, it can be inferred that community leaders' support for CCB in tourism development is positively related to their economic benefits from tourism industry. Moreover, the findings of this study could be explained by theory of social exchange. Based on the social exchange theory community residents' support for tourism development depends on the outcome of this cost-benefits equation (Andriotis, 2005). Findings from these studies have suggested that local people will act to maximize benefits and minimize costs in different situations. They also weigh total benefits against total costs that effect their decision to participate in tourism decision making and tourism development planning (Kayat, 2002; Lawler, 2001; Yoon et al., 2001). The findings of this study also emphasize on role community leaders in CCB for tourism development. The findings are supported by Austen (2003), who stated that without the community leaders effort in building the community capacity in local communities, the tourism development would not materialized. Littrell and Hobbs (1989) also confirmed the importance of community leader's role in their discussion of the self help approach to building capacity in communities. According to Israel and Beaulieu (1990), without powerful leaders, it was virtually impossible for local communities to tackle problems. Taylor (2003) also believed that without the significant role of community leaders, building capacity cannot be developed. Therefore, tourism development planners should take into considerations the community leaders' characteristics as important elements in the development of tourism in local communities.

CONCLUSION

The main purpose of this chapter is to illustrate and discuss variables related to the CCB for the tourism development. Although, there are several studies which discuss the construct of CCB, particularly in health promotions and agriculture, however, there seems a very few studies that discuss the CCB in the context of community tourism development. In relation to this, the present researchers have attempted to embark a study in order to understand CCB in tourism development. The data presented in this chapter demonstrate that there is a need for the development of CCB in local communities of Shiraz. In terms of assessing levels of CCB; three main findings have been discovered. First, CCB in tourism development in the study area is generally low. Second, the CCB in the Old District is higher than the New District of Shiraz. Third, the level of sense of community is the dominant factor compared to other dimensions. Moreover, the results also show that the levels of CCB are different according to the perception of types of impacts of tourism. These findings have also been supported by FGD. The study also proves that a high percentage of the answers stressed the positive aspects of socio-cultural, environmental and economic impacts of tourism in local communities. The results of the study also show that there is a relationship between the level of CCB and community leaders' perception of tourism impacts as well as leaders' characteristics. The findings show that perception of economic impacts has a positive significant relationship with the level of CCB. Furthermore, some leaders' characteristics also had significant relationships with levels of CCB in tourism development. Meanwhile, the results from the multiple regression analysis indicated that

CCB can be predicted by community leaders' income, tourism income, extra activities form tourism, duration of residence, educational level, and number of members family engaged in tourism activities. According to the result, the largest beta coefficient is for the perception of income. In sum, regression analysis indicated that approximately 74 percent ($R^2 = 0.737$) of the variance in CCB was predicted by those variables. It is hoped that the findings of this study could be used to assist community leaders in the design and implementation of tourism development strategies in local communities that are undertaking tourism planning. Moreover, it is expected that the findings of this study could be utilized by the leaders and tourism developers for their future follow-up studies and reassessment of CCB for tourism development.

KEYWORDS

- **Community capacity building**
- **Local communities**
- **Tourism development**

Chapter 3

Local Communities and Tourism Development

Fariborz Aref and Ma'rof Redzuan

INTRODUCTION

This chapter attempts to identify the relationship between the community leaders' perceptions toward tourism impacts and their effort in building the capacity for tourism development in local communities of Shiraz, Iran. The chapter is based on the study carried out among 175 communities' leader. The analysis of data uses Pearson correlation to determine the relationship between variables involved. The findings reveal that two impacts (economic and environmental) have the most significant relationship with the level of community capacity building. The findings of the study imply that those leaders who perceived the tourism activities could bring economic benefits would have the higher tendency to be actively involved in building the capacity of their communities in relation to the development of tourism, whereas those who perceived tourism could bring negative impact to the environment, would put less effort in the capacity building.In many countries, tourism is a fast growing industry and a valuable sector. Tourism contributes significantly to the countries' economy. Moreover, tourism plays an increasingly important role in the development of communities. The benefits of tourism include both tangible (e.g., job creation, state and local tax revenue, etc.) and less tangible (e.g., social structure, quality-of-life, etc.). In addition, tourism can, and often does, result in less desirable effects on the economic, social, and environmental fabrics of communities. These benefits and costs provide ample opportunity for creative public policy debate. In other words, tourism affects the economy and lives of communities. There are real and perceived fears that are sometimes attributed to tourism. These impacts of tourism on communities could influence the communities' effort to develop the industry. In relation to this, the main focus of this chapter is to identify the relationship between communities' perception towards the impacts of tourism and their effort to build their community capacity in relation to tourism development.

Community perception towards the tourism impacts on a community can vary significantly. According to Sharma (2004), positive attitudes towards tourism impacts among communities residents will result in more successful tourism development. Thus, understanding the community perception can help to access community support for continued tourism development through community capacity building. Gursoy and Rutherford (2004) suggested that tourism developers need to consider the perception and attitude of residents before they could start investing scarce resources. Moreover, understanding of community perception towards tourism impacts can also help to identify types of tourism which have the potential for building community capacity

(Moscardo, 2008, p. 86). Meanwhile, several studies indicate that people who have an economic gain from tourism perceive more positive impact from it (Chon, 2000). In this present study, it is assumed that community perception towards tourism impacts does have a considerable effect on the level of community capacity building in tourism development. In the study, the researchers employ exchange theory in order to explain the relationship between perception towards tourism impacts and the level of community capacity building. Tourism has been proved as one of the most ingeniously crafted and expedient opportunities for social exchange (Singh et al., 2003). Thus, in this study, social exchange theory is considered as a conceptual sociological approach to the study of leaders' perceptions towards tourism impacts and its relationship with their effort for community capacity building in tourism development. However, the researcher did not find any study about the relationship between the perceptions towards tourism impacts and level of community capacity building.

LITERATURE REVIEW

The tourism industry has human and environmental costs, besides its benefits to communities involved. Thus, some communities have to make a choice whether to adopt tourism or reject it as a source of income. For the communities which adopted tourism as one of the development alternatives, they would put more effort in developing the tourism industry. Some local communities would attempt to build their community capacity in relation to tourism development. Community capacity building can be seen as the capacity of community residents to participate in community development activities, both as individuals and through groups and organizations. In relations to tourism development, community capacity building is a necessary condition for improving the process of tourism development and enhancing its benefits for local communities. Hence, the main objective of this study is to investigate relationship between community leaders' perceptions of tourism impacts and their effort for building capacity in tourism development.

A number of theories have been suggested to explain the nature of residents' perception towards tourism impacts and their support to tourism development. Among the theories are conflict theory, community attachment theory, dependency theory, and social exchange theory. However, most of studies utilize the social exchange theory, which has been considered as the most appropriate framework to develop and understand community residents' perception (Ap, 1992). Social exchange theory is used predominately in the literature on assessing tourism impacts for a particular destination (Andereck and Vogt, 2000; Andriotis, 2005; Ap, 1992; Chen, 2000, 2001; Gursoy et al., 2002; Vogt and Jun, 2004). Social exchange theory can strengthen the belief that a need exists to measure the level of active participation of community residents in the community development planning process associated with tourism development (Wang and Pfister, 2008). In the tourism literature, a number of studies have utilized the social exchange theory to explain community perception and reactions to tourism development (Ap, 1992; Jurowski et al., 1997; Yoon et al., 2001). Most of these studies evaluate community residents' perception and assessments of cost and benefits of tourism and their effort for further tourism development in their particular regions. The social exchange theory explains how people react and support tourism development (Ap, 1992; Yoon et al., 2001). In other words, social exchange theory supports that community residents calculate the costs and benefits of tourism development, and their effort for tourism development depends on the outcome of this cost-benefits calculation (Andriotis, 2005). Moreover, according to Andriotis and Vaughan (2003), social exchange theory allows the investigation of positive and negatives perception towards tourism impacts in a community. It is more than likely, that residents will be aware of the positive and negative implications of tourism and whether to support or not to support the tourism development is based on their perception of the benefits and costs (Andriotis and Vaughan, 2003). Thus, in the present study, social exchange theory could explain the relationship between community perception towards tourism impacts and their action to get involved in the community capacity building in tourism development. The Figure 1 illustrates this issue.

Tourism industry not only provides means of recreation to the tourists but offers assistance to the ailing and developing economies of the world. Many countries depend on tourism for income. The entrepreneurs, communities and states find immense commercial opportunities in tourism and have made intense efforts to reap the benefits. The net result is the generation of wealth. But this wealth generation is not without a price. For the development of tourism, environment, societies, and cultures at the destination has paid a heavy price. The present cause of concern is not only the development but also to tackle the challenges posed by development (Chaudhary et al., 2007). In the case of the impacts of tourism, Ming and Wong (2006) have studied the homestay operators perception towards the tourism impact on their community and how their social demographics influence their perception towards tourism. Using factor analysis the impacts on the local community perceived by the homestay operators were condensed into seven factors: economic impacts, the interaction between tourism and other sectors, life quality improvement, general physical environment deterioration, beach degradation, sea water pollution, and interruption to quiet life. However, the economic and social impacts of tourism are a big subject that cannot be covered thoroughly here. Economically, tourism can create jobs for local people and bring money into the country. Since tourists spend money on travel, hotels, food, entertainment, and recreation, they can be an important source of income and thus of economic development for the communities with few other possible sources of revenue. Meanwhile, a study by Nyaupane and Thapa (2006) indicates that generally, on comparison of descriptive and statistical analyses, local residents were consistently more likely than managers to perceive fewer negative and greater positive impacts of tourism on the environment. Quite a number of studies are related to the studying the impacts of tourism, however, seldom could we find studies that deal the relationship between community leaders' perception towards tourism impacts and community capacity building in relations to tourism development.

RESEARCH METHODOLOGY

The study was carried out in 175 local communities in Shiraz. Shiraz is the capital of the Iranian province of Fars, the ancient homeland of the Achemenian (ca.549–330 B.C.E) and the Sassanian (ca.224–651 C.E) dynasties. The Greeks called this area Persia, from which came their beloved national language, Farsi, from the name of this province (Limbert, 2004, p. 3). Shiraz is a central area for Persian civilization and culture. Shiraz has a population of more than 1,000,000 people. It is situated in the south western region of Iran, in the inlands of about 200 km from the Persian Gulf at an elevation of 1,800 m above sea level. Shiraz also is one of the most popular cultural tourism destinations in Iran with a long interesting history of the Roman Empire (Cultural Heritage News Agency, 2006). Throughout history, foreign visitors to Shiraz have praised the city's gardens, its site, its clear air, its wines, and the charm of its people. Iranians themselves, however, have long treasured Shiraz as a city of Islam. Its traditional Iranian name is Dar al -Elm (Abode of Knowledge) (Limbert, 2004).

The data for this study were collected from community leaders. Community leadership was identified as a key factor in developing tourism in local communities (Aref and Ma'rof, 2009; Moscardo, 2008). According to Eyler et al. (1999), Thompson et al. (2000), and Von et al. (1992) community leaders are able to speak for the community because of their knowledge and their roles in the community. For this study, community leader is defined as those who can influence policy, or opinion, or action on community because of their roles and positions in the community (Aref et al., 2009). For the purpose of this survey, questionnaire was designed for data collection. Moutinho (2000) believed that questionnaire is the most commonly used in tourism marketing research. The items in the questionnaire for this survey were measured using Likert scale. The Likert scale commonly used in marketing research (Grover and Vriens, 2006). Pearson Coefficient Correlation was used to measure relationship between the variables. Pearson correlation statistic is a statistical technique to measure the strength of the association that exist between two quantitative variables (Ary et al., 1996). The purpose of the study is to measure the strength of relationship between two main variables (the perception towards the tourism impacts and the level of community capacity building). In statistics, correlation (often measured as a correlation coefficient) indicates the strength and direction of a linear relationship between two random variables. In this study community capacity building is a composite variable, consisting of eight domains, namely, participation (7 items), community leadership (6 items), community structure (5 items), skill and knowledge (5 items), community power (5 items), sense of community (7 items), resource mobilization (5 items), and external support (5 items). Meanwhile, there are three variables of tourism impacts, namely social-cultural impact (10 items), environmental impacts (5 items), and economic impacts (5 items). The study used Likert scale to measure every item. In the analysis, the community capacity building variable was correlated with the three variables of perception of tourism impacts in order to determine the strength of their relationships. Meanwhile, descriptive statistics were applied to describe the variables understudied.

Table 1. Means and standard deviation of the studied variables.

Variables	Mean	Standard Deviation
Perception towards cultureal impact	37.77	3.114
Perception towards econonic impacts	17.24	2.346
Perception towards environmental impacts	17.45	2.935
Total perception	72.46	6.002
Community capacity building	81.02	23.763

THE FINDINGS OF THE STUDY

As have been mentioned above, the main objective of the study is to determine the relationship between community leaders' perception towards tourism impacts and their effort for community capacity building in tourism development. Pearson correlation was used to identify these relationships. Table 1 shows the findings of the study in relations to means and standard deviations of the studied variables. For the three variables related to impacts of tourism (environmental, economic, and socio-cultural), the data reveal that generally, the leaders have high perception scores for every variable. This is reflected by the means of every variable—socio-cultural impacts (M = 37.77, SD = 3.114), environmental impacts (M = 17.45, SD = 2.935), economic impacts (M = 17.24, SD = 2.346), and total impacts (M = 72.46, SD = 6.002). These findings imply that most of the leaders have agreed with the impacts of tourism on the economy, environment, and socio-cultural of their communities. Moreover, the standard deviations reflect that there are relatively small deviations (differences) between respondents (leaders) in terms of their perceptions towards the impacts of tourism. Meanwhile, the mean of leaders' effort of community capacity building in relation to tourism development is relatively low (M = 129.47, SD = 19.445). It implies that majority of the leaders have less effort in the development of tourism activities. In Iran, tourism industry is not one of main focuses of development of the country. Thus, it is understood that majority of the communities in Iran have given less focus on the development of the industry.

The second analysis for this chapter focuses on the relationships between the perception towards tourism impacts and the effort of community capacity building in relation to tourism development. The results of the analysis are shown in Table 2. The correlation between socio-cultural impacts and level of community capacity building is found to be non significant (r = –0.092, N = 175, p = 0.224, two-tailed). Meanwhile, the correlation between economic impacts and the level of community capacity building is found to be positively significant (r = 0.252, N = 175, p < 0.001, two-tailed), whereas the correlation between perception towards environmental impacts is negatively significant (r = –0.257, N = 175, p < 0.001, two-tailed). Lastly, the correlation between the overall (total) perception of the tourism impacts and the level of capacity building is statistically non significant (r = –0.075, N = 175, p = 0.325, two-tailed).

When comparing the socio-cultural, environmental, and economic impacts of tourism and total tourism impacts descriptively, economic impacts show positive relationship with the level of community capacity building in tourism development. However, environmental impacts have negative significant relationship with community capacity building in tourism development. These findings support the assumption that the communities will support the tourism development if the development bring about benefits, such as economic benefits that outweigh the costs of sharing environmental and social resources with tourists (Harrill, 2004). In addition, Martin et al. (1998) found that retirees were less supportive of tourism development and identified more with the negative impacts of tourism. They conclude that those who did not receive real economic gain from the tourism growth would not support further development. The findings from this study supported the previous studies in terms of positive tourism impacts and their support for tourism development. The findings of studies related to economic impacts are consistent with the past studies that have been conducted by Ap (1992) and Yoon et al. (2001). These studies evaluated community residents' perception and assessments of cost and economic benefits of tourism and their support for further tourism development in their communities.

Table 2. Pearson correlation matric among tourism impacts and level of CCB.

	1	2	3	4	5
1. Socio-cultural impacts	1				
2. Environmental impacts	.354**	1			
3. Economic impacts	.166*	.240*	1		
4. Total impacts	.757**	.767**	.594**	1	
5. Community capacity building	−.092	−.252**	.252**	−.075	1

$*P<.05$ $**p<.01$.

Social exchange theory supports that community residents balance the costs and benefits of tourism development, and their support for tourism depends on the outcome of this cost-benefits equation (Andriotis, 2005). Thus, according to Mason (2003), the economic impacts of tourism are the most widely researched impacts of tourism on a destination. Studies by Andereck and Vogt (2000) also support the findings of the present study. According to their studies, there is a relationship between community residents' support for tourism development and their perception toward tourism impacts. However, it can infer that community leaders' support for community capacity building in tourism development is positively related to their benefits from tourism development. Empirical findings from these studies have suggested that people will act to maximize benefits and minimize costs in different situations. They also weigh total benefits against total costs that effect their decision to participate in tourism decision making and tourism development planning (Kayat, 2002; Lawler, 2001; Yoon et al., 2001). Andriotis and Vaughan (2003) also found that when the exchange of the economic, social, and environmental resources is at least perceived as balanced by the local communities, only the then tourism is perceived positively by residents. However, they caution that the benefits of tourism may be experienced by only a handful of individuals in the community, and only those who benefit will be more likely to support tourism development. In order to have tourism supported by all community members of the community, the benefits of tourism must be evenly distributed (Andriotis and Vaughan, 2003).

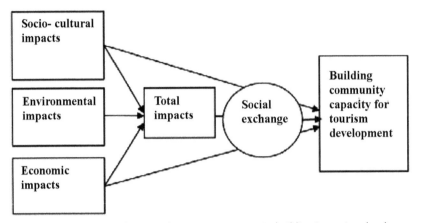

Figure 1. Tourism impacts and support for community capacity building in tourism development.

CONCLUSION

By using social exchange theory framework, this chapter attempts to illustrate the relationship between perception towards tourism impacts and the level of community capacity building. This theory helps to create a clear understanding about the relationship between perceived impacts and support for tourism development (Perdue et al., 1990). From the study, it is found that the correlation between perception of economic impacts and level of community capacity building is positively significant, whereas the correlation between environmental impacts of tourism and the level of community capacity building is negatively significant. Thus, it could be concluded that the higher the perception of the communities leaders towards the economic impacts, the higher their tendency that to put their effort in building their community capacity in relation to tourism development. On the other hand, if the leaders perceived that tourism could bring environmental damage to their communities, there is a tendency that they will not put their effort in the tourism development. These findings have an implication on the understanding and managing tourism impacts. It is suggested that the well managed tourism can make a positive contribution to destinations, and thus it could received a support from the local communities. As one of the world's largest industries, tourism carries with it significant social, environmental, economic, and political impacts. Although tourism can provide significant economic benefits for some destinations, however, the image of tourism as a benign and environmentally friendly industry has often been challenged. There is a clear and growing body of evidence suggests that the effects of tourism development are far more complex than policy-makers usually suggest and that the impacts of tourism occur not just at the destination, but at all stages of a tourist's trip. Furthermore, tourism does not exist in a vacuum. Broader social and environmental changes also shape the form, growth, and experience of tourism development. Meanwhile, according to Moscardo (2008), a lack of entrepreneurial capacity, limited understanding of tourism markets and a lack of community understanding of tourism and its impacts have been identified as barriers to effective tourism development in peripheral regions. Thus, the findings of this study could assist community leaders in the design and implementation of tourism development strategies in communities that are undertaking tourism planning.

KEYWORDS

- **Community capacity building**
- **Community perception**
- **Local communities**
- **Tourism impacts**

Chapter 4

Rebuilding After Catastrophe

Hejiang Shen, Limei Yuan, Yana Liu, Zhang Ying, and Wei Fei

INTRODUCTION

The thing about the tourism industry's restoration and rebuilding after catastrophe has a great influence not only on sustainable development of tourism destination, as the tourism destination is concerned highly by public, but also on the social judgment on the accessibility of stricken area, except those, it even influences the works which are the restoration and rebuilding of the stricken area's various constructions and the important criterion, depending on that, the international community determines if the stricken area should be rebuilt completely. So, the restoration and rebuilding of stricken area after catastrophe has the great value and profound meaning on reducing the tourists' fear and worries about the area happened crisis, and exerting the tourism industry's effect on all-round social development, which spurs the relevant industries to be reconverted as before.

OBJECTIVE VANTAGE OF THE TOURISM INDUSTRY'S RESTORATION AND REBUILDING AFTER CATASTROPHE

Tourism industry has suffered a lot from the calamitous events' outburst is no doubt. But, "the tourism industry itself possesses great power for the recovery of elasticity instead of showing weakness," and "with the crisis controlled and eliminated effectively," "the tourism industry will burst into much more vitality and energy," therefore "the tourism industry is known as the industry with stronger recovery power by itself". According to that, to restore and rebuild the tourism industry after catastrophe has the objective vantage.

The Advantage of the Tourism Industry Sell-repairing Capability

It is known to us, as the comprehension industry which takes the tourists as the core, that the tourism industry provides all kinds of services for tourists for their tourist activities relying on the tourism attractors. Basically, it is known as the economic sociocultural service-type business. Tourist activity becomes the key to this industry for the tourist plays the most important role. In the other hand, whether the tourist can make their tourist activities into truth smoothly or not becomes the key for the tourist industry's trouble-free running. The paroxysmal calamitous events not only lead to the discontinuing of the various tourist activities in tourist destination, but at once affect the tourists enter the tourist destination from the place where they live, those directly affect the tourism industry in the tourist destination "normal" operation, however, "with the crisis being eliminated gradually, the tourism industry will be soon recovery as before, which has shown its elasticity's level". So as the result of the crisis eliminated, objectively, the external safe factor to tourists realizing their tourist activities has been ready, if improving the speed to restore and perfect the various basic facilities, such as tourist communications, tourist hotel and tourist attraction, for developing the tourist activity in tourist destination, then the tourism industry will shows the powerful recovery ability. Just as, Frans Gallie, the secretary-general of WTO said that the tourism industry has the powerful recovery ability, and it will be more mature after experiencing one crisis.

The Comparative Vantage of Tourism Industry's Recovery and Rebuilding

Compared with the other industries, the tourism industry is one comprehension service industry, most important is that "it has the obvious comparative vantage". Compared with agriculture, steel industry, and building material industry and so forth, which need long-term restoration and rebuilding and take the damage to local recourse and environment, tourism industry has the comparative vantage in restoration and post-disaster reconstruction. To restore and rebuild the tourism industry firstly has the much effect on promoting and furthering the development of related industries, and also set a good example to the other industries. In brief, bring the tourism industry's comparative vantage into full play has the magnitude to promote the society all-round development in tourism destination after catastrophe.

The Vantage of Foundation of Restoring and Rebuilding the Tourism Industry in Tourism Destination

The tourism industry's recovery and rebuilding has the certain vantages of foundation. Firstly, there are rich and unique tourism resources in tourism destination, on the basic of restoration of tourist attractions and evaluating the damage caused by catastrophe to tourist attractions, the tourist attractions may be opened to the public with measured strokes; secondly, the fairly perfect system of travel reception and supply built after long-term development and construction, the same as the first, on analyzing the damage caused by crisis to tourist system, may be perfected with measured stroke, therefore, the capability of travel reception should be recovered fast; Thirdly, according to the present industry structure in tourist destination, tourism industry usually is prioritized, even taken as the cornerstone industry. So, to rebuild the tourism industry after catastrophe is objectively necessary to perfect industry structure and adjust industrial pattern in tourist destination. Comparing with the tourism industry, either manufacturing or agriculture's development has much more limiting factors, furthermore, the added value and spur of this industry are also much lower, first developing the tourism industry not only optimizes industry structure, but also restores the damaged tourist resources and environmental deterioration so that improving and enhancing the tourist destination's ecological functions.

THE VALUE OF SIGNAL TRANSMISSION EFFECT OF TOURISM INDUSTRY'S PRIORITY TO RECOVERY AND REBUILDING AFTER CATASTROPHE

Safety Information Transfer

The basic value of effect embodied in tourism industry's recovery after catastrophe indicates to the public that the tourist destination has been one safe place, which is the fundamental, also the main factor to tourists to realize their tourist activities. Whether the tourist destination is safe or not has directly respect to the tourist's security of the lives and property, because which the tourist destination's accessibility has been influenced. It has been proved that the tourism industry does not exist without safety, and safety is the critical element to the tourism industry, if crisis, especially the catastrophe, happens to the tourist destination, which makes the tourists in passenger origin district always be fear and scared, at last, cancel the plan to travel to tourist destination. So the basic information of tourism industry's priority to recover and rebuild is to indicate to the world that the crisis has gone, the fear and hidden trouble caused by crisis has been removed, now the tourist destination is safe so the tourists can travel there relievedly. The effect produced by that information has the great value to recover the tourist's confidence and eliminate their fears.

The Transfer of Tourist Destination's True Information

The outburst of the disastrous crisis incident directly takes the enormous impact and great bodily injury to tourism industry. Although crisis takes partial failure to local tourism industry, it takes the global influence to tourism economy, whose "amplification effect" has gone beyond people's imagination, inducing public's psychological crisis in various degree, such as abandoning the choice to travel to this tourist destination, abandoning the investment to tourist destination and so on. As a result, the influence taken by crisis has certain extensibility, therefore, to eliminate all kind bodies' including investor, tourist, and so forth anxiety, to rebuild tourism industry, to show the public the practical action of rebuilding the tourism industry, to transfer the true information to public is regarded as the important tropism of tourism industry's rebuilding after catastrophe.

The transfer of tourist destination's true information mainly reflects the spirit of combating a nature disaster to save oneself displaying in tourism system, which will produces one vital effect on helping the tourist, tour investor, and tour operator recover their confidence to tourism industry. So as to crisis happening to some areas produce global negative effect and immediate impact on tourism consumer's visiting and tourism investor's confidence. In result, rebuilding tourism industry has the critical compact on boosting investor's confidence or eliminating tourist anxiety on tourist consumption in order to reset their confidence. In addition, disastrous crisis incident happening make it be a huge and careful systematic engineering to rebuild the tourism industry. So in a sense, the work to rebuild the tourism industry also conveys the spirit of disaster resistance displaying in the progress of tourism system exerting and striving hard without any let up.

THE VALUE OF PROMOTION-DEMONSTRATION EFFECT OF REBUILDING AND RECOVERING TOURISM INDUSTRY FIRSTLY AFTER CATASTROPHE

The Promotion Effect of Tourism Industry

Economically, tourism industry with high degree of association and strong promotion effect is "a inter-industrial and inter-regional industry, whose territorial scope covers tourism-generating region and tourism destination, the integration of those two regions forms the structure of spatial system of tourism industry, within this system, the related industries which fits the tourism demand including transportation industry, hospitality industry, scenic spot service industry, commerce, catering industry, entertainment industry, travel service industry and so forth make up the tourism industry". As a result, the economic multiplier effect tourism industry producing overpasses the other industries so that becomes a comprehension industry with strong promotion effect, whose comprehension and promotion directly promotes transportation industrial, communications,' commercial, building industrial, and energy industrial and so forth development, with calculating, the income of tourism industry's increases 1 yuan, which leads tertiary industry's income to increase over 4 yuan. Thus its promotion effect to national economy is more obvious. Meanwhile, tourism industry also known as the industry to rich public, which expands the peasant's income channel and leads the peasants in tourism destination to increasing income, but supply the jobs to labors, accord with calculation, tourism industry indirectly offers five jobs for absorbing one employee. In one word, developing tourism industry expands the employment channel but also offers lots of job opportunities.

The outburst of the disastrous unexpected crisis incidents may cause multiple loss, even numerous industries may face a fatal strike. For example, Great Sichuan Earthquake caused disastrous loss in the districts such as Wenchuan, Qingchuan, Beichuan, and Dujiangyan. With roundly unfolding the work of disaster relief and eliminating the effect crisis causing, resuming production and rebuilding the homes become the most important thing after the disaster. Thus, during the progress of rebuilding and recovering, being the cornerstone industry, new-type industry, or the leading industry in tourist destination, it should play its role to lead other industries. It is a great meaning for promoting relevant industries' development and enlarging the job opportunity to public, and so forth.

Demonstration Effect of the Tourism
Tourism industry known as Sunrise Industry or Smokeless Industry, under the theme of industrial structure adjustment and building conservation-oriented society, tourism industry becomes the one which is called the environment-friendly industry or energetic conservation-oriented industry. Therefore accelerating tourism industry development will has the congenital demonstration effect on sustainable utilizating resource, promoting the harmonious co-existent between human beings and environment and changing economic growth mode.

The tourism industry's recovery and rebuilding can also show a good demonstrative effect, and it can be a dynamically developing leading industry in roundly recovering and rebuilding the stricken areas. With recovering and rebuilding the society and economics in tourism destination, tourism industry must be the harmonious industry which improves people's life and strengthens the stability of the society, and then the industry benefiting people which increases income and enlarges the employment. The destructed sceneries, the roads, communication facilities, tourists-receiving facilities, and public facilities will be recovered with the primitively rebuilding of tourism, and will recover rapidly and develop better because of scientific arrangement.

THE IMAGE-SHOWING EFFECT VALUE OF THE POST-CATASTROPHE AREA

Tourism is export oriented industry. Being the tour destination, its good surroundings, excellent service, pretty resources, and well-prepared service facilities etc. are of lot meanings for opening the tour destination, absorbing investment and strengthening the popularity of the destination. The occurrence of the catastrophe unexpectedly causes tremendous pessimistic effects on the fatal economic loss and the damage of the tour destination's brand image, which sends to the international society the information that it's been a dangerous place to go. However, after the catastrophe, building a good image, a safe destination and a reliable brand would be the main work. Absorbing more domestic and broad tourists to travel to the stricken area is most persuasive, and it the most important responsibility tourism industry can take.

Rebuilding the tourism industry priorly after catastrophe should be carried out gradually according to extent of the disaster after detailed investigation and carefully planning. Meanwhile the chargers should faithfully transmit the information of the disaster area and make it well known, and they also should develop and design some new tour products relating to catastrophe, carry forward the spirit of combating on the earthquake disaster in the stricken area, and build new brands. Therefore the primitive rebuilding of the tourism industry is very important, which would be a window to show the area and the national image to public and it also be the wind vane of the economic development and social order as well as the sign of eliminating the effect of the earthquake.

KEYWORDS

- **Catastrophe**
- **Rebuilding**
- **Restoration**
- **Tourism industry**

Chapter 5

Tourist Preferences Study Using Conjoint Analysis

Shalini N. Tripathi and Masood H. Siddiqui

INTRODUCTION

Tourism and hospitality have become key global economic activities as expectations with regard to our use of leisure time have evolved, attributing greater meaning to our free time. While the growth in tourism has been impressive, India's share in total global tourism arrivals and earnings is quite insignificant. It is an accepted fact that India has tremendous potential for development of tourism. This anomaly and the various underlying factors responsible for it are the focus of our study. The objective being determination of customer preferences for multi attribute hybrid services like tourism, so as to enable the state tourism board to deliver a desired combination of intrinsic attributes, helping it to create a sustainable competitive advantage, leading to greater customer satisfaction and positive word of mouth. Conjoint analysis (CJA) has been used for this purpose, which estimates the structure of a consumer's preferences, given his/her overall evaluations of a set of alternatives that are pre-specified in terms of levels of different attributes. Tourism is a service industry; therefore, there are inherent challenges with service marketing that affect how the tourism product is communicated to the consumer public. According to Williams (2006), tourism and hospitality have become key global economic activities as expectations with regard to our use of leisure time have evolved, attributing greater meaning to our free time. This results in marketing having potentially greater importance in tourism than in other industries but sadly potential that is not always fulfilled (Morgan and Pritchard, 2002). Williams (2006) believes that a major reason for such unfulfilled potential lies in most tourism marketing focusing on the destination or outlet (in other words the products being offered) and lacking focus on the consumer. Therefore, while tourism boards may already use a number of planned and controlled marketing activities, this chapter purports that they could also exploit the destination image enhancement opportunities that exist through developing an insight about the customer/tourist preferences and delivering the desired service package.

THE INDIAN TOURISM INDUSTRY

Tourism in India has registered significant growth in the recent years. In 1951, International Tourist Arrivals stood at around 17,000 only while the same has now gone up to 3.91 million in 2005. The upward trend is expected to remain firm in the coming years. Tourism is the third largest net earner of foreign exchange for the country recording earnings of US$5731 million in 2005, a growth of 20.2% over 2004 (Tourism Overview in 2005–2006). It is also one of the sectors which employ the largest number of manpower. The first ever Tourism Satellite Accounts for India compiled by NCAER for the year 2002–2003 showed that tourism employed 38.8 million persons, directly and indirectly, which was 8.3% of the total employment in the country and who contributed 5.8% of the gross domestic product (GDP) (Tourism Satellite Accounts for India, NCAER). These figures are estimated to have increased to 41.85 million employed in 2003–2004 with a GDP contribution of 5.9%. Various studies have also shown that tourism generates the highest employment per unit of investment for the skilled, semi-skilled, and unskilled. The World Travel and Tourism council (WTTC) has identified India as one of the foremost growth centers in the world in the coming decade (WTTC Travel and Tourism Economy Research).

India's share in international tourist arrivals has increased from 0.46% in 2004 to an estimated 0.55% in 2007. Foreign Tourist Arrivals (FTA) has increased from 3.46 million in 2004 to an estimated 5 million in 2007. The contribution of tourism to India's foreign exchange earnings has grown from $6.17 billion (Rs. 279,440 million) to an estimated $11.96 billion (Rs. 494,130 million) in 2007. India's share in world earnings from tourism has increased from 0.98% in 2004 to 1.21% in 2006. There is a significant increase in the domestic sector also, as number of domestic tourists has increased from 366.23 million in 2004 to an estimated 462 million in 2006. (Tourism Statistics for India: Annual report on the status of tourism in India, published by Ministry of Tourism, Government of India).

While the growth in tourism has been impressive, India's share in total global tourism arrivals and earnings is quite insignificant. It is an accepted fact that India has tremendous potential for development of tourism. The diversity of India's natural and cultural richness provides the basis of a wide range of tourist products and experiences, which embrace business, leisure, culture, adventure, spirituality, eco-tourism, and many other pursuits. Apart from acknowledging the traditionally recognized advantages of developing tourism for the promotion of national integration, international understanding, earning of foreign exchange, and vast employment generation, it can play a major role in furthering the socio-economic objectives of nation.

The Ministry of Tourism adopted a multi-pronged approach in order to achieve this growth. Providing a congenial atmosphere for tourism development, strengthening the tourism infrastructure and hospitality related services, integrated development of identified destinations and circuits, integrating elements of tourism, emphasizing on culture and clean civic life marketing of tourism products in a focused manner along with a branding exercise and positioning India as a high value destination in the new key markets and giving thrust on the human resource development activities have been the hallmarks of this strategy. The focus of product development in the states also underwent a change by enhanced outlays for "destination development up to an amount of Rs. 50 million and circuit development" up to an amount of Rs. 80 million (Tourism Policy). A new proposal was moved to allocate up to Rs. 500 million for individual destinations with high tourist footfalls in order to totally redesign the experience of the tourist through greater organization and provision of civic facilities.

The important initiatives taken by the Government to improve the flow of foreign tourists into the country and thereby increasing the country's share in the world tourism included the following:

- Beginning of cruise tourism by an international shipping firm.
- Direct approach to the consumers through electronic and print media through the "Incredible India" Campaign called "Colours of India" (Incredible India Campaign)
- Creation of World Class Collaterals.
- Centralized Electronic Media Campaign.
- An integrated campaign in South East Asia to promote Buddhist sites in India, and so forth.

Among the most favored tourist destinations in India, Kerala for its scenic beauty, Agra for Taj Mahal, Khajuraho for its sculptures and temples, Goa for its beaches, Lucknow for its historical significance, and some pilgrimages are the most important.

TOURISM IN UTTAR PRADESH

The state of Uttar Pradesh is situated in the northern part of India and is one of the most fascinating states of the Union of India. The state of Uttar Pradesh offers immense tourism delights and an endless array of attractions, to the visitors in the state by way of its rich and varied topography, vibrant culture and captivating festivities, monuments, and ancient places of worship. Agra, Ayodhya, Sarnath, Varanasi, Lucknow, Mathura, and Prayag combine religious and architectural marvels.

The state tourism department has reviewed the existing Tourism Policy and finalized the new Tourism Development Policy for the state of Uttar Pradesh (Tourism Policy for Uttar Pradesh) (www.up-tourism.com/policy/new_policy.htm; planning-commission.nic.in/plans/stateplan/upsdr/vol-2/Chap_b5.pdf). The objectives of the policy are:

- Providing economic benefits to the local population and enhancement of employment opportunities.
- Improving and diversifying the tourism product base, with focus on adventure, religious and monument based travel.
- Increasing the hotel capacity of the region.
- Increasing the visitation number.
- Enhancing the investment in the tourism industry.
- Increasing revenue per visitor through superior visitor profile, better facilities and value addition to the tourism product.

These aspirations as projected by the State Tourism Policy have the following strategies for development:

- Development of basic infrastructure, to be undertaken by the government bodies.
- Planning tourist circuits through a master plan.
- Enhancing and encouraging the participation of the private sector in efforts of the state government for providing necessary facilities to domestic and international tourists.
- Dovetailing development funds from different sources.

- Improving the product diversity to attract a range of tourists.
- Coordination between various government departments.
- Proper restoration of heritage properties and their publicity.
- Providing cheap, clean, and satisfactory facilities to tourists in matters of transport, accommodation, food, and recreation.
- Organizing cultural shows on occasion of different fairs, festivals, and seminars with a view to attracting more and more tourists.
- Setting standards and quality benchmarks.
- Extensive and effective marketing.

In 2002, the foreign exchange earning for the state was Rs. 28,390 million which increased to Rs. 50,344 in the year 2005 (Malviya, 2008).

According to the AC Nielsen ORG-MARG "Collection of Tourism Statistics for the State of Uttar Pradesh" report (UP Tourism Statistics), the total number of tourists visiting the State of Uttar Pradesh for the period of April 2005—March 2006 was 17.8 million. Out of this, 4.5 million were domestic overnight visitors, 0.5 million foreign overnight visitors and 12.8 million were day tourists. Domestic overnight visitors spent 8.3 million bed nights and foreign overnight visitors spent 0.97 million bed nights in this period at various accommodation units in the state. Taking a holistic view, major heads of expenditure for the visitors to the destination were accommodation services, food and beverage services, as well as transport equipment rentals.

The glaring anomaly to be noted over here is that despite its rich cultural heritage and high potential for tourism, the growth of tourism in the state of Uttar Pradesh has not been very significant (UP Tourism Statistics). This anomaly and the various underlying factors responsible for it are the focus of our study.

MARKETING OF TOURISM

Tourism being a service industry presents inherent challenges with service marketing that affect how the tourism product is communicated to the consumer public. There is, according to Clow et al. (2006, p. 404), a "difficulty in communicating effectively the attributes of a service because of the unique characteristics of services, especially intangibility." Indeed, the intangible nature of any service presents immense challenges to marketers in so much as communicating a product's offering favorably to a potential market. Consider trying to communicate the thrill of a rollercoaster ride; the buzzing atmosphere in a busy city restaurant; the range of emotions felt while watching a theatre production. Travel-based products also have uniqueness in that they are not of a "tangible" nature. Information constitutes the bulk of travel products and transactions.

Tourism and travel, as Zhou (2004) states, are about the experiences and memories that tourists will have for a lifetime, but there is an inherent difficulty in promoting something largely intangible in this way. "Tangibilising the intangible" (Levitt, 1981 cited in Kotler, 2000) to engage your target audience is understandably complex. However, the buyer decision-making process for the service product compounds marketing challenges even further (Hoffman and Turley, 2002). In the absence of being able to touch, see, or test a service, pre-purchasing decisions are much riskier than for goods

(Palmer, 2000). In many ways, it is venturing into an unknown and untested territory unless the consumer has purchased the product before or the product has received a positive word of mouth (File and Prince, 1992).

Gilmore et al. (2007) discuss sustainable tourism marketing in the context of a world heritage site and contend that a strategic marketing approach for the development of sustainable tourism is vital to the management of a world heritage site. This concept of tourism incorporates social, economic, and environmental perspectives in a given region.

Hence, although the various State Tourism Departments may be deploying a number of marketing activities, but this study proposes developing an in depth understanding of tourist preferences and delivering the desired tourism packages ensuring greater customer satisfaction.

GAINING INSIGHT INTO CUSTOMER PREFERENCES

Knowing where consumer preferences and their values reside, companies can develop the necessary marketing strategies to increase customer satisfaction, loyalty, and retention, thus strengthening their competitive position. It is impossible today to remain cost competitive and offer every feature desired by customers (Pullman et al., 2002). Therefore, marketing, engineering and operations need to work together to determine the profit-maximizing bundle of product features.

The tourism industry has some specific characteristics that impact upon any tourism marketing management activity. Both public and private sector companies are involved in the planning, management, and delivery of tourism services (Font and Ahjem, 1999) and small companies often provide many fundamental services within tourism regions (Dewhurst and Thomas, 2003; Go et al., 1992). So the industry is an amalgam of companies and organizations with different purposes and agendas and this has an influence on the overall tourism offering.

It is widely recognized that the tourism industry is fragmented and many authors have asserted the need for some form of co-operative arrangement between stakeholders (Boyd and Timothy, 2001; Bramwell and Lane, 1999; Butler, 1991; D'Amore, 1992; McKetcher, 1993). Integrated, co-ordinated tourism is seen to be desirable, if not essential, for the implementation of sustainable tourism (WTO, 1993).

Marketers are more likely to use CJA to help design new product feature sets. Green and Krieger suggest the use of the CJA technique, for the detection of competitive actions and reactions in the case of introducing new products or services and extensions, through the analysis of consumers' preferences and perceptions (Green and Krieger, 1997).

The CJA is a survey-based multivariate technique that measures consumer preferences about the attributes of a product or a service. The goal is to identify the most desirable combination of features to be offered or included in the product or the service. The underlying theoretical premise of the CJA process is that consumers simplify the complexity of a purchasing decision, selecting for themselves a subset of features/attributes for which they give individual subject values, depending on the characteristic structure of those values.

In their working paper, Green and Rao (1969) discussed briefly the conjoint methodology. However, the first detailed consumer oriented paper appeared only in 1971 by Green and Rao. Later, Green and Srinivasan in 1978 developed it as a major set of techniques for buyer's trade-offs among multi-attributed products and services.

Conjoint broadly refers to any decompositional method that estimates the structure of a consumer's preferences, given his/her overall evaluations of a set of alternatives that are pre-specified in terms of levels of different attributes. Hence, is best suited for understanding consumers' reactions to and evaluations of predetermined attribute combinations that represent potential products or services. While maintaining a high degree of realism, it provides the researcher with insight into the composition of consumer preference. The CJA is based on the simple premise that consumers evaluate the value of a product/service by combining the separate amounts of value provided by each attribute. Here, first a set of real or hypothetical products or services are constructed by combining selected levels of each attribute. These combinations are presented to respondents, who provide only their overall evaluations. Thus, the respondents are asked to perform a very realistic task choosing among a set of products/services by rating/ranking. Because of construction of the hypothetical product/service in a specific manner, the influence of each attribute and the worth of each level as judged by respondent can be determined by the respondents' overall ratings. Figure 1 gives a proposed conceptual model for this chapter, illustrating the step wise process followed to arrive at the most desirable tourism package (as per tourist preferences), so that it can be conveyed further to the state tourism department for implementation.

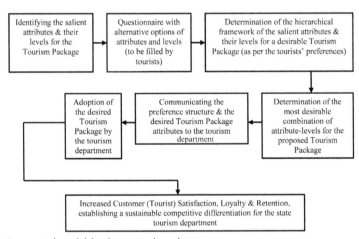

Figure 1. Conceptual model for the research study.

DESIGNING A CONJOINT ANALYSIS EXPERIMENT

Specifying Attributes and Levels

Although CJA places minimal demand on the respondents in terms of both the number and types of responses needed, a number of key decisions need to be made, in designing the experiment and analyzing the results (Figure 2). The first step of the conjoint decision process is specification of objectives of the CJA. The objective of the present study was determination of customer preferences for multi attribute hybrid services like tourism, so as to enable the state tourism board to deliver a desired combination of intrinsic attributes, helping it to create a sustainable competitive advantage, leading to greater customer satisfaction and positive word of mouth. Accordingly, in formulating the CJA problem, six categories of salient attributes were identified (Table 1). These attributes were identified by a detailed identification process consisting of discussion with tourism industry experts, secondary analysis of reports of the tourism department, content analysis of the pilot survey.

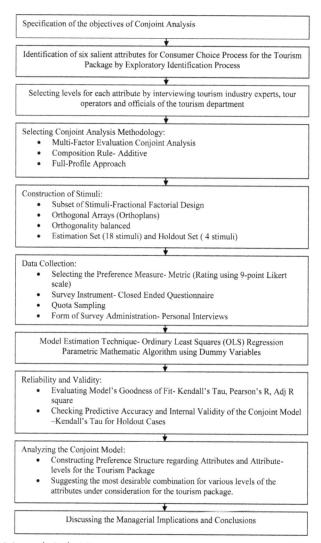

Figure 2. Conjoint analysis decision process.

After identification of salient attributes, their appropriate levels were selected. The number of attribute levels determines the number of parameters that will be estimated and also influences the number of stimuli (attribute combination) to be evaluated by the respondents. So, following the in-depth interview with tourism industry experts, tour operators, and officials of Uttar Pradesh Tourism Department, the levels estimating the attributes were selected in such a way that they covered the whole spectrum of product and services that are actually offered or are plausible. We have taken three different levels for each of the six attributes (Table 1). These attribute levels satisfied all the requirements for sufficiency, appeal, and application, simultaneously it was kept in mind that when operationalizing either features or levels, they should be both communicable and actionable (can be implemented).

Table 1. Investigated attribute and their levels.

1. Information

1.1 Web & Tele Media

1.2 Print Media

1.3 Tour Operator & Tourism Office

2. Security

2.1 Luggage Safety

2.2 Medical Insurance

2.3 Family Safety

3. Choice

3.1 Natural Sites

3.2 Modern Architecture

3.3 Historical/Religious Monuments

4. Access

4.1 Airways

4.2 Roadways

4.3 Railways

5. Complaint Redressal

5.1 Ombudsman

5.2 Feedback Form

5.3 Govt Officials/Tourism Dept

6. Value for Money

6.1 Greater Quality of Sightseeing

6.2 Greater Comfort in Lodging

6.3 Comfortable Lodging and Extensive Sightseeing at Premium Price

Selecting Conjoint Analysis Methodology and Construction of Stimuli

After determining the basic attribute and their levels, we have decided to use multi-factor evaluation CJA methodology (Green and Srinivasan, 1990). The reason behind this choice revolved around three basic characteristics of the proposed research: number of attributes, level of analysis and the permitted model form. Here we are dealing with six attributes, our level of analysis would be aggregate; and the model form to be used would be additive. Hence, full-profile approach, involving construction of complete profiles of the service/product offerings for all the attributes, was used here. We have three levels for each of the six attributes. Hence there will be total 36 = 729 product descriptions (stimuli). However, number of stimuli profiles were greatly reduced from 729 to 22 stimuli by means of fractional factorial design. This appeared to be a manageable number for the respondents and also exceeds the minimum number of stimuli (Total number of levels across all attribute—Number of attributes + 1 = 13) that must be evaluated by the respondent to ensure the reliability of the estimated parameters. A special class of fractional design, called orthogonal arrays was used. It assumes that all interactions present in stimuli are negligible. It allows for efficient estimation of all main effects of interest (Green et al., 2001; Kuhfeld et al., 1994). Here, two sets of data were obtained. One, estimation set, consisting of 18 stimuli, was used for calculating part-worth functions for the attribute levels. The other, holdout set, consisting of four stimuli, was used to assess reliability and validity. The orthogonal arrays (orthoplan) were generated by SPSS-15.0 software. So, total 22 design cards resulted and therefore respondents (tourists) have to evaluate questionnaires consisting of 22 cards.

Deciding on the Form of Input Data

For the survey purpose, we have used Metric Conjoint Analysis. Here, respondents were required to provide preference ratings for the tourism package described by 18 profiles in the estimation set and four profiles in the holdout set. The ratings were obtained using nine-point Likert scale (1 = Least preferred, 9 = Most preferred).

Survey Administration

The survey instrument was a closed ended questionnaire. The questionnaire had 22 stimuli profiles for preference rating. There were also questions related to demographic and behavioral information of the tourists. The 1080 questionnaires were found complete in all respects. "Quota Sampling" was deployed, so as to make the sample representative of the population of tourists visiting Uttar Pradesh. The quotas have been constructed on the basis of various demographic characteristics like age, gender, marital status, occupation, income, city of residence, and so forth (Table 2). The information was collected from the tourists at different tourist places and hotels in the state of Uttar Pradesh. The questionnaires were administered personally to ensure the authenticity of information provided by the respondents. The questionnaires were pre-tested to check the orthogonality and other aspects and thereafter suitably modified.

Table 2. Demographic characteristics of respondents.

Demographic Characteristics		Frequency	Percentage
Age	Below 25	216	20.0
	25-35	297	27.5
	36-45	291	27.0
	Above 45	276	25.5
Gender	Male	627	58.0
	Female	453	42.0
Marital Status	Single	420	39.0
	Married	660	61.0
Annual Income	Below 0.2 million	138	13.0
	0.2 million -0.4 million	411	38.0
	0.4 million -0.6 million	288	26.7
	Above 0.6 million	243	21.3
Profession	Student	114	10.5
	Services	390	36.1
	Business	399	36.9
	Housewife	177	16.5
Total		1080	100

Conjoint Analysis Procedure

The basic CJA model may be represented as (Carroll and Green 1995; Haaijer et al., 2000):

$$U(X) = \sum_{i=1}^{m} \sum_{j=1}^{ki} \alpha_{ij} x_{ij}$$

where,

$U(X)$ = Overall utility (importance) of an attribute

α_{ij} = part-worth utility of the jth level of the ith attribute

$i = 1, 2..., m$ $\qquad\qquad$ $j = 1, 2..., k_i$

x_{ij} = 1, if the jth level of the ith attribute is present

$\qquad$ = 0, otherwise.

The basic model was estimated with the ordinary least squares (OLSs) regression parametric mathematic algorithm (Fox, 1997) using dummy variable regression. The preference ratings were the predicted (dependent) variable and predictor variables consist of dummy variables for the attribute levels. This algorithm calculates partial values by homogenizing the rate fluctuations based on the normal distribution (Green and Krieger, 1993). Partial values were then used to calculate the total mean perceptual values.

RELIABILITY AND VALIDITY

The CJA results should be assessed for accuracy, reliability, and validity. The objective is to ascertain how consistently the model predicts the set of preference evaluations under different situations. Our results derived from the CJA are reliable and valid as:

1. While evaluating the goodness of fit of the estimated conjoint model, we found out that value of Kendall's tau is 0.943, value of Pearson's R is 0.977, and the value of adjusted R square is 0.843. Both these values are reasonably high and these results are significant at 5% level of significance (asymptotic significance = 0.014) (Tables 3.1–3.3)

2. The value of Durbin–Watson statistic is 2.227 (Table 3.2), which lies in the range (1.25–2.75), showing that auto-correlation is not present.

3. The correlation table (Table 4) shows that there is small correlation among different predictors. So, multicollinearity is not present in the data.

4. We have also used four stimuli as validation or holdout stimuli to determine internal validity. Parameters from the estimated conjoint model (using 18 stimuli) were used to predict preferences for the holdout set of stimuli and then they were compared with actual responses by calculating correlation. Considering the table (Table 3.1), we have found out that value of Kendall's tau is 0.712 for the four holdout cases. This value is significantly high (asymptotic significance = 0.009). So, we can say that our conjoint model has high predictive accuracy and internal validity.

Table 3.1. Model Summary (a).

	Value	Sig.
Pearson's R	.977	.014
Kendall's tau	.943	.004
Kendall's tau for Holdouts	.712	.009

Table 3.2. Model Summary (b).

Model	R	R Square	Adjusted R Square	Std. Error of the Estimate	Durbin-Watson
1	.977(a)	.954	.843	.15993	2.227

Table 3.3. ANOVA (b).

Model		Sum of Squares	df	Mean Square	F	Sig.
1	Regression	2.645	12	.220	8.616	.014(a)
	Residual	.128	5	.026		
	Total	2.773	17			

a. *Predictors:* (Constant), d12, d10, d7, d6, d1, d9, d4, d8, d3, d2, d11, d5
b. *Dependent Variable:* MEAN_SCORE

Table 4. Correlations among predictors.

		MEAN SCORE	d1	d2	d3	d4	d5	d6	d7	d8	d9	d10	d11	d12
Pearson Correlation	MEAN SCORE	1.000	0.325	0.188	-0.287	-0.212	-0.065	0.308	-0.095	-0.149	0.181	-0.023	0.088	0.322
	d1	0.325	1.000	-0.500	0.000	0.000	0.000	0.000	0.000	0.000	0.000	0.000	0.161	0.000
	d2	0.118	-0.500	1.000	0.000	0.000	0.000	0.000	0.000	0.000	0.000	0.000	0.161	-0.250
	d3	-0.287	0.000	0.000	1.000	-0.500	0.000	0.000	0.000	0.000	0.000	0.000	0.161	-0.500
	d4	-0.212	0.000	0.000	-0.500	1.000	0.000	0.000	0.000	0.000	0.000	0.000	-0.0181	0.500
	d5	-0.065	0.000	0.000	0.000	0.000	1.000	-0.500	0.000	0.000	0.000	0.000	0.645	-0.500
	d6	-0.308	0.000	0.000	0.000	0.000	-0.500	1.000	0.000	0.000	0.000	0.000	-0.322	0.000
	d7	-0.095	0.000	0.000	0.000	0.000	0.000	0.000	1.000	-0.500	0.000	0.000	-0.081	0.000
	d8	-0.149	0.000	0.000	0.000	0.000	0.000	0.000	-0.500	1.000	0.000	0.000	0.161	0.250
	d9	0.181	0.000	0.000	0.000	0.000	0.000	0.000	0.000	0.000	1.000	-0.500	-0.081	0.000
	d10	-0.023	0.000	0.000	0.000	0.000	0.000	0.000	0.000	0.000	-0.500	1.000	-0.081	0.000

Table 4. *(Continued)*

							Correlations						
	MEAN SCORE	d1	d2	d3	d4	d5	d6	d7	d8	d9	d10	d11	d12
d11	0.088	0.161	0.161	0.161	-0.081	0.645	-0.322	-0.081	0.161	-0.081	-0.081	1.000	-0.564
d12	0.322	0.000	-0.250	-0.500	0.500	-0.500	0.000	0.000	-0.250	0.000	0.000	-0.564	1.000
MEAN SCORE	–	0.094	0.320	0.124	0.199	0.399	0.107	0.354	0.277	0.236	0.464	0.365	0.096
Sig. (1-tailed)													
d1	0.094		0.017	0.500	0.500	0.500	0.500	0.500	0.500	0.500	0.500	0.261	0.500
d2	0.320	0.017		0.500	0.500	0.500	0.500	0.500	0.500	0.500	0.500	0.261	0.159
d3	0.124	0.500	0.500		0.17	0.500	0.500	0.500	0.500	0.500	0.500	0.261	0.017
d4	0.199	0.500	0.500	0.017		0.500	0.500	0.500	0.500	0.500	0.500	0.375	0.017
d5	0.399	0.500	0.500	0.500	0.500		0.017	0.500	0.500	0.500	0.500	0.002	0.017
d6	0.107	0.500	0.500	0.500	0.500	0.017		0.500	0.500	0.500	0.500	0.096	0.500
d7	0.354	0.500	0.500	0.500	0.500	0.500	0.500		0.017	0.500	0.500	0.375	0.500
d8	0.277	0.500	0.500	0.500	0.500	0.500	0.500	0.017		0.500	0.500	0.261	0.159
d9	0.236	0.500	0.500	0.500	0.500	0.500	0.500	0.500	0.500		0.017	0.375	0.500
d10	0.464	0.500	0.500	0.500	0.500	0.500	0.500	0.500	0.500	0.017		0.375	0.500
d11	0.365	0.261	0.261	0.261	0.375	0.002	0.096	0.375	0.261	0.375	0.375		0.007
d12	0.096	0.500	0.159	0.017	0.017	0.017	0.500	0.500	0.159	0.500	0.500	0.007	

FINDINGS AND MANAGERIAL IMPLICATIONS

The most important aspect of the relationship between service providers and customers is that the service providers lack an in depth insight into customer preferences. There is often a disconnect between what customers want and what service providers offer. This is particularly true in case of services like tourism because of the intangibility element associated with it. The present study was undertaken to determine hierarchical framework of salient attributes in a desirable tourism-package (as per tourists' preferences) and thereafter to identify the most desirable combination of attributes that can be offered to tourists visiting the state of Uttar Pradesh. The results as presented in Figure 3 represent the mean preference structure or the grading provided by the tourists visiting state of Uttar Pradesh. These preference scores are based on the data collected from 1,080 tourists through a structured questionnaire.

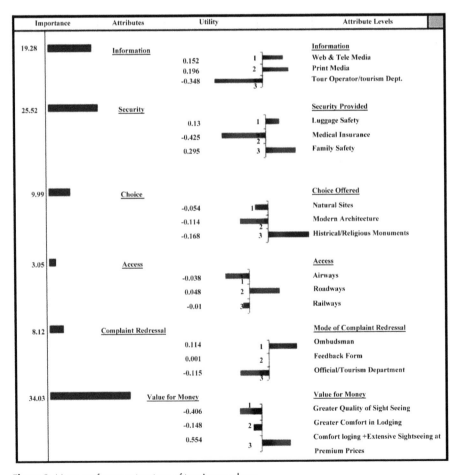

Figure 3. Mean preference structure of tourism package.

Here six salient attributes and their levels were identified for consumer choice process in the tourism package by exploratory identification process. Full Profile CJA was used for construction of preference structure. Analyzing the preference structure or the relative importance accorded (by tourists) to the six salient attributes, the tourists accorded the maximum utility/importance to the attribute "value for money" (with importance as 34.03%). Hence the state tourism board needs to comprehend "value" in customer terms and deliver the same. Taking into account the part worth functions, the tourists have primarily defined value in terms of comfortable lodging and extensive sightseeing (even at a price premium). Sightseeing and comfortable lodging as attributes rank very high as per tourist preferences.

The second most important attribute in the desirable tourism-package is "security expected during the visit" (importance 25.52%). Ensuring safety and security of all tourists is function of paramount importance for the state tourism board. Within the purview of this attribute the tourists accorded the highest priority to family safety. In recent times, with a sudden spurt in terrorist related activities and attacks on tourists in particular, there is a sense of insecurity among tourists. Appropriate security should be steadfastly ensured by the state law enforcement authorities. In absence of requisite security measures, any substantial progress in development of tourism of a destination may not be possible.

Thereafter at the third place in the worth hierarchy is the attribute of "information" with a utility percentage of 19.285. The most preferred form of accessing the relevant and required information is "print-media" and then "web-media". For informed decision making, prospective tourists seek host of information (related to accessibility, tourist packages on offer, lodging, sightseeing, etc.). And print media provides detailed and permanent (in the consumer's perception) information about the alternative tourism packages on offer. The web media is probably preferred because of its convenience and easy accessibility. This information can be made available via brochures, newspapers, travel magazines, and informative websites.

Then at the fourth place of the hierarchical framework, is the attribute "choice offered" (worth 9.99%) to tourists (in terms of sightseeing options). Here the tourists accorded the highest priority to historical and religious monuments. The state of Uttar Pradesh possesses as its major attractions, some important historical and religious monuments. Hence there should be coordinated efforts by the state tourism board, archaeological department, and state government towards proper maintenance and upkeep of these monuments.

Next in the hierarchical preference structure is the attribute representing complaints handling and redressal mechanism for tourism and related services (worth 8.12%). Here tourists stressed upon a dedicated "ombudsman", who would be empowered to suitably address tourist grievances.

The last attribute was the "mode of access" but the tourists did not accord much important to it (3.05%). The decision pertaining to the mode of travel is generally governed by monetary constraints, time constraints, and available options.

Binary Logistic Models

As a post hoc implementation to the application of CJA for developing a desirable tourism package, binary logistic regression model was constructed to examine the effect of demographic and socio-economic factors upon the utilities assigned to different levels of the attributes (constituent components of the tourism package). Consumers being heterogeneous, with differing perceptions, may attach different degree of importance to various attribute-levels and this in turn would affect the nature and size of the utilities. These considerations may be incorporated while designing customized tourism service packages for different groups of customers.

In binary logistic regression models, levels of the salient attributes are taken as predicted (dependent) variables. To convert the utilities values into dichotomous variables, we have taken the value "one" if utility of the attribute level is above the mean and "zero" otherwise. So, the total number of binary logistic regression models to be estimated was 18. The predictor variables for each of the regression model were age, gender, marital status, family income, and profession. These 18 models were estimated and the results are presented in the Table 5.

Table 5. Logistic regression model results for attribute levels.

Dependent Variable	Constant	Age	Gender	Marital Status	Annual Income	Profession
Web & Tele Media	−.812	.116	−.088	−.098	.083	.078
	(−1.376)	(2.732)*	(−.473)	(−.632)	(1.679)	(.634)
Print Media	.989	.009	−.798	−.031	−.129	.027
	(1.886)	(.132)	(.043)	(−.911)	(−.911)	(.392)
Tour Operator & Tourism Office	.143	.232	−.436	−.009	−.211	−.143
	(.332)	(.088)	(−.684)	(−.241)	(−1.112)	(−1.045)
Luggage Safety	−.430	.094	−.017	.435	−.043	.084
	(−.989)	(1.020)	(−.563)	(.678)	(−.075)	(.273)
Medical Insurance	−.383	.127	.005	−.112	.065	.106
	(.996)	(1.746)	(.032)	(−.958)	(.697)	(.546)
Family Safety	−.574	.125	−.057	−.066	.017	.072
	(−.838)	(1.563)	(−2.261)*	(−1.877)	(.447)	(.118)
Natural Sites	.507	.089	−.008	−.043	.003	−.149
	(1.274)	(1.569)	(−.937)	(−.978)	(.583)	(−.781)
Modern Architecture	−.649	−.036	.087	.038	−.073	.037
	(−1.029)	(−2.469)*	(.390)	(.769)	(−.0870))	(1.161)
Historical/Religious Monuments	.467	.049	−.012	.005	−.083	−.003
	(1.243)	(.889)	(−.054)	(.054)	(−.278)	(−.761)
Airways	.503	.037	−.051	−.014	.622	−.032
	(.799)	(.064)	(−.286)	(−.039)	(1.274)	(−.238)
Roadways	−.159	.318	−.107	.067	−.058	−.054
	(−.756)	(.137)	(−.700)	(.092)	(−1.06)	(−.687)
Railways	−.892	.144	−.069	.002	−.062	.032
	(−.994)	(.039)	(−.671)	(.077)	(−1.16)	(.041)

Table 5. *(Continued)*

Dependent Variable	Constant	Age	Gender	Marital Status	Annual Income	Profession
Ombudsman	.133	.106	.022	-.332	-.159	-.031
	(.548)	(.9650)	(.049)	(-.965)	(-.254)	(-1.43)
Feedback Form	.386	-.038	.018	-.015	-.139	.064
	(1.003)	(-.511)	(.756)	(-.834)	(-.376)	(.186)
Govt. Officials/Tourism Dept	-.302	.069	.059	-.068	-.029	.008
	(-.756)	(.365)	(.829)	(-.949)	(-.586)	(.030)
Greater Quality of Sightseeing	-.247	-.522	.033	-.066	-.069	.088
	(-.635)	(-.604)	(.749)	(-.956)	(-.945)	(1.044)
Greater Comfort in Lodging	-.139	-.049	.258	.017	-.035	.138
	(-.447)	(-.165)	(.132)	(.867)	(-1.22)	(.744)
Comfortable Lodging and Extensive Sightseing at Premium Price	-.139	.382	-.149	.112	.129	-.261
	(-.292)	(2.389)*	(-1.867)	(1.236)	(2.567)*	(-.843)

Note: 1. Figures in parentheses are t-ratios.
2. *Significance at 5% level of significance.

According to the above table (Table 5), most of the explanatory variables (demographic and socio-economic characteristics) do not show significant effects on the dependent variable (utilities) barring some variables which have a significant impact and may contribute to higher perception value for certain attribute-levels. For web-media, age show significant effect upon the importance attached to web-media. The younger generation being more technically savvy, may enjoy greater comfort level using web and tele-media for accessing information in comparison to traditional methods like print media and tourism office. However the older generation may perceive information from these traditional sources as being more authentic hence greater reliance on these sources, so the utility values may vary accordingly. Gender as an explanatory factor shows significant effect on dependent variable family-safety, probably contributing to the high utility value. Females tend to assign higher importance to the family safety *vis-à-vis* any other factor during a holiday. Predictor age contributes to higher utility value being assigned to the sightseeing option of modern architecture, an option probably finding favor with the younger age group, whereas the timeless treasures that is the historical and religious monuments are equally preferred by all age groups. Family income and age as predictors have a significant effect in the model analyzing comfortable lodging and extensive sightseeing at premium prices, and are mainly responsible for contributing high utility value to this service option. The rationale being that people in the older age group (40 years and above), with higher disposable income, would prefer a tourism package incorporating extensive and exclusive sightseeing, greater comfort in lodging, with a willingness to pay a price premium for a package customized to suit their preferences.

Age appears to be most important explanatory variable or predictor, as it was found to be significant in three binary logistic regression models.

CONCLUSION AND MANAGERIAL IMPLICATIONS

The chapter attempts to provide Uttar Pradesh Tourism department, with information about specific attributes to be incorporated in the tourism services provided by them, as per tourists' preferences.

The study focuses on the relative importance accorded to the identified six salient attributes value for money, information, security, choices offered, complaint redressal, and modes of access.

The CJA results reveal that the tourists accord the greatest importance to the "value for money" attribute, followed by "security" and thereafter "information". They however place relatively less value on "variety of sightseeing options", "complaint redressal", and "modes of access".

The binary logistic regression analysis results however reveal that some socio-economic variables of the tourists played a significant role in shaping the importance of the underlying utilities, indicating that the utilities would probably be sensitive to the structure of these variables.

The study has important management and marketing implications. From the management perspective, the study can empower the state tourism departments with information (about tourist preferences), so that they can add value to their relationship with the tourists, by incorporating the preferred combination of features. The decision making authorities in the tourism department can also assess the information provided by the study, to appropriately bridge the gaps between their perception of value (of services provided) and the tourists' perception of value (desired services), by developing corrective action plans. Such corrective actions will ensure greater customer satisfaction as well as a differentiable competitive advantage, *vis-à-vis* the other tourist destinations.

Although this study focuses on tourism department of the state of Uttar Pradesh, however the premise of this chapter can be successfully implemented by the tourism authorities of other national environments. Worldwide the most important factor governing the relationship between service providers and customers is the service providers' lack of insight into customer preferences. This leads to a lacuna between what customers want and what service providers' offer, especially in case of services like tourism. In order to bridge this lacuna tourism authorities (of any country) can determine the preference structure of the tourists (visiting the tourist destinations of that country), and offer customized tourism packages. The attributes and their levels used for CJA could be adapted in accordance with the socio-cultural environment of a country.

There are, however, certain limitations in the present study, as well as some avenues for further research. Specific product combinations have not been analyzed in this study that could possibly end in modified or niche marketing strategies. Further research could examine the usefulness of promoting specific product characteristics in everyday practice, such as promoting an ideal tourism package. It is difficult to develop combinations with more than three levels of product characteristics as well as use of a variety of examined factor variables. This weakness is based on the difficulty that individuals had in replying to the standardized questionnaires, thus resulting in choosing variable categories very carefully and after in-depth interviews. In the present research, the limitation was six factor categories each with three analysis levels. Thus, the conclusions of CJA focus on the levels of product characteristics and on the factor variables that were used in this research.

Taking into cognizance the above limitations, the basic premise of the study was to enable the state tourism departments to not only create high absolute value, but also to develop a competitive advantage which will be perceived as a customer advantage by customers. This will in turn ensure delivery of high customer value and satisfaction.

Key Policy Implications

This study aims to provide Uttar Pradesh Tourism Department, valuable information about tourist preferences, so that they can design customized tourism packages; consequentially furthering the socio-economic objectives of the state like enhancement of revenue from tourism.

As far as the policy implications related to implementing such a study are concerned, the Ministry of Tourism, Government of India has a scheme/plan titled "Market Research Study and Preparation of Perspective Plans". The objectives of this scheme are preparation of master plans, conduct surveys and studies and accept research studies which are useful for tourism planning. It receives proposals from various state governments/Union Territory administrations and issue guidelines stemming from various market research studies. (Tourism Policy and Schemes implemented by M/o Tourism).

Further Department of Tourism and U.P. State Tourism Development Corporation Ltd. also accept research proposals and consider relevant research studies for planning and implementation purposes. After due deliberations, useful research proposals are accepted for implementation, for furthering development of tourism in the state. (Tourism Policy for Uttar Pradesh)

KEYWORDS

- **Binary logistic models**
- **Conjoint analysis**
- **Tourist preferences**
- **Uttar Pradesh tourism**

Chapter 6

Tourist Satisfaction and Destination Loyalty Intention

Patricia Oom do Valle, Joro Albino Silva, Jьlio Mendes,
and Manuela Guerreiro

INTRODUCTION

This study explores the relationship between travel satisfaction and destination loyalty intention. The research was conducted with 486 tourists visiting Arade, a Portuguese tourist destination. Taking as the basis the use of structural equation modeling (SEM), the results substantiate the importance of tourism satisfaction as a determinant of destination loyalty. Also, a categorical principal components analysis (CATPCA) provides a detailed analysis of this cause-effect relationship by establishing that greater levels of satisfaction (measured by overall satisfaction in terms of holiday experience, destination attributes, and met expectations) result in increased likelihood of future repeat visits and a keen willingness to recommend the destination to others. Clusters of tourists were also identified and characterized in relation to satisfaction levels and loyalty intentions. These analyses provide a useful background in the planning of future tourist marketing strategies.

Tourism represents a key industry in the Portuguese economy. In 2004, Portugal received more than 12 million tourists with tourism representing approximately 8% of the gross domestic product (GDP). Tourism also plays an important role in the Portuguese employment marketplace since more than 10% the population is employed in tourism-related sectors. Located in the south of Portugal, Algarve belongs to the top 20 travel destinations worldwide with the local economy relying mostly on the tourism-related activities. Despite the exceptionally favorable conditions for tourism (quality beaches, warm climate, hospitable and friendly community, and multiculturally-attuned), Algarve has recently experienced some difficulty in maintaining its position as a preferred travel destination. Compared to 2004, the number of tourists entering Algarve decreased by 0.8% with lodging demand decreasing by 4.8% (AHETA, 2005). Although several external factors could be mentioned as passive reasons for this occurrence, the current condition of tourism in Algarve is much the result of emerging new holiday destinations that offer lower prices and, in some cases, higher quality facilities (AHETA, 2005).

Even though, the study of consumer loyalty has been pointed out in the marketing literature as one of the major driving forces in the new marketing era (Brodie et al., 1997), the analysis and exploration of this concept is relatively recent in tourism research. Some studies recognize that understanding which factors increase tourist loyalty is valuable information for tourism marketers and managers (Flavian et al.,

2001). Many destinations rely strongly on repeat visitation because it is less expensive to retain repeat tourists than to attract new ones (Um et al., 2006). In addition, Baker and Crompton (2000) show that the strong link between consumer loyalty and profitability is a reality in the tourism industry.

The study of the influential factors of destination loyalty is not new to tourism research. Some studies show that the revisit intention is explained by the number of previous visits (Court and Lupton, 1997; Mazurki, 1989; Petrick et al., 2001). Besides destination familiarity, the overall satisfaction that tourists experience for a particular destination is also regarded as a predictor of the tourist's intention to prefer the same destination again (Alexandros and Shabbar, 2005; Bigné and Andreu, 2004; Bigné et al., 2005; Bowen, 2001; Kozak and Rimmington, 2000; Oh, 1999). Other studies propose more comprehensive frameworks. Bigné et al. (2001) model return intentions to Spanish destinations through destination image, perceived quality and satisfaction as explanatory variables. Yoon and Uysal (2005) use tourist satisfaction as a moderator construct between motivations and tourist loyalty. Recently, Um et al. (2006) propose a model based on revisiting intentions that establishes satisfaction as both a predictor of revisiting intentions and as a moderator variable between this construct and perceived attractiveness, perceived quality of service, and perceived value for money.

More complex models have the advantage of allowing a better understanding of tourist behavior since more variables and their interactions can be taken into account. However, for more effective marketing interventions it is important to assess whether the destination models also consider the tourist's personal characteristics (Um and Crompton, 1990; Woodside and Lysonski, 1989). In fact, despite the use of more comprehensive models, so far, they have left unspecified the main personal characteristics (socio-demographic and motivational) of the more potentially loyal and satisfied tourists. The contribution of this study lies in bridging this research gap. This study integrates the main stream of previous research on destination loyalty intention proposing a causal relationship between this construct and satisfaction. However, besides estimating this causal model, the chapter aims to identify how observed variables of the latent constructs are related and, next, find and describe segments of tourists based on these relations.

The study relies on the use of a SEM procedure, through a CATPCA and a cluster analysis. The model is estimated using data from a questionnaire answered by tourists visiting Arade, a Portuguese tourism destination, located in Algarve, in the western part of the province, which includes four municipalities Portimão, Lagoa, Monchique, and Silves (Figure 1). On the one hand, this type of approach can help destination managers to determine segments of tourists which require special attention in the definition of future tourism intervention strategies. On the other hand, the complementary use of CATPCA and cluster analysis can be applied in further research in order to develop more complex models in which an increased number of latent variables and relations among them are considered.

This study is organized as follows. The next section provides an overview of previous research that has focused on destination loyalty and tourist satisfaction. A structural model that establishes the causal relationship between these constructs and defines the set of research hypotheses. Next section describes the research methods adopted. The final two sections discuss the results obtained and summarizes the more important conclusions and implications of the study.

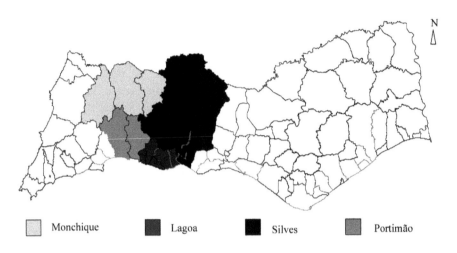

| ▢ Monchique | ■ Lagoa | ■ Silves | ▨ Portimão |

Figure 1. Algarve, Arade and its municipalities.

LITERATURE REVIEW

The concept of loyalty has been recognized as one of the more important indicators of corporate success in the marketing literature (Bauer et. al., 2002; La Barbara and Mazursky, 1983; Turnbull and Wilson, 1989; Pine et. al., 1995). Hallowell (1996) provides evidence on the connection between satisfaction, loyalty, and profitability. The author refers that working with loyal customers reduces customer recruitment costs, customer price sensitivity, and servicing costs. In terms of traditional marketing of products and services, loyalty can be measured by repeated sales or by recommendation to other consumers (Pine et al., 1995). Yoon and Uysal (2005) stress that travel destinations can also be perceived as a product which can be resold (revisited) and recommended to others (friends and family who are potential tourists).

In his study about the desirability of loyal tourists, Petrick (2004) states that loyal visitors can be less price sensitive than first time visitors. This study shows that less loyal tourists and those visiting the destination for the first time tend to spend more money during the visit. However, these tourists report a high value in the measure "risk-adjusted profitability index", proposed by the author, and as such are not as desired as loyal tourists.

The determining factors of loyalty have been studied in the marketing literature. Bitner (1990), Dick and Basu (1994) and Oliver (1999) show that satisfaction from products or services affect consumer loyalty. Flavián et al. (2001) add that loyalty to a product or service is not the result of the absence of alternative offers. Instead, loyalty occurs because consumers increasingly have less free time available and therefore try to simplify their buying decision process by acquiring familiar products or services.

As referred to above, research shows that the satisfaction that tourists experience in a specific destination is a determinant of the tourist revisiting. Baker and Crompton (2000) define satisfaction as the tourist's emotional state after experiencing the trip. Therefore, evaluating satisfaction in terms of a traveling experience is a post-consumption process (Fornell, 1992; Kozak, 2001). Assessing satisfaction can help managers to improve services (Fornell, 1992) and to compare organizations and destinations in terms of performance (Kotler, 1994). In addition, the ability of managing feedback received from customers can be an important source of competitive advantage (Peters, 1994). Moreover, satisfaction can be used as a measure to evaluate the products and services offered at the destination (Bramwell, 1998; Noe and Uysal, 1997; Ross and Iso-Ahola, 1991; Schofield, 2000).

Recently, more holistic models have been used to explain destination loyalty in tourism research. Yoon and Uysal (2005) propose a model which relates destination loyalty with travel satisfaction and holiday motivations. This study finds a significant cause-effect relationship between travel satisfaction and destination loyalty as well as between motivations and travel satisfaction. Oh (1999) establishes service quality, perceived price, customer value, and perceptions of company performance as determinants of customer satisfaction which, in turn, is used to explain revisit intentions. Bigne et al. (2001) identify that returning intentions and recommending intentions are influenced by tourism image and quality variables of the destination. Kozak (2001) model intentions to revisit in terms of the following explanatory variables: overall satisfaction, number of previous visits and perceived performance of destination. In a recent chapter, Um et al. (2006) propose a SEM that explains revisiting intentions as determined by satisfaction, perceived attractiveness, perceived quality of service, and perceived value for money. In this study repeat visits are determined more by perceived attractiveness than by overall satisfaction.

Another important conclusion from the study carried out by Um et al. (2006) is that the revisit decision-making process should be modeled in the same way as modeling a destination choice process. This implies that the personal characteristics of tourists, such as motivations and sociodemographic characteristics also play an important role in explaining their future behavior. Despite sharing equal degrees of satisfaction, tourists with different personal features can report heterogeneous behavior in terms of their loyalty to a destination (Mittal and Kamakura, 2001).

Motivations form the basis of the travel decision process and therefore should also be considered when analyzing destination loyalty intentions. Beerli and Martín (2004) propose that "motivation is the need that drives an individual to act in a certain way to achieve the desired satisfaction" (Beerli and Martín, 2004:626). Motivations can be intrinsic (push) or extrinsic (pull) (Crompton, 1979). Push motivations correspond to a tourist's desire and emotional frame of mind. Pull motivations represent the attributes of the destination to be visited. Yoon and Uysal (2005) take tourist satisfaction to be a mediator variable between motivations (pull and push) and destination loyalty.

The effect of socio-demographic variables in the tourist decision process is also an issue which has received some attention. Some studies propose that age and level of education influence the choice of destination (Goodall and Ashworth, 1988; Weaver et al., 1994; Woodside and Lysonski, 1989; Zimmer et al., 1995). Font (2000) shows that age, educational level, nationality and occupation represent determinant variables in the travel decision process.

CONCEPTUAL MODEL AND RESEARCH HYPOTHESES

The proposed SEM of the tourist loyalty intention is presented in Figure 2. The model establishes a direct causal-effect relationship of tourist satisfaction on destination loyalty intention. This connection is supported by earlier studies as those carried out by Kozak and Rimmimington (2000), Bigné et al. (2001, 2005), Gallarza and Saura (2005), Yoon and Uysal (2005), and Um et al. (2006).

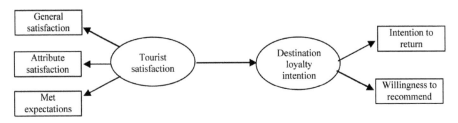

Figure 2. The proposed hypothetical model.

The model also shows the observed variables used to measure the latent constructs tourist satisfaction and destination loyalty intention. As will be described in the following section, the observed variables were chosen based on previous research. In addition, the application of the SEM procedure will demonstrate that these variables adequately represent the corresponding constructs.

As stressed by Yoon and Uysal (2005), satisfaction should be perceived from a multidimensional perspective, that is, more than one observed variable should be considered. Chon (1989) demonstrates that both the perceived evaluative outcome of the holiday experience at the destination and associated expectations are important elements in shaping tourist satisfaction. Customer satisfaction can be estimated with a single item, which measures the overall satisfaction (Bigné et al., 2001; Fornell, 1992; Spreng and Mackoy, 1996). Besides the global perception about the outcome alone, the degree of satisfaction can be evaluated through specific service attributes (Mai and Ness, 2006). Additionally, satisfaction can be evaluated using the theory of expectation/confirmation in which expectations and the actual destination outcome are compared (Bigné et al., 2001; Chon, 1989; Francken and Van Raaji, 1981; Oliver, 1980). That is, if expectations exceed perceived outcome then a positive disconfirmation is obtained, leaving the tourist satisfied and willing to repeat the visit; if a negative disconfirmation occurs the tourist feels dissatisfied and will look for alternative travel destinations. Based on these studies, three observed variables (also referred to as indicators) are used in order to measure tourist satisfaction in this chapter: (1) general destination satisfaction; (2) mean satisfaction level in terms of destination attributes; and (3) whether destination expectations were met.

Oliver (1999) states that, loyalty is a construct that can be conceptualized by several perspectives. Cronin and Tayler (1992), Homburg and Giering (2001) measure the construct "future behavioral intention" by using two indicators: the intention of repurchase and the intention to provide positive recommendations. In tourism research, similar approach is adopted and tourist loyalty intention is represented in terms of the intention to revisit the destination and the willingness to recommend it to friends and relatives (Bigné et al., 2001; Cai et al., 2003; Chen and Gusoy, 2001; Niininen et al., 2004; Oppermann, 2000; Petrick, 2004). Therefore, two indicators, "revisiting intention" and "willingness to recommend" are used as measures of destination loyalty intention.

As referred to in the literature review, socio-demographic variables and motivational variables can influence the travel decision. This study also aims to analyze whether this relationship is true when considering revisiting a destination. In specific, besides estimating the conceptual model proposed in Figure 2, this study looks to show that tourists, stating a more favorable revisiting intentions and recommendation behavior, are expected to be the most satisfied, possessing different sociodemographic characteristics and motivations to travel.

Accordingly to the above considerations, the following research hypotheses are formulated:

H_1: Tourist satisfaction holds a positive influence on tourist loyalty

H_2: "General destination satisfaction," "mean satisfaction level in terms of destination attributes," and "the extent to which expectations were met" are adequate measures of tourist satisfaction

H_3: "Revisiting intention" and "willingness to recommend" are adequate measures of destination loyalty intention

H_4: Destination loyalty intention is different according to socio-demographic characteristics of tourists

H_5: Destination loyalty intention is different according to travel motivations

METHODOLOGY

The Questionnaire

The data for this study were collected from 486 personal interviews based on a structured questionnaire carried out from March to July 2004. The questionnaire, comprising five sections, was designed to analyze tourist motivations and perceptions towards Arade. Section 1 enquired about the basic background data on the tourist's vacation at this destination, that is, lodging municipality (Portimão, Lagoa, Monchique, or Silves), type of lodging (hotel, apartment, private home, other), length of the stay, main push motivation to travel to Arade (leisure/recreation/holidays, visiting friends, business, health) and main form of transportation used in the region (rental car, private car, public transports, other).

Sections 2 and 3 involved 30 attributes of the destination that were assessed in terms of importance (Section 2) and satisfaction (Section 3). The assessed attributes, which represent the attributes of the destination (pull factors) included: beaches, spas, hospitality, authenticity, accessibilities, historical centers, traffic, forms of transportation, sports facilities, landscape, monuments, urban planning, restaurants, traditional architecture, animation, lodging, shopping areas, cultural events, tourist information, food, leisure areas, public safety, gardens/green spaces, pedestrian areas, competence and kindness, parking, water supply system, waste recovery system, cleanliness, and traffic signs. These attributes were selected because they are the most quoted in the tourism literature (Cossens, 1989; Fodness, 1994; Iso-Ahola and Mannel, 1987; Mohsin and Ryan, 2003; Shoemaker, 1989; Uysal et al., 1996). In both cases, the attributes were assessed with a five-point Likert type scale. This scale ranged from "totally irrelevant" (1) to "extremely important" (5) in terms of importance and from "very unsatisfied" (1) to "very satisfied" (5) in terms of satisfaction.

Section 4 looked to measure the overall tourism experience in Arade by asking respondents about the overall satisfaction with the journey, intention to revisit and recommendation intention, and whether the expectations about the journey were met or not. Finally, Section 5 draws on questions about socio-demographic characteristics: gender, age, marital status, occupation, educational qualification, and nationality.

Sample Procedures and Participants

The target population of this study involves Portuguese and foreigner tourists visiting Arade and stating in one of the four municipalities of this tourist region. From this population, a sample was selected using a quota sampling method with interviews performed by trained interviewers, instructed to select respondents as randomly as possible (not based on personal preferences), at different locations and at different times. This sampling method was applied because it is not possible to obtain a list of all tourists visiting Arade during this period, which would enable the use of a stratified sampling method (the random version of the quota sampling method). The number of tourists to be included in each quote was defined proportionally to the type of tourist in the target population (Portuguese and foreigner) and its distribution according to the four municipalities. A minimum of 30 interviews in the smallest quote (Portuguese tourists lodged in Monchique) was anticipated in order to perform statistical tests, if necessary. The sample dimension for the remaining quotes was determined proportionally giving rise to a total of 486 interviews.

Since non-random sampling does not ensure a representative sample, the main socio-demographic features of the target population of tourists (INE-National Institute of Statistics, 2004) were compared with the analogous features of the sample. Three socio-demographic characteristics of the target population were available for this comparison: gender, age, and educational qualifications. This analysis shows that the sample is not significantly different from the target population in terms of gender because in both cases the majority of tourists were female (around 51% of the population; around 54% of the sample). In terms of age and educational qualifications, older tourists with lower qualifications were expected. In fact, the proportion of tourists older than 65 in the target population was 16.5% although this percentage represents only 3.2% in the sample. Similarly, 19.4% of target tourists have a degree whereas in the sample this percentage was much higher (50.6%). Note that the sample represents a target population for both Portuguese nationals and foreign tourists according to the municipality where they were lodged. Around 30% of respondents were Portuguese tourists, around 59% were lodged in Portimão, 29% in Lagoa, 6% in Silves, and 6% in Monchique. Table 1 shows the main socio-demographic characteristics of respondents and also some features of the visit. Most tourists were female, possessed college or high school qualifications, belonged to the 25–44 age interval, were foreign (mainly English), and married. In the majority of cases, tourists were lodged in Portimão, in a hotel, motivated mainly by reasons related to leisure/recreation and holidays and travelled by rental car during their stay.

"Runs tests" were carried out in order to assess whether the observations for each variable could be considered as having a random pattern. For all variables in the table, this hypothesis was not rejected (runs tests: p > 0.05). This observation is required in order to form statistical inferences, though absent in sub-represented groups, namely, older tourists with lower education qualifications.

Table 1. Demographic characteristics of the sample and journey features.

Characteristic	Distribution of Answers
Tourist's gender	Female: 53.6%; male: 46.4%
Tourist's age	15–24: 19.1%; 25–44: 50.0%; 45–64: 27.7%; older than 65: 3.2%
Tourist's educational qualification	Elementary: 6.2%; Secondary: 44.2%; College or higher: 50.6%
Tourist's nationality	Portuguese tourists: 28%; Foreign tourists: 72% (45% English)
Tourist's marital status	Married: 62.4%; single: 32.2%; divorced: 4.5%; widowed: 0.8%
Tourist's occupation	Managerial and professional occupations: 20.6%; associate professional and technical: 18.3%; students; 17%; sales and customer services or administration and secretarial: 14%; skilled trades: 13.3%; other: 16.8%
Lodging municipality	Portimão: 59%; Lagoa: 29%; Monchique: 6%; Silves: 6%
Type of lodging	Hotel: 48.3%; apart hotel: 9.6%; private house: 18%; other: 24.1%
Length of the stay	Mean = 12 days; standard deviation = 6 days
Main travel motivation to *Arade*	Leisure/recreation/holidays: quoted by 91.6% of respondents; visiting friends: quoted by 10.9% of respondents; business: quoted by 3.7% of respondents; health: quoted by 3.9% of respondents
Main form of transportation used in the journey	Rental car: 39.8%; private car: 29.3%; public transports: 26.8%; other: 4.1%

Latent Constructs and Observed Variables

Table 2 shows the latent constructs, observed variables, and questionnaire items used to measure each observed variable of the proposed model and the corresponding scales.

Table 2. Latent construct, observed variables, questions, and scales.

Latent Constructs	Observed Variables	Questions	Scale
	General satisfaction	What is your overall satisfacton level as a tourist experiencing *Arade*?	1– very unsatisfied 2– unsatisfied 3– not satisfied nor unsatisfied 4– satisfied 5– very satisfied
Tourist satisfaction	Attribute satisfaction	In terms of satisfaction, how would you rate the following *Arade attributes*? (*)	1– very unsatisfied 2– unsatisfied 3–not satisfied nor unsatisfied 4– satisfied 5– very satisfied
	Met expectations	Were your expectations met?	1– no 2– yes
Destination loyalty	Intentions in revisiting	Do you intend to revisit *Arade* in the future?	1– no 2– may be; 3– yes
	Willingness to recommend	Would you recommend *ARADE* to your friends and family?	1– no 2– may be; 3– yes

(*) Mean of satisfaction level with the thirty attributes.

Statistical Data Analysis Procedures

This study applies three methods of multivariate statistical analysis: SEM, CATPCA, and cluster analyses. The research hypotheses H1–H3 are tested according to the SEM procedure. By describing the tourist segments produced by the cluster analysis, H4 and H5 are assessed.

Firstly, the proposed hypothetical model is estimated by using a SEM procedure via the Analysis of Moment Structures software (AMOS 5) (Arbuckle and Wothke, 1999). This software package is used because it works inside the software SPSS 14, which was available to the research team and used to treat the data. The AMOS has a simple interface, and only requires the path diagram to specify the model, generating indexes and tests that are necessary to assess the estimated model.

Questionnaire items described in Table 2 represent observed variables for tourist satisfaction and destination loyalty intention. To correct for non-normality of the observed variables, the Weighted Least Squares (WLS) method of estimation (Schumacker and Lomax, 1996) is adopted. The model fit analysis follows similarly to Hair et al.'s approach (1995). According to this study, the measurement model and the structural model should be evaluated separately, after examining the overall model fit. Three types of overall model fit measures are examined: absolute fit, incremental fit, and parsimonious fit. The Chi-square goodness-of-fit test is the best known index of absolute fit and used as a general indicator of how well the proposed model complies with the available data. Chi-square values should be low and not statistically significant for the purpose of goodness of fit. In addition to the Chi-square test, other measures of overall model fit are also used. Excluding the cases of the root mean square residual (RMSR) (Steiger, 1990) and the root mean square residual of approximation (RMSEA) (Steiger, 1990), in which lower values are considered desirable (zero suggesting a perfect fit), the remaining measures range from 0 (no fit) to 1 (perfect fit) and the normed Chi-square measure (Joreskog, 1969) range from 1 to 5, ideally.

The measurement model specifies the relationship between the latent constructs and the corresponding observed variables. The measurement model fit assesses the reliability and validity of the latent variables (García and Martinez, 2000; Hair et al., 1995;). Reliability analysis refers to whether the observed variables, chosen to indicate the construct, are really measuring the same (unobserved) concept. In this study, we determine two measures of reliability for each construct: the construct composite reliability and the variance extracted from each construct. Scharma (1996) considers 0.7 as the adequate minimum acceptance level for the composite reliability and 0.5 for the variance extracted. On the other hand, validity focuses on whether one observed variable truly measures the construct intended by the researcher. The validity of the observed variables holds true if these are significant, or at least moderately significant, on hypothesized latent variables (Bollen, 1989).

The structural model specifies the relationships between the latent constructs. In analyzing the structural model fit, we test the standardized parameter estimate that links the two latent constructs in terms of its sign and statistical significance. In addition, the squared multiple correlation coefficient for the structural equation associated to the latent variables is examined. This coefficient is similar to the coefficient of determination used in multiple regression analysis and shows how well the data supports the proposed relationship.

Next, using CATPCA, we explore the relationship between each observed variable measuring the latent constructs tourist satisfaction and destination loyalty intention. The use of this technique complements information taken from the SEM. As reported in Table 2, all observed variables are qualitative (categorical) and CATPCA is a multivariate technique developed to analyze categorical variables (Meulman and Heiser, 2004). This method is basically an exploratory technique that uncovers the associations among the categories of qualitative variables in large contingency tables. The CATPCA uses a mathematical algorithm that provides an optimal quantification to each category of the qualitative variables that allows for their graphical representation. As the name of the method suggests, CATPCA performs a principal components analysis (PCA) for categorical variables. Through this method, each category of the qualitative variables have an optimal quantification in each dimension (or component) produced by this special type of PCA. For each category, the optimal quantifications in the retained dimensions are the coordinates that allow the representation of the category in the geometrical display. These geometrical displays make data interpretation easier since they reveal similar variables or categories. Specifically, categories that are related are represented as points close together on the graph. Unrelated categories appear distant on the graph.

As the classic PCA, CATPCA produces dimensions which are quantitative variables that capture the information (variability) contained in the initial observed variables. Standard outputs of both methods include the eigenvalue associated to each retained dimension and the total amount of explained variance. Each eigenvalue is perceived as a measure of the importance of the corresponding dimension in capturing the information provided by the original observed variables. In turn, the total amount of explained variance informs how well the set of retained dimensions captures, as a whole, the initial set of qualitative variables. In this study we follow the Kaiser (1960) criterion that suggests that only dimensions with eigenvalues higher than 1 should be retained.

Lastly, the graph produced by CATPCA suggests distinct groups of tourists based on scores obtained from this method. We validate these groups via a cluster analysis through a k-means cluster optimization method. The use of a cluster analysis in this context is recommended because although CATPCA can identify specific groups present in the data it is unable to specify their common features (Maroco, 2003). The statistical analysis concludes with a description of the main features for each group (segment) of tourists. In this study, CATPCA and cluster analysis were performed with SPSS 14.

Structural Equation Modeling

Figure 3 shows the estimated standardized path coefficients on the model itself. All estimates are statistically significant (p = 0.000). The selected overall fit indices are reported in Table 3. As can be observed, the Chi-square statistic is low and non-statistically significant (p > 0.01), suggesting that the model is a good description of the data. Auxiliary measures of overall fit also report the desired levels, indicating a good overall model fit: the GFI is high and exceeds the recommended level of 0.9; the RMSR and the RMSEA are close to 0. In addition, the proposed model reports high levels for the remaining measures (close to 1), suggesting an adequate incremental and parsimonious fit.

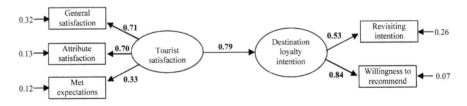

Figure 3. Standardized estimates of hypothetical model.

Table 3. Goodness-of-fit indices for the estimated structural model.

Absolute fit measures	Incremental fit measures	Parsimonious fit measures
Chi-square = 13.34 (p=0.015)	AGFI[3] = 0.93	Normed Chi-square[8] = 3.085
RMSR[1] = 0.02	NFI[4] = 0.879	
RMSEA[2] = 0.067	TLI[5] = 0.774	
	IFI[6] = 0.915	
	CFI[7] = 0.909	

[1] RMSR: root mean square residual (Steiger, 1990); [2] RMSEA: root mean square residual of approximation (Steiger, 1990); [3] AGFI: adjusted goodness of fit index (Joreskog and Sorbom 1986); [4] NFI: normed fit index (Bentler and Bonnet, 1980); [5] TLI: Tucker and Lewis index (Tucker and Lewis, 1973); [6] IFI: incremental fit index (IFI) (Bollen, 1988); [7] CFI: Comparative fit index (Bentler, 1990); [8] Normed Chi-square measure (Joreskog, 1969).

Table 4 shows the results of the measurement model in terms of the constructs' reliability and variance extracted. These measures exceeded the recommended levels of 0.7 and 0.5, respectively, for both tourist satisfaction and destination loyalty intention. This means that the latent constructs are reliable, that is, the observed variables selected to indicate each construct measure the same (unobserved) concept (Scharma, 1996). As seen in Figure 3, significant standardized loadings of each observed variable on the corresponding constructs (p = 0.000) were reported, thus validating the proposed constructs. As explained in the methods section, validity refers to whether the observed variables truly measure the latent construct intended by the researcher (Bollen, 1989). In short, hypotheses H2 and H3 should not be rejected.

Table 4. Results of the measurement model.

Latent Constructs	Construct reliability	Variance extracted
Tourist satisfaction	0.84	0.66
Destination loyalty	0.81	0.75

After assessing the measurement model, we observed the structural model. As presented in Figure 3, the findings indicate a positive relationship between tourist satisfaction and destination loyalty intention, as shown by a high and statistically significant loading between the two constructs (0.785; p = 0.000). This implies that satisfaction has a positive influence on the tourist loyalty intention, that is, H1 is supported. The squared multiple correlation for the structural equation relating the two constructs is moderately high (0.616), suggesting that 61.6% of the variability of loyalty destination intention is explained by the variability of tourist satisfaction.

Categorical Principal Components Analysis

In general terms, CATPCA is traditionally used to reduce the dimensionality of an original set of categorical variables (nominal and ordinal) into a smaller set of quantitative variables (components or dimensions) which account for most of the information (variance) in the original variables. As explained above, once this method has been applied, each category of each qualitative variable will have an optimal quantification in the retained dimensions. These quantifications are coordinates that allow the categories to be represented in a geometrical display, making data interpretation easier.

In having estimated the structural model, CATPCA was performed to explore the joint relationships among the five observed variables of the model: general satisfaction, attribute satisfaction, met expectations, revisiting intention, and willingness to recommend. Based on the observation of the eigenvalues in a higher number of dimensions, we retained only the first two dimensions (those with eigenvalues higher than 1) which account for 62.1% of the total variance of the original data.

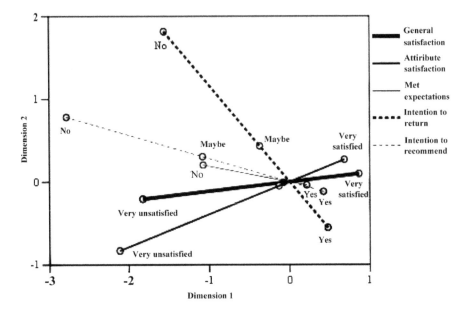

Figure 4. Joint plot of category points for tourist satisfaction and destination loyalty intention.

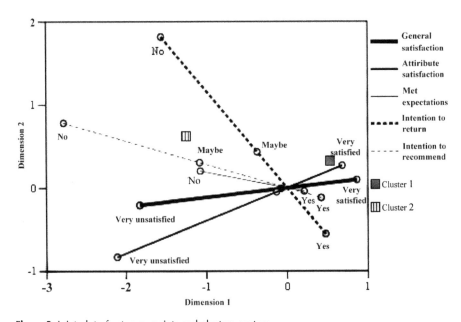

Figure 5. Joint plot of category points and clusters centers.

Figure 4 is the geometrical display that allows a visual interpretation of how the categories of the observed variables are related. The horizontal axis represents dimension 1 and the vertical axis shows dimension 2. In the graph, the variables measuring tourist satisfaction are indicated by solid lines and the variables measuring destination loyalty intention are captured by the dashed lines. In each line, the displayed points represent the categories of variables. As can be observed, the graph shows that the categories indicating higher level of satisfaction (general satisfaction: 5—very satisfied; attribute satisfaction: 5—very satisfied; met expectations: 2—yes) and higher level of loyalty intention (revisiting intention: 3—yes; willingness to recommend: 3—yes) are represented close to each other (on the right-hand side of the graph). These results show that tourists generally satisfied with their experience in terms of specific attributes of the location and whose expectations were met are more likely to return to Arade and recommend it to family and friends.

Another aspect that the graph clarifies is that the direction of the line representing willingness to recommend is not very different than the directions of the lines representing level of satisfaction. When comparing these lines, however, the line indicating revisiting intention has a somewhat different direction. Since in the graphs produced by CATPCA, similar points/lines suggest related categories/variables, this study reveals that higher levels of satisfaction are more related to willingness to recommend than intention to return.

Cluster Analysis

The graph produced by CATPCA suggests that two groups of tourists can be determined as a result of the relations between the categories of variables measuring tourist satisfaction and variables measuring destination loyalty intention. As indicated by the map, these groups display the following characteristics: on the right-hand side of the graph, we can observe more satisfied tourists willing to return and recommend Arade; the left-hand side shows tourists who are less satisfied and uncertain about revisiting or recommending Arade as a holiday destination.

In order to validate these groups, a cluster analysis was performed. Final cluster centers are presented in Table 5. Figure 5 displays these centers (also referred to as centroids) on the graph produced by CATPCA (dark square and lined square). These centroids are clearly at the centre of the groups suggested by CATPCA, establishing the presence of these groups. The centroid of Custer 1 appears on the right-hand side of the graph and the centroid of Custer 2 is represented on the left-hand side. Thus, the clusters can be referred to as "more satisfied and more loyal tourists" (cluster 1) and "less satisfied and less loyal tourists" (cluster 2). Note that 349 (72%) tourists were included in cluster 1 and 137 (28%) in cluster 2.

Table 5. Final cluster centers and number of tourists in each cluster.

Dimensions from CATPCA	Cluster 1	Cluster 2
Dimension 1	0.50	−1.27
Dimension 2	−0.15	0.37

An advantage of running a cluster analysis after CATPCA is that it allows a new variable that identifies which tourist belongs to which cluster. In particular, the tourists included in cluster 1 were identified with code 1 and code 2 was used to identify tourists belonging to cluster 2. This new variable (named as cluster membership) can then be related with other variables measured in the questionnaire in order to provide a detailed description of the groups.

Table 6 shows the distribution of tourists for each group across the categories of variables used in the CATPCA. As expected, there is a significant dependence relationship reported between each of these variables and cluster membership (chi-square independence tests: $p > 0.000$). The values in bold allow us to identify the tourist profile in each cluster according to these variables. As expected, the first cluster includes the most satisfied (70.3%) and very satisfied tourists (98.6%), whose travel expectations were met (79.6%) and whose intentions to recommend and return to Arade were stated (93.6% and 92.3%). The second cluster displays opposing characteristics in terms of these variables.

Table 6. Frequency distribution of variables used in the CATPCA in the two clusters solution.

Variables used in the CATPCA	Cluster 1	Cluster 2	Total
Overall satisfaction with holiday experience			
1 – very unsatisfied	25.0%	**75.0%**	100.0%
2 – unsatisfied	8.3%	**91.7%**	100.0%
3 – not satisfied nor unsatisfied	8.6%	**91.4%**	100.0%
4 – satisfied	**70.3%**	29.7%	100.0%
5 – very satisfied	**98.6%**	1.4%	100.0%
Mean satisfaction with the attributes of the destination			
1 – unsatisfied	0.0%	**100.0%**	100.0%
2 – not satisfied nor unsatisfied	6.5%	**93.5%**	100.0%
3 – satisfied	**69.3%**	30.7%	100.0%
4 – very satisfied	**90.7%**	9.3%	100.0%
Where your expectations met?			
1 – no	31.6%	**68.4%**	100.0%
2 – yes	**79.6%**	20.4%	100.0%
Do you intend to revisit *Arade* in the future			
1 – yes	**93.6%**	6.4%	100.0%
2 – may be	54.5%	45.5%	100.0%
3 – no	3.8%	**96.2%**	100.0%
Would you recommend *Arade* to friends and family?			
1 – yes	**92.3%**	7.7%	100.0%
2 – may be	10.4%	**89.6%**	100.0%
3 – no	0.0%	**100.0%**	100.0%

Clusters were also described in terms of socio-demographic characteristics. In this analysis, no significant dependence relationships are identified between cluster membership and the variables: "gender," "occupation," "marital status", and "type of lodging" (chi-square independence tests: $p > 0.1$). This means that tourists in each cluster have approximately the same demographic profile reported in Table 1 according to these variables. Besides these variables, the groups do not report significant differences in terms of "age" (independent samples t-test: p = 0.268), despite the average age being higher in cluster 1 (37.19 years; standard deviation = 13.2 years) than in cluster 2 (35.72 years; standard deviation = 13.68 years).

Table 7 clarifies the variables in which the clusters report significant differences. For a 10% significance level, tourists in both clusters are statistically different in terms of "educational qualification level" (chi-square independence test: p = 0.058). As can be observed in the Table, 58.1% of tourists belonging to cluster 2 hold a degree. This percentage decreases to 46.2% with tourists included in cluster 1. "Nationality" is an important variable that differentiates the groups (chi-square independence test: p = 0.000): cluster 1 includes 77% of foreigner tourists whereas this proportion is 59.6% in cluster 2. That is, the weight of Portuguese tourists is higher in cluster 2 (40.4%) than in cluster 1 (23%). The analysis shows that H4 is only partially demonstrated. Another variable that distinguishes clusters is the "length of the stay." Tourists in cluster 1 stay, on average, 12.56 days in Arade, whereas tourists in cluster 2 remain, on average, 10.56 days (independent samples t-test: p = 0.001). In both cases, the "length of the stay" has a standard deviation of around 6 days. Finally, the clusters also differ in terms of the main form of transportation mainly used during stay (chi-square independence test: p = 0.072). Around 40% of tourists in cluster 2 use a private car, whereas most tourists in cluster 1 rent a car (43.8%) or use public transports (26.8%).

Table 7. Frequency distribution of selected variables in the two clusters solution.

Selected variables	Cluster 1	Cluster 2
Educational qualification level		
Elementary	6.9%	4.4%
Secondary	46.8%	37.5%
College or higher	46.2%	58.1%
Total	100%	100%
Nationality		
Portuguese	77%	59.6%
Foreigner	23%	40.4%
Total	100%	100%
Length of the journey (mean and standard deviation)	12.56 (6)	10.56 (6)
Main mean of transportation used in the journey		
Rental car	43.8%	30.1%
Private car	25.6%	39.0%
Public transports	26.8%	19.8%
Other	3.8%	11.1%
Total	100%	100%

Another finding that deserves attention is the fact that the push motivations behind traveling to Arade do not differentiate the groups (chi-square independence tests: p > 0.1). In both clusters, only 10.9% of tourists indicate "visiting friends" as the main motivation for visiting this destination. The same occurs with respect to the remaining motivations: only around 4% of tourists in the two clusters indicate reasons relating to "business" or "health". For both groups, "leisure/recreation and holidays" is the main motivation for traveling to this destination (reason indicated by 92% of tourists in cluster 1 and by 90.5% of tourists in cluster 2).

Figure 6 shows the thirty attributes of Arade that were graded by the respondents in terms of importance, that is, the pull motives for visiting this destination. This analysis was done by each cluster. Regarding importance, a first finding reveals that tourists in both clusters do not report significant differences for any of the attributes (independent samples t-tests: $p > 0.15$). In other words, pull motivations do not distinguish the clusters. Figure 6 also clarifies the attributes that tourists in both clusters consider more important (beaches, hospitality, landscape, restaurants, lodging, food, public safety, competence and kindness, water supply system, waste recovery system, and cleanliness) and those that are less valued (spas, sports facilities, and monuments). Because motivations (whether pull or push) do not differentiate the clusters, H5 is not supported.

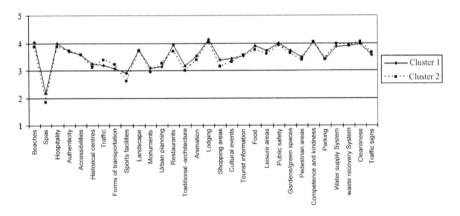

Legend: 1 – totally irrelevant; 2 – little important; 3 – indifferent; 4 – important; 5 – extremely important

Figure 6. Mean importance of the attributes (by cluster).

Figure 7 provides a similar analysis as Figure 6 but includes the satisfaction with the attributes. The first aspect that should be noted is that tourists in cluster 1 report a higher level of satisfaction in all attributes than tourists in cluster 2. All differences between groups are statistically significant (independent samples t-tests: $p = 0.000$). The figure also clarifies the attributes in which the differences between groups are higher (such as, hospitality, urban planning, competence and kindness, and cleanliness) and those that are perceived more similarly (beaches, food, and monuments). For both clusters, the attributes more positively perceived are beaches, hospitality, landscape, restaurants, food, lodging and the competence, and kindness of the locals. The attributes more negatively assessed are traffic, urban planning, parking zones, and traffic signs. Attributes such as spas, traditional architecture, cultural events, waste recovery system, and cleanliness also report low levels of satisfaction, especially among tourists in cluster 2.

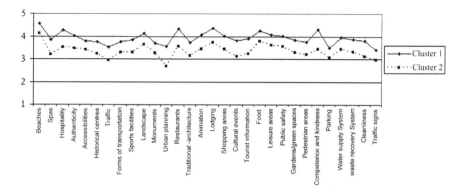

Legend: 1 – very unsatisfied, 2 – unsatisfied, 3 – not satisfied nor unsatisfied, 4 – satisfied, 5 – very satisfied

Figure 7. Mean satisfaction according to the attributes (by cluster).

DISCUSSION AND CONCLUSION

As living standards increase around the world, more people find themselves able to travel to different destinations. This study establishes the direct causal relationship between tourist satisfaction and destination loyalty intention by exploring the case of tourists visiting Arade, a Portuguese tourism destination.

The results of this study validate the research hypothesis that tourist satisfaction is one contributing factor to destination loyalty intention. This conclusion is mainly based on the findings of the estimated SEM. Through CATPCA and cluster analyses, results were fully explored establishing that two clusters of tourists could be identified and then described. Cluster 1 includes the most satisfied tourists who are more determined in revisiting and suggesting the destination; cluster 2 embraces those with worst perceptions of the destination and with weak intentions of returning and recommending. Moreover, observation of the graph produced by CATPCA allows us to conclude that a higher level of satisfaction is more associated to willingness to recommend than to intention to return. This information could not be provided by the SEM procedure. In fact, the estimated model only indicates that tourist satisfaction and loyalty intentions are adequately measured (which is informed by the measurement model results) and are related (which is informed by the structural model results) but do to put forward how the observed variables are jointly correlated. Thus, the sequential data analysis procedures used in this study enables an indepth look at the relationship between satisfaction and loyalty in the tourism framework.

The results of this study have important implications for marketers and managers of Arade as a travel destination. In specific, there is a need to improve the perceived quality of the tourist offer, which is the basis of tourist satisfaction (Bigné et al., 2001). Most attributes of the destination services may be controlled and improved by tourism suppliers. The improvement of these services is important and worthwhile because, as this study shows, tourists experiencing higher satisfaction levels reveal favorable intentional behavior, that is, the willingness to return to Arade and to recommend it to others. Moreover, this study also shows that the most satisfied tourists (cluster 1) spend more time, on average, in this destination than the least satisfied tourists with weaker intentions of returning or recommending the region (cluster 2). This is an important finding because a longer stay brings potentially added economic advantages to the region.

Figure 7, and in particular the line representing tourists in cluster 2 (the least satisfied), provides useful indications in improving Arade's competitiveness. The weaknesses of the destination can be summarized, in decreasing order of importance, into four areas: (1) urban planning problems (indicated by the attribute "urban planning"); (2) traffic problems (indicated by the attributes "traffic", "parking", and "traffic signs"); (3) cleanliness problems (indicated by the attributes "cleanliness" and "waste recovery system"); and (4) cultural initiative problems (indicated by the attributes "traditional architecture" and "cultural events"). The most critical attributes can be considered those related to traffic and cleanliness because these are important pull motivations that go beyond destination choice (Figure 6). The Destination Management Organization (DMO) of Arade should consider a priority trying to establish solutions for these problems. Some of these weaknesses can be resolved in the short term through the involvement of the municipalities. The lack of traffic signs, inadequate waste recovery system, the need for old building renovation and the development of the absence of cultural initiatives are good examples. The provision of more and ideally located parking spaces also deserves urgent attention. Finally, it is of strategic importance to review and improve the region's urban planning in order to enhance the overall attractiveness of this tourism region.

Taking into account the country's natural conditions, Portugal, and in particular Arade, has all the requirements necessary to be at the forefront in tourism of the future. Figure 7 also clearly shows is that tourists in cluster 1 provide a very good evaluation of the natural conditions of the destination ("beaches", "landscape"), as well as of the social environment ("hospitality", "authenticity", "public safety" and "competence and kindness"). Facilities more related to tourism activity are also greatly appreciated ("restaurants", "lodging", "shopping zones", "food", "leisure spaces"). These are also the most positively assessed attributes by tourists in cluster 2, even lower levels of average satisfaction are observed. It is fundamental that marketers of this destination take advantage of this information in order to project the region's image, either nationally or internationally. In general, the perceptions about this destination (Figure 7) surpass expectations (Figure 6), a characteristic that may be further explored in future marketing communication plans.

By evaluating each attribute individually Figure 7 exhibited statistically significant differences between the two clusters for all attributes, more positively graded by tourists belonging to cluster 1. Despite the attributes being different in terms of perceptions, tourists in both groups assess them similarly when focus is on importance rather than satisfaction. This means that the groups are not significantly different in terms of the pull motivations behind the destination (Figure 6). In addition, this study shows that tourists in the two clusters present a quite similar profile in what concerns the push motivations behind the Arade region. In both cases, the main and almost single intrinsic motivation in choosing this destination is associated to the need for a vacation/

holiday. Arade, therefore, should focus on this global segment—tourists that choose the destination for leisure motives—taking advantage of the unique natural and social conditions of the region, offering recreation and rest and at the same time work out the problems mentioned above that threaten the destination's image.

This study also establishes that no significant socio-demographic differences exist between the two groups of tourists in terms of gender, age, marital status, and occupation. By working with a significance level of 10%, we can conclude that clusters differ in terms of qualification level. As mentioned, around 60% of tourists belonging to cluster 2 hold a degree (the least satisfied). This percentage is lower in cluster 1. This result suggests that higher qualification levels may be related to higher demanding levels 1 terms of services offered by the destination. It is not atypical that tourists with higher qualification levels are potentially more judgmental when assessing places they are visiting since, very likely, they are already aware of alternative holiday destinations and, therefore, more critical in terms of assessment. However, this is a characteristic that clearly deserves further research.

Another relevant finding is that cluster membership and nationality are significantly dependent. In specific, cluster 2 registers an increased proportion of Portuguese tourists than cluster 1. This may be a consequence of the generalized feeling among Portuguese citizens that foreign tourists are better welcomed and treated than Portuguese tourists. This sentiment has some foundation because some cities of Algarve—those most dependent on tourism-related activities—resemble foreign surroundings. There are many English pubs, restaurants displaying English cable television, eateries selling only familiar English food, and tourist information only in English. Moreover, most Portuguese come to Algarve at least once a year, and so are very familiar with the region. One consequence of this fact is that national tourists do not perceive the region's strengths as positively as foreign tourists. For example, the English tourist more easily appreciates the warmer climate and high quality beaches in Algarve than the national tourists do. The latter tend to be more intolerant and criticizing.

This characteristic provides empirical evidence of the need for a more careful marketing approach towards national tourists. Centering promotional campaigns on sun and beach is not enough to attract Portuguese tourists. Instead, the DMO should invest in employing more highly qualified staff in the tourism and hospitality industry, and become more involved with those responsible for arising regional problems (those depicted in Figure 7), stimulating and supporting initiatives that induce positive changes in the more critical aspects of the tourism product. Moreover, the DMO should develop specific promotional actions leading to an upgrading of the destination image since this is always an important segment of the market. First, marketing messages can be directed to show that destination problems are being addressed, demonstrating that effort is being made by municipalities to answer to expectations by visitors. Second, it becomes equally important to stimulate greater participation from those involved in the evaluation process on the tourist experience as well as more efficient management of opinions, complaints, and suggestions. Finally, because image change is a slow process, DMO should consider stakeholder involvement in developing publicity campaigns commitment aimed at the mass media at regular interval periods. Aside from major campaigns initiatives, it would be essential to represent the region under the "friendly destination concept" with marketing messages aimed at low season tourism, when the region is less congested and less marked by some of the drawbacks (such as traffic and litter problems).

Furthermore, we can also observe in the CATPCA graph that high satisfaction levels are more related to willingness to recommend than intentions to return. This result is understandable. If a tourist classifies the tourism experience as positive and pleasant it is expected that he/she recommends the destination to friends and relatives. However, revisiting destinations carries some costs, even when a previous visit was highly satisfactory. These costs can be financial, if the tourist feels that the overall travel expenses are too high and, therefore, conditioning him/her to return, or they can be opportunity-related. In fact, the tourism offer is so large that returning to an already familiar place can imply not visiting a different destination, a high opportunity cost.

This study has some limitations whose overcoming provides directions for further research.

As shown in Section 5, the data matched the estimated model. Nevertheless, and because any model is always an approximate description of reality, a different model with other observed variables could produce a similar or even improved global fit. In the proposed model, the latent constructs are measured by observed variables dictated by the previous research. As described, the analysis of the measurement model shows that, in general, they are reliable and valid measures of the corresponding constructs, even though the observed variable met expectations had reported a low loading (0.33) on tourist satisfaction (although statistically significant), especially when compared to those associated with the satisfaction variables (0.71 and 0.70, respectively). It would certainly be preferable to achieve a higher loading in this variable. However, as explained in Section 3, assessing whether tourist expectations are met or not should be considered in terms of satisfaction with the destination experience. Moreover, removing met expectations from the model yields worse results in almost all indices produced by the SEM analysis. Therefore, future research should contemplate met expectations on a more detailed scale, rather than the adopted binary approach.

Based on the SEM results, we can conclude that the first three proposed research hypotheses cannot be rejected. Some care, however, should be taken when interpreting the first hypothesis. In effect, this study only shows that tourist satisfaction is one contributing factor to tourism loyalty intentions. In other words, what is being evaluated is "destination loyalty intentions" and not "actual destination loyalty" because the observed variables only consider revisiting and recommending intentions. This aspect of how "destination loyalty intentions" leads to "actual destination loyalty" (measured for instance by a revisiting experience and whether the destination was effectively recommended as a result of a previous visit) is another topic of considerable ground for further investigation.

A final underlying detail of this study is the moderate squared multiple correlation value which was reported in the SEM (61.6%). Despite the model's goodness-of-fit evidenced by all analyzed indicators, there is empirical support that destination loyalty intention is explained by additional constructs besides satisfaction. This finding suggests that further work on the predictors of destination loyalty is necessary. By extending the proposed model to include other constructs in the satisfaction-loyalty relationship (such as motivations, perceptions, expectations and destination image), further examination can be made, through the use of combined statistical data analysis procedures, to better understand the tourist behavior.

KEYWORDS

- **Clusters**
- **Loyalty**
- **Satisfaction**
- **Tourism**

Chapter 7

Recreation, Tourism, and Rural Well-being

Richard J. Reeder and Dennis M. Brown

INTRODUCTION

The promotion of recreation and tourism has been both praised and criticized as a rural development strategy. This study uses regression analysis to assess the effect of recreation and tourism development on socioeconomic conditions in rural recreation counties. The findings imply that recreation and tourism development contributes to rural well-being, increasing local employment, wage levels, and income, reducing poverty, and improving education and health. But recreation and tourism development is not without drawbacks, including higher housing costs. Local effects also vary significantly, depending on the type of recreation area. With their high rates of growth, rural recreation counties represent one of the main rural success stories of recent years. During the 1990s, these places—whose amenities attract permanent residents as well as seasonal residents and tourists—averaged 20% population growth, about three times that of other nonmetropolitan counties, and 24% employment growth, more than double the rate of other nonmetro counties. However, tourism- and recreation-based development has been viewed as having negative as well as positive economic and social impacts, leading some local officials to question recreation development strategies.

What is the Issue?

Critics argue that the tourism industry—consisting mainly of hotels, restaurants, and other service-oriented businesses—offers seasonal, unskilled, low-wage jobs that depress local wages and income. As more of a county's workforce is employed in these jobs, tourism could increase local poverty and adversely affect the levels of education, health, and other aspects of community welfare. Meanwhile, the rapid growth associated with this development could strain the local infrastructure, leading to problems such as road congestion.

On the other hand, if tourism and recreational development attracts significant numbers of seasonal and permanent residents, it could change the community for the better. For example, the new residents could spark a housing boom and demand more goods and services, resulting in a more diversified economy with more high-paying jobs. Even low-paid recreation workers could benefit if better employment became available. Income levels could rise, along with levels of education, health, and other measures of community welfare, and poverty rates could be expected to decline.

This study quantifies the most important socioeconomic impacts of rural tourism and recreational development.

What did the Study Find?

Rural tourism and recreational development results in generally improved socioeconomic well-being, though significant variations were observed for different types of recreation counties.

Rural tourism and recreational development leads to higher employment growth rates and a higher percentage of working-age residents who are employed. Earnings and income levels are also positively affected. Although the cost of living is increased by higher housing costs, the increase offsets only part of the income advantage.

Rural tourism and recreational development results in lower local poverty rates and improvements in other social conditions, such as local educational attainment and health (measured by mortality rates). Although rates of serious crimes are elevated with this kind of development, this may be misleading because tourists and seasonal residents, while included as victims in the crime statistics, are not included in the base number of residents. Rapid growth brings its own challenges, particularly pressures on infrastructure. The one growth-strain measure examined in the study, commuting time to work, revealed little evidence of traffic congestion in rural recreation areas.

Rural recreation counties have not benefited equally. Rural counties with ski resorts were among the wealthiest, healthiest, and best educated places in the study, while those with reservoir lakes or those located in the southern Appalachian mountains were among the poorest and least educated. Rural casino counties had relatively high rates of employment growth and large increases in earnings during the 1990s.

How was the Study Conducted?

The study assessed the effect of recreation and tourism development on 311 rural US counties identified by ERS as dependent on recreation and tourism. The findings here, showing largely positive effects, pertain mainly to places already dependent on recreational development. Counties just beginning to build a tourism- and recreation-based economy may not benefit to the same extent.

The authors used multiple regression analysis to determine the degree to which socioeconomic indicators in the 311 counties had been affected by recreational development. The key variable in the regression analysis was recreation dependency, a composite measure reflecting the percentage of local income, employment, and housing directly attributable to tourism and recreation. For each socioeconomic indicator in the study, two regressions were computed to explain intercounty variations—one for a single point in time (1999 or 2000) and one for variations in changes that occurred during the 1990s. A descriptive analysis, supplementing the regression analysis, compared recreation, and other nonmetro county means for each of the socioeconomic indicators and trends, and then made socioeconomic comparisons among the different types of rural recreation counties.

While the economies of many rural areas in the US have been sluggish in recent years, rural communities that have stressed recreation and tourism have experienced significant growth. This has not gone unnoticed by local officials and development organizations, which have increasingly turned to recreation and tourism as a vehicle for development. However, not all observers are convinced that the benefits of this approach are worth the costs. There are concerns about the quality of the jobs created, rising housing costs, and potential adverse impacts on poverty, crime, and other social conditions. This report assesses the validity of these concerns by analyzing recent data on a wide range of socioeconomic conditions and trends in US rural recreation areas. The purpose is to gain a better understanding of how recreation and tourism development affects rural well-being.

Recreation and tourism development has potential advantages and disadvantages for rural communities. Among the advantages, recreation and tourism can add to business growth and profitability. Landowners can benefit from rising land values. Growth can create jobs for those who are unemployed or underemployed, and this can help raise some of them out of poverty. Recreation and tourism can help diversify an economy, making the economy less cyclical and less dependent on the ups and downs of one or two industries. It also gives underemployed manufacturing workers and farmers a way to supplement their incomes and remain in the community. Benefiting from growing tax revenues and growth-induced economies of scale, local governments may be able to improve public services. In addition, local residents may gain access to a broader array of private sector goods and services, such as medical care, shopping, and entertainment. While other types of growth can have similar benefits, rural recreation and tourism development may provide greater diversification, and, for many places, it may be easier to achieve than other kinds of development—such as high-tech development—because it does not require a highly educated workforce.

Many of the potential disadvantages of recreation-related development are associated with the rapid growth that these counties often experience; on average, "recreation counties" grew by 20% during the 1990s, nearly three times as fast as other rural counties. Rapid growth from any cause can erode local natural amenities, for example, by despoiling scenic views. Cultural amenities, such as historic sites, can also be threatened. Growth can lead to pollution and related health problems, higher housing costs, road congestion, and more crowded schools, and it may strain the capacity of public services. Small businesses can be threatened by growth-induced "bigbox" commercial development, and farms can be burdened by increased property taxes. In addition, newcomers might have different values than existing residents, leading to conflicts over land use and public policies. Growth can also erode residents' sense of place, which might reduce support for local institutions, schools, and public services.

Aside from these general growth-related issues, some specific problems have been linked to tourism and recreation industries. These include the potential for higher poverty rates associated with low-wage, unskilled workers who are attracted to the area to work in hotels, restaurants, and In this chapter, "tourism" and "recreation" refer to the development process in which tourists, seasonal residents, and permanent residents are attracted to the community to take part in recreation and leisure activities.

With this mix of positive and negative impacts, it is understandable why experts on development policy may be uncertain about the value of rural tourism and recreation development strategies. Hence, it is important that policymakers have access to information about the nature and extent of the socioeconomic impacts of this type of development.

Past research has examined some of the impacts (Brown, 2002). Much of that research, however, is in the form of case studies, with only a few empirical studies examining nationwide rural impacts, such as the articles by English et al. (2000) and Deller et al. (2001). English et al. examined the impact of tourism on a variety of measures of local socioeconomic conditions (local income, employment, housing, economic structure, and demographic characteristics). Deller and his colleagues examined recreational amenities (including recreational infrastructure), local government finances, labor supply characteristics, and demographic demand characteristics, estimating their effects upon the growth of local population, employment, and income.

Our research used an approach similar to that of English and his colleagues, which identified a group of tourism-dependent counties and then used regression analysis to estimate the effect of tourism on various indicators of local rural conditions. Using the new ERS typology of rural recreation counties developed by Kenneth Johnson and Calvin Beale (2002), we identified differences between rural recreation counties and other nonmetro counties for various indicators of economic and social well-being. We also examined socioeconomic variations by type of recreation county. We then used regression analysis to test statistically for the effect that dependence on recreation (including tourism and seasonal resident recreation) has on local socioeconomic conditions. Details about the regression analysis are provided in the appendix.

We hoped to shed light on several important questions about this development strategy. Among these are:

- How does rural recreation development affect residents' ability to find jobs?
- How are local wages and incomes affected?
- How does recreation development affect housing costs and local cost of living?
- What effect does recreation development have on local social problems such as crime, congestion, and poverty?
- How are education and health affected?
- How do various types of recreation areas differ in socioeconomic characteristics?

What is a Recreation County?

In 1998, Beale and Johnson identified 285 nonmetropolitan recreation counties based on empirical measures of recreation activity, including levels of employment and income in tourism-related industries and the presence of seasonal housing (Beale and Johnson, 1998). They modified and expanded their typology a few years later (Johnson and Beale, 2002). Their 2002 typology identified 329 recreation counties that fell into 11 categories, varying by geographic location, natural amenities, and form of recreation. It is this typology that ERS has adopted as its recreation county typology. We used the 2002 typology, which covered only nonmetropolitan counties. To simplify our analysis, we excluded Alaska and Hawaii. This reduced the number of recreation counties in our study to 311.

One of the advantages of this typology is that it includes not only places with significant tourism-related activity but also those with a significant number of seasonal residents. (See "How Were Recreation Counties Identified?") Like tourists, most seasonal residents are attracted by opportunities for recreation, including some who come simply to relax in a scenic rural setting. In theory, seasonal residents should have a bigger economic impact on the local community than tourists because they stimulate the housing industry and their season-long presence significantly increases the demand for a wide range of local goods and services. In addition, seasonal residents often later become permanent residents. Because many seasonal residents first came to the area as tourists, it is difficult, if not impossible, to separate the long-term impact of tourists from seasonal residents. Our use of the ERS typology, which covers both tourism and seasonal recreational/residential development, thus seems ideal for estimating the long-term, overall impacts of tourism and recreation combined.

Another advantage of this typology is that it is derived from a continuous variable—a weighted average of tourism and seasonal housing dependence. In theory, this continuous variable may be used more effectively to estimate impacts than a simple recreation/other nonmetro dichotomous variable because it allows us to examine variations in the extent of recreation. Similarly, the different types of recreation counties in the Johnson/Beale typology can be used to further elucidate and estimate the impacts of recreational activity on local socioeconomic conditions.

General Characteristics of Recreation Counties

The 311 recreation counties in our study are located in 43 States, but tend to be concentrated in the West, the Upper Great Lakes, and the Northeast (Figure 1). In the West, this reflects the ample opportunities for hiking, mountain climbing, fishing, and wintertime sports found in the many national parks and ski resorts there. By contrast, the high concentration of recreation counties in the Upper Great Lakes and Northeast—especially in New England and Upstate New York—is largely due to the popularity of long-established second homes in areas with lakes. Many of these areas also have significant wintertime recreation activities, including snowmobiling and skiing. Not surprisingly, recreation counties score higher (4.25) on ERS' natural amenities index than other nonmetro counties (3.34).

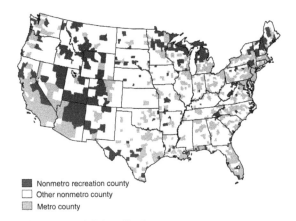

Nonmetro recreation county
Other nonmetro county
Metro county

Note: Excludes counties in Alaska and Hawaii.
Source: Adapted from Kenneth M. Johnson and Calvin L. Beale, 2002. "Nonmetro Recreation Counties: Their Identification and Rapid Growth," *Rural America*, Vol. 17, No. 4:12-19.

Figure 1. Nonmetropolitian recreation counties, 2002. Counties are concentrated in the West, Upper Midwest, and Northeast.

How Were Recreation Counties Identified?

The 2002 Johnson/Beale typology covered only nonmetropolitan counties, using the 1993 Office of Management and Budget (OMB) definitions of metropolitan areas. Johnson and Beale began by examining a sample of well-known recreation areas to determine which economic indicators were most appropriate for identifying other such counties. They then computed the percentage share of wage and salary employment from the Census Bureau's 1999 County Business Patterns data and personal income from Bureau of Economic Analysis data as these data apply to recreation-related industries, that is, entertainment and recreation, accommodations, eating and drinking places, and real estate. They also computed a third measure: the percentage share of housing units of seasonal or occasional use, from 2000 Census data. They then constructed a weighted average of the standardized Z-scores of these three main indicators (0.3 employment + 0.3 income + 0.4 seasonal homes). Counties scoring greater than 0.67 on this recreation dependency measure were considered recreation counties. Next, they added several large nonmetro counties that did not make the cut but had relatively high hotel and motel receipts from 1997 Census of Business data. Additional counties were accepted if the weighted average of the three combined indicators exceeded the mean and at least 25% of the county's housing was seasonal. Then Johnson and Beale deleted 14 counties that lacked any known recreational function but appeared to qualify "either because they were very small in population with inadequate and misleading County Business Patterns coverage or because they reflected high travel activity without recreational purpose, i.e., overnight motel and eating place clusters on major highways." These calculations produced their final set of 329 recreation counties. In 2004, ERS established these recreation counties as one of its county typologies (available at http://www.ers.usda.gov/Briefing/Rurality/Typology/). By 2004, some of these counties had changed their metropolitan status based on the new 2003 OMB definitions of metropolitan areas.

Data from the 2000 Census reveal that recreation and other nonmetro counties average similar population sizes (Table 1). However, during the last decade, the population of recreation counties has grown almost three times as fast (20% vs. 7%, on average). Recreation counties also have relatively low population densities, and more of their residents tend to live in rural parts of the county (those with less than 2,500 population).

Using the ERS 1993 county economic and policy typologies (Cook and Mizer, 1994), we found that the economies in recreational counties were generally more diverse than in other nonmetro counties. For example, only 30% of recreation counties were highly dependent on a single major industry (agriculture, mining, or manufacturing), while 58% of other nonmetro counties were highly dependent on just one of these industries. Recreation counties also were slightly less dependent on neighboring counties for employment; only 13% of recreation counties were identified as commuting counties (with a high percentage of their resident workforce commuting outside the county for employment), compared with 17% of other nonmetro counties.

We also found that about a third (32%) of recreation counties were retirement-destination places versus only 4% of other nonmetro counties.

Table 1. Demographic characteristics of recreation and other nonmetro counties.

Indicator	Type of country	
	Recreation	Other nonmetro
Nonmetro counties in our study	*Number*	
	311	1,935
Average county population in 2000	*Persons*	
	26,256	24,138
Population change 1990–2000	*Percent*	
	20.2	6.9
Population density in 2000	*Persons per square mile*	
	35.9	40.2
Rural share of county population in 1990	*Percent*	
	79.9	72.4

Note: These are county averages (simple means).
Source: ERS calculations using data from the U.S. Census Bureau and Bureau of Economic Analysis, U.S. Department of Commerce.

Many recreation counties (38%) were Federal land counties, meaning that at least 30% of the county's land was federally owned; only 7% of other nonmetro counties had that much Federal land. In addition, relatively few recreation counties (10%) had experienced persistently high levels of poverty (from 1950 to 1990), whereas about a fourth (26%) of other nonmetro counties fell into this category. Because recreation counties are not homogeneous with respect to these and other characteristics, the averages we present for all recreation counties mask considerable variation.

ECONOMIC IMPACTS

The conventional wisdom among researchers in recent years has been that recreation and tourism have both positive and negative economic impacts for recreation areas. On the positive side, recreation development helps to diversify the local economy (English et al., 2000; Gibson, 1993; Marcouiller and Green, 2000), and it generates economic growth (Deller et al., 2001; Gibson, 1993). It achieves this partly by acting as a kind of export industry, attracting money from the outside to spend on goods and services produced locally (Gibson, 1993). It also stimulates the local economy through other means. Infrastructure, such as airports and highways and water systems, often must be upgraded to meet the needs of tourists, and such improvements can help foster the growth of nonrecreation industries in the area by attracting entrepreneurs and labor and by providing direct inputs to these industries (Gibson, 1993).

Recreation development can involve significant economic leakages, however, in that many of the goods and services it requires come from outside the community—for example, temporary foreign workers often are drawn to the area to fill jobs in hotels, ski resorts, and so forth—and many of the recreation-related establishments (restaurants, hotels, tour, and travel companies) are owned by national or regional companies that export the profits (Gibson, 1993). Thus, part of the money from tourists and seasonal residents ends up leaving the locality. Another economic drawback involves the seasonality of recreation activities, which can create problems for workers and businesses during off-seasons (Galston and Baehler, 1995, Gibson, 1993), though this may actually be a plus for places where seasonal recreation jobs are timely, coming when farmers and other workers normally have an off-season.

The greatest economic concern is that recreation development may be less desirable than traditional forms of rural development because it increases the incidence of service employment with relatively low wages. According to Deller et al. (2001), "There is a perception that substituting traditional jobs in resource-extractive industries and manufacturing with more service-oriented jobs yields inferior earning power, benefits, and advancement potential" and that this may lead to "higher levels of local underemployment, lower income levels, and generally lower overall economic well-being." In addition, many researchers are concerned that recreation may result in a less equitable distribution of income (Gibson, 1993; Marcouiller and Green, 2000). These problems may be compounded by the higher housing costs in some recreation areas (Galston and Baehler, 1995).

These concerns reflect findings from individual case studies. Only a few studies have attempted to estimate how rural recreation areas nationwide differ on economic measures. Deller et al. (2001) found that rural tourism and amenity-based development contributed to growth in per capita income and employment, and concluded that as a result of the positive impact on income "the concern expressed about the quality of jobs created ... appears to be misplaced." English et al. (2000) also found that rural tourism was associated with higher per capita incomes, and with a higher percent increase in per capita income, although they found no significant relationship for household income. English and his colleagues also found housing costs and the change in housing costs over time to be significantly related to rural tourism. On the other hand, they found no evidence that the distribution of income was less equal due to rural tourism.

To address these economic issues, we examined a variety of indicators reflecting employment, earnings, income, and housing costs.

Employment

Two employment measures, the local employment growth rate (percent increase during the 1990s) and the local employment-population ratio (percentage of working-age resident population employed in 2000) are particularly illuminating.

Recreation counties, on average, had more than double the rate of employment growth of other rural areas during the 1990s: 24% versus 10%. The regression analysis, moreover, indicated that the extent to which a recreation county was dependent on recreation was positively and significantly related to the rate of local employment growth (see Appendix for details on regression analysis). Employment growth generally offers residents more job opportunities, enabling some unemployed residents to find jobs and employed residents to find better jobs. However, job growth does not necessarily improve job conditions for current residents. If too many people come into the area seeking employment, and if those newcomers aggressively compete with locally unemployed (or underemployed) residents, the resident job seekers may end up having greater difficulty gaining employment. Thus, we need to look closely at employment data to determine how recreation affects the local ability to find jobs.

Data Sources

The source for most of our data is the Decennial Census (Census Bureau, U.S. Department of Commerce). Other sources include:

- The Bureau of Economic Analysis, U.S. Department of Commerce, for data on earnings per job, and the Bureau of Labor Statistics, U.S. Department of Labor, Local Area Unemployment Statistics, for employment growth.
- The Uniform Crime Reporting Program (an unpublished data source available on an annual basis from the Federal Bureau of Investigation (FBI)), for data on serious crimes. Note: These data have not been adjusted by the FBI to reflect underreporting, which could affect comparability over time or among geographic areas.
- The area resource file (a county-specific health resources information system maintained by quality resource systems, under contract to the Health Resources and Services Administration, U.S. Department of Health and Human Services), for the age-adjusted death rate, the number of physicians, and the area (in square miles) used to compute population densities for regression analysis.
- Kenneth Johnson and Calvin Beale for the recreation county types and the measure of recreation dependency used in their 2002 article.

To measure the ability of residents to find jobs, we examined the percentage of the working-age population that was employed. For our study, we broke this into three separate rates covering three groups of the working-age population: ages 18–24, 25–64, and 65 and over. We hypothesized that recreation counties might be particularly advantageous for younger and older populations that may have a harder time competing in places with less job growth. In addition, younger and older groups may find it more convenient to work in recreation counties, which are thought to provide more part-time and seasonal jobs than most other places.

As expected, we found higher employment-population rates in recreation counties for both the younger and older age groups. However, the difference was less than 1 percentage point. The main working-age employment rate (ages 25–64) was roughly the same for both recreation and other nonmetro counties in 2000. However, for each of these age groups, the upward trend in the employment-population rate during the 1990s favored recreation counties. Our regression analysis indicates that recreation had a positive and statistically significant impact on the employment rates for all three age categories in 2000. Recreation also had a positive and statistically significant impact on the increase in the employment rate during the 1990s, except for the older age group.

Earnings

Conventional wisdom suggests that a main drawback of tourism is that many of the jobs it creates are in restaurants, motels, and other businesses that tend to offer relatively low wages and few fringe benefits. But does this mean that rural recreation development generally leads to low-paying jobs? To address this question, we examined average annual earnings per job (which include wages and salaries and other labor and proprietor income, but exclude unearned income and fringe benefits). We found that average earnings per job were $22,334 in 2000 for recreation counties—about $450 less than in other rural counties (Figure 2, Table 2). The difference, though only about 2%, is consistent with the low-wage hypothesis. On the other hand, our finding that earnings per job increased faster in recreation counties than in other rural counties in the 1990s was not consistent with the conventional wisdom, but again, the difference was relatively small ($200).

Our regression analysis, however, found no statistically significant relationship between earnings per job and recreation dependency, at least no simple linear relationship. With regard to change in earnings per job during the 1990s, the regression analysis found that recreation had a positive and statistically significant impact on earnings per job. So these findings do not support the conventional wisdom that recreation results in generally low-paying jobs.

The data on earnings per job covered all jobs in the county, including those filled by nonresidents. A different picture emerges when we look only at earnings per resident worker. Aside from excluding nonresidents employed in the county (who, in theory, might be lowering the average earnings per job in recreation counties), this measure totals the income workers receive from all the jobs they have. This is important because recreation counties often provide numerous part-time and seasonal jobs, potentially allowing more of their residents to have multiple jobs than the residents of other counties. The average worker's earnings from multiple jobs exceeded the average earnings per job. In recreation counties, earnings amounted to $29,593 per resident worker (16 years or older) in 1999—about $2,000 more than in other rural counties—an 8% difference. Our regression analysis found recreation had a positive and statistically significant effect on earnings per resident worker. Thus, some residents may work more hours in recreation counties, but on average they end up earning more than residents of other nonmetro counties.

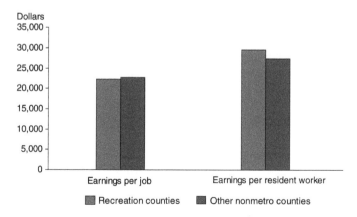

Source: Calculated by ERS using data from U.S. Census Bureau and Bureau of Economic Analysis, U.S. Department of Commerce.

Figure 2. Earnings in recreation and nonrecreation counties, 1999. Recreation counties have significantly higher levels of earnings per resident worker.

Table 2. Economic conditions in recreation and other nonmetro counties.

Indicator	Type of country	
	Recreation	Other nonmetro
Emplyment gowth	Percent	
1990–2000	23.7	9.8
Employment/population ratio in 2000		
Ages 16-24	67.4	66.7
Ages 25-64	70.3	70.3
Ages 65 and over	13.6	13.4
Change 1990–2000	Percentage points	
Ages 16-24	0.7	0.0
Ages 25-64	0.7	0.3
Ages 65 and over	1.5	1.4
Earnings per job in 2000	Dollars	
Change 1990–2000	22,334	22,780
	5,340	5,140
Earnings per resident worker in 1999	29,593	27,445
Income per capita in 2000	35,001	31,812
Change 1990–1999	11,952	10,531
Median monthly rent in 2000	474	384
Change 1990–2000	134	104

Note: These are county averages (simple means).
Source: ERS calculations using data from the U.S. Census Bureau and Bureau of Economic Analysis, U.S. Department of Commerce, and Bureau of Labor Statistics, U.S. Department of Labor.

INCOME

Earnings are only one source of income. Other sources include interest receipts, capital gains, and retirement benefits like social security. Because many recreation areas have attracted wealthy individuals—including retirees, whose earnings are only a small part of their incomes—we expected recreation county income levels to be higher than in other rural areas. Consistent with this expectation, we found average per capita income was 10% higher in recreation counties than in other nonmetro counties (Figure 3). Moreover, per capita income levels were growing more rapidly during the 1990s in recreation counties than in other nonmetro counties. These findings were reflected in our regression analysis, which found recreation had a positive and statistically significant effect on both the level of per capita income and the change in per capita income over time. This should also benefit the community as a whole, because higher incomes mean an increase in demand for local goods and services, as well as increased local government tax collections and contributions to local charities and other social organizations.

One problem in interpreting per capita incomes is that they average together the incomes of the wealthiest and the poorest individuals. Thus, a small number of extremely wealthy people could make the community seem much better off than with other measures, for instance, the income of the typical (or median) person in the county. If recreation counties had more wealthy individuals than other rural counties, the per capita measure might be a misleading indicator of how the average family or household in each of these counties differed in income. For this reason, we include a second income measure: median household income in the county in 1999.

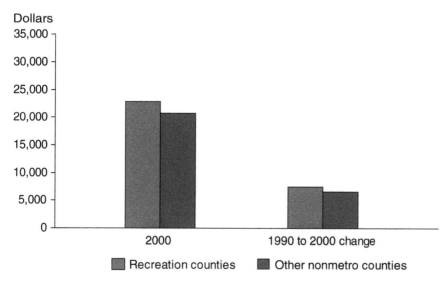

Source: Calculated by ERS using data from U.S. Census Bureau and Bureau of Economic Analysis, Department of Commerce.

Figure 3. Per capita income in recreation and nonrecreation counties, 2000, and change during 1990s. Recreation counties have significantly higher levels of income and had more income growth in the 1990s.

Using this measure, we found that median household income was 10% higher in recreation counties than in other rural counties. The recreation county advantage amounted to $3,185 per year for the median household. The regression analysis reflected this finding, showing a positive and statistically significant relationship between recreation and both the level and change in median family income.

Housing Costs

One of the main complaints about recreation areas is that the cost of living in them is often higher, offsetting much of the advantage that residents might obtain from their higher incomes. Of particular concern is that high living costs could become a significant hardship for people struggling to raise families on minimum-wage jobs (Galston and Baehler, 1995). A high cost of living could force some lower paid workers (including some longtime residents) to look for housing outside the area.

The cost of housing is one of the most important contributors to the cost of living. According to Census data in 2000, median monthly rents for housing averaged $474 in recreation counties, 23% higher than the $384 median rent in other nonmetro counties (Figure 4). Our regression analysis also found a positive and statistically significant effect of recreation on median rent. Rents also increased faster during the 1990s in recreation counties, with the extent of recreation positively and significantly related to the extent of rent increase.

Though recreation counties had higher rents than other nonmetro counties, over the course of a year this amounted to a difference of only $1,080 per household—about a third of the $3,185 advantage we found in median household income in recreation counties. So after deducting for their higher rents, we found that households in recreation counties still had a significant income advantage over those in other rural counties.

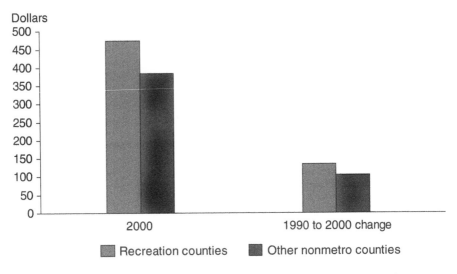

Source: Calculated by ERS using data from U.S. Census Bureau, Department of Commerce.

Figure 4. Median monthly rents in recreation and nonrecreation counties, 2000, and change during 1990s. Recreation counties have significantly higher rents and had more growth in rents in the 1990s.

It is difficult to draw conclusions from this kind of information, for several reasons. First, rents show only part of the housing cost picture. Most housing units in the nonmetro counties we studied (in both recreation and other nonmetro counties) are owner-occupied rather than rented. Assuming that higher rents reflect higher home prices and greater equity in homes, higher home prices should increase the wealth of homeowners in recreation counties. In addition, higher rents and home prices may reflect better housing quality in recreation counties, rather than simply higher costs. This might be expected because more of the housing in these rapidly growing places is likely to be relatively new (and hence more valuable), and recreation county residents, having generally higher incomes, may demand better housing than residents of other nonmetro counties. Higher home values also increase the local tax base, which may lead to higher tax collections, enabling local governments to increase public services.

Thus, on balance, it is unclear whether these higher housing costs are a plus or minus for the community.

SOCIAL IMPACTS

Various researchers have examined the relationship between nonmetro recreation and social conditions in a community. Page et al. (2001) note that rapid population growth in nonmetro recreation counties has resulted in overcrowded conditions and traffic congestion. Recreation may also affect local poverty rates. Some authors have argued that recreation activity creates new sources of employment, helping to raise the poor from poverty (Gibson, 1993; Patton, 1985). Others have pointed to the low-wage, seasonal, and part-time nature of many tourism jobs, arguing that tourism may actually add to the number of poor in the community (Galston and Baehler, 1995; Smith, 1989). Recreation affects social conditions in other ways. For example, Page et al. argue that tourism and recreation activity may help to maintain or improve local services, such as health facilities, entertainment, banking, and public transportation, because of the increased demand that tourists generate for these activities. The relationship between recreation and crime has also been explored by a number of researchers (McPheters and Stronge, 1974; Page et al., 2001; Rephann, 1999), with a popular question being whether casinos increase criminal activity (Hakim and Buck, 1989; Rephann et al., 1997).

To address social impact concerns, we identified eight social indicators. Two involve conditions associated with rapid population growth; one identifies a population subgroup (persons in poverty) that may present special challenges; two relate to education; two deal with health-related concerns; and one measures crime.

Population Growth

The first social variable we examined was the county population growth rate during the 1990s. Population growth can be beneficial for stagnant or declining rural areas looking for new sources of employment and income, but in some places it can bring problems. This is particularly true if growth occurs rapidly and haphazardly, contributing to sprawl, traffic congestion, environmental degradation, increased housing costs, school overcrowding, a decrease in open land, and loss of a "sense of place" for local residents.

Perhaps because of their natural amenities and tourist attractions, recreation counties experienced a 20.2% rate of population growth between 1990 and 2000, nearly triple the 6.9% rate for other nonmetro counties during the same period (Table 3). These results are consistent with our linear regression analysis, which found a positive and statistically significant relationship between recreation and the county population growth rate. Further analysis revealed an apparent curvilinear relationship, in which recreation counties with moderate recreation dependencies experienced higher growth rates than those with smaller and larger recreation dependencies.

Table 3. Social conditions in nonmetro recreation and other nonmetro counties.

Indicator	Recreation	Type of country	Other nonmetro
Population growth		Percent	
1990–2000	20.2		6.9
Mean travel time to work		Minutes	
in 2000	22.7		23.0
Change 1990–2000	4.4		4.3
Poverty rate		Percent	
in 1999	13.2		15.7
Change 1989–1988		Percentage points	
	−2.6		−3.1
Residents without a high school diploma		Percent	
in 2000	18.4		25.0
Change 1990–2000		Percentage points	
	−7.4		−8.4
Residents with at least a bachelor's degree		Percent	
in 2000	19.2		13.6
Change 1990–2000		Percentage points	
	4.0		2.4
Physicians		Number	
per 100,000 residents in 2003	123.0		83.4
Age-adjusted deaths per 100,000 residents in 2003	817.3		898.3
Rate of serious crime per 100 residents in 1999	2.8	Percent	2.4

Note: These are county averages (simple means).
Source: ERS calculations using data from the U.S. Census Bureau and Bureau of Economic Analysis, U.S. Department of Commerce, Department of Health and Human Services, and the FBI.

Travel Time to Work

This variable was included to test the hypothesis that growth in recreation counties may lead to increasing traffic congestion (Page et al., 2001). We found that mean commute times for recreation and other rural counties were not significantly different in 2000. Moreover, during the 1990s, commute times increased at roughly the same rate (4.4% for recreation counties versus 4.3% for other rural counties). The regression analysis, however, revealed a significant negative relationship between recreation dependence and change in travel time to work during the 1990s. One explanation may be that expanded economic opportunities in recreation counties during the 1990s meant that residents had to travel shorter distances for jobs.

Poverty Rate

Poverty poses a problem for communities by increasing the costs of providing public services and contributing to crime rates, health problems, and neighborhood blight. Previous research has found that an expanding tourist industry is linked with a decreasing rate of poverty (John et al., 1988; Rosenfeld et al., 1989). Given that many recreation counties have attracted well-off retirees and that average income levels have risen in recreation counties, the counties might, on average, be expected to have fewer individuals living in poverty than other nonmetro counties. However, as noted earlier, some have argued that tourism, by expanding the number of low-paying, part-time jobs, could increase the number of individuals living in poverty in these counties (Galston and Baehler, 1995; Smith, 1989).

We found that the poverty rate was substantially lower in recreation counties than in other rural counties. In 1999, 13.2% of all residents in recreation counties were living in poverty, compared with 15.7% in other nonmetro counties. Mirroring the national trend of declining poverty rates during the 1990s, the proportion of residents living in poverty during the decade declined (at approximately the same rate) in both recreation and other rural counties. Our regression analysis also found a significantly negative relationship between recreation and the poverty rate. In addition, the regression analysis found a statistically significant negative relationship between recreation and the change in the poverty rate.

Educational Attainment

Previous research has identified the central role that education plays in rural poverty (McGranahan, 2000). Education is important, not only because it contributes to the economy, but also because it can affect the quality of life in rural communities and can help raise people out of poverty. Nonmetro areas with lower levels of education tend to be poorer and offer fewer economic opportunities for their residents. Migration (movement to another area) tends to increase with higher levels of education (Basker, 2002; Greenwood, 1975, 1993). Hence, recreation counties, which have had many in-migrants in recent years, may be expected to have higher levels of educational attainment than other nonmetro counties. English et al. (2000) found rural tourism to be associated with higher levels of educational attainment. We examined educational attainment at two levels: high school and college.

Our results show that residents in recreation counties have higher levels of education than other nonmetro residents (Figure 5). Recreation counties have both a smaller share of residents 25 years or older without a high school education, and a higher share of those with at least a bachelor's degree, than residents of other nonmetro counties. In 2000, 18.4% of residents age 25 or older in recreation counties did not have a high school diploma, compared with 25% in other nonmetro counties. For the same year, 19.2% of recreation county residents age 25 or older had a 4-year college degree or higher, compared with 13.6% in other nonmetro counties. During the 1990s, educational attainment on both measures improved in recreation as well as other nonmetro counties. These findings are supported by our regression analysis, which found that recreation had a significant negative correlation with the share of residents without a high school diploma and a significant positive correlation with the share of residents with a bachelor's degree or higher. In addition, a statistically significant relationship was found between recreation and an increase in the share of college-educated residents during the 1990s. However, the change in the share of high school graduates during the 1990s, although positive, was not significantly related to recreation.

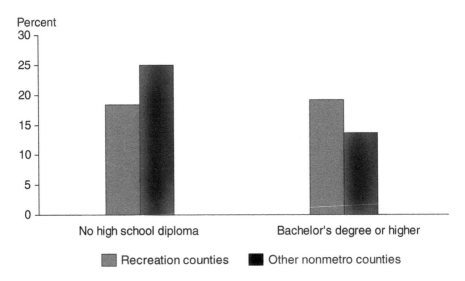

Source: Calculated by ERS using data from U.S. Census Bureau, Department of Commerce.

Figure 5. Educational attainment in recreation and nonrecreation counties, 2000. Recreation counties have significantly higher levels of educational attainment.

HEALTH MEASURES

Health is important for quality of life. In some recreation counties, many individuals moving in are retirees who demand more from health services than younger people; this could result in improved health services in these places. Many recreation counties are in pristine locations with clean air and water, which might also lead to better overall health. In addition, residents in recreation areas are probably more likely to be involved in outdoor activities than individuals in other nonmetro areas, which may also promote better overall health.

Our indicators of local health conditions—the number of physicians available and the age-adjusted mortality rate—support the view that recreation county residents have better health and health services than other nonmetro residents. In 2003, recreation counties had 123 physicians per 100,000 residents, compared with 83.4 per 100,000 residents in other nonmetro counties. The analysis also shows that the age-adjusted death rate (computed as a 3 year average) was almost 10% lower in recreation than in other nonmetro counties.

Our regression results show that recreation had a significantly negative correlation with the age-adjusted death rate. However, the relationship between recreation and the number of physicians, although positive, was statistically insignificant.

Crime Rate

Many researchers have looked at the link between recreation activity and crime (McPheters and Stronge, 1974; Page et al., 2001; Rephann, 1999). Some types of recreation counties attract criminals who prey on tourists in-season and rob unoccupied houses during the off-season. Also, some low-income residents of these counties may commit crimes of opportunity, taking advantage of the influx of well-off outsiders. Some researchers have argued that crime may be particularly associated with casinos (Hakim and Buck, 1989, Rephann et al., 1997).

The results of our analysis indicate that recreation counties had nearly a 17% higher rate of serious crime (murder and non-negligent manslaughter, forcible rape, robbery, and aggravated assault) than other nonmetro counties. In 1999, the overall rate of serious crime in recreation counties was 2.8 incidents per 100 residents, compared with 2.4 incidents per 100 residents in other nonmetro counties, a statistically significant difference. These results are consistent with our regression analysis, which found that a significantly positive relationship exists between recreation and the crime rate.

However, the meaning of this finding is not clear because the crime rate is a biased measure in recreation areas, due to the fact that crimes committed against tourists and seasonal residents are included in the total number of crimes (the numerator of the crime rate), while tourists and seasonal residents are not included in the base number of residents (the denominator of the crime rate). So the crime rate is expected to be higher in recreation areas, even if residents of these areas are not more likely to be crime victims than residents of other rural areas.

VARIATIONS BY TYPE OF RECREATION COUNTY

As noted, Johnson and Beale (2002) categorized each recreation county as belonging to one of 11 mutually exclusive recreational groupings, a classification that provides greater insight into the recreational component of each county (Figures 6 and 7). The single most common category is the Midwest Lake and Second Home, accounting for 70 counties and overwhelmingly concentrated in central and northern Michigan, Minnesota, and Wisconsin (Table 4). The Northeast Mountain, Lake, and Second Home group, a closely related category, is mainly concentrated in northern New England (Maine, New Hampshire, and Vermont) and in portions of New York and Pennsylvania. Together, these two similar categories account for more than a quarter of all recreation counties. Both categories are relatively prosperous: Northeast counties had the highest level of earnings per job among all recreation types, and the Midwest category experienced sharp increases in household income during the 1990s (Table 5). Both regions had rates of poverty among the lowest of all recreation categories (Table 6).

Although almost every type of recreation county registered at least double-digit population growth during the 1990s (the exception being the Northeast Mountain, Lake, and Second Home), Ski Resort counties grew the fastest (increasing 38%), continuing a trend from the 1980s. Other recreation categories in the West (West Mountain and Other Mountain) also experienced rapid population growth. Ski Resort counties stand out in other ways, measuring substantially higher than other recreation counties on a number of economic variables, including ratio of employment to population, earnings per job, earnings per worker, per capita income, and median household income. Ski Resorts also had the lowest poverty rate among all recreation categories, but had substantially higher housing costs—nearly 40% higher than the average for other nonmetro counties—which grew rapidly during the 1990s. Ski Resort counties also stand out in terms of social indicators, having the highest levels of educational attainment, the largest number of doctors, the lowest death rates, and the highest rate of crime among all recreation categories.

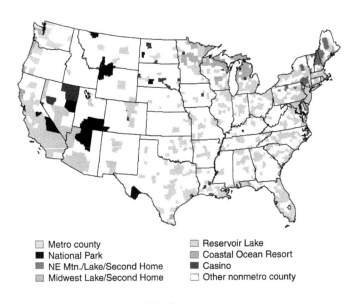

Metro county
National Park
NE Mtn./Lake/Second Home
Midwest Lake/Second Home

Reservoir Lake
Coastal Ocean Resort
Casino
Other nonmetro county

Note: Excludes counties in Alaska and Hawaii.
Source: Adapted from Kenneth M. Johnson and Calvin L. Beale, 2002. "Nonmetro Recreation Counties: Their Identification and Rapid Growth," *Rural America*, Vol. 17, No. 4:12-19.

Figure 6. Nonmetropolitian recreation categories by type (part 1), 2002.

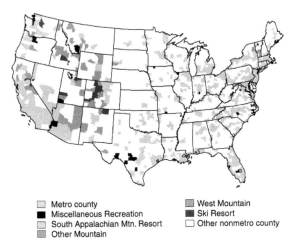

Metro county
Miscellaneous Recreation
South Appalachian Mtn. Resort
Other Mountain

West Mountain
Ski Resort
Other nonmetro county

Note: Excludes counties in Alaska and Hawaii.
Source: Adapted from Kenneth M. Johnson and Calvin L. Beale, 2002. "Nonmetro Recreation Counties: Their Identification and Rapid Growth," *Rural America*, Vol. 17, No. 4:12-19.

Figure 7. Nonmetropolitian recreation categories by type (part 2), 2002.

Table 4. Recreation county categories.

Recreation category	Number of counties
Midwest Lake and Second Home	70
Northeast Mountain, Lake, and Second Home	19
Coastal Ocean Resort	35
Reservoir Lake	27
Ski Resort	20
Other Mountain (with Ski Resorts)	17
West Mountain (excluding Ski Resorts and National Parks)	46
South Appalachian Mountain Resort	17
Casino	21
National Park	18
Miscellaneous	21
Total	311

Source: Kenneth M. Johnson and Calvin L. Beale, "Nonmetro Recreation Counties: Their Identification and Rapid Growth," *Rural America*, Vol. 17, No. 4, 2002:12-19.

In contrast, Reservoir Lake counties and South Appalachian Mountain Resort counties are among the most economically challenged recreation county types. Reservoir Lake counties, which are mainly located in the Midwest and Great Plains regions, and South Appalachian Mountain Resort counties—in the upland areas of Georgia, North Carolina, Virginia, West Virginia, and Maryland—have among the lowest earnings per worker and lowest median household income levels. They also have among the lowest rents. Both of these regions have among the lowest levels of educational attainment. Further, they have higher-than-average age-adjusted death rates, but relatively low crime rates. The South Appalachian Mountain Resort category also has a significantly longer commute than other other nonmetro counties, possibly a reflection of its mountainous topography.

Casino counties also have relatively low levels of economic development, with the highest rate of poverty—over 40% higher than for all recreation counties—as well as below-average levels of per capita income, median household income, and earnings per worker. Still, during the 1990s, Casino counties, which are mainly located in the Upper Midwest, the Dakotas, the Mississippi Delta region, and Nevada, collectively had sharp employment growth (a third faster than the average for all recreation counties). Casino counties, which benefited from the establishment of gambling on Native American reservations during the 1990s, had a lower level of educational attainment, fewer physicians, a higher-than-average age-adjusted death rate, and a significantly higher rate of crime than most other recreation counties.

CONCLUSION

This study provides quantitative information on how tourism and recreation development affects socioeconomic conditions in rural areas. Specifically, we wanted to address economic issues related to employment, income, earnings, and cost of living,

Table 5. Economic conditions and trends by type of recreation county.

Indicator	Casino	Ocean Resort	Reservoir Lake	MW Lake Home	NE MT/LK Home	Nat. Park	West MT	Ski Resort	Other MT	South AP MT Resort	Rec. Misc.	Rec. total	Non-rec. Total
Employment growth 1990–2000	*Percent*												
	31.7*	19.2*	24.9*	23.3*	3.5	19.0*	25.0*	35.3*	26.0*	18.7*	29.2*	23.7*	9.8
Employment/population ratio in 2000													
Ages 16–24	66.0	67.5	64.6	67.3	68.8	66.3	66.5	74.3*	67.2	66.1	68.1	67.4	66.7
Ages 25–64	70.4	69.9	67.3	69.4	72.1	69.9	69.7	77.4*	70.6	69.4	71.0	70.3	70.3
Ages 65 and over	16.0*	13.8	13.3	10.0*	11.6*	15.3	15.5*	19.3*	13.5	11.1*	14.8	13.6	13.4
Change 1990–2000	*Percentage points*												
Ages 16–24	1.0	-1.4*	0.2	2.7*	1.3	0.7	0.0	0.8	0.5	-0.1	-0.7	0.7*	0.0
Ages 25–64	0.7	-1.4	0.6	2.8*	1.1	0.5	-0.0	0.4	0.6	-0.7	-0.4	0.7*	-0.3
Ages 65 and over	2.2	1.6	1.2	2.0	0.8	0.9	0.5	3.0	0.8	1.3	0.9	1.5	1.4
Earning per job	*Dollars*												
in 2000	24,372	23,698	19,630*	22,710	25,255*	21,233	20,058*	24,294	23,560	22,412	20,604	22,334	22,780
Change 1990–2000	6,748	5,761	4,264	5,359	5,100	4,383	3,487*	7,394*	5,342	5,848	4,887	5,340	5,140
Earning per worker													
in 1999	28,249	31,905*	27,033	29,314*	28,968*	28,346	28,618*	34,992*	30,391*	28,596	30,089*	29,593*	27,445
Income per capita													
in 2000	21,865	26,628*	20,002	21,485	23,718*	21,891	20,717	29,552*	22,898*	21,895	24,215*	22,810*	20,727
Change 1990–2000	7,457	8,813*	5,802*	7,243*	7,566*	7,363	5,704	11,080*	7,323	7,834*	8,419*	7,471*	6,564

Table 5. *(Continued)*

Indicator	Casino	Ocean Resort	Reservoir Lake	MW Lake Home	NE MT/LK Home	Nat. Park	West MT	Ski Resort	Other MT	South AP MT Resort	Rec. Misc.	Rec. total	Non-rec. Total
Median household income in 1999	33,325	37,239*	29,635*	34,896*	34,447*	33,215	33,905*	44,521*	36,128*	32,843	36,396*	35,001*	31,812
Change 1989–1999	11,477	11,475*	10,280	13,495*	9,411*	11,231	11,146	16,220*	11,630*	11,244	11,677*	11,952*	10,531
Median monthly rent in 2000	440*	556*	384	421*	460*	445*	473*	660*	535*	431*	488*	474*	384
Change 1990–2000	115	140*	110	111	85*	126	151*	228*	142*	129*	150*	134	104

Note: These are county averages (simple means).

MW=Midwest; NE=Northeast; MT=Mountain; LK=Lake; Nat.=National; AP=Appalachian; Misc.=Miscellaneous; Rec.=Recreation.

*Significantly different from nonrecreation county mean at 5-percent error level.

Source: ERS calculations based on data from U.S. Census Bureau and Bureau of Economic Analysis, U.S. Department of Commerce, and Bureau of Labor Statistics, U.S. Department of Labor. Recreation types from Johnson and Beale (2002), USDA, Economic Research Service.

Table 6. Social conditions and trends by type of recreation county.

Indicator	Casino	Ocean Resort	Reservoir Lake	MW Lake Home	NE MT/LK Home	Nat. Park	West MT	Ski Resort	Other MT	South AP MT Resort	Rec. Misc.	Rec. total	Non-rec. Total
Population growth							*Percent*						
1990–2000	16.7*	18.8*	20.4*	15.8*	5.8	13.3*	27.6*	38.0*	24.9*	18.4*	23.3*	20.2*	6.9
Mean travel time to work							*Minutes*						
in 2000	21.7	22.3	24.3	22.3	23.3	20.3*	23.1	22.1	21.2	26.3*	23.5	22.7	23.0
Change 1990–2000	2.7*	3.8	4.8	4.8*	4.8	4.1	5.1*	4.6	3.9	5.3	3.6	4.4	4.3
Poverty rate							*Percent*						
in 1999	18.8*	12.4*	15.2	10.7*	12.0*	16.2	14.0*	10.2*	13.9	13.2*	13.3	13.2*	15.7
							Percentage points						
Change 1989–1999	-4.3	-1.6*	-2.9	-4.4*	0.0*	-4.4	-1.3*	-1.6*	-1.5*	-2.6	-2.1	-2.6	-3.1
Residents without high							*Percent*						
school diploma in 2000	21.2*	19.0*	23.6	18.0*	18.7*	17.7*	16.1*	11.8*	14.5*	24.7*	19.8*	18.4*	25.0
							Percentage points						
Change 1990–2000	2.7	4.7*	2.8	3.4*	2.7	4.2*	4.5*	6.5*	4.8*	3.4*	4.2*	4.0	2.4
Physicians per 100,000							*Number*						
residents in 2003	78.0	166.6*	52.8*	97.5	181.9*	110.1	109.9*	192.0*	190.7*	149.7*	114.4	123.0*	83.4
Age-adjusted death rate per 100,000 residents													
in 2000–02	955.6	839.5*	858.8	829.7*	869.0	809.1*	766.3*	661.7*	759.3*	869.7	772.7*	817.3*	898.3
Rate of serious crime													
per 100 residents in 1999	3.2*	3.2*	2.0	2.6	2.6	2.5	2.6	3.8*	3.0	2.0	3.3*	2.8*	2.4

Note: These are county averages (simple means). MW=Midwest; NE=Northeast; MT=Mountain; LK=Lake; Nat.=National; AP=Appalachian; Misc.=Miscellaneous; Rec.=Recreation.

*Significantly different from non-recreation county mean at 5-percent error level.

Source: ERS calculations based on data from U.S. Census Bureau and Bureau of Economic Analysis, U.S. Department of Commerce, and Bureau of Labor Statistics, U.S. Department of Labor. Recreation types from Johnson and Beale (2002), USDA, Economic Research Service.

and social issues such as poverty, education, health, and crime. A summary follows of our main findings on the socioeconomic impacts of rural recreation and tourism development.

Employment
Our regression analysis found a positive and statistically significant association between recreation dependency and the percentage of working-age population with jobs. We also found that, with the exception of the older (65 and over) population, recreation dependency positively affected the change in this employment measure during the 1990s.

Earnings
We examined earnings per job and earnings per resident to measure the value of the jobs associated with rural recreation development. We found that the average earnings per job in recreation counties were not significantly different than in other nonmetro counties, and we found no direct (linear) relationship between local dependency on recreation and local earnings per job in our recreation counties. However, our regression analysis found a positive relationship between recreation and growth in earnings per job during the 1990s. Thus, the trend seems to favor the pay levels for jobs in these recreation counties.

These findings concern earnings of all who work in the county, including nonresidents. They report earnings per job, not per worker—an important distinction because workers may have more than one job, and the availability of second jobs (part-time and seasonal) may be greater in recreation counties than elsewhere. When we focused on total job earnings for residents of recreation counties, we found these earnings were significantly higher ($2,000 more per worker) than for residents of other rural counties. The regression analysis also found a significant positive relationship between recreation and resident-worker earnings. So the earnings picture for recreation counties appears positive for the average resident.

Cost of Living
Our research suggests recreation development leads to higher living costs, at least with respect to housing. We found that the average rent was 23% higher in recreation counties, and it was positively and significantly associated with the degree of recreation dependency in our regression analysis. While this may reduce some of the economic advantages for residents of recreation counties, it does so only partially. Median household incomes, on average, were $3,185 higher in recreation counties than in other rural counties. Annual costs associated with rent were $1,080 higher in recreation counties, offsetting only about a third of the recreation county income advantage.

Growth Strains
We found recreation led to significantly higher rates of population growth. In theory, this can aggravate social problems, such as school crowding, housing shortages, pollution, and loss of identification with the community. The one growth-related social

problem we addressed was road congestion. Examining the time it takes to commute to work, we found little evidence that congestion was presenting undue problems for residents in recreation counties. Moreover, our regression analysis found that recreation was associated with smaller increases in average commute times in the 1990s than in other rural counties.

Poverty

Another social problem that appeared to be reduced in recreation counties was poverty. Our regression analysis found recreation was associated with lower poverty rates and with larger declines in the poverty rate during the 1990s.

Crime

There may be some cause for concern with regard to crime. We found crime rates (for serious crimes) were higher in recreation counties than in other rural counties, and our regression analysis also found a statistically significant positive relationship between crime rates and recreation dependency. However, crime statistics may be biased in recreation areas because crimes against tourists and seasonal residents are counted in the crime rate, while tourists and seasonal residents are not counted as part of the population base upon which the rate is calculated. Thus, even if people in recreation areas do not face a higher chance of becoming victims of crimes, the crime rates of these areas will appear higher than elsewhere. Nonetheless, one may still argue that recreation-related crime adds to the local cost of policing and incarcerating criminals, just as recreation-related traffic—even though it may not create congestion—adds to the cost of maintaining roads.

Education and Health

Our analysis found that recreation is associated with a more educated population, particularly with a higher percentage of college-educated people. We also found relatively good health conditions (measured by age-adjusted death rates) in recreation counties. This might be expected from the higher numbers of physicians per 100,000 residents that we found in recreation counties. However, our regression analysis did not find a statistically significant relationship between recreation dependence and the local supply of physicians. So some other explanation must be posited for the general good health in recreation counties, such as greater opportunities for physical exercise or residents who are more health-conscious.

Variations by County Type

Conditions vary significantly by recreation county type. For example, Ski Resort counties have among the wealthiest, best educated, and healthiest populations of all recreation county types. Ski Resort counties also have relatively high rates of crime. In contrast, Reservoir Lake counties and South Appalachian Mountain Resort counties have among the poorest and least educated residents of all recreation county types, along with relatively high age-adjusted death rates, but they have relatively low crime rates. Casino counties—which had among the highest rates of job growth and the largest absolute increases in earnings per job during the 1990s—also had among the highest rates of growth in employment per person for seniors, perhaps reflecting the greater need for jobs among those over age 65 in these relatively high-poverty communities.

IDEAS FOR FUTURE RESEARCH

We focused mainly on conditions facing residents of mature rural recreation counties, that is, places that already have a substantial amount of recreation. Additional insights may come from expanding the analysis to include emerging recreation areas and neighboring places that may be affected by spillover impacts from recreation areas. Future research might also address issues related to specific population subgroups, such as low-paid workers, who may face more significant problems related to the high cost of housing in recreation areas. The analysis might also be expanded to examine recreation impacts on other aspects of community well-being, such as the environment, public services, institutions like churches and charitable foundations, and small business formation and entrepreneurial activity.

Our knowledge of rural recreation impacts might also benefit from different formulations of the regression model. For example, models could be fine-tuned to focus on individual indicators, or they could be estimated separately for individual regions and types of recreation areas. Feedback effects might be incorporated into the model— for example, recreation can lead to higher housing costs, which in turn can lead to reduced tourism and recreation development. More sophisticated models may be able to separate out these two effects. The models might also be examined over different time periods to test for cyclical effects and robustness over time.

Research might also measure the effects of specific State and local policies, along with other factors thought to affect the level of rural recreation and tourism (such as the availability of natural amenities and proximity and access to nonmetro areas). This might help state and local officials assess their potential for recreation and tourism development and identify strategies to further this development.

APPENDIX: REGRESSION ANALYSIS

Making inferences from simple comparisons of recreation and other nonmetro county means can be misleading because it is possible that much of the observed socioeconomic difference between the two groups could be coincidental and not directly related to the extent of recreation.

For example, during the 1990s, many recreation counties in the Rocky Mountains benefited from an unusual regional phenomenon associated with the outflow of population from metropolitan California. This raises a question: How much of the difference in growth that we observed between recreation and other nonmetro counties nationwide was region-specific, associated with this one-time outflow of population?

Similarly, the decade of the 1990s was one of rapid economic improvement, which may have particularly benefited places with high poverty rates, providing job opportunities to many who, under normal conditions, would have had a hard time finding jobs. Many of these high-poverty rural areas are in the South in other nonmetro counties. This largely regional phenomenon could have led to our finding that recreation counties nationwide benefited less from poverty rate reduction than did other nonmetro counties. But would we find the same thing if we looked at each region separately?

Other factors unrelated to recreation might also be expected to differentially affect recreation and other nonmetro areas and lead to a potential bias in the differences observed between the two types of counties. For example, counties that are more urban in nature may have had developmental advantages over more rural and isolated areas. While recreation is expected to add to the level of urbanization, recreation counties are still less urban than other nonmetro counties on average, so this potential bias could mask the beneficial impact of recreation in simple comparisons.

Regression Methodology

In an attempt to overcome potential biases, we narrowed our analysis to recreation counties and conducted a regression analysis to see how a recreation county's extent of recreation dependency might affect the socioeconomic indicators examined in this report. Our measure of recreation dependency is the weighted average of a county's Z-scores covering tourism-related employment and income shares of the local economy and the recreational home share of total county homes, as developed by Johnson and Beale (2002): the larger the average, the more dependent a county is on recreation and tourism. In addition, we included 10 dichotomous variables reflecting the Johnson and Beale recreation county types (for statistical reasons, we excluded the miscellaneous recreation county type). This allows for significant socioeconomic variations by type of recreation county (but it assumes that impacts associated with changes in recreation dependency do not vary with recreation type).

Following the approach of English et al. (2000), we also included several control variables that were not highly correlated with recreation dependency but that might be expected to affect local socioeconomic conditions. For example, we included eight dichotomous (0, 1) variables identifying the Census regional subdivisions. We did not include a dichotomous variable for one of the nine subdivisions—the Southeast—to avoid statistical problems.

We also included several demographic measures related to urbanization that are often included in empirical studies explaining regional socioeconomic variations. One was a dichotomous variable indicating whether the county was influenced by a nearby metropolitan area (based on adjacency as defined in the ERS 1993 Beale Codes, which requires both physical adjacency and significant commuting to the metro area). The other two demographic measures were county population density and percentage of county population residing in the rural portion of the county.

Ideally, an attempt to explain cross-county variations in socioeconomic indicators would involve separate models for each indicator, using theory to identify the explanatory variables and the form of the regression most relevant for a particular indicator. Given the large number of indicators in this study, we decided a simpler approach was expedient, so we followed English et al. in using just one set of explanatory variables for all of the indicators examined in our study. This results in some imprecision.

One of the ways our analysis differed from that of English and his colleagues was that our regressions only explained variations among our 311 recreation counties (rather than including all nonmetro counties as English did). In addition, we ran two ordinary least-squares regressions explaining intercounty variations rather than one. One of our regressions explained intercounty variations in the year 2000 (or the most recent year the data were available). The other regression explained intercounty variations in the change in the indicator over the previous 10 years. The change regression, which used the identical set of explanatory variables, may be viewed as a check on the year 2000 regression. In most cases, the regressions produced similar results: if recreation dependency was significant in the 2000 regression, it usually had the same sign and was significant in the change regression.

We also ran additional regressions for each indicator, adding a "squared" version of the recreation dependency variable to allow for a curvilinear relationship. We do not show the results of these additional regressions because in most cases they did not affect our results—the squared variable either explained little or no additional variation, or it only replaced the non-squared recreation dependency variable in significance with the same sign. In discussing our findings, however, we mention two cases where these curvilinear recreation factor regressions provided interesting results.

Regression Findings

Space limitations prevent us from showing the complete regression results here, including estimated coefficients for the many control variables we used in our regressions. However, we can summarize our findings by showing only the regression coefficients for the recreation dependency variable in the linear regressions we ran to explain variations for each of the socioeconomic variables of interest. For example, each horizontal row in Table 7 summarizes the results of one or two regressions covering a particular socioeconomic variable. Results for the 2000 regression refer to regressions that explain socioeconomic variations in the year 2000 (or in the next-closest year available). Results for the 1990s change regression refer to regressions that explain variations in the change in socioeconomic variables during the 1990s. Thus, Table 7 summarizes the results for 29 regressions. In addition, the regression statistics shown are unstandardized, and one should not attempt to draw inferences about their relative importance based on their magnitudes.

These regression coefficients are generally consistent with what we previously found when comparing simple means for recreation and other nonmetro counties (Tables 2 and 3). Dependency on recreation was significantly related to most of our economic indicators, and the recreation dependency regression coefficients were also generally consistent with most of our prior findings with regard to social indicators.

In addition, we found statistically significant relationships that were not apparent from comparisons of means for recreation and other nonmetro counties. For example, the regression analysis showed significant positive relationships between recreation and the employment-population ratios for all three age groups studied, whereas there was little or no difference in the means for these ratios.

In some cases, the regression analysis raises questions about previously observed statistical differences. For example, we earlier found that recreation counties were statistically different from other nonmetro counties with respect to number of physicians per 100,000 residents, but the regression analysis found no statistically significant relationship between this indicator and recreation dependency.

Table 7. Linear regression analysis measuring the effect of recreation dependency on economic and social indicators.

	2000 regression		1990s change regression	
Dependent variables	**Recreation dependency B estimate**	**Regression's explanatory power[1]**	**Recreation dependency B estimate**	**Regression's explanatory power[1]**
Economic indicators:				
Job growth rate	NA	NA	5.50**	0.184
Employment-population ratio:				
Ages 16-24	1.13**	0.209	0.56**	0.115
Ages 25-64	0.92**	0.211	0.48**	0.139
Ages 65 and over	1.04**	0.364	0.30	0.013
Earnings per job	−7.95	0.396	482.77**	0.265
Earnings per worker[2]	846.49**	0.317	NA	NA
Income per capita	1,044.52**	0.265	487.73**	0.207
Median household income[2]	1,474.40**	0.393	907.59**	0.339
Median rent	32.59**	0.516	10.74**	0.377
Social indicators:				
Population growth rate	4.59**	0.282	2.85**	0.245
Travel time to work	−0.25	0.327	−0.44**	0.157
Poverty rate[2]	−0.84**	0.249	−0.43**	0.242
Percent without HS diploma	−1.37**	0.468	0.22	0.341
Percent with bachelor's degree	2.24**	0.491	0.65**	0.211
Physicians per 100,000 population[3]	0.69	0.280	NA	NA
Age-adjusted death rate				
per 100,000 population[4]	−24.20**	0.290	NA	NA
Crime rate[2]	0.68**	0.264	NA	NA

NA=Not applicable.
* The coefficient is statistically different from zero at the .05 level.
** The coefficient is statistically different from zero at the .01 level.
[1]Adjusted R-square statistic (fraction of variation explained by regression).
[2]Data are reported for 1999
[3]Data are reported for 2003
[4]Data are reported for 2000-02
Source: ERS calculations, based on data from U.S. Census Bureau and Bureau of Economic Analysis, U.S. Department of Commerce, and Bureau of Labor Statistics, U.S. Department of Labor.

For travel time to work, we had previously found no statistically significant difference between recreation and other nonmetro counties, either for the year 2000 or for the trend during the 1990s. However, the regression analysis revealed a statistically significant negative relationship between recreation dependence and change in travel time to work during the 1990s.

One of the more interesting findings was recreation dependency's negative and statistically significant relationship with the change in poverty rate. This means that the more recreation dependent a county is, the bigger its decline in poverty rate during the 1990s, controlling for other factors. The finding contrasts with our simple descriptive analysis, which found that recreation counties had, on average, a smaller decline in poverty than other nonmetro counties during the 1990s. This suggests that, as we suspected, the smaller average decline in poverty for recreation counties may have been simply a geographic coincidence, because when we controlled for regional differences and other factors in our regression analysis we found that the higher a county's recreation dependency, the more its poverty was reduced during this decade.

Another interesting finding involved earnings per job. We initially found that recreation dependency had a negative but statistically insignificant coefficient for earnings per job (in the 2000 model). When we ran the curvilinear version of the first regression (the 2000 model), we found a significant negative coefficient for recreation dependency and a significant positive coefficient for recreation dependency squared. This implies that the recreation counties with moderate degrees of recreation dependency had relatively lower earnings per job, while those with higher or lower recreation dependency had higher earnings. Taken together, these findings present a somewhat muddled picture with respect to recreation impacts on earnings per job—there is no clear indication that recreation hurts a county in this regard. We got a clearer regression finding regarding the change in earnings per job during the 1990s, which revealed a positive and significant relationship between recreation dependency and the growth in earnings per job.

Two other indicators had different results for the 2000 regressions and the 1990s change regression: the employment population ratio for the elderly and the percent of adult (ages 25 and older) residents without high school diplomas. In both cases, the regressions explaining the change in the indicator produced insignificant coefficients for recreation dependency. For the employment-population ratio for ages 65 and up, the change regression performed very poorly, explaining less than 6% of the variation—less than any other regression in our analysis. This suggests that we might find a significant relationship if we were to improve the model to explain the behavior of the elderly. For the other indicator, the percentage without high school diplomas, we may need to find some other explanation, since the regression explaining change for this indicator performed better in terms of explaining variation than all of our other change-form regressions. Perhaps something unusual was going on in the 1990s that kept places with higher recreation dependencies from experiencing more significant declines in the percentage lacking high school degrees.

We have already mentioned recreation's curvilinear relationship with earnings per job. The other case where we found a curvilinear relationship involved recreation's effects on population growth rates in the 1990s. The linear regression explaining population growth rate had a statistically significant positive coefficient for recreation dependency. The curvilinear regression had a statistically significant positive coefficient for recreation dependency and a statistically significant negative coefficient for recreation dependency squared. This implies that counties with moderate recreation dependencies have higher growth rates than counties with smaller or larger recreation dependencies.

KEYWORDS

- **Economic indicators**
- **Recreation**
- **Recreation counties**
- **Rural development policy**
- **Social indicators**

ACKNOWLEDGMENTS

The authors wish to thank the following reviewers for their helpful comments: Calvin Beale and Pat Sullivan of the Economic Research Service and Rick Wetherill of Rural Development, all of USDA, as well as Steven Deller of the Department of Agricultural and Applied Economics, University of Wisconsin at Madison. Thanks also go to Courtney Knauth for her editing assistance, and to Anne Pearl for the graphic design and text layout of the chapter.

Chapter 8

Rural Tourism

Dennis M. Brown

INTRODUCTION

This annotated bibliography summarizes studies on rural tourism. Primary emphasis is on studies dealing with the US, but some international studies are also included. Topics covered include tourism planning and development, tourism marketing, tourism and rural development, tourism and sustainable development, economic and other effects of tourism, heritage tourism, nature-based tourism/ecotourism, and agritourism.

This bibliography summarizes studies dealing with tourism in rural America. Material is drawn from a wide range of academic disciplines, including economics, planning, geography, and history. Emphasis is given to those studies conducted since the early 1990's.

A number of studies highlight the important role that tourism can play in rural development, with some authors describing the potential benefits in purely economic terms—for example, by citing the impact of tourism on jobs created, income added, or local tax revenues. In contrast, other studies stress the positive effects that tourism can bring to quality of life issues, including a greater "sense of place" for rural residents, an upgrading of local cultural facilities, or an enhancement of regional conservation efforts. Frequent mention is made of different strategies employed in rural tourism, including heritage tourism, nature-based tourism/ecotourism, and agritourism.

Other studies caution that effective rural tourism requires careful planning and development and typically employs well thought-out marketing approaches. Even well-designed tourism strategies can have potential negative side-effects, including higher taxes for local residents, escalating real estate prices, increased sprawl, and a degradation of local natural resources. Frequently, effective rural tourism requires regional or State-level coordination since many rural areas, especially those that are more isolated or more sparsely populated, lack the resources required to establish a successful tourism program.

Rural America is a popular tourist destination. According to a recent study, nearly two-thirds of all adults in the Nation, or 87 million individuals, have taken a trip to a rural destination within the past three years (Travel Industry Association of America, 2001a). Almost nine out of 10 of these trips were for leisure purposes. Overall, the travel industry is big business in America. Travel expenditures within the US totaled nearly $564 billion in 2000, making the travel and tourism industry the third largest in the Nation (after health services and business services), and accounting for total direct employment of over 7.8 million (Travel Industry Association of America, 2001b).

Tourism has many potential benefits for rural areas (Frederick, 1992). Tourism can be an important source of jobs for nonmetro communities, especially for those that are economically underdeveloped. Because jobs in the tourist industry often do not require advanced training, local residents with few skills can readily work as food servers, retail clerks, and hospitality workers. Tourism also not only offers business opportunities to local residents, but it can serve as a vehicle for marketing a place to potential residents and firms, as today's tourist may return later to retire or start a business locally.

Tourism can also enhance local quality of life. For example, tourism can serve as an important source of tax revenues for local jurisdictions. Some rural areas may be more willing to levy higher taxes on tourists because they are transitory, and, hence, may be perceived by local authorities as being more captive to user fees and other forms of taxation. This can lead to higher quality public services and lower local tax rates. Tourism can also support local culture in rural areas by encouraging restoration of local and regional historic sites. And tourism, which is generally considered to be a relatively clean industry, may foster local conservation efforts.

Benefits deriving from tourism development must be balanced against potential negative effects. Jobs in the travel and tourism industry are frequently low-paying and seasonal and often offer limited benefits. In some cases, particularly where tourism strategies are ineffectual, local residents may have to pay for tourism marketing and infrastructure through higher taxes. Tourism can also increase demand for land in rural areas, which may inflate real estate prices, potentially putting the cost of housing beyond the reach of the average local resident. This is the case for some amenity-rich tourism destinations (particularly in the West) experiencing growth in recent years stemming from recreation-based activities (Brown and Fazzone, 1998). Tourism may directly lead to unsightly sprawl in rural areas by creating a demand for development. Other negative side effects include potentially higher rates of crime and greater demand for local services, such as police and fire protection and sanitation services, which can be expensive to provide. Also, tourism can risk changing the rural "sense of place" for some communities. Increased crowding and traffic congestion may also result with an influx of tourists into an area. Greater demand for local arts and crafts can also potentially lead to a lowering of the quality of these products. Finally, tourism risks degrading natural resources in rural areas unless environmental sustainability efforts are undertaken. Many of these risks, however, can be mitigated if proper planning is employed at the outset of tourism development.

This chapter covers a wide range of studies dealing with different aspects of tourism. The citations are not intended to be exhaustive but rather to provide a sampling of different emphases in the literature. Two major types of studies are covered in the review. First, studies describing general concepts of rural tourism are reviewed. These include studies dealing with: the planning and/or development of tourism; the marketing of tourism; tourism and rural development; sustainable tourism development; and economic and other effects of tourism. Second, major tourism strategies are covered, with special attention on: heritage tourism, ecotourism, and agritourism. Other miscellaneous studies, including those dealing with multiple topics, are also listed.

Most studies reviewed in this chapter deal exclusively with rural areas, although some urban citations have been included when the issues involved had relevance to nonmetro America. The focus is community-based tourism development, with an emphasis on how local communities can more effectively develop a viable tourism strategy. Also, while the studies were mainly conducted since the early 1990's, some citations from the 1980's have also been included.

In recent years, rural tourism has gone through significant changes. What was once an activity primarily focused on usage of national parks has evolved into an area of interest now deemed to have considerable potential for rural development. One aspect of this change in status is the vocabulary used to describe various types of rural tourism activities. For example, some studies refer to outdoor-based tourism as "ecotourism", while other publications use the term "nature-based tourism". Although, these two terms are not technically synonymous—the term "ecotourism" suggests activities that promote conservation of nature, while "nature-based tourism" is evocative of a broader spectrum of outdoor-based recreation, including hunting, fishing, camping, and the use of recreational vehicles—they reflect a change in perspective in the tourism industry. For the purposes of this publication, however, both terms are used interchangeably.

The remainder of this chapter is divided into two sections. First is a discussion of the main issues related to rural tourism and tourism strategies, with relevant research cited. Second is the annotated bibliography, organized by topic. All references cited in the discussion section can be found in the area of the annotated bibliography addressing the topic described.

Research on Rural Tourism

Comprehensive planning and development represents one of the key components of most successful rural tourism strategies. Long and Nuckolls (1994) underscore the need for effective planning, and stress that technical assistance can prove crucial to tourism development success for many small communities with limited resources. Weaver (1991) argues that many nonmetro communities would also benefit from an expanded Federal role in rural tourism, as well as greater State involvement. Marcouiller (1997) stresses that tourism planning need not occur in a vacuum, but may be of more use to a rural community when the planning is tied to broader regional development efforts.

Marketing of tourism poses special challenges for many rural areas. Frequently, rural communities lack the name recognition associated with more populated areas. Different strategies can be pursued to achieve greater name recognition among potential visitors. Commonly, this involves targeting potential visitors to an area. For example, Henning (1996) demonstrates that survey methods in a rural Louisiana community have been effective in targeting the area to seniors, who are among the most frequent visitors. Often regional marketing makes the most sense given the limited resources available to many rural areas (Shields and Schibik, 1995). However, Sadowske and Alexander (1992) caution that prior to implementing an expensive marketing strategy, communities should be aware of other costs associated with tourism development. They also argue that the key to success in tourism often lies in communities striking a balance between the private and social costs and benefits of rural tourism development.

Tourism can be an important force for developing disadvantaged rural areas. In particular, rural communities with few other options for development may perceive that tourism represents a panacea for growth. While tourism can certainly be an important component of a sound development plan, this is not always the case. For example, Bontron and Lasnier (1997) note that the local tourism impact varies greatly among rural regions and depends on a host of factors including work force characteristics and seasonality issues. Local support, however, is usually a necessary component for a successful tourism strategy, as noted by Bourke and Luloff (1995), and echoed by Brass (1996), Burr (1995), and Woods (1992). That is why tourism strategies must be consistent with local goals and be sensitive to sustaining a community's character and traditions.

Developing tourism that works in concert with nature is a goal of sustainable development, which generally refers to development that "meets the needs of the present without compromising the ability of future generations to meet their own needs" (Rátz and Puczkó, 1998). Culbertson, Turner, and Kolberg (1993) note that sustainability both contributes to human well-being and is in harmony with the natural environment. Stabler (1997) provides a thorough treatment of sustainable tourism development in terms of economic, ethical, and environmental perspectives from the standpoint of a variety of academic disciplines, including geography, sociology, economics, management, marketing, and planning.

Measuring the economic effects of tourism is a popular topic in the literature. Chang (2000) provides an excellent summary of a broad range of economic impact studies utilizing a variety of estimation techniques, including input-output analysis, economic base theory, econometric techniques, hybrid models, and non-survey methods. Stynes (2000) notes that most impact analyses are concerned with measuring changes in local sales, income, and regional employment resulting from tourism activity, although specific economic effects are difficult to generalize since they depend on a variety of local factors. Goldman and Nakazawa (1994) provide a nine-step process for determining income multipliers to estimate local economic impacts resulting from tourism, while Johnson and Thomas (1990) offer a framework for estimating local employment effects of a museum in England.

Weaver (1986) notes that tourism can not only result in enhanced employment opportunities, increased income potential for local residents, diversification of the local economic base, and additional tax revenues for rural areas, but it can also raise community visibility, and add cultural opportunities for residents. These non-economic benefits are also discussed by Jurowski (1996), who argues that tourism, if well planned, can enhance local environmental resources.

Some have cautioned that while tourism has been a high-growth industry in recent years, it often produces low-paying, part-time, and seasonal jobs (Bontron and Lasnier, 1997). However, others point out that such part-time positions offer important opportunities for those rural residents lacking higher education and advanced training since these individuals would generally not qualify for higher-paying, professional positions

(Frederick, 1992). Moreover, in many places people may already have part-time or seasonal jobs and tourism can help supplement these workers' salaries. For example, many farm laborers and some farmers only work during part of the year and can use another job at a different time of the year to make more money. Part-time tourism jobs may also provide needed income to a parent who needs time off to care for family members. High school-age children may also prefer such jobs since their schedules would not accommodate full-time positions. Hence, part-time and seasonal jobs may make the most sense for important segments of the rural population.

Tourism can offer rural residents business opportunities in activities that cater to the tourist trade. Such locally-operated businesses, which may be seasonal, can provide local residents with valuable opportunities to develop business skills and can give local crafters, farmers, and food processors, among others, outlets to sell their products to local retail establishments. Farmers growing fresh produce can take advantage of tourism to establish direct marketing channels for ready-to-eat products, which may also serve as outlets for processed foods such as jams, jellies, breads, and preserves.

Rural Tourism Strategies

This review focuses on several different types of tourism strategies, including: heritage tourism (sometimes referred to as cultural heritage tourism), nature-based tourism/ecotourism, agritourism, as well as partnership-based approaches, such as scenic byways and heritage areas.

Heritage tourism refers to leisure travel that has as its primary purpose the experiencing of places and activities that represent the past. A principal concern of heritage tourism is historical authenticity and long-term sustainability of the attraction visited. Active local involvement is also typically a key component of successful heritage tourism endeavors. Baldwin's (1994) study of a local heritage festival in northeastern Tennessee represents a good example of a successful heritage tourism program that fostered community involvement in an economically underdeveloped rural community. A different heritage tourism focus is provided by DeLyser's (1995) article on ghost towns, which emphasizes that such towns in the West may have rich histories that can be attractive to potential tourists.

A second major type of rural tourism activity is nature-based tourism/ecotourism (sometimes called recreation-based tourism), which refers to the process of visiting natural areas for the purpose of enjoying the scenery, including plant and animal wildlife. Nature-based tourism may be either passive, in which observers tend to be strictly observers of nature, or active (increasingly popular in recent years), where participants take part in outdoor recreation or adventure travel activities. McDaniel's (2001) article of southwestern Virginia, which highlights the tourism potential of the region's scenic and abundant recreational activities, is a representative example. Guglielmino (1998) cautions that although ecotourism represents a viable economic development strategy for rural areas with natural resources, even successful ventures require patience for local communities. Also, as noted by King and Stewart (1996), undertaking ecotourism, unless managed carefully, can sometimes pit people against local natural resources. This suggests a strong need for pursuing sustainable development in ecotourism activities, as suggested by Lash (1998), who argues that the needs of the local community, visitors, and the environment can best be met through a synergistic approach between development and the environment that will not degrade the resource base.

A third major form of tourism is agritourism, which refers to, "the act of visiting a working farm or any agricultural, horticultural or agribusiness operation for the purpose of enjoyment, education, or active involvement in the activities of the farm or operation" (Lobo, 2001). It includes taking part in a broad range of farm-based activities, including farmers' markets, "petting" farms, roadside stands, and "pick-your-own" operations; engaging in overnight farm or ranch stays and other farm visits; and visiting agriculture-related festivals, museums, and other such attractions. (See Dane (2001b) for a discussion of agritourism, including a listing of some examples of this type of tourism.) Hilchey's (1993a) publication provides a detailed discussion of various farm-based tourism enterprises available to farmers in New York State. He notes that long-term trends in consumer demand for tourism and recreation suggest that agritourism enterprises can help provide an important niche market for farmers throughout the Nation. Hilchey (1993b) also notes that three factors are often the key to successful agritourism activities: social skills of farm-based entrepreneurs, farm aesthetics, and proximity of farms to urban centers.

KEYWORDS

- **Agritourism**
- **Ecotourism**
- **Heritage tourism**
- **Rural tourism**

Chapter 9

Development and Research of Rural Tourism

Hejiang Shen, Xuejing Wang, and Min Wang

INTRODUCTION

Based on the existing results in the academic circles, from the point of the basic cognition on leisure experience, the author analyzes the true essence of leisure experience and levels of rural area and the rural tourism, it has analyzed the theme of the rural tourism which is "new tourism," "new rural," "new experience," and "new prevailing custom." The chapter also takes "leisure" and "experience" as the core, and elaborates value-orientation on the development of the rural tourism. Namely, at the same time, it views the harmonious as the foundation of the development of rural tourism and then demonstrates the dialectical relationship on "leisure, experience, harmonious" of the rural tourism.In recent years, the development and research of rural tourism has been the focus of academic circles in domestic and abroad. And with the implementation of new countryside strategy, it has become the hot topic of academic circles and professional fields once again. Based on the existing achievement, the author analyzes the core notion on the theme of the year of rural tourism from the point of the basic cognition and the judgment of rural areas. And on this view, with taking "the leisure, the experience and the harmony" as the essential factors, the author has explained the value orientation and the dialectical relationship in the rural tourism development.

THE ELEMENTARY COGNITION AND JUDGMENT

The True Essence of Leisure Experience

Leisure experience is a kind of happy desire which people diligently strive after for a long time, and it's an important symbol of the human culture and evolution. From the ancient days, the thought has become a formidable power to defeat the nature and to conquer the world. As a result, because of the differences of historical epoch, the thought has displayed its class nature intensively. In our country, leisure experience once with "idleness" and "depression" was placed on a par. But the process of the historical development has already indicated that people in pursuit of happy life will become the final determinant and the great power to impel the improvement of social society.

Nowadays, with the fast development of economy in our country, the increasing living standard of people and the demand to achieve the genius culture and to get the leisure experienced feeling are even stronger than ever. There are various causes in forming the kind of phenomenon. But actually the uppermost cause is the true essence of leisure experience which is used to reflect the living condition and manifest people's qualities of life.

The Recognition of Countryside

First, the countryside is a geographical concept. The geographic scope of a village differs from another because of the different division standard. In China, the geographical scope of countryside is the result of national administration division. That is to say, suppose an area beyond the urban district including city suburb, organic town, and other rural areas. Popularly speaking, countryside is a vast region beyond the urban.

Second, countryside often refers to village. This is a custom appellation which people have formed for a long time. The famous sociologist Fei-xiaotong, who had engaged in social studies for many years used "rural" as a term frequently, such as "Rural China," "Rural Society." His book *"The Investment in Jiangcun"* published in October 1986 takes villagers' life in Yangtze valley as the studying object and "the research goal of it lies in understanding people's life" (Fei, 1986) (The subtitle of the book is *"the Peasant's life in China"*). The famous sociologist Yang-maochun equated "the rural society" with "the life in countryside." He considered: an only village cannot represent the whole rural society. A complete rural society must include a group of farmer families, several or more than ten villages, a market town, and the market town area which is formed by the market town and the periphery of various villages. This kind of countryside society is called "rural community." It "takes the family as the unit, the village as the backbone and the market town area as its scope" (Yang, 1980, pp. 49–58). Therefore, rural area means countryside in this sense.

Third, "rural" is a term which is relative to "urban." Being two kinds of different social organized forms, there are great differences between countryside and the city no matter in the way of production or the style of life. Therefore, "the rural society is a sociological concept which contrasts to urban area (or metropolis) correspondingly," the information it transferred, has only indicated "a specific aspect of today's human society's," but all of them are the important compositions of the entire society. Of course undeniably, with increasing development of the rural economy, especially under impetus of the city to the suburb and the countryside economy, and with the increasing urbanization degree of rural area enhanced, the productive way and life style of countryside are having a profound transformation to get more assimilation with city. But the situation of our country has caused insurmountable difficulties to overcome the contradiction between "the particularity" and "the universality." There are great differences between the theoretic countryside and the earthy countryside. Therefore, "the identical form of social structure system although is the same in nature, actually it can be differentiate in the social system of urban area and the social system of countryside. They are two relatively independent parts and display different characteristics" (Yuan, 1990, pp. 47–49).

Relating to Rural Tourism

According to "the Sustainable Development of Tourism—the Guiding Traveling Plan for Local Area" which was sent by the world Traveling Organization issued for the governments of various countries, the local communities and traveling operators. And the countryside can also be the base which "the tourists explore the regions nearby"

(1997). On the basis of related understanding about countryside, the rural tourism should include several aspects naturally as follow:

First, on the view of tourism destination, the rural tourism refers to so many villages beyond the city (including city suburb). And if from the point of area range, this is the largest tourist district in our country. The situation indicates that China is a great country which is famous for its agriculture. The acreage of rural area occupies the national territory area above 90%, and the population of rural area accounts for 70%. Without a doubt, with the development of the agricultural economy, it has greater significance to construct the well-off society comprehensively. Moreover, developing rural tourism has inestimable functions to construct the new countryside socialism, impel the village economy, lead the farmer to increase production and income and optimize the industrial structure of countryside. So the rural tourism will become the largest and the most potential market of tourism development in our country.

Second, on the point of view of the development process of tourism history, rural tourism is one kind which appeared lately. From the actual development angle, the rural tourism has been developing since the middle of 1980s under the reform and open policy of our country. But the system of arrangement which was truly led by the government and impelled by the market has been just started. With the implementation of new rural reconstruction strategic in our country, the theme of "rural tourism" of the year 2006, indicates the comprehensive start of our rural tourism and also symbolizes the general countryside will play a very important role in the tourism development because of its vast area and distinguished landscapes. So "paying great attention to the benign interaction between the rural development and the tourism development will achieve tremendous profits without doubt" (Liu, 2006).

Third, on the view of the rural tourism market, because countryside is a definition which is related to city, there is a certain deviation on the cognition to rural tourism market in the academic circles. It corresponds to the regional relationship between the countryside and the city with the rural tourism and the urban tourism unilateral. In fact, exploring from the market mechanism that the rural tourism is interlinked with the urban tourism and it does not simply exchange them. Indeed, destination of the rural tourism is villages. So we can estimate that the consumers who constitute the rural tourism market should be all tourists who are satisfied with the traveling conditions. That is to say, a man who has "the motive of body, the culture motive, interpersonal (society) association and the motive of status and the fame" (Mcinttosh and Goeldner. 1984, pp. 171–172) will be the potential source of rural tourism destination. Therefore, the rural tourism market should "recover the regions whose landscapes have great differences with the destination" (Liu, 2005). Although the current tourists of rural tourism present "the character of unidirectional flow, the citizen—rural resources" (Dai, 2005), the flow of the rural tourism market should be similar to the urban (or metropolis) which should include the villagers to create a paralleled new pattern "the urban area to the rural area" and "the rural area to the urban area" on the true essence of rural tourism.

THE ACADEMIC ANALYSIS TO THE DEVELOPMENT OF RURAL TOURISM

Because the rural tourism in our country has just started, the key of keeping the sustainable and harmonious development of rural tourism is how to develop the rural tourism and perfect the core idea and the value orientation naturally.

The Appearing of Ideas

The construction of new countryside is an important content to construct the harmonious society of socialism. But the harmonious tourism is an important connotation to realize the harmonious society of socialism. Without any doubt, it is also the embodiment to construct the new countryside. Therefore, it's not only necessary but also feasible to be engaged in rural tourism with developing rural economy, adjusting the structure of agriculture, exploring the development way of rural area and helping the farmers to increase the production and income. Regarding this, the 5th CCP Plenary Conference of the Central Committee of the CCP 16th session and in 2005 the Central Economy Working Conference has already made "the solid advancement to the new rural reconstruction of socialism, and ulteriorly arrange the strategic work of 'three rural problems (rural economy, rural areas and rural residents)' well." It is obvious to realize the strategic target with the developing rural tourism vigorously. To ulteriorly impel the development of traveling industry in full scales, cause the traveling industrial structure to hasten reasonably, and adapt with the new rural reconstruction strategic target, the National Travel Agency at the right moment has placed the working emphasis on the construction of new countryside and named the theme of the year 2006 of the rural traveling. And the agency took "new countryside, new traveling, new experience, new prevailing custom" as the basic idea to develop rural tourism. So it has initiated a new complexion in developing rural tourism.

The Academic Analysis to the Development of Rural Tourism

New countryside: China is regarded as a large agricultural nation in the world, and the agriculture has always been the basis of social economy in our country. Since the reform and open policy, the rural area in our country has obtained great progress. The problems of the general farmers' food and shelters have been solved basically, but the "three rural problems" has been puzzling us in the process of economic development and construction of well-off society. Therefore, the new countryside will become a new growth point "through the implementation of bringing along prosperity of agriculture with the help of tourism." And the transformation of economic conformation from the traditional planting economy to service economy has caused the phenomena: "the farmers become employees of tourism," "it urges millions of farmers transformed to the non-agricultural domain, and parts of peasant's house turned to family hotels" etc. (Shao, 2006) To alter the way of life and traditional production drastically is an important embodiment for new countryside reconstruction.

New traveling: Rural tourism, it is novel for its ruralism and localization. Looking from the type of resources, the rural traveling resources are provided with traditional cultural atmosphere and great attraction to citizens. These are also advantages which the urban tourism and the commercial tourism do not have. Consequently, developing rural tourism has greatly enriched the product types in new traveling system.

New experience: To the tourists from city, participating in rural tourism which appeared as a new style of tourism product will achieve brand-new feeling and experience. Such as the tourists may enter the old-time farmyard, degust delicious food cooked by the peasants, and also may take the achievement of rural modernization.

New fashion: Tourism once became privilege of the minorities. But now with the increasing living standard of people and the coming of normal tourism, it has been a kind of living modes. Especially with the enhancement of the individuality traveling, the rural life, the rural culture and the rural view have become new voguish luminescent spots. To people who lived in cities, they are weary of sustaining flow of cars and the deterioration of environment. They are longing for the regression to near nature no matter who was born in city or lived in the metropolis for making a live at early time. Thereupon, the new fashion of tourism for advocating the nature and returning rurality has quietly emerged.

"LEISURE EXPERIENCE" AND THE VALUE ORIENTATION FOR RURAL TOURISM DEVELOPMENT

The Behavior State Under Local Environment: Leisure Oxygenic Bar

Leisure means amusement and entertainment if we want to understand it from its surface. If we analyze the word from psychological angle, leisure is a state which one can relax one's body and mind. And from the angle of tourism research, leisure is an activity through which people may wander in nature, satisfy one's individual hobby and relax body and soul. Leisure, just like American leisure scientist called John Kaili claimed, "Essentially speaking, leisure should be understood as a kind of state of becoming, the state of becoming prefers a kind of orientation to define it simply by the time, space, form and result." The subaudition is that "leisure is not the current reality, it is dynamic. It includes many factors facing the future, but not merely indicates the existing form, the scene and the significance." So "Any too static pattern should superinduce dynamic analysis on the existence of person and the scene" (Kaili, 2000). On this view, to develop rural tourism, the core of value orientation is exploiture, the product supply and the psychology of consumers. All of these should take leisure state as the goal, and try to make the rural area as the "Leisure Oxygenic Bar" for tourists.

Leisure tourism in rural area is not to connect leisure and rural simply, and also not the simple sublimation of traditional sightseeing. It is the humanities connotation which was determined by the characteristics of rural tourism destination resources. That is, via exploring and planning carefully, provides a thematic thought of tourism product which includes rural culture, rural life, rural natural conditions and social customs for tourists. Therefore, rural tourism is considered as a brand-new traveling state which is dynamic, sustainable and can participate in joyfully. And the leisure atmosphere of tourism which includes enjoying nature and delighting with people will be "a Soundless Leisure Oxygenic Bar" forever.

The Experience of Localization: Value Experience

Rural tourism is considered as the best way to experience leisure directly. And the localization is the fountainhead which it grows. The reason is very simple. The most prominent character of rural tourism is "the ruralism" and "the localization." So an experienced travel will remind the tourists of the villagers, the river and the hill. And it will take infinite aftertaste and feelings for tourists in order to achieve the most devoted state "flow." This is "a feeling who may forget time flies" Kaili, John R. (2000).

Certainly, there are also problems about rural tourism on how to provide with charm and how to realize the goal of experience for tourists. All of these are up to the true sentiment that the tourists received. The sentiment "must be the direct feeling and sudden enlightenment to the innermost feeling's world and corresponds to the nonego in the syncretic process" (Xie, 2005). Obviously, the assimilation here is determined by the elements of rural tourism and the accordance degree between the actuality of procedure and the cognition of tourists. Namely, that is "to create an unforgettable experience and the valuable recollection activities encircling consumers" (Gilmore and Pine, 2002). Although there are different degrees of cognition, the consuming process and the yielding process of rural tourism production will bring the sense of experience which will be recalled by tourists.

The Dialectical Relationship Among Leisure, Experience, and Harmony

The rural tourism takes the ruralism and the localization as its characteristics. And it makes clear to all that the core of rural tourism is "leisure and experience." But the premise and foundation to realize the value is "harmony." So leisure, experience and harmony are mutually interdependent.

In the developing process of rural tourism, leisure is the goal, and experience is the process. Leisure and experience supplement and interact with each other. It is the premise and foundation to build up the harmonious traveling standpoint and carry out the scientific development view to realize the sustaining development of rural tourism. Although leisure experience is a compass which has been aspired after for a long time, in the view of the traveling activity, harmony actually is really the life line and groundwork of tourism. Without it, the process of leisure experience will be disorderly and barbaric. And what the operators and consumers display will become "the behavior pollution" inevitably. It is fatal to the sustainable development of tourism. Accordingly, the essential factors for constructing the harmonious countryside must be placed on primacy. And it is also important to pay equal attention to the economic benefit, social benefit, environment benefit, scientific planning, and the ordinal harmony, the innovation of system, operators' standardization and the consumers' behavior. Otherwise, leisure experience between man and nature, man and society will be hard to accrete together, and also hard for rural tourism to create "valuable experience for customers" (Leng, 2005).

In brief, rural tourism is an important embodiment for adjusting agricultural structure, transforming the increasing way of agricultural economy and developing domestic tourism in the round. Under the value orientation of leisure and experience, the scientific, ordinal, and harmonious development is the life-line and fundamentality of rural tourism beyond all doubt. And it also symbolizes the coming era of the leisure and experience economy. On this view, they are mutually interdependent in the development of rural tourism.

KEYWORDS

- **Experience**
- **Harmony**
- **Leisure**
- **Rural tourism**

Chapter 10

Cultural Tourism: Gold Mine or Land Mine?

Christina Cameron

INTRODUCTION

In one way, cultural tourism is the raison d'être of our heritage institutions; yet in another way, it threatens their very existence. Our challenge is to get the right balance.

The concept of cultural tourism is new in Canada. Our knowledge of available products and the expectations of the international and domestic markets is somewhat limited. Research conducted by Tourism Canada clearly shows that our international visitors are no longer just interested in our magnificent landscapes, but also want to discover Canadian society with its different cultural manifestations.

CULTURAL TOURISM AS GOLD MINE

Tourism Canada conducted a number of market studies in the late 1980s. The 1986 Longwoods study found that Canada's cultural distinctiveness was the single most important factor attracting Americans to Canada. The 1987 study concluded that culture is a major draw to urban areas: "The concentration of museums, galleries, theatres, historic sites ... forms a vital component of an urban experience, capable of attracting large numbers of visitors. Cultural activities, while not always the prime motive for travel to an area, may help to lengthen the stay and enrich the trip experience." The 1989 study, again by Longwoods, revealed a relatively high degree of interest among American urban tourists, touring visitors, and business/pleasure travelers in heritage institutions, in particular historic sites. The 1991 study from Tourism Canada reaffirmed the desire from international tourist markets for more opportunities to discover the nature of the people of Canada. There is a consistent pattern here. And finally, to round off this overview of market studies, in March 1993 the Canadian Tourism Research Institute, part of the Conference Board of Canada, reported that there is an emerging trend in the important Japanese travel market towards "an increase in history- or culture-related tours."

In support of the thesis that cultural tourism in Canada will continue to grow are the emerging demographic and psychographic trends. I refer here to the rising education level of the world's population, the most significant factor in cultural participation. I refer also to the increasing age of the population of the Western world. Statistics show that cultural and heritage activities increase through middle age to peak between 45 and 65. By way of example, the number of Americans aged 55 or older will increase by over 40% in the next 20 years. Moreover, a new factor, environmental degradation, may further lead to greater demand for cultural tourism. There is no doubt that factors such as ozone depletion and exposure to ultraviolet radiation will affect leisure patterns as people move from outdoor activities to indoor pursuits.

Unfortunately, there is little scientific information from which we can clearly understand the exact part the heritage institutions play in the cultural tourism industry.

We do have statistics on the economic benefits of tourism in general. In 1990, for instance, international and domestic travelers spent approximately $26 billion while traveling in Canada. It is estimated that tourism generated nearly $18 billion in direct income and provided direct employment for more than 600,000 Canadians. As well, it generated $12 billion in revenue for all levels of government.

But we do not have good statistics on the economic benefits of cultural tourism. This is not to say that heritage institutions have paid no attention to measuring these benefits. I know that the museums and art galleries do undertake such analyses from time to time, as does CPS. Take, for example, the 13 national historic sites administered by CPS in Nova Scotia (the Fortress of Louisbourg, Halifax Citadel, Fort Anne, and the Alexander Graham Bell complex at Baddeck, among others). The overall economic impact of these 13 sites amounts to $30 million and 650 person-years of employment. In the Annapolis Valley alone, the four CPS-administered sites generate $3.5 million and 75 person-years of employment. What we have failed to do is estimate the global contribution of heritage institutions to the economic benefits of tourism. The job is not a simple one. It may be easy enough to estimate the impacts of the 1,200 museums in Canada with their 24 million visitors, or the impacts of our 800 heritage institutions, as defined by Statistics Canada. It is feasible to capture the economic benefits of the 115 national historic sites administered by the federal government, with their 7 million visitors, and even the cultural dimensions of our 36 national parks, with their 20 million visitors.

But then it gets more complicated. There are another 600 or so national historic sites in Canada, not administered by the government, not statistically identified as "heritage institutions," but nonetheless important generators of cultural tourism. I'm thinking here of historic streetscapes and districts like Rennie's Mill Road in St. John's, historic Lunenburg, and, of course, the historic centre of Québec City, a listed world heritage site. I'm also thinking of landmarks like Christ Church Cathedral in Fredericton, Bonsecours Market in Montréal, the Parliament Buildings here in Ottawa, Union Station in Toronto, the Fort Garry Hotel in Winnipeg, and Stanley Park in Vancouver. Taken together, this network of nationally-significant sites contributes greatly to attracting and retaining visitors, both domestic and international.

I am convinced that heritage institutions are a gold mine for the tourism industry. Even with the inadequate data available, studies indicate that heritage institutions attract more tourists than the performing arts do. Museums and historic sites are portals to the cultural landscape, offering tourists authentic experiences of our regions and country. This appears to be what the markets of the future will be seeking. So I conclude this section by affirming that, yes, cultural tourism is a gold mine for the country, and heritage institutions are an essential element. I would suggest that we would be well advised, in times of scarce resources, to work with the tourism industry to identify clearly the contribution that heritage institutions make to the tourism economy.

CULTURAL TOURISM AS LAND MINE

The concept of cultural tourism as land mine deserves some nuancing. This is a "good news, bad news" scenario. Most heritage institutions have been founded to serve the public. Visitors are the lifeblood of most heritage institutions I know. We take pride in our visitors and strive to ensure that they both enjoy and learn from our special places. At a more pragmatic level, we are all in the game of counting numbers of visitors, to prove that these institutions are wanted and needed by the constituency that ultimately pays for them.

On the positive side of the ledger, it can be argued that tourism has done as much as any government or industry to protect the heritage of this country. Whether it is the establishment of museums and galleries, the renovation of old buildings, the setting aside of conservation areas, or the establishment of historic sites, all these efforts are due in part to their accompanying tourism potential. It may please us to believe that funding for the protection and presentation of heritage resources is driven by the spirit of social good. But the reality is that it is more often the promise of economic benefits through tourism development that loosens the purse strings of investors, be they from the private or the public sector.

It can be a virtuous circle. Visitors spend money that in turn is spent, among other things, on improving the "heritage product" on offer. These improvements help to attract more visitors, greater expenditure, further improvements, and so on. Given proper management, this cycle is good for the heritage institutions and the economy.

On the other hand, there is the issue of wear and tear. Without proper management, environmental problems can result from large volumes of traffic and people; historic fabric can become eroded; and heritage resources can be spoilt by unsympathetic alterations or by being "over-restored" in the name of enhancing the visitor experience.

We who are responsible for heritage institutions are charged with protecting that heritage for the benefit of this and future generations. Cultural tourism has come under attack for undermining, alienating, and sometimes enslaving local cultures through its intrusive infrastructure, its commoditization of meaningless cultural products, and its creation of staged unauthentic experiences. But perhaps the biggest downside of tourism is that, if successful, it can destroy through excessive use not only the heritage resources of a site, but also the quality of the cultural experience that brought the visitor in the first place.

There are many examples in Europe, where cultural tourism has thrived for centuries, examples that show how excessive tourism has led to overcrowding and ultimately to the destruction of the heritage resources. Floors and paths are particularly vulnerable. The rare black and gold marble floor at St. Paul's in London, the mosaic floor at St. Mark's in Venice, and the stone floor at Notre-Dame in Paris are all disappearing under the footfalls of thousands of visitors each day. Hiking trails on the Devon coast and the historic footpath beside Hadrian's Wall look like tracks from dune-buggy races. The issue here is one of physical carrying capacity.

Excessive tourism not only puts pressure on the physical resources; it can also destroy the cultural experience that drew the tourists in the first place. Let us take the example of Stonehenge. Until recently, this circle of megaliths stood magnificently alone in an open field. Visitors used to be able to stop their cars and walk up to it without bother. But because of vandalism and the pressure of too many people, this world heritage site is now surrounded with a wire fence. It receives over a million visitors a year. At any moment there are several hundred visitors milling around the site. Lost forever is the haunting, quiet experience of this mysterious, ancient temple. This is what I refer to as spiritual carrying capacity.

I have chosen these examples from Europe because these countries have enjoyed—or endured—intensive cultural tourism for so long. And the pressure continues to mount. In the UK, for example, over the past decade visits to heritage attractions have increased 21%. Canada has an advantage in that we are on the rising wave of cultural tourism that is far from its crest. We still have time to do things differently.

But lest we get too complacent, here are some Canadian examples. Québec City's historic district received over 4 million visitors in 1990, a 25% increase in the last decade. Clearly this outnumbers the permanent residents by a six-to-one ratio, as residents and former residents know only too well. Or take Green Gables in Prince Edward Island National Park. During the summer months, this small, two-storey wooden cottage that inspired the Anne stories groans under the weight of 5,000 visitors a day. Surely this is well above both its physical and its spiritual carrying capacity. Then there are the upper lockstations of the Trent-Severn heritage waterway, say around Bobcaygeon or Fenelon Falls, on a warm summer weekend. The search to tie up cruisers, houseboats, and runabouts has stripped the bark off all the trees at water edge and eroded the shoreline. Moreover, onshore facilities in these small communities are completely overwhelmed. Or take the example of the West Coast Trail in Pacific Rim National Park. Overcrowding and deterioration of the trail have led CPS to limit its use. Like golfers, hikers now have to reserve starting times, sometimes weeks in advance. And then there is Banff.

SUSTAINABLE TOURISM

If we accept the premise that cultural tourism in Canada will increase, then those of us who manage heritage institutions will be challenged to find the balance between consumption and conservation; we will be challenged to attain sustainable tourism.

Inherent in this concept is the notion of trusteeship. Those entrusted with the management of heritage institutions have a responsibility to pass them on in good condition to future generations. This approach is consistent with the goal of sustainable development, a concept given global endorsement as a result of the Brundtland report, *Our Common Future*. In line with our discussion of sustainable tourism is Brundtland's definition of sustainable development: "meeting the needs of the present without compromising the ability of future generations to meet their own needs."

The UK has taken the lead in examining this issue of sustainable tourism. In 1991, government sponsored a task force, with members from the private and public sectors involved in industry, environment, heritage, and employment. Their work resulted in a key report entitled *Tourism and the Environment: Maintaining the Balance*. It is an important declaration for sustainable tourism, based on maintaining the balance among the three poles: tourism, environment, and local communities.

The task force developed a set of principles to manage the relationship among the visitor, the place, and the host community. Reading some of these principles will give you the flavor of this forward-looking approach.

- The environment has an intrinsic value which outweighs its value as a tourism asset. Its enjoyment by future generations and its long term survival must not be prejudiced by short term considerations.

- Tourism should be recognized as a positive activity with the potential to benefit the community and the place as well as the visitor.

- Tourism activities and developments should respect the scale, nature and character of the place in which they are sited.

- In any location, harmony must be sought between the needs of the visitor, the place and the host community.

- The tourism industry, local authorities and environmental agencies all have a duty to respect these principles and work together to achieve their practical realization.

The UK report goes on to describe case studies and suggested techniques for controlling excessive tourist use, conserving heritage resources, and ensuring maximum benefit for host communities. Its fundamental message is the need to create strategic alliances and partnerships among all those who have stakes in attaining sustainable tourism.

In Canada there are hints of this kind of activity. The heritage institutions are wrestling individually with notions of carrying capacity. The management of blockbuster exhibitions and the West Coast Trail are examples. But it will require more effort and a systematic application of conservation science before we have credible standards of carrying capacity.

What about the tourism industry? As part of the National Round Table on the Environment and the Economy, Canada's Tourism Industry Association has recently produced a Code of Ethics for Sustainable Tourism. The code is based on the belief that a high-quality tourism experience depends on the conservation of natural resources, protection of the environment, and preservation of our cultural heritage. There are separate codes for the industry and the tourists.

For the industry, the code calls for members to encourage an appreciation of heritage, to respect the values and aspirations of the host communities, and to strive to achieve tourism development in a manner that harmonizes economic objectives with the protection and enhancement of heritage.

For the tourists, the code calls on visitors to enjoy our diverse heritage and help in its protection and preservation, and to experience our communities while respecting our traditions, customs, and local regulations.

In addition to these codes of ethics, the package also includes detailed guidelines for all participants, including accommodations, food services, tour operators, and ministries of tourism. These are fine words and the basis for sustainable cultural tourism. What remains to be seen is whether the tourism industry will take them to heart and translate them into meaningful action.

A promising model is the emerging ecotourism movement. Ecotourism combines travel experiences with low impact on natural resources, environmental conservation, sustainable economic activity, and learning by the consumer. Ecotourism recognizes that the natural and cultural resources of a region are the key element of the travel experience and accepts therefore that there are limits on use. It requires that there be an educational experience for all participants associated with the activity—visitors, travel agents, and local communities. Finally, ecotourism promotes environmental ethics and seeks that all participants abide by an ethical framework.

What has not yet happened in Canada is the development of the strategic partnerships that cut across various sectors of activity. There is lots of sporadic ad hoc partnering springing up. For example, many of our park and site superintendents become members of local Chambers of Commerce or tourist boards, giving them opportunities to forge partnerships with neighboring heritage institutions and infuse heritage concerns into the decision-making process. The CPS's well-known public consultation process for its management or master plans for field units also provides a forum to exchange views and develop shared values for sustained use of the parks or sites. And there are the newly formed interdepartmental and intergovernmental committees tasked with ensuring that heritage is factored into decisions on land use around the world heritage district at Québec City.

But these are mere beginnings. If we are going to meet the challenge of sustainable tourism in a postindustrial era, we will need to develop broadly based alliances to integrate competing conservation and development goals. The individual interests of the heritage conservationists and the tourism industry are converging.

Collectively we need to demonstrate the economic benefits of tourism, so that our heritage institutions enjoy stable financial support. We need to develop meaningful standards of carrying capacity to ensure conservation of the heritage resources for this and future generations. We need to develop marketing and de-marketing strategies in light of carrying capacity. And we need to ensure that cultural tourism is managed in such a way that it enhances, not destroys, the environment that is its key attraction.

KEYWORDS

- **Cultural tourism**
- **Excessive tourism**
- **Heritage institutions**
- **Sustainable tourism**

ACKNOWLEDGMENTS

I wish to thank Robert Moreau, Visitor Activities, Interpretation Branch, Canadian Parks Service, for his support in the preparation of this chapter.

Chapter 11

Heritage Tourism

Cheryl M. Hargrove

INTRODUCTION

Visiting historic and cultural sites is one of the most popular tourist activities today. Families, seniors, groups, and even international visitors choose to frequent historic attractions when on vacation. As a result, destinations are paying attention to one of the fastest growing niche market segments in the travel industry today—heritage tourism.

What is heritage tourism? The National Trust for Historic Preservation defines heritage tourism as "traveling to experience the places, artifacts and activities that authentically represent the stories and people of the past and present."

Why has heritage tourism captured so much attention during the past decade? Primarily, economics drive the interest in heritage tourism. According to a recent study by the Travel Industry Association of America, people who engage in historic and cultural activities spend more, do more, and stay longer than other types of US travelers. Last year, visiting historic and cultural sites ranked second to shopping in the list of activities engaged in while on holiday. Baby boomers in particular wish to experience history through travel, visiting the authentic places where significant events occurred or made relevant contributions to the development of America. Even international visitors to the US desire America's heritage; one of three tour a historic or cultural attraction during their holiday. The potential is huge, not only to attract more visitors to lesser-known sites but also to increase the monies generated from existing or new visitors. Heritage tourism also uses assets—historic, cultural, and natural resources—that already exist. Rather than creating and building attractions, destinations look to the past for a sustainable future. Indeed these assets need preservation and often restoration or interpretation, but the foundation for creating a dynamic travel experience lives on in the stories and structures of the past. Often, the opportunity to create a tourist product is more easily attained by using existing heritage sites than if the destination had to develop new attractions.

An obvious way for destinations to identify heritage resources is to tap the National Register of Historic Places. About 74,000 listings make up the National Register, including all historic areas in the national park system, over 2,300 National Historic Landmarks and properties—sites, buildings, districts, structures, and objects—deemed significant to the nation, a state, or local community. For inclusion in this esteemed group, places must pass rigorous state and national review, providing documentation as to their significant architecture, archeology, age, or association with an individual or event. The prestige associated with national designation elevates these properties above all others, and creates the premier foundation for designing heritage tourism programs.

Photo 1. Museum of Coastal History, St. Simons Island, Georgia. Photo by Tommy E. Jenkins.

As the popularity of heritage tourism increases, so does the competition. In the past decade alone, more than half of US states have established formal cultural heritage tourism programs. A January 2001 *Wall Street Journal* article reported that more than a dozen African-American museums either opened to the public or broke ground in the US in 2000. Even theme parks and casinos are focusing on history to promote their attractions: Disney California and several Las Vegas casinos built replicas of major heritage sites to attract visitors to their facilities.

Identifying and promoting real heritage attractions is just the first step in attracting heritage travelers—and their spending. To counter increased competition and manufactured "heritage" experiences, destinations often join together to create theme tours and trails that link sites like a string of pearls. The National Register of Historic Places maintains an immense database of information related to listed properties, providing a handy resource for tour planners and destination marketers to research potential sites and attractions that serve as the basis for a heritage trail or loop tour.

Individual travelers will also find the National Register database as a source to rediscover familiar places or unveil information about new heritage destinations. They can click on <www.nr.nps.gov> for access to America's heritage chest. Information is available by name, location, agency, or subject. For instance, to explore the Georgia coast, guests can navigate the site a few different ways. For tour operators and local organizers familiar with the destination, a listing of all the National Register properties near Brunswick and the Golden Isles of Georgia may be adequate for trip planning. The site can be searched by state and then by county (Glynn) to get information on Fort Frederica National Monument located on St. Simons Island. Travel planners can retrieve information on Brunswick's Old Town Historic District and the Jekyll Island Club, a Historic Hotel of America, to create a customized itinerary. In fact, 12 historic sites and districts are listed—a solid foundation for a heritage tour of the coastal area.

Photo 2. Jekyll Island, Georgia. Photo courtesy Golden Isles Visitors Bureau.

Register travel itineraries. Full of photos and maps, the itineraries provide comprehensive information to navigate the voyage along a particular heritage route or theme (see Andrus article, p. 48). *Along the Georgia-Florida Coast* transports the traveler through Brunswick and the Golden Isles, visiting familiar sites accessed through the general database, and 40 other places of historic significance from St. Augustine to Savannah. The section on Colonial History describes early settlers' encounters with indigenous peoples, European occupation and settlement, plantation agriculture based on African slavery, African-American culture, and even the early days of tourism. This itinerary is just one of some two dozen produced by the National Register of Historic Places in partnership with the National Conference of State Historic Preservation

Officers. Whatever the interest may be—a heritage tour of Detroit or Charleston, the civil rights movement, places where women made history, lighthouses, military history, cultural landscapes—the National Register of Historic Places provides information to customize travel to any US destination.

Heritage tourism's popularity, though, also stems from the opportunity to educate. The American heritage traveler is older, better educated, and more affluent than other tourists. Mission-driven institutions managing historic sites recognize that heritage tourism provides a unique opportunity to inform people on the importance of preserving and protecting America's treasures. The National Register of Historic Places is our country's list of sites, buildings, structures, districts, and objects worthy of preservation and promotion. Awareness through tourism can ensure that America's most valued treasures are conserved and maintained for the enjoyment not just of heritage travelers today, but also by future generations. Through appropriate funding, sensitive development, and promotion, heritage tourism affords a solid foundation that sustains the resource as well as offering a social and economic impact.

KEYWORDS

- **Heritage attractions**
- **Heritage tourism**
- **National Register of Historic Places**

Chapter 12

A Position Paper on Cultural and Heritage Tourism

US Department of Commerce

INTRODUCTION

Ten years ago a seminal blueprint for cultural and heritage tourism was adopted by the more than 1,500 dedicated political and industry leaders and practitioners as part of their national agenda for the travel industry, which they developed at the 1995 White House Conference on Travel and Tourism. Recognizing the extraordinary opportunity presented by this landmark event to expand the creative dialog between this industry and America's cultural and heritage institutions, a coalition representing the arts, historic preservation, humanities organizations, and the federal cultural agencies—the National Endowment for the Arts, the National Endowment for the Humanities, the Institute of Museum Services, and the President's Committee on the Arts and the Humanities—submitted a white paper, Cultural Tourism in the US, to provide specific responses to the industry's nine issue areas and outline goals for the culture and heritage tourism segment.

In that paper, the authors encapsulated a definition for cultural and heritage tourism—"travel directed toward experiencing the arts, heritage, and special character of a place. America's rich heritage and culture, rooted in our history, our creativity and our diverse population, provides visitors to our communities with a wide variety of cultural opportunities, including museums, historic sites, dance, music, theater, book and other festivals, historic buildings, arts and crafts fairs, neighborhoods, and landscapes."

Its adoption at the 1995 conference initiated new relationships between unlikely partners—the cultural, heritage, and tourism sectors—who sought to fulfill its key values and vision of a sustainable industry with appropriate growth. Collaborations spread across the country following the white paper's roadmap of action steps, and the results have surpassed expectations: six regional forums that catalyzed state action on cultural and heritage tourism; cultural and heritage tourism staff positions established at convention and visitors bureaus (CVBs), in state agencies and regionally; groundbreaking research by the Travel Industry Association of America (TIA) on the impact of cultural and heritage tourism that spawned subsequent national and local studies; and broad-based multisector initiatives such as North Carolina's awardwinning Blue Ridge Heritage Initiative, Maine's New Century program and the White House's Preserve America program.

Over the last decade, travel industry research confirms that cultural and heritage tourism is one the fastest growing segments of the travel industry. For some travelers, cultural and heritage experiences are "value added," enhancing their enjoyment of a place and increasing the likelihood that they will return. For a growing number of visitors, however, who are tired of the homogenization of places around the world, authentic experiences are an important factor and motivator for their travel decisions and expectations.

CULTURAL AND HERITAGE TOURISM TODAY

The industry today encompasses cultural and heritage specialists, who are an important resource for the travel and tourism industry in providing these customers with accurate, insightful interpretation of local assets. Communities throughout the US have developed successful programs linking the arts, humanities, history, and tourism. Cultural and heritage organizations—such as museums, performing arts organizations, festivals, humanities, and historic preservation groups—have formed partnerships with tour operators, state travel offices, CVBs, hotels, and air carriers to create initiatives that serve as models for similar efforts across the US.

An integral but often invisible component of the cultural and heritage sector are the artists, performers, writers, and other creative workers whose skills and vision bring to life our nation's genius and ideas. These living traditions are often supported by the cultural and heritage tourism infrastructure of institutions, galleries, performance spaces and other community venues that make a significant contribution to economic and community development. The arts, humanities, and heritage involve and benefit local residents in developing the narrative that creates a sense of place, which the travel and tourism industry can promote, market and brand. Cultural and heritage tourism also provides a means of preserving and perpetuating our nation's cultural heritage through education, increased revenues and audiences, and good stewardship.

Yet cultural and heritage tourism is different from other "mass market" travel industry segments in several ways. First, many cultural and heritage institutions are nonprofit organizations where tourism is only one strategy that meets their mission. In many cases, funds are dedicated to an artistic or educational mission or the preservation, interpretation, and management of a resource rather than to marketing. Second, limited capacity or the fragility of cultural, natural, and heritage resources and sites sometimes constrains the number of visitors that can be hosted annually or seasonally. Overuse or excess capacity can result in negative impact on resources and can diminish the quality of the visitor and resident experience. Many cultural and heritage sites are open year round, but some resources—including performance groups—have limited schedules or operations.

Finally, cultural and heritage assets are traditionally "one of a kind" and seek to provide unique experiences not replicated in any other community. Additionally, the artistic or educational missions of these institutions, as well as the interests and work of the artists, performers and artisans, all contribute to a place's authenticity. Hence, authenticity is a key value and influencer in branding a destination that includes, but is not limited to, its events, architecture, music, dance, cuisine, craft, and artistic traditions. This uniqueness is ill-suited to cookie-cutter programming and marketing. The travel and tourism industry must work closely with cultural and heritage organizations and the community to provide quality visitor experiences without compromising the integrity of message or negatively affecting these authentic resources and living traditions. Each constituent group should be proactive in helping its partners in learning more about how their respective industries work.

A SNAPSHOT OF CULTURAL AND HERITAGE TOURISM

Domestic

- Eighty-one percent of the 146.4 million US adults who took a trip of 50 miles or more away from home in the past year can be considered cultural and heritage tourists. Compared to other travelers, cultural, and heritage tourists:
- Spend more: $623 versus $457
- Use a hotel, motel or B&B: 62% versus 55%
- Are more likely to spend $1,000+/–: 19% versus 12%
- Travel longer: 5.2 nights versus 3.4 nights
- Historic/cultural travel volume is up 13% from 1996, increasing from 192.4 million person-trips to 216.8 million person-trips in 2002.
- The demographic profile of the cultural heritage travel segment today is younger, wealthier, more educated and more technologically savvy when compared to those surveyed in 1996.
- The 35.3 million adults say that a specific arts, cultural, or heritage event or activity influenced their choice of destination.

(*Source*: Travel Industry Association of America and Smithsonian Magazine, The Historic/Cultural Traveler, 2003 Edition.)

International

In 2004, according to the US Department of Commerce, there were over 10.6 million overseas visitors who participated in cultural and heritage tourism activities while within the country. The top five markets interested in cultural and heritage tourism as a share of their total visitors are: UK, Japan, Germany, France, and Australia.

- The average overseas cultural and heritage tourism traveler visits the country for over 19 nights (16 nights for all overseas travelers).
- More than 72% are here for leisure/holidays as one of the purposes of their trip (62% for all overseas travelers).
- They are more willing to visit more than one state (41%) compared to only 30% for all overseas visitors.

THE OPPORTUNITY TODAY

The 2005 US Cultural and Heritage Tourism Summit is another watershed moment for growing this industry sector. There has never been a more important time to convene key leaders and decision makers, whose sectors and efforts have contributed to its current success. Cultural and heritage tourism has been an engine of growth over the last decade, and we can learn much from each other in developing strategies to sustain that growth into the future. This Summit also comes at a time when many believe that as a global power the US has a vital interest in welcoming visitors from abroad and sharing with them a rich and nuanced picture of the diversity of America's cultural heritage.

The goal of the Summit is to forge a new vision and design a national 5-year strategy that will expand and develop cultural and heritage tourism for the benefit our nation's economy, residents, traveling consumers, cultural and heritage institutions, and the travel and tourism industry.

To enhance and sustain this industry segment, we believe the recommendations set forth in this chapter must be addressed and adopted. Each citizen, practitioner, and elected and appointed official plays a pivotal role in developing this industry segment.

PRODUCT DEVELOPMENT

Uniquely American Experiences

Product development encompasses the preservation, enhancement, and promotion of our nation's natural, historic, and cultural resources. Cultural and heritage specialists can assist the travel and tourism industry in developing new tour itineraries, regional circuits, and thematic packages of attractions and activities. However, we must first assure that the natural, historic, and cultural resources that are the basis of such products are identified, preserved, and enhanced.

Sustaining and developing these historic and cultural resources, which are often within the public domain, depends in part on the need to increase public and private sector investment. For cultural and heritage organizations such investment depends on: (1) adopting sound business practices; (2) increasing advocacy of the economic and social benefits of their assets; and (3) diversifying both their product mix and partnerships.

Over the last decade, the success of cultural and heritage tourism has prompted many states, regions and cities to undertake a comprehensive look at their cultural and heritage industry as a tool for economic and community development. This holistic policy and investment approach to nurturing the physical and human resources of culture and heritage, both its for-profit and nonprofit sectors, has been labeled the creative economy, which includes (but is not limited to) the arts, preservation, design, film, and music industries. Such a holistic investment by the public and private sectors will create a more competitive economy and a more vibrant community.

Every place in America—rural area, small town, Native American reservation, urban neighborhood, and suburban center—has distinctive cultural and heritage assets that can potentially attract visitors and their spending. Each must discover and value its own culture and heritage and decide for itself what kind of tourism and how many visitors are appropriate/desired to meet their tourism goal, and what assets it wants to share with visitors. Each must tell its own collection of stories to visitors using various traditional media such as maps, publications, the Internet sites, and tours and through creative expressions including exhibits, songs, paintings, dance demonstrations, and interpreters. Each community seeking to develop its tourism potential can build on its foundation of cultural and heritage resources by engaging local residents—from an existing network of volunteers who contribute services to their local cultural and heritage institutions, to artists and other experts employed in these disciplines—to help tell its story, which can be packaged in numerous ways.

Authenticity and Quality

Historic and cultural attractions express, interpret, and preserve our national cultural heritage. Their contribution to the visitor experience is twofold: first, the interpretive programs and materials they present must be of high quality, providing accurate information in engaging and memorable ways. Second, the artisans, performers, writers, and artists that bring a place to life for visitors should meet the highest standards of that community. The cultural and heritage segments should fulfill their important role in the travel and tourism industry by increasing understanding of the significance of authenticity and its effect on visitation, marketing, and branding. Travel and tourism industry professionals should recognize visitors' desires to experience the "real America," which can best be done through its historic sites and monuments, its living traditions and landscapes, museums, and other cultural organizations, and, above all else, its people.

Tourism Planning

Comprehensive planning for cultural and heritage tourism development is crucial to assuring positive visitor experiences with minimal adverse impacts on local residents and resources. Tourism planning must be locally driven and focused on the connections between natural, historic, and cultural resources and the life of the community itself. Expertise provided by local cultural and heritage organizations and specialists can help the tourism industry satisfy visitor interest in "real places" by providing accurate interpretation of a destination's history and assuring the continued vitality of community life for residents and visitors alike.

The tourism planning process should take advantage of technology in coordinating and assisting efforts among the different sectors in the cultural and heritage tourism industry. It should also recognize and encourage the growth of small businesses—both for-profit and nonprofit services, such as local guided tours, cooperatives selling authentic arts and crafts, galleries, bed and breakfasts, museum shops, and ethnic restaurants, which are all important components that reflect and support the local culture. Training and education will assist these institutions and self-employed creative artists to improve their business success, which furthers their sustainability and contribution to the tourism industry. Capital investments and technical expertise can enhance the cultural and heritage experiences for all audiences through increased programming and special attention to the requirements and spirit of the Americans with Disabilities Act.

Public–private Partnerships

Cultural and heritage organizations; federal, state, local, and tribal arts, and humanities agencies; other federal, state, local, and tribal government agencies; and the travel and tourism industry should establish public–private partnerships to identify opportunities for cultural and heritage tourism development. A foundation of these collaborations should be the implicit recognition of the value of cultural and heritage tourism to a community's quality of life and economic well-being. Equally important to partnerships is the recognition of the value of public sector leadership since many of these cultural and heritage resources belong to all Americans. As part of a knowledge base, there is a need to increase understanding and use of partnership examples at the local, state, and federal levels that reflect broad coordination in delivering needed human, technical and financial resources. These partnerships can implement cooperative programs and projects and ensure the preservation of unique resources by creating greater incentives to attract private sector investment whether it be human, financial or technical. Such collaborations can leverage the potential of existing institutions, expand the economic impact of cultural and heritage tourism, and ameliorate or even avoid adverse effects of unplanned tourism.

PROMOTION
Revealing Our Character
Historic and cultural attractions and their living traditions make each destination unique. Promotional campaigns must follow a thoughtful product development process to ensure that quality services, attractions, or experiences are in place before a destination is promoted.

Success will depend on all sectors—tourism, culture, heritage, nature—seeing themselves as part of the cultural and heritage tourism industry. Given the technological and media savvy of the next generation of consumers, the industry needs to reinvent and reposition itself in promoting cultural and heritage resources. Promotion will need to stay current with trends in technology in reaching new consumers, and be committed to cooperative messaging, programming and marketing that cuts across sectors, generations, and interests.

Building Blocks for Tours and Conventions
Cultural and heritage assets, as well as natural resources, should be primary ingredients for group tour experiences that seek to develop new regional and thematic packages. Cultural, natural, and heritage resources are also important components for individual travelers and groups who create their own itineraries by drawing on the Internet and other resources. Cultural and heritage institutions also represent a resource for destination management organizations, meeting and convention planners seeking to promote shoulder season and offseason travel.

Destination USA
Promotional campaigns for US tourism should feature our nation's unique natural, historic, and cultural resources, as well as the creative talent, that define and sustain our country's distinctive character. The US needs a well-funded international presence that draws on the richness of these resources and artists. A successful international promotional effort depends on a proactive approach to developing new international markets and expanding public and private sector support for cooperative marketing at the local, regional, and national levels. National branding campaigns need to be localized and involve community leaders and residents in articulating their heritage, culture, and image.

Thematic Tourism

Thematic tours should be inclusive of natural, cultural, and historic assets to maximize the opportunities for attracting a cross-section of audiences to multiple sites and events that transcend geographic boundaries. The stories, themes, and partners should reflect the diversity of the US and include the broader cultural and historic tourism industry. Linking similar assets together as a linear "strings of pearls" allows consumers to travel by motivation and interests—such as military history, ethnic settlements, music, commerce and industry, architecture, or landscapes—to expand opportunities for these visitors to stay longer and spend more.

RESEARCH

A Lens on the Landscape

Research supports and intersects with all the key issue areas in cultural and heritage tourism. It helps identify the consumers and key trends in the industry and supports case making, advocacy, and policy efforts. Although an abundance of information is being collected, there is a continuing need to increase access to the information and improve distribution of research and consistency in findings.

Data Collection and Dissemination for Domestic Tourism

Communities, their cultural and heritage institutions, and the tourism industry need national market research that identifies domestic travelers' interest in cultural and heritage activities and tracks their actual visitation to specific sites and organizations. The tourism industry and relevant federal agencies should better publicize and make easily available existing travel and tourism data, using existing Internet sites and other vehicles to publish and distribute studies and key information. All the sectors in the cultural and heritage tourism industry should examine using new tools to measure the impact of the industry, from the North American Industry Classification System (NAICS), to travel and tourism satellite accounts and current employment data, to the broader examination of culture, heritage and tourism's contribution to the creative economy.

International Visitors

The Office of Travel and Tourism Industries, a division of the US Department of Commerce's International Trade Administration, conducts important and relevant research on international inbound visitation to America. Given that international consumer understanding of cultural and heritage tourism is different from that of their counterparts in the US, it is recommended that the federal agency broaden its research and develop more detailed international visitor surveys to identify and analyze foreign visitors' motivations and activities regarding culture and heritage. Specifically, the research should capture information on interest in and visitation to national parks, heritage sites, and areas; historic buildings, neighborhoods, and districts; and performing arts centers, museums, and other arts organizations, as well as rural and multicultural tourism experiences, including the appeal of regional and thematic tours. Public access to this additional detailed information is vital for cultural and heritage tourism practitioners to proactively develop and market desired experiences.

Data Collection by Cultural and Heritage Institutions
Individual cultural and heritage institutions, and their national affiliates, should collect meaningful data about their visitors including, but not limited to, projected visitation, actual visitation, and economic and cultural impacts and make it available to the travel industry. Cultural and heritage institutions involved in regional or thematic promotion should improve the quality, consistency, and frequency of their respective regional data. Cultural and heritage institutions should share the results of their research with their local destination marketing organizations (DMOs) including CVBs, chambers of commerce, and other like entities. These DMOs should use their surveys to obtain information that will assist their local heritage and cultural institutions in promoting themselves as visitor attractions and activities.

Return on Investment Studies
The initiatives currently defining and measuring the for-profit and nonprofit sectors of the creative industry should incorporate, examine and build on the travel industry's studies of the economic impact of tourism. All sectors in the cultural and heritage tourism industry should agree on a set of common data points so that comparisons can be made and impacts measured between these sectors. All data should be collected and analyzed to demonstrate how investments, activities, and visitation contribute to the overall cultural heritage tourism goal and benefit cultural and heritage resources, residents, customers, institutions, and industry.

TECHNOLOGY

Communications Tools for Today and Tomorrow
The explosive growth in technology has made a significant impact on every aspect of the cultural and heritage tourism industry. Striking a balance between keeping current with technology and having the resources to deploy these tools, as well as using these tools to enhance and not undermine an authentic experience, are key considerations for all the sectors in cultural and heritage tourism. Technology in this case encompasses three areas: (1) technology that supports business/industry strategy; (2) programmatic technology to deliver content; and (3) operational efficiency technology that helps administrators and experts work smarter.

Delivering Content
Using technology to map assets, analyze impact of potential infrastructure improvements and interpret sites will streamline the planning and development process. The design of interfaces, hyperlinks, calendars, and other Internet information systems should make it easier for both individuals and groups to access, organize and customize thematic, rural and regional trip itineraries. Management software will allow practitioners to track visitation and sources of revenue and to monitor capacity.

Business Application
Technological advancements should be shared among all the sectors in the cultural and heritage tourism industry, from creating and expanding shared databases to

developing new partnerships with other businesses to exploit smart card and other emerging technology. With an ultimate goal of efficiency and effectiveness, technology can help cultural and heritage institutions provide customers greater flexibility in accessing information and making purchases. Mentoring programs and tapping specific technical assistance will help level the field of knowledge among all sizes of cultural and heritage institutions.

Enhanced Experiences

Cultural, heritage, and tourism partners should collaborate on developing content for a broad range of high- and low-tech vehicles to meet customer preferences for information. Technology offers many opportunities to assist visitors in planning and experiencing the cultural, natural, and historic riches of this nation. Exploiting the use of handhelds and other devices to overcome barriers in language and wayfinding offers potential areas of collaboration for the public and private sectors in the cultural and heritage tourism industry. Geographic Information Systems (GISs) mapping tools, assistive audio devices, wireless machines, handhelds, and other technological hardware and software provide customers the flexibility, affordability, and convenience they desire.

INFRASTRUCTURE

Access to Excellence

The cultural and heritage tourism industry comprises many components large and small, ranging from heritage corridors and living landscapes to downtowns and scenic byways to cultural centers and parks. Accurately assessing the physical needs and threats to these resources; engaging in thoughtful planning to address capacity, access, and service issues; and acknowledging that infrastructure improvements should benefit both residents and visitors, requires careful delineation and coordination of the roles and responsibilities of the various levels of government, as well as the private sector. Assuring the physical preservation and viability of all of these facilities and maintaining a healthy relationship between a place's natural, cultural and heritage resources is crucial to the continued vitality of the industry, to creating a multidimensional and dynamic customer experience and to preserving the spirit of the community and its residents.

The Visitor and Resident Experience

The travel and tourism industry and cultural and heritage organizations must work together to ensure that the visitor experiences available in the US are memorable, visually attractive, and rewarding. Quality design of environmentally sensitive signage, entryways, streetscapes, and public facilities—combined with good interpretation—can illuminate the landscape for the visitor, provide coherence to the visitor's experience, and ensure that the tourism infrastructure is itself a part of a high-quality tourism and resident experience. Good design can also make an important contribution to safety and security, mitigating the physical and intangible barriers to visitors by creating a sense of welcome for visitors.

Transportation and the Visitor Experience

The cultural and heritage tourism sectors should strengthen partnerships with transportation agencies at the local, state, regional, and federal levels to address how transportation affects the visitor experience. In urban areas, public transit agencies can improve the visitor experience by working with the cultural and heritage tourism partners in addressing visitor issues through cooperative marketing and wayfinding, particularly for the international market. In sensitive landscapes and historic areas, especially in rural areas, public transport can help address the carrying capacity issues of these sites. Cultural, heritage, tourism, and natural resource managers should collaborate in examining the opportunities presented by the web of bikeways, trails, historic roads, and horse paths in telling the story of a place. Increasing local flexibility in developing signage and wayfinding systems that knit together sites and institutions by using trails, roads, and bikeways allows communities to develop a more positive resident and visitor experience.

Transportation facilities in rural areas should be designed in a way that does not threaten the very attributes that make rural areas attractive places to live in or visit. Where possible, infrastructure development should use art, architecture, and site design to reflect or be compatible with local culture and landscape. Transportation plans should be sensitive to the value of historic buildings and neighborhoods and to the need to preserve local communities. Transportation facilities should include services for travelers and be integrated with surrounding buildings that serves both visitor and resident needs. Finally, transportation enhancement and other highway funds should be used to address these and other issues, as well as leverage more public and private investment.

Impact of Infrastructure Design

Cultural and heritage organizations should ensure that their activities and facilities are accessible for travelers with disabilities. Advances in the "universal design" of products, programs, graphics, buildings, and public spaces can enhance America's competitive edge if tapped by all sectors of the cultural and heritage tourism industry.

The cultural impact of infrastructure improvements must be considered in the planning and development of infrastructure design standards. For example, in rural areas the landscape/natural environment contributes to the traditions and cultural values of the people who settled there. Tourism infrastructure planning and development must address broader cultural and geographic regions, not just one specific tourism destination such as a park or resort. Heritage area partnerships and regional tour routes such as scenic and historic highways and themed corridors are excellent mechanisms for such planning and development.

Natural, Cultural, and Historic Infrastructure

The authenticity of the visitor experience includes many pieces that encompass downtowns, living landscapes, heritage corridors, cultural institutions, and historic structures and sites. We must make sites as accessible as possible to both international and domestic visitors while minimizing adverse impacts on these natural, historic, and cultural resources. The natural resource, historic preservation, and cultural organizations should work with the travel and tourism industry to assure the preservation and appropriate promotion of these resources.

Addressing both the capital needs and threats to these resources and demonstrating how these resources contribute to job creation and other economic benefits requires new leadership in developing public and private investment. Creating new models in economic and community development that focus on the needs of the cultural and heritage tourism entrepreneurs and organizations benefits visitors, residents, communities, and the industry.

Wayfinding and Visitor Orientation

Advances in technology have created numerous opportunities to guide and orient visitors and residents to cultural, natural, and historic sites and attractions. The growth in technology has many benefits, but it also threatens to create a digital divide between visitors and sites trying to meet ever-increasing technological changes. Leadership at the local, state and federal levels that includes communities, transportation and the various sectors in the cultural and heritage tourism industry should explore how to integrate and harness technology into a consistent wayfinding and orientation system. Wireless wayfinding and orientation strategies must complement maps and highway signage, which should use consistent symbols nationwide to identify cultural, historical, and natural attractions.

EDUCATION/TRAINING

Cultural Conversations

Education and training forms a bridge between the educational missions of most nonprofits and the commercial for-profit sectors in the cultural and heritage tourism industry. Community residents should be among the first contingent of cultural and heritage visitors, finding out about themselves, their neighbors and their cultural and heritage assets. In the process of educating residents about the value of its own place, the for-profit and nonprofit interests in the cultural and heritage tourism industry can address opportunities to educate their leaders and staff in crafting a cultural and heritage tourism product that integrates all the ingredients of place—natural, cultural, and historical resources, and living traditions. Educating community residents is an effective means of using local citizens as tourism ambassadors for a region.

Knowledge Base

A comprehensive set of training objectives, tools, and materials should be developed for all sectors in cultural and heritage tourism. While the knowledge base in each segment of the cultural and heritage tourism industry is different, education and training needs to be coordinated to create a unified team, bringing the different sectors together.

Education and training programs should include the significance and value of natural, historic, and cultural resources, as well as an awareness of community development techniques such as land use planning, historic preservation and community cultural planning. Educators should involve cultural, heritage, and business specialists in their training programs. Programs should include cultural sensitivity training for cultural and ethnic etiquette.

All segments in the cultural and heritage tourism industry should identify current training materials and toolkits, address the gaps with new materials and put all this material into a collective national toolkit. This information should be made broadly available in user-friendly formats through the Internet, conferences, and training programs.

Visitor and Resident Education and Training

Hospitality issues and concerns should be part of the education and training of all sectors of the cultural and heritage tourism industry. In addition to tourism planning and development issues, this should include visitor service issues. All the sectors should assure that needed information about the destination community, including any safety issues, reaches front-line staff such as ticket sellers, hotel clerks, concierges, bus and taxi drivers, tour guides, and others who interact with the traveling public every day.

The cultural and heritage tourism industry should facilitate cooperation and understanding among the marketing and communications staffs to broaden awareness and promotion of area attractions, and keep them informed about visitor interests, needed visitor services, and planned promotional campaigns.

All the interests in cultural and heritage tourism should join together in celebrating the diversity and uniqueness of place. This includes preparing communities to receive visitors, addressing fears and concerns, as well as enhancing their appreciation of the value of their own traditions, heritage, culture, and institutions. In particular, educational efforts should assist smaller organizations in participating as equal and full partners. It also means educating the community about the benefits of cultural and heritage tourism and educating travelers about the culture of their destinations. Finally, training and education should assist residents and visitors in understanding and welcoming different cultures in a sensitive and respectful way.

Cultural and Heritage Tourism Entrepreneurs

Recognizing and supporting cultural and heritage entrepreneurs—business owners, self-employed artists, and artisans and others—as legitimate and important to local economies should be part of the training programs developed by the cultural and heritage tourism industry. These include identifying public and private sources of seed funding or training assistance for new or existing businesses or artists and artisans. All sectors should cooperate in encouraging university or college arts administration and tourism management programs, both undergraduate and graduate programs, to develop and integrate curricula that address cultural and heritage tourism and entrepreneurship.

SUSTAINABILITY

Preserving a Viable Sense of Place

The 1995 White House Conference on Travel and Tourism's issue paper states, "The responsibilities of the travel and tourism industry, the states and communities, and the federal government include making certain that tourism development and activities are carried out in such a way as to sustain or improve the natural, social, and cultural foundations of a destination."

The stewards of natural, cultural, and historical assets must be assured that cultural and heritage tourism respects the traditions, values, and sensitivities associated with these assets. They must believe that tourism and other development activities provide sustainable benefits that do not sacrifice the integrity of a community's assets for greater marketability. Sustainability addresses both programmatic needs, and the viability of the resources themselves. Strengthening local leadership and support from all the stakeholders is key to striking a balance between an optimal visitor experience and economic opportunity and the needs of the community to preserve and sustain its historic, cultural, and natural resources.

Sustainability

The implications of tourism and other development should include impacts not just on natural resources, but also on historic and cultural resources such as the built environment and local ways of life that attract visitors to a destination. In planning for tourism, the stakeholders should anticipate developmental pressures and apply limits and management techniques that sustain natural resources, heritage sites, and local culture and institutions.

Sustainability should conserve resources; respect local culture, heritage, and tradition; focus on quality balanced with economic opportunity for residents; optimize the visitor experience through a creative mix of cultural, natural, and historic resources; and measure success not only in numbers alone, but also in the integrity of the experience that contributes to economic viability of the institutions, resources, community, and its residents.

Access with Minimum Impact

The cultural and heritage tourism industry should work with local communities to find ways to ensure visitor access to natural, historic, and cultural resources in ways that will avoid damaging or destroying those resources. New technologies (e.g., lightweight viewing platforms in fragile landscapes, specialized vehicles, software) and creative management practices (e.g., conservation easements, design guidelines) should be used wherever possible to minimize impact. Representatives of the industry should be a voice for resource protection as well as promotion.

Cultural Stewardship

Poorly planned tourism development can endanger not only a destination's environment, but also the very culture of the people who live there. Local cultural organizations should: (1) work with the travel and tourism industry to improve visitor awareness of the need to preserve natural, historic and cultural resources by minimizing the impacts of visitation; (2) expand or develop training and outreach programs for all the stakeholders in cultural and heritage tourism to address planning, marketing, product development, technology, economic opportunity, and their effects on sustainability; and (3) focus on educating government agencies, civic leaders, natural resource managers, and others on the inherent potential of cultural, natural, and heritage assets, and the need for investment in these assets, to provide educational value, recreation opportunities, and a stimulus for community and economic development.

Stakeholders in Stewardship

In planning and executing development, the involvement of stakeholders—local community leaders; resource managers; cultural and heritage institutions; artists, interpreters, and performers; tourism, business; and other representatives—is key to creating and sustaining cultural and heritage tourism projects and resources. Sustainability requires investment in fine-tuned assistance like micro-lending institutions, common venues, and the Internet sales and marketing, as well as in other areas to help communities and individuals participate and stay viable in the tourism economy. Sustainable cultural and heritage tourism should strive to give local stakeholders more control over their product mix and their story, and instill an ethic of inclusiveness and sense of participation in a larger global enterprise.

KEYWORDS

- **Convention and visitors bureaus**
- **Cultural and heritage tourism**
- **Historic and cultural attractions**
- **Promotional campaigns**
- **White paper**

ACKNOWLEDGMENTS

A Position Paper on Cultural and Heritage Tourism in the United States is the work of many talented people who were brought together to review the original 1995 white paper, Cultural Tourism in the United States, published by the President's Committee on the Arts and the Humanities and the American Association of Museums. The resulting document reflects their experience and success in developing a thriving cultural and heritage tourism industry. A debt of gratitude is also due the National Endowment for the Arts, the National Endowment for the Humanities, and the Institute of Museum and Library Services, whose vision and leadership in meeting the goals of the original white paper has contributed to this success and affirmed the public sector's role in supporting the nation's cultural life.

Finally, my thanks to the members of Partners in Tourism and the Cultural and Heritage Tourism Alliance for their contributions to revising this white paper, to the Shop America Alliance for their support of the 2005 Summit and to Cheryl Hargrove, Helen Marano, and Barbara Steinfeld for their help in realizing this document. Thanks as well to the National Assembly of State Arts Agencies for editorial assistance —Kimber Craine, Editor President's Committee on the Arts and the Humanities

Chapter 13

Historical Authenticity in Heritage Tourism Development

Craig Wiles and Gail Vander Stoep

INTRODUCTION

A review of heritage tourism literature reveals a fundamental tension over the use, function, and degree of authenticity of historic resources used for tourism development. Using a case study approach, this chapter explores how stakeholder beliefs regarding historical authenticity influence the heritage tourism products, services, and experiences created for visitors and the value of historical authenticity to community stakeholders relative to other factors involved with heritage tourism development. Heritage tourism stakeholders in Manistee and Ludington, Michigan consider historic preservation and historical authenticity to be important components of heritage tourism development; however, other factors, such as providing an engaging and entertaining experience, have resulted in the creation of inauthentic contexts, stories, and experiences at some sites. Enhanced development of interpretive services is suggested as a way to preserve authenticity while also providing a more engaging experience.

Recognizing the current and potential economic benefits of tourism, both heritage resource managers and economic development professionals have advocated collaborative partnerships to develop historic resources for heritage tourism. Despite the intent to work together, philosophical tensions regarding the nature and function of historic resources have hampered collaboration. There is evidence in the heritage tourism literature of a fundamental tension over the use, function, and authenticity of historic resources; this tension is especially evident regarding the use of historic resources as a commodity within the tourism industry (Ashworth, 1994; Garrod and Fyall, 2000; McKercher and du Cros, 2002). By using history to create experiences for tourists, the history of a site can be altered and, in some cases, recreated into something completely false (Cohen, 1988; Herbert, 1995).

Defining History and Authenticity

During the past century, there have been changes in methods of historical research, and some have questioned the motivation and purpose for history to be written at all. The notion of objective truth or reality has been challenged by the idea that historians, and the sources of historical information with which they work, have inherent biases that influence what can be known about the past. Despite claims to objectivity, the previous domination of historical narratives from a white, male, heroic perspective is seen to have served more as a nation-building, identity-creating, or status quo-preserving device than as an objective source of information about how things occurred in the past (Loewen, 1995; Lowenthal, 1998). As a result, considerable effort has been made by historians under the social constructivist philosophy to study less powerful, disadvantaged, and exploited members and groups within society (Iggers, 1997). This definitional and conceptual debate also presents a quandary for heritage tourism planners and developers: Which resources, stories, events, and perspectives accurately present a community's history and associated culture? Which should be developed and presented to tourists?

Heritage resource organizations that have advocated partnerships with heritage tourism have been explicit in their calls for authenticity. The National Trust for Historic Preservation (Green, 1993), for example, cites authenticity as a way to promote the true story of an area by giving the destination real value and appeal. While she does not explicitly define authenticity, Hargrove (1999, 2002) describes it in terms of objective truth, a significant or distinctive asset, something real and tangible that visitors can experience and that is supported by historical fact. Visitors to heritage sites across the US, she argues, have come to value and expect authenticity as part of a meaningful, quality educational experience. In calling for a focus on authenticity, McKercher and du Cros (2002) clarify this point by saying, "the days have well and truly passed where low-quality experiences can satisfy the gullible tourist" (p. 127).

Within the context of heritage tourism, Wang (1999) provides an important differentiation between the competing definitions of authenticity. Authenticity in tourism can be applied to both the visitor experience (activity-related authenticity) and the toured objects themselves (object-related authenticity). Where Wang's existential definition of authenticity deals with the activities or experience of the visitor, both objective and constructive definitions of authenticity focus more on objects, or the heritage tourism product that has been developed. Because the goal of this study is to better understand the role of authenticity in the heritage tourism development process (creating objects or products for consumption), Wang's objective and constructive definitions of object-related authenticity are used as the basis for exploring stakeholder beliefs and opinions.

Heritage Tourism and Authenticity
While historians are becoming more apt to recognize the limits of objective truth in their field, some are nonetheless critical of the heritage industry as presenting false and untrue stories. "Heritage," argues Lowenthal (1998), which is based more on faith than on fact, "passes on exclusive myths of origin and continuance, endowing a select group with prestige and common purpose" (p. 128). Ashworth (1994) suggests that this is the result of a selective process between competing messages. The end result of this process, he argues, is a heritage product that has a meaning specific only to its intended audience and separate from its actual, tangible artifacts. This meaning can be manipulated in endless ways to cater to any potential audience, turning history into a commodity rather than a source of objective truth. In this sense, generating revenue and providing entertainment value could be considered more important than accurately representing history in its authentic context.

Several studies have shown a link between planning decisions and a lack of authenticity in the heritage tourism products and experiences created for visitors. Tilley (1997) showed how the Wala Island Tourist Resort in Malekula, Vanuatu (located off the coast of Australia), selectively chose portions of the historical record that would best attract their target market tourists from neighboring islands. Similarly, Waitt (2000) described how deliberate decisions were made by heritage tourism developers in Sydney, Australia, to select parts of the historical record that would avoid issues of conflict, oppression, and racism that were authentic to the area in order to attract a certain type of tourist. Barthel-Bouchier (2001) also described how the Amana Colonies (Iowa, US) deliberately ignored authentic aspects of their history, as well as recommendations of historic preservationists, to develop a commercialized "German" product to attract more tourists rather than tell the authentic story of their culture.

PURPOSE OF STUDY

The purposes of this study are: (1) to explore how stakeholder beliefs regarding historical authenticity influence heritage tourism products, services and experiences created for visitors; and (2) to explore the value of historical authenticity relative to other factors involved with heritage tourism planning and development. The following major questions guided the research:

- How is heritage tourism represented in the communities and how do stakeholders define historical authenticity?
- Do stakeholders use objective reality to help shape heritage tourism products, or is history considered a commodity that is molded to fit their target audiences?
- Is authenticity a lower priority than attracting visitors, generating revenue, or providing an entertaining experience?

RESEARCH METHODS

Following expert consultation with Bill Anderson, Director of the Michigan Department of History, Arts and Libraries (HAL), the Michigan communities of Manistee and Ludington (see Figure 1) were selected as case study sites for this research. Manistee and Ludington were part of the HAL Cultural Tourism Visitor Experience Pilot Project because of their demonstrated commitment to creative partnerships for developing historic resources by both heritage resource managers and economic development professionals. Manistee and Ludington are independent communities, but they have used similar economic development strategies through heritage tourism. They are examined in this research as a single case because they function as a single collaborative entity for regional product development and promotion in the HAL Pilot Project.

The primary sources of data for this case study were 13 individual in-depth interviews with stakeholders involved in the heritage tourism development process, including six heritage resource managers, five economic development professionals, and two other participants identified through a snowball sampling technique. This was supplemented by a document review, including primary and secondary sources of historical information, planning documents, marketing and promotional materials, and other relevant secondary sources such as newspapers, magazines, and electronic media. In addition, tour guide training manuals, historical markers, and exhibit texts were documented by the researcher to assess the existing heritage tourism landscape and provide context for the comments of the interviewees.

Figure 1. Location of case studies.

Interviews were audio recorded using a tape recorder and then transcribed by the researcher for later analysis. Three hundred seven images of historical markers and exhibit text were also transcribed, along with marketing and promotional materials. Analysis primarily involved thematic text analysis using text coding as described by Crabtree and Miller (1992), with the goal of organizing the large volume of text from the interviews into categories of meaning.

RESULTS FROM PRIMARY DATA

Interview participants primarily defined historical authenticity as objective reality, emphasizing the importance of original buildings, historic homes, and tangible artifacts. The sights, smells, and sounds of a cruise aboard the Lake Michigan carferry S.S. Badger or the Victorian flair of the National Register Historic District in downtown Manistee are examples of this objective definition. The perception of historical authenticity as objective reality is related to an overall appreciation for historic resources among participants, an appreciation that puts value on preservation and restoration efforts. In the case of the Ramsdell Theater in Manistee, for example, the intangible benefits of preserving the theater outweighed the economic costs of the project. "There is absolutely no way that the Ramsdell Theater, by virtue of the improvements that we have made, will ever have an increase in revenue to compensate for the dollars being dumped in," explained one participant, "but it was important to this community that that theater be preserved."

While interview participants felt that historical authenticity was important, there were limits to its importance when considered against other factors such as providing a fun and engaging visitor experience. More than half of the interview participants mentioned the importance of the visitor experience when developing heritage tourism products, illustrating the struggle to balance authenticity as objective reality with the need to create revenue-generating experiences for tourists. "It's not like a history class," explained one participant. "People are there to be entertained; they are there for an experience." While some participants did state that embellishing stories to create an engaging context was acceptable, inappropriately altering a building to improve the visitor experience was not. "We're willing to make some changes as long as it doesn't affect the character of the building," explained one participant. "In other words, we don't want to destroy one of the staircases—the main staircases—to put in an elevator because it's one of the key design elements of the building."

Collaborative Process

Heritage tourism development began in Manistee with the Uniqueness Committee, an arm of the Manistee Chamber of Commerce, that coordinated efforts between community members, civic organizations, museum members, and local churches to identify, promote, and preserve Manistee's historic resources. Beginning during an economic downturn in the 1980s, the Uniqueness Committee helped to integrate historic preservation efforts with tourism as part of an alternative economic development strategy. One outgrowth of these efforts is an annual preservation recognition award given to local homeowners in the Manistee historic district. The city of Manistee also has chosen to refurbish existing government buildings, such as the firehouse and city hall, rather than tear them down to build new ones. This preservation ethic was apparent among participants, and is likely a direct outgrowth of the successful early efforts of the Uniqueness Committee.

Mutual respect for the skills, priorities, and perspectives of the two primary stakeholder groups represented in this study—heritage resource managers and economic development professionals—is evident in study results. Economic development professionals believe in the value and importance of historians and other experts in the heritage tourism development process, and heritage resource managers demonstrate a clear understanding of the fiscal realities of their organizations within the heritage tourism landscape. Therefore, in the case of Manistee and Ludington, the relationship between heritage resource managers and economic development professionals appears less adverse than in other cases described in the literature.

The Visitor Experience

Although this research did not assess the experiences of visitors from their point of view, study participants expressed clear views on the importance of creating an engaging visitor experience as part of the tourism development process. One participant shared ideas about a lumber museum concept in which visitors could experience walking on logs that simulated floating them down the Manistee River, or could breathe in the smells of a bunkhouse filled with sweaty lumberjacks. Some participant comments indicated a belief that authentic history was not fun or engaging and that some license was needed to make visitor experiences more desirable. "In order to attract people to the historical story being told, it has to be made as entertaining as possible," explained one participant, "and that means there is certain embroidery that has to go on." For example, examples of ghost stories were shared by stakeholders and several stories were told about the lunettes (architectural feature of a vaulted ceiling) in the lobby of the Ramsdell Theater that were not authentic, according to the local historians. At the same time, several participants implied that a fun and engaging experience was somehow different than an authentic one. "You need to engage them somehow," explained one participant, "and sometimes you're not going to engage them with the pure authentic form."

The need for balance between authenticity and the visitor experience often resulted in compromise and was apparent in decisions made at individual heritage tourism sites. In the case of Manistee and Ludington, there was an appreciation for the physical remains of history that transcended the visitor experience. For example, putting in a larger bed and carpet in the captain's quarters of the S.S. City of Milwaukee would make overnight visitors more comfortable, but would not permanently alter the ship or run counter to its National Historic Landmark status. Therefore, such modifications were deemed reasonable and justified. On the other hand, modifications that destroy historic character or resources are considered inappropriate. As an example, ongoing restoration efforts at the First Congregational Church of Christ in Manistee are done in consultation with a historic preservation expert. Possible alterations are considered only if the initial design of the building is preserved. In this case, a suitable location had been found for a new elevator to provide improved access for all visitors to the magnificent view from the sanctuary's balcony.

RESULTS FROM SECONDARY DATA

Despite the coordinated regional efforts of Manistee and Ludington, more could be done to enhance the visitor experience through interpretive services. Some interpretive messages are outdated, and some interpretive signs present historical topics that are not promoted as they once were. Ludington is one of several communities to claim the "exact spot" where Father Jacques Marquette died in the 17th century. Despite recent publications on this topic by local authors, the Father Marquette story is not part of the current theme developed for tourists and is noticeably absent from current promotional materials, even though multiple sites were built in the 1950s to commemorate him. These sites and monuments are easily accessible by tourists, with one monument prominently displayed in the Ludington marina. The memorial erected in his honor has enduring qualities beyond the scope of tourism, so is justified in that way. However, when this and other older sites may be considered as tourism attractions, challenges to presentation of authentic stories and images may become problematic. Some of the sites contain outdated and inaccurate messages, and some use language that could be considered offensive or politically incorrect to current audiences. As Loewen (1999) suggests, some of these historical markers and interpretive texts could either be re-interpreted in a modern context, or simply stored in a museum as part of the historical record.

There was also evidence of a lack of coordination between some entities and the region's coordinated heritage tourism development efforts. One of the local gift shops, for example, displays a unique set of murals covering the entire length of the store adjacent to the street. Despite their artistic merits, the murals depict scenes of the American West, including several of Native Americans that are not authentic to the eastern shore of Lake Michigan. As with outdated historical markers, these murals could have value in other contexts, but as tourist attractions attempting to portray an authentic image and story about the region's history, they fail. More coordination among planners, tourism businesses, and other stakeholders is needed to present authentic messages that would enhance local historic themes and topics identified as important to the development and portrayal of the region's heritage.

In some cases, interpretation at sites related to the developed topics and themes of the region simply does not exist. The Udell Rollways, for example, is a site where lumber was rolled several hundred feet and then into the Manistee River so it could be floated down river to the lumber mills. The location was promoted in the early 20th century as a picnic site and still provides a picnic pavilion today. However, there are no historical markers or interpretive services at the site, and the historic context of its original purpose would likely be missed by most visitors. Another site in a park south of Manistee contains two large rocks with the inscription "be kind to animals." According to a local historian, these used to contain water for horses and other small animals to drink. The park used to be the home of a gazebo and was a popular site for concerts, picnics, and events during Manistee's early history. Again, without interpretive signage, these facilities and historic events are easily lost among the modern playground equipment currently at the site.

CONCLUSION AND RECOMMENDATIONS

Manistee and Ludington were chosen as a case study for this research because of their history of collaborative heritage tourism development efforts among diverse stakeholders. This process began independently in the two cities and has grown into a collaborative regional effort. As stated above, the primary tension between authenticity and heritage tourism identified by participants is created as a result of wanting to provide a "fun and engaging visitor experience" and to enhance economic gain. Despite the desire among some participants to provide amusement park theatrics to visitors, significant progress could be made by more fully and appropriately developing interpretive services at heritage tourism sites.

The following improvements to interpretation could improve the visitor experience in Manistee and Ludington:

- More coordinated organization of themes around historical topics, at individual sites and especially between venues across the region,
- Improved signage that links more clearly to the historical topics and developed themes of the region,
- Guided experiences led by trained volunteers or Certified Interpretive Guides, and
- Development of multi-sensory, participatory visitor experiences.

In Manistee and Ludington, the tension between authenticity and other factors has resulted in compromise, but not at the cost of the physical historical remains in the region. Tangible, historical artifacts, and buildings were identified as a primary link to the past by interview participants. Despite continued economic difficulties in the region, an ethic of historic preservation continues to thrive and is an integral part of the region's heritage tourism and economic development decision making.

In both cities there is evidence of both Wang's (1999) objective and constructive definitions of authenticity. An emphasis on historic preservation and presentation of tangible, authentic artifacts to visitors demonstrate the objective realm, while creating stories and fabricating inauthentic contexts represent the constructive realm. As in other cases in the literature (Barthel-Bouchier, 2001; Tilley, 1997; Waitt, 2000), history has been developed as a commodity in what Lowenthal (1998, p. 128) calls a "creative commingling of fact with fiction."

Primarily defining authenticity as objective reality based on actual buildings and historical artifacts is a natural fit with historic preservation efforts. In the case of Manistee and Ludington, there seems to be a direct relationship between the success of historic preservation and heritage tourism development. At the same time, creating inaccurate stories could actually have negative impacts on the quality of the visitor experience and visitors' perceptions of the heritage tourism venue (Hargrove, 1999; McKercher and Du Cros, 2002). Additional research should focus on the elements of a fun and engaging experience and the impact of embroidered or inaccurate stories on visitors' perceptions of experience quality and value, and on their understanding of the region's history.

KEYWORDS

- **Authenticity**
- **Heritage tourism**
- **Manistee and Ludington**
- **Primary and secondary sources**
- **Ramsdell Theater**

Chapter 14

Tourism Image Orientation Study of Tianjin

Li Jin and Liming Zhao

INTRODUCTION

Starting with the status quo of tourism development of Tianjin, this chapter analyzes the factors restricting the tourism development of this city, as well as the characteristic of tourism resources and market perception of this city by conducting questionnaire investigation into the tourism image of Tianjin. Basing on the above, it discusses the establishment of tourism image of Tianjin, and puts forward the theme words of whole image of tourism and tourism attractive matter image.As one of the four cities directly under the central government, Tianjin is a city possessing abundant historical and cultural heritages of 600 years. Meanwhile, it is an important industrial and commercial harbor city, in which multiple kinds of culture gathered, in north China. But the reputation and attraction of tourism in this city is not proportional to its rich cultural connotation and modern achievement. People's impression of Tianjin is that it is just a common city guarding Beijing. So the obscurity of tourism image is the bottleneck restricting the development of tourism in Tianjin.

Table 1. The tourism development index comparison of Tianjin with surrounding cities.

	Tianjin	Beijing	Dalian	Shenyang	Yantai	Weihai
Gross income in 2002	363.94	1178.00	135.60	144.20	79.12	55.50
Gross income in 2003	422.26	858.00	125.60	144.60	71.54	57.52
Gross income in 2004	485.14	1398.60	170.10	181.30	92.93	71.40
Total tourists in 2002	3313.66	11810.00	1450.11	2138.50	1079.09	725.00
Total tourists in 2003	3800.00	8912.00	1189.30	2272.40	932.98	778.17
Total tourists in 2004	4483.01	12315.00	1652.00	2845.30	1192.34	866.70

Source: Annual tourism statistics of China.

STATUS QUO OF STUDIES ON TOURISM IMAGE OF TIANJIN

As far as the tourism image of Tianjin concerned, different people have different opinions on how to build it in recent years. Simin Liu thinks that building central commercial and tourism leisure region is a short way to improve the charm of Tianjin, while the city committee and the city government put forward the idea of "understanding Tianjin from modern history", Xiaoying Fu and Qunchao Ran think that the whole tourism image of Tianjin should be "the emperor's port in the past and millions of people's Eden today".

In our opinion, the basic principles for orientation of whole tourism image are that, basing on the resources and environment and their characteristics, give prominence to the whole image of city in the region it belongs to, and pay attention to the tourists' image perception and differentiation. Starting with the characteristic of resources and environment in the core district of city, and combining the survey on tourist to Tianjin, this chapter made a further study on tourism image of Tianjin, so as to enrich the studies on city tourism management and promote the healthy development of tourism in Tianjin.

Table 2. The growth rate of tourism index (%).

	Tianjin	Beijing	Dalian	Shenyang	Yantai	Weihai
Foreign exchange income growth in 2002 compared to the same period last year	1.30	4.06	22.71	53.70	16.77	19.00
Foreign exchange income growth in 2003 compared to the same period last year	16.00	−27.00	−8.20	0.30	−10.00	4.00
Foreign exchange income growth in 2004 compared to the same period last year	22.80	63.00	25.44	25.40	29.90	35.40
Tourist number growth in 2002 compared to the same period last year	0.24	4.65	8.00	25.20	16.94	13.00
Tourist number growth in 2003 compared to the same period last year	15.00	−15.00	−22.00	6.30	−14.00	7.00
Tourist number growth in 2004 compared to the same period last year	19.50	38.00	38.90	25.20	27.80	27.80

Source: Annual tourism statistics of China.

STATUS QUO OF TOURISM IN TIANJIN

General Situation

During the 10th 5-year plan, Tianjin took tourism as the keystone of the tertiary industry, actively implemented the exploitation and optimization of tourism resources, and accelerated the development of tourism. According to the statistical data issued by Tourism Bureau of Tianjin, the gross income of tourism in 2003 was 42.226 billion yuan although influenced by SARS, increased by 16% compared with 36.394 billion yuan in 2002, and the total tourists were 38 million, increased by 15% compared with 33.1366 million in 2002. In 2004 and 2005, Tianjin continuously maintained good momentum of growth in tourism. In 2004, the gross income of tourism is 48.514 billion yuan, and the total tourists are 44.8301 million, increased by 22.8% and 19.5% respectively compared with the corresponding period last year, of which foreign tourists are 620 thousand and foreign exchange are 420 million dollars. The gross income of tourism in 2005 is 58.27 billion yuan, and the total tourists are 50.87 million, increased by 20.02% and 13.25% respectively compared with the corresponding period last year, of which foreign tourists are 740 thousand and foreign exchange are 510 million dollars.

Comparison of Tourism of Tianjin with Those of Surrounding Cities

Tourism Income and Tourist Number are Higher than Surrounding Cities
Compared with other cities surrounding Bohai Sea, the tourism development in Tianjin is better. Tourism income and tourist number are higher than Dalian, Shenyang, Yantai, Weihai, except Beijing.

Low Development Speed and Low-level Opening-up

Although tourism of Tianjin made much progress in recent years, its development speed is much lower than other cities surrounding Bohai Sea. From the angle of foreign exchange income and tourist number, growth speed of Tianjin in 2002 and 2004 is much lower than other five cities, with the exception of the period of SARS in 2003. During the period of SARS, the foreign exchange income and tourist number in Beijing, Dalian, and Yantai were in a state of negative growth, the foreign exchange income, and tourist number in Shenyang and Weihai declined greatly. The proportion of foreign exchange to total tourism income of Tianjin is at middle or low level too, to a certain extent, it told us that the opening up of tourism of Tianjin is at low-level.

Table 3. The proportion of tourism foreign exchange income to the total tourism income of some cities around Tianjin (%).

	Tianjin	Beijing	Dalian	Shenyang	Yantai	Weihai
2002	0.94	2.63	2.43	0.95	1.14	0.94
2003	0.78	2.21	2.00	0.77	1.06	0.73
2004	0.85	2.27	2.05	0.79	1.13	0.70

Source: Annual tourism statistics of China.

CHARACTERISTIC OF TOURISM IN TIANJIN

There are Abundant Important Historical Persons and Events in Tianjin

From the era of Jin, Yuan, the development of industry and commerce of Tianjin were accelerated because of the prosperity of water transport, accordingly, its culture boomed. Tianjin played an important role in Chinese modern history, a lot of important events has relationship with Tianjin such as the Boxer rebellion, Battle of Dagukou, Signing of Tientsin treaty, Way station training, Zhongshan Sun traveled north, Juewu society, and so forth. Many historical persons such as Hongzhang Li, Shikai Yuan, Qichao Liang, Fu Yan, Yi Pu, Zhongshan Sun, Enlai Zhou, Shutong Li, and so forth left their footmarks in Tianjin, and it is too numerous to mention one by one. These important historical events and famous historical persons left a lot of historic sites and former residences of celebrities in Tianjin.

Architecture of Different Countries Gathered in Tianjin

Before the foundation of China, the area of concessions of England, France, USA, Germany, Japan, Russia, Italy, Belgium, and Australia in Tianjin is up to 1,556 hectares. Thousands of big and small foreign buildings of different styles are left in these concessions, so Tianjin has another name of "museum of architecture of ten thousand countries". There are more than 230 well preserved buildings of different styles, of which 89 are English style, 41 are Italian style, six are French style, two are Spanish style, 46 are courtyard style, 40 are apartment style, five are western bungalow style, and one is Chinese and western style. These buildings can be classified into Revival of Learning style, Greek style, Gothic style, romantic style, eclectic style, and Chinese and western style. All of these buildings have important historical, cultural, artistic, and academic values. Much data show that Tianjin is the most outstanding city in respect of combination of Chinese modern culture and historical culture, and in respect of combination of eastern culture and western culture. Tianjin not only preserved the profound national culture essence well, but also deposited rich and colorful world culture, the city style of combining western and Chinese characteristic, and combining historical and modern characteristic is unique to Tianjin.

Special Folkway and Folk Custom

Tianjin is always said to be "a city whose residents are from various places". Tianjin not only has sense of era, but also preserved the traditional historical custom well. Opera and drama of Tianjin is very good, there are various drama such as Beijing style drum, Plum blossom style drum, and Western river drum. There are four world famous civil arts, the craftwork of special characteristic such as Yang Liuqing's annual painting, Clay figure Zhang, and Tianjin Wei kite are much favored by lots of people. Besides, the residents of Tianjin are passionate, hospitable, greathearted, and humorous, and these characteristics attracted a lot of tourists from other places.

There are Rivers, Sea, Mountains, and Cities in Tianjin

The outstanding characteristic of tourism resource of Tianjin is that it has rich water system. The saying of "where nine rivers converge, seventy two Gu" is from the ancient era. The rivers which pass Tianjin are main branch of Haihe River, the South Canal, the North Canal, Ziya River, Daqing River, Yongding River, Chaobai River, Ji Canal, and so forth. Tianjin is an important seaside city in the region surrounding the Bohai Sea. In the north of Tianjin, there lies the famous Pan Mountain National Landscape Area, Huangyaguan Great wall, Jiulong Mountain National Forest Park, Baxian Mountain National Nature Protection Area, and Green Screen Lake Landscape Area. Of the four big cities directly under the central government, some have mountains, rivers but have no sea, such as Beijing and Chongqing, some have sea and rivers but have no mountains, such as Shanghai, only Tianjin possesses all of them.

Natural Resources Comparison of Tianjin and Cities Around

Although Tianjin has rivers, sea, mountains, and various sites, it lacks fully developed tourism spots that can be the number one of China or number one of the world. The Pan Mountain which is praised as "the most spectacular mountain unparalleled elsewhere in the world", and the Haihe River scenic line which embodies the scenery of modern metropolis are not so famous as Taishan Mountain and Baotu Spring in Shandong. Geography advantage of closely nearing Bohai Sea does not bring good development momentum to seaside tourism. On the contrary, Tianjin is defiladed by the tourism image of Qingdao, Dalian, and Beidai River. Dalian and Qingdao exhibit themselves as fresh and neat seaside cities, while the Beidai River is famous because it is a summer resort. Compared with Beijing, the tourism resources of Tianjin are less famous, and arc small in scale. It is difficult to realize the idea of doing well in cultural relic and historic sites tourism because its distance from Beijing is only 120 km.

Table 4. Advantages and disadvantages of tourism development in Tianjin compared to Beijing.

Item	Content and identical rate	
Advantages	Reasonable price 78.4%,	Abundant dietary culture 35.1%
Disadvantages	Bad environment 69.7%,	Dull tourism product 63.0%
	Inconvenient communication 40%	

Source: The results of questionnaire investigation into tourism image of Tianjin.

The results of questionnaire investigation into the advantage and disadvantage of tourism in Beijing and Tianjin showed that, compared with Beijing, the advantage of Tianjin is its low-level consumption standard, so shopping tourism will bring tourists from Beijing and surrounding regions to Tianjin.

ANALYSIS OF TOURISM IMAGE MARKET PERCEPTION OF TIANJIN

Two approaches were used to investigate and research the tourism image market perception of Tianjin, one is questionnaire investigation into the tourism image of Tianjin, and the other is collecting theme word for tourism image of Tianjin.

Results of Questionnaire Investigation into the Tourism Image of Tianjin

One hundred eighty students and 20 teachers of Tianjin university of commerce were chosen as the investigation objects, 180 questionnaires were handed out to students and 165 valid questionnaires were handed in. Twenty questionnaires were handed out to teachers and all of them were handed in the proportion of investigation objects who are from Tianjin is 30.3%, and 69.7% are from other provinces.

Table 5. The investigation results of Tianjin tourism beneficial image.

Problem	Item						
What impressed you in Tianjin:	Tianjin snacks	Folkway and Folk custom	City Scenery	Natural landscape	Cultural relic and historic sites	Shopping	Average identical rate
Identical rate:	67.0%	43.2%	7.0%	4.3%	19.9%	24.3%	27.28%
What deserves travelings:	Road of Binjiangdao	Former Residence of celebrity	Old cultural street	Food street	Seaside beach	Landscape of Ji County	
Identical rate:	24.3%	33.5%	35.7%	19.5%	17.9%	47.6%	29.75%
Advantage compared to Beijing:	Convenient communica-tion	Reasonable price	Abundant natural and hu-manistic resources	Dietary culture			
Identical rate:	8.1%	78.4%	14.1%	35.1%			33.93%
What is unique in Tianjin:	City scenery	Natural scenery	Humanis-tic sight	Special architec-ture	Shopping for leisure		
	13.0%	10.3%	37.3%	33.0%	27.65		24.25%
Tourism image of Tianjin:	Seaside city	Exposition of foreign architecture	Unique folk custom culture	Modern historical, cultural city	Paradise for shop-ping		
Identical rate:	16.2%	24.9%	39.0%	33.5%	13.0%		25.32%

The investigation results showed that of the 26 questions about the tourism beneficial image of Tianjin, only the identical rate of reasonable price and Tianjin snacks are over 50%, they are 78.4% and 67.1% respectively. The average identical rate of the 26 beneficial images is 25.65%.

Collecting Theme Word for Tourism Image of Tianjin

Thirty-four students, whose major are tourism management of Tianjin university of commerce, were chosen to collect tourism image theme words, and we got 28 items which can be classified into four kinds, that is seaside scenery, historical culture, folk custom and dietaries, and city scenery. Of the 28 items, two are seaside scenery, 10 are historical culture, six are folk custom and snacks, eight are city scenery. The proportion of the above four kinds are 7.14, 39.28, 21.43, and 32.15% respectively. We can see from these results that the informants have different opinions about the tourism image of Tianjin, and no theme word is over 50%, which can represent the whole tourism image of Tianjin.

Table 6. The results of theme words investigation of Tianjin tourism image.

Seaside scenery	Historical culture	Folk custom and dietaries	City scenery
Seaside tourism and leisure city; Seaside metropolis	Looking at former residences of celebrities; Bright pearl of Bohai Sea, epitome of modern history; With whom to bear the honour and disgrace, view history of Tianjin of a hundred years; Former stories of Tianjin, modern China; A hundred years' dream, historic retrospect; Condense culture of modern age-old city, keep on route of tourism; Know Tianjin from modern China; Tianjin, window of modern culture; Tianjin, modern city with a hundred years' history; Leisure travel to historical and humanistic scenery; City for Olympic games;	Delicious food inherited from folk society; Sweet Tianjin; Palatable humanistic charm; Cheap and useful merchandise, eat in Tianjin; Taste delicious food, retrospects history; Folk custom, culture, snacks;	New look of old city; Old Tianjin, foreign style; Tianjin, pretty image of European architecture; Modern China, pretty Tianjin; Longtime culture of old city, profound foreign characteristic; Beautiful scenery, enjoy youself in Tianjin; Tianjin characteristic, Haihe River scenery; Tour Tianjin, view and admire rivers, sea, cities, climb mountains;

THEME WORDS OF TIANJIN TOURISM IMAGE

According to the basic principle of tourism orientation, together with the above analysis, we put forward the theme word of whole tourism image and tourism attractive matter image.

Theme Word of Whole Tourism Image of Tianjin

"Display styles of different countries, enjoy multiple cultures."

This theme not only gives prominence to the characteristic of natural resources in Tianjin, but also embodies the humanistic charm of cultural relics of 600 years. "Styles of different countries" means the thousands of foreign modern buildings, which genuinely recorded the process of social development and evolvement of Tianjin even China. It is the epitome and evidence of modern city history and modern Chinese history. It is said that architecture is always the product of culture, that is to say, architecture and culture has indivisible relationship between each other. The existent modern foreign buildings are carrier of substance and spirit, they not only reflect the industry and wisdom as well as the long historical culture of Chinese people, but also reflect the complementarities and blend of Chinese and western culture, they are indications of diversity of human culture.

Tianjin also has a tradition of holding tourism celebrations, which fully reflect the characteristic of multiple cultures. First is spring festival folk custom temple fair, which is a performance of folk custom culture characterized by "annual culture"; second is Mazu culture tourism festival, which is held biennially and attract numbers of tourists from Taiwan, Hongkong, Macao, and Fujian; the third is the Sea Fair of Tanggu, which exhibits culture of fishery; the fourth is drum tower tourism festival, which is an celebration festival combining folk custom culture, modern art, tourism, and commercial activities as one.

Theme Word of Tourism Attractive Matter Image

Overall orientation is to generalize the tourism image of whole city by a simple slogan, but it is always abstract. The image of Tianjin tourism, that is "Display styles of different countries, enjoy multiple cultures" should be proved and enriched by the orientation of tourism attractive matters which are special characteristics of Tianjin.

Landscape Culture, Displaying the Beauty of Environment

The landscape area of Ji County in the north of Tianjin consists of famous mountain, that is the Panshan Mountain, famous pass, that is the Huangyaguan Great Wall, and famous temple, that is Temple of Paradise. Panshan Mountain, which has profound and rich cultures, is the most famous tourism region, Qianlong emperor had been to Panshan Mountain for 32 times and left 1,300 poems there. Ecological environment is the life of tourism in Ji County, so, much importance should be attached to Ji County to make it become a green tourism region which contains famous mountain, quiet woods, beautiful water, impregnable pass, and ancient temple.

Historical Culture, Displaying China's 100 Years

As one of the 99 famous historical and cultural cities, the historical and cultural resources of Tianjin are of high quality. In the modern history of 100 years, a lot of historic sites were left, such as Dagu emplacement, church of Wanghailou, Lvzu hall, Li Dazhao's site for revolution, site of "12.9" student movement, site of "north bureau" of communist party of China. We can say that Tianjin is the epitome and eyewitness of modern 100 years history of China.

Dietary Culture, Enjoying Delicious Food of World

The snacks which are praised as "the three unique snacks of Tianjin" are Goubuli steamed dumplings, the 18th street fried dough twist, and the ear-hole lane fried glutinous cakes, They are so famous that to a certain extent they have become the symbol of Tianjin in people's eye. All the three snacks are of 100 years history, many times of innovations and changes were done to them so as to make them fit for the taste of modern people. As a matter of fact, besides the three famous snacks mentioned above, there are a lot of other snacks such as "Parched spiced peanuts Zhang", "Parched crisp broad beans Zhang", "Pitang Zhang", "Chinese pancake sandwich", "Dafulai crispy rice with vegetables". These snacks originated from the folk society and are prevalent in folk society, they are representatives of "dietary culture" of Tianjin, and are important tourism attractive matters.

Commercial Culture, Cheap but Useful Goods

Commerce in Tianjin is prosperous, there are various styles of commercial streets and commercial districts, such as Heping Road which is crowded with monopolization stores, Binjiangdao commercial street, Dahutong Market which wholesales small general merchandizes, drum tower Commercial Street which has characteristic of Tianjin folk custom, and Guyi Street, Xiaobailou Commercial Street, as well as foreign product market in Tanggu. These commercial streets provide tourists with broad space for shopping. Besides, the consumption standard of Tianjin is relatively low compared with that of the same kind of cities, so it is a good choice to go shopping in Tianjin.

The core of tourism development of a city is to establish special, clear tourism image so as to attract tourists, Tianjin has advantage in tourism because of its special humanistic scenery, fully developed commerce, dietary culture, and inexpensive merchandize. Tianjin will surely be one of the best tourist destinations in China.

KEYWORDS

- **Market perception**
- **Tianjin**
- **Tourism image**
- **Tourism resources**

Chapter 15

Management Strategy for China Group Hotel

Junfeng Li

INTRODUCTION

In recent years, the enterprise management pattern has been changed greatly due to the rapid development of China economy. There are emerging many big group enterprises by adjustment and union. Some star class hotels have purchased other hotels to form group hotels in order to expand their scales. The small hotels, especially the ones with ill-management, purchased by the star class ones, have faced the problems of reconstructing and reforming after their enrollment. In particular, the reform is mainly concerning the consciousness. Besides, there are personnel reform, management reform, and software and hardware improvement, and so forth how to reform the purchased small hotels and predetermine the future under the present policy and situation is the main point in this thesis. I do I hope this chapter can make a contribution for China's group hotel in bringing in more foreign exchange income.

A NEW UNDERSTANDING OF THE ORIGINAL HOTEL AND THE CONSCIOUSNESS REFORM

Recognizing a new to the purchased hotel and reforming its consciousness is very important beginning for the purchased hotels waiting for reconstruction and reform. In the purchased hotel, both the top managers and the bottom employees are part of the group hotel. But if their consciousness do not unit together with the group, the favorable suggestions and theories proposed by chief managers will not be carried out all right. The reason is very simple. They just treat the jobs assigned by the new group as usual, for the shortage of a new sense of responsibility. The differences in consciousness might be brought into the new group hotel, with some evil habits. That might form an evil circle which will make it impossible to carry out any innovative plan and program.

Usually, the original personnel welcome new management system. Especially if the new management strategy is meeting their taste, it will be more evident. But if the new management system is as common as the original, the personnel will feel nothing for it is just a change in form but not in content. Generally speaking, the personnel are looking forward to the new manager. If this attitude is in a normal state, it will exert a positive effect on later management. But if not, it will exert absolute damage. If the new manager disappoints the personnel gradually, then the more replacement of managers, the more disappointment in personnel will appear.

At the very beginning, the personnel possess an indifferent attitude toward the new management system after being purchased. This attitude is fit for the interest need of the personnel in the changing stage. They want to avoid frustration of "hope greatly and disappoint heavily," so being indifferent is the best choice. Meanwhile, the new management system after coalition is far different from top manager replacement. Although the former has a sense of threatening, it is companied by hope and fancy. So it is the best time to make the original personnel to recognize their hotel and perform consciousness reform. The group manager should grasp this chance to give the personnel a clear introduction of new business policy and instruct them with new management system which will help the personnel to have a new understanding of original hotel and accept the consciousness reform. The personnel in management layer must achieve this goal. Only by this way, the new policy can be carried out successfully.

THE IMPORTANCE OF CULTIVATING "BEING TOGETHER" SPIRIT

After the group reconstruction, the original hotel will reopen. In another words, it is "ole hotel, newly open." It should be appearing brand-new. As establishing the improvement of management strategy, the manager should take the "cultivation of being together spirit" into consideration and regard it as an important content. Without a faith of "honor or disgrace, being together," the big group hotel will cannot pursue a long-term development. If the original hotel cannot reach a common faith at this point, it will fall into failure again and will not come back to life.

China economy mechanism reform is at the deep development stage. It is not easy to change thoroughly the old corrupt customs. But we have to change sooner or later. And it is comparatively easy to change now rather than later. The changing time forces people to change. If not, people will be lagged behind time and will be kicked out. Only if identify and solve problems as soon as possible, people can grasp the possibility of development and the capability of competitiveness. With an active attitude toward reform, people might build and understand the "being together spirit". The group hotel manager must impose a deep understanding of the importance of "being together spirit" on the whole personnel. In the severe market competition, all the employees may be out of work. They have to change the indifferent attitude to take part in the group hotel work with a more active spirit.

ESTABLISHMENT OF MANAGEMENT SYSTEM AND RESPONSIBILITY MECHANISM

Achieving the initial success in psychological construction, the hotel can formally establish the management system and improve business strategy. The method of management by layer what has clear allocation of responsibility should be applied in the whole business activities. Each unit has its own jobs and responsibilities. That will form a favorable circle.

As making the business decisions, the manager should observe the capabilities of employees to make full use of the most capable one. The ineptitude workers should be handled with properly and replaced. In dealing with business, the manager should obey and respect the administration layers and avoid contacting with the common employees to guarantee the middle and lower managers' authority. But in life, the manager can express their care for the personnel.

The managers in every layer should not only stick at their department jobs but also take detailed records and make work reports in time for any accidence and service items in business. That will help the top manager to know and analyze the situation. Once identify problems, the manager in every layer should immediately correct faults and make improvement and provide guidance. It can fully exert the effect of management by layers. Only if each unit can perform its responsibility altogether, the top managers can allocate their energy to think over more important program concerning with all group.

MODIFICATION OF MANAGEMENT RULES AND REDUCTION OF PERSONNEL

After the achievement of spirit cultivation and the establishment of management system it is the turn to modify management rules and to execute the new policy fitting for new management system.

To modify management rules must obey some basic ideas, such as "the shallow rules must be modified," "sharp difference between rewards and punishments," "fair and reasonable," and "strict but not severe." With the gist of "no consider for impossible," the principle of "everything for public," and "getting rid of selfishness," the goal of "perfect service, increase benefits," the management rules can be constructed seriously, completely, reasonably.

Once the modification has been done, it is better to publicize and carry it out as soon as possible. A try-out period, one to 3 months or 3–6 months for example, is welcome for all employees to have time to change themselves to meet the rules. Once coming into the formal execution period, the management rules should be performed strictly. The personnel arrangement and reduction must be based on the new rules. Usually the original hotel has a large personnel trouble. The modified management rules can effectively restrain the personnel expanding and the organization ill-management. If the unwanted employees or the units with no profits cannot accomplish the tasks assigned by superiors, they have to be kicked out or canceled. Otherwise, they might harm the hotel operation. At the same time, the modification of management rules should take consideration of laws which show the rationality of new leader mechanism.

RELATION OF IMPROVING HARDWARE OR SOFTWARE AND EARNING FOREIGN EXCHANGE

High standard software and hardware can benefit the group hotel to produce highest interests. If the success of hotel relies on the standard of software and hardware, it is acceptable to say the software determines the 70% share, and the hardware 30%. Because the software is "practical" and it is the leading actor in daily hotel operation. The hardware is "empty" in a sense. Although it is important, it serves as a minor role in function. People are the instructors after all. And the software changes greater than hardware. People are alive, and they are more active. But buildings are dead, and they are comparatively less active. Nothing can change a building but rebuilding or nature disasters. That is to say the software is a decisive factor to well-manage a hotel.

Take the Japan tourists in China for example. According to a research, although there are near one and half million Japan tourists visiting China main land, ranking fourth in Japan's transnational travel, there is only about a one hundred thousand increase annually. Why such a low increase in China with such a great travel market? The Japan tourists visited China highly praised its beauty, but seldom kept a favorite impress on China hotel services. So, it is urgent to improve on the software aspect.

Generally speaking, the software of star class has reached certain level. Only if all the sections keep to their jobs and fully performed their responsibilities, the defects are not difficult to overcome.

At present, the following three aspects should be improved for the software aspect of big group hotel.

Shortage of Professional Dedication

The short of professional dedication often result in rapid decreasing in service. The cause lies in the lax management of manager and the poor quality of employees. For example, the pervasion of evil habits in managers leads to many unfavorable accidents. And quite a lot employee comes here just for jobs with no any idea of "service" and "dedication." For these employees, it is impossible to be professional dedication. So, the group hotel leaders and managers in every layer should pay attention on the employees' thoughts, arranging professional dedication education. Only if to educate them constantly with the thoughts of "professional dedication is the basic requirement in service industry and it is the highest manifest for the personnel," the professional dedication could root in the whole hotel.

Shortage of Professional Sensitivity

The professional sensitivity means the employees should equipped with high capability of immediate response to changes happened around. The employees should be capable of seeing everything, hearing everything and remember everything. They should be pay attention to the customer's intention at any time in service to provide amiable service instead of being asked.

The customers cannot forgive the employees without professional sensitivity and often criticize such kind of deeds. That might result in conflicts and part on bad terms. If it happens in star class hotel, the honor of the hotel will be heavily damaged. On the contrary, if the employees can response quickly and deal with problems properly, the hotel's honor will be defended and will win positive evaluation.

Shortage of Professional Train

This is an urgent task. Every employee should take up different type of professional train. All behavior unfit for professional standards must be corrected. The best way is to give instructions by professional train. The employees should accept new knowledge and service theory and technology to meet the star class hotel requirement.

As designing the hotel hardware aspect, many factors should be taken into consideration. In theory, it seems that the design of hotel hardware aspect should be quite reasonable. It has experienced so many years and has been established after detailed research. And its advantages or disadvantages might be opposite for customers' different habits in practical.

Hot to reach its highest utilization rate for the hotel hardware in such a contrary condition? First, the building that cannot be rebuilt and repaired should be modified with low-cost ornaments to add its beauty in appearance. For example, to beautify the park environment to make the customers feel be reluctant to leave. Second, the interior equipments should be protected and kept maintenance to ensure clearance and decency. If have to perform fitment, to ensure beautiful color and convenient use and safe performance. Besides, the equipment of preventing noises release should be installed on certain facilities.

After the improvement of software and hardware, the hotel should adopt the "X" and "X + 1" star class evaluation method to assess the service level which can ensure the customers enjoy high quality and super level service. That will contribute to the group hotel's operation and bring much more foreign exchange.

Importance of Resuming Confidence and Building Confidence

Removing all difficulties and building confidence are important qualification to do a nice job. The employee without confidence will work in low spirit and feel 1 day seems like a year. The employee with confidence will work in high spirit and feel everything is in spring. Those two polarizations are inappropriate in hotel. It will harm the whole performance if not be corrected. To enhance the employee's morale education is the best way to make them feel honorable for the work in hotel and to promote their centripetal force. If everyone has confidence, the group hotel's prosperity will be expected soon.

The operation of hotel cannot be short of team spirit. The inspiration and construction of team spirit relies on whether the employees are equipped with professional dedication and centripetal force. These potential forces have to be aroused by the group hotel's daily training besides the individual personality. The cultivation of team spirit belongs to consciousness reform field. Apparently, the consciousness reform is important and meaningful for the re-united big hotel group.

In hotel's operation process, to improve service technology should be regarded as a long-term program to be executed. Especially the middle and top managers should have chances to communicate with hotels that have won high praises. If budget permits, they had better pursue further study in foreign countries to understand their management technologies and customs by which they can improve their own service technology. It all depends on human effort. If only hard work, it will success. With the cooperation and hard work of all employees, the original hotel and the whole group hotel will come into the success way together.

KEYWORDS

- **Group hotel**
- **Improvement**
- **Management strategy**

Chapter 16

Education Tourism Market in China

Bin Wang and Shen Li

INTRODUCTION

Educational tourism, a burgeoning section in China's tourism market, has attracted great attention from both industry and researchers, however, the focus always falls on young people, the educational demands of other tourists are largely neglected. The chapter, firstly does a comprehensive analysis of situation and problems of Chinese inbound, outbound, and domestic education tourism markets, and then, based on an investigation made in Dalian with common residents as subjects, attempts to identify basic characteristics of education tourists demands. In light of information obtained from both supply and demand sides, some useful conclusions are reached, from which derive some marketing policies to cultivate Chinese education tourism markets.

Education tourism is a kind of special short-term tourism whose purpose is learning and knowledge gaining and whose major participants are students with minor participants teachers (Guo, 2000, pp. 4–6). The activities involved in education tours are various, ranging from getting to know a school, custom or culture, studying a language, attending a symposium or seminar to attending an academic or research project (Yuan, 2003, pp. 10). Anyway, the chief purpose of education tourism is about education and study. So the destinations of education tour are always set in reputed schools, institutes, universities, or some historical sites and famous scholars' residence. It is expected that each participant can gain skills or knowledge in education tours. It is believed that education tour can enrich a person's knowledge and upgrade tourists products for the local tourism industry, therefore, greater attention are being given to this market nowadays in China.

Education tourism has been prevailing in developed countries. In its initial stage in foreign countries, most of its participants are students. They would take advantage of their vocation time to take tours abroad for sightseeing and knowledge gaining. In countries of Europe and America, education tourism has become a tradition and been considered to be a crucial part of modern education. On the contrary, education tourism had a relative late start in China. An early one can be dated back to 1989, in which a tour to Confucius residence was launched. And most of the tourists in that tour were foreign guests. Besides, the content of the itinerary was about cultural exchange. After that, training tourism gradually starts to take shape. In 1995, travel agencies specializing in the organization of education tours were founded while in December 1995, all these education established a syndicate, which signified the epoch of education tourism (Wen, 2005, pp. 25–29).

CURRENT SITUATION OF CHINESE EDUCATION TOUR MARKET

In 20th century, tourism industry developed at a dramatic pace. Meanwhile it comes into the new age of diversity, with the drastically increasing number of tourists, activities, and themes. Among this large tourist population, young students take up a big portion. According to the statistics, education tourism is overwhelmingly popular especially in developed countries. In 1991, totally 42 schools in Japan launched education tour in China and the student participators were 8,417 (Yuan, 2003, pp. 10). However when it came to 2004, the number rose up to 217 schools and 38,204 students, which just accounts for 24.4% of the total number of Japanese education tourists that year (Wen, 2005, pp. 25–29). Though the market is big, it is now just confined within students and young tourists. Education for people with other occupations is still at its initial stage. And this probably results from the inappropriate market segregation of education tourism.

Because China is a country with vast territory and culture, a stable society and a rising status across the world, more and more foreign education tourists choose China as their education tour destination. At the same time, outbound tour operations with study as the main purpose are also on the increase. Touring for studying languages and experiencing cultures in other countries is becoming one of the top choices for outbound tour among younger generation.

Current Situation of Inbound Education Tourism in China

Take the Chinese International Travel Service (CITS) for instance. Organization of inbound education tour has been its traditional service. Each year, CITS has guests from Italy, Germany, Austria, UK, and Japan. Last year, around 205 batches of tour parties, up to 40,000 Japanese students, came to China for education tours. Over years, China has been the first destination choice for Japanese education tourists and Beijing hosts almost 85% of them (Dong, 2004, pp. 15). It is said that there are 104 schools opening to the Japanese students for education tours in Beijing, including senior high schools, skill training schools, and universities. In addition to these academic exchanges, Japanese students also participate in the so-called experiencing education tour, like technology tour, alley tour, and environment protection tour. And these Japanese would prefer to live with locals during the education tours so that they may further experience the authentic culture.

Though there is no doubt that inbound education tourism contains tremendous potential, doubt should really be cast onto the discrepancy between the product supply and the demand, because there is indeed a misconception. For example, there are totally 900,000 Japanese tourists taking tour in Shanghai while there are only 10,000 education tourists. The figures indicate that such a potential market each travel agency should have competed for is not attractive to Chinese travel services. It is mainly because travel services in Shanghai suppose that since most of the education tourists are students whose purchasing power is not strong, the profits travel agencies could make may be limited. As a matter of fact, though the expenditure per day by students is relatively low, the periods of the education tours are significantly longer. In turn, the total net profits travel services can make through education tours are actually larger than expected. Besides, here are some in-depth relevant effects to enable the inbound education tourists' consumption to grow. Most of the time, students in inbound education tours are always accompanied by their parents or teachers, and the consuming capacity of this group of people should never be ignored. What is more important is that those young students are the potential consumers in the future, so over the long pull, an excellent organization of student education tour can be conducive to the future. In addition, Olympics and World Expo in China are approaching. Tens of 1000 foreigners are going to swarm into China. Then we may expect another wave of growth in tourism industry. And an appropriate product and itinerary design would lead to a rise in education tourism in China, too.

Current Situation of Outbound Education Tourism

The living standard in China has been changed drastically since the open and reform. More and more parents prefer to have their children study abroad, because they believe competent people in 21st century should have a broad perspective and global view. And all these attributes can be obtained through overseas study. Propelled by this upsurge of overseas study, Chinese outbound education tourism also takes shape.

Travel agencies doing business on the outbound education tourism specially target on students. Generally, students need to get to know the universities or schools they are going to before they actually study abroad. In 2005, which is the hottest year for education tourism, this kind of "school tour" is popular. However, tons of problems jumped out of these school tours: time is too short and limited for students to improve their foreign languages or to have a complete idea about the school; price of the tours is at large high and unacceptable; it is not guaranteed to secure the visa. That means sometimes tourists can not travel abroad though they have got enough money. All these risks made the outbound education tourism shrink a lot after 2005. Yet now the market seems to revivify gradually. Travel services are not only now thinking about making a cut on the price of each tour but also adding something new and informative activity items into the tour itinerary so that students can really benefit or gain some useful knowledge in the tours. There is an advertisement reading "8088 ¥ for 5-day education tour in Japan." The price listed is just the half of that a few months ago (Wang, 2005, pp. 16.). And there are also some scenic cities included into education tours as tourist attraction. In this trend, we may expect revitalization in the Chinese outbound education tourism.

Current Situation of Domestic Education Tourism

The number of university, middle school, and primary school students is between 0.2 billion and 0.3 billion. Yet compared with this figure, the number of student tourists in education tour is nothing. It is not because students are not willing to take education tour or because they are short of money to take tours. Generally it is because none of the travel services has now a large-scale exploration of this market and tour products virtually specializing in student education are rare. In other words, there is a great imbalance of supply and demand in education tourism market.

AN INVESTIGATION INTO EDUCATIONAL TOURISM MARKET IN DALIAN CITY

Dalian, one of Chinese 10 best tourism cities, have attracted tourists from all over the world for its mild coastal climate, spectacular seascape, fascinating theme parks, and festivities. Owing to its desirable location neighbored with Japan and Korean and proximity to Beijing, capital of China. It has been attracting overseas students from Japan, Korean, Russia, and other countries to study Chinese or pursue degrees in its many notable universities and high schools.

Compared with strong demands, supply of domestic education tourism in Dalian lags far behind, mainly because the product and itinerary are not as various as expected and most of them are intended for students. Travel agencies now do not care about other education groups, like teachers or scholars. As for the contents of the itinerary, it is still far from satisfaction of tourists. Most of the time, travel agencies only base their domestic education tourism on historical and natural sites touring, which essentially is not that much "knowledge gaining". Yet there is still something new about domestic education tourism. In recent years, travel agencies are aware of the demand for prospective university tours. They organize several tour parties with the chief purpose visiting the reputed universities in Beijing and Shanghai, which prove to be welcomed. Yet domestic supply still has a long way to go to catch up with the up-to-date demands. Travel agencies need not only more detailed market segmentation but also an innovative itinerary with a fair price.

However, in China as a whole, educational tours conducted nowadays basically cater to teenagers, while those programs designed for other groups of people are largely neglected (Wang, 2005, pp. 16.). In fact, educational tour, as a style of traveling with the aim of enlarging knowledge and mastering skills, should be a popular traveling style suitable for all ages. Thus, it would be enormously meaningful for practitioners and researchers to examine the educational tour intentions of common people. To fulfill this objective, between September and October, 2007, a convenience survey was conducted among Dalian residents of all ages to gain an insight into their demands for educational tours. Six hundred questionnaires were administered to residents randomly selected in public places such as parks, squares, and campuses, during which 564 valid questionnaires were collected with a valid rate of 94%.

The Relationship between Profiles of Urban Residents and their Demands for Educational Tour

The 62.1% of the interviewees express liking of educational tours and are willing to make an educational tours in near future which indicates ordinary urban residents have strong intentions for educational tour.

Residents Gender and Age and Their Demands of Educational Tour

Totally 564 people's survey information is valid. Among these 564, 350 are willing to participate in an education tour, with the proportion of 62.1%. And among 285 male interviewees and 279 female interviewees, male tourists who would like to take education tours are up to 202, taking up the proportion of 70.9%; female tourists who would like to take education tours are up to 148, taking up the proportion of 53%. In terms of different age groups, among all the interviewees who are willing to take education tours, 6.6% of the interviewees are younger than 12; 10.5% are between 12 and 18 years old; 16.7% are between 19 and 25; 28% are between 25 and 40; 21.5% are between 40 and 55; 16.8% are older than 55 years old. Based on the data, we can obviously reach a conclusion that male tourists like education tourism more and the major education tourists' age is from 12 to 40, which can be well demonstrated in Table 1.

Table 1. Relation between residents' age and their intentions for educational tour.

Age	<12	12-18	19-25	26-40	41-55	>56
A (%)	6.6	10.5	16.7	28.0	21.5	16.8
B (%)	86.5	89.8	79.8	44.3	51.2	25.1
C (%)	9.1	19.1	21.5	20	17.7	12.8

A: represents proportion of samples based on age
B: represents percentage of those who have intentions for educational tour within each age group
C: represents proportion of people with intentions for educational tour based on age

Occupation and Demands
People with different occupation are in favor of education tours in different extents. Here is a list on ratios of number of potential education tourists with different jobs to the total amount of the interviewees with the correspondent occupation: students 89%; scholars 65%; teachers 73%; government officials 42%; corporation managers 34%; enterprise owners 30%; soldiers 32%; workers 21%; mechanics 45%; sales clerks 33%; pension takers 25%. So we may conclude that students, scholars, and teachers are more likely to take education tours.

Level of Education and Demands
Among the interviewees who had working experiences (excluding those who are still at schools), 39% interviewees with primary school education are willing to take educational tour, while 46% of those with secondary school education, 92% with college education and 89% with graduate education are intent to take educational tour, which clearly indicates that people with higher education are prone to make educational tour.

Interviewees Demands Characteristics
Traveling Style
The 60.6% of interviewees prefer package tour over individual tour when making educational tour for they would benefit from sharing and communicating, thus optimizing their traveling experience.

Expected Expenditure on Education Tours
In the survey of expenditure of a 5-day education tour, we have got the expected expenditure of tourists in different gender, age and occupation. Table 2 well demonstrates the differences.

From the Table 2, we may tell that people at the age from 26 to 55 have the strongest purchasing power and teachers, scholars and students are the education tourists with the biggest consuming capacity. Generally, it is estimated that since teachers, scholars and students have more access to culture and splendor of history and think highly of those, they would prefer to spend more on education tours so as to gain more knowledge than education tourists with other occupations do. In the meantime, residents with higher education are willing to spend more on education tour programs and those with college education or higher have the stronger purchasing power in touring for education.

It can be concluded that expenditure people are willing to pay for education tours is relatively low compared to expenditures on other tourism products. Although younger people constitute the main body of educational tourists, their purchasing power is rather limited. On the other hand, people at other ages also like educational tour and they have larger consuming capacity, but their demands are basically neglected in practical tour operations nowadays. Moreover, scholars and teachers, though having strong desire and purchasing power for education tour, are given little attention from tour operators. In short, people aged from 19 to 55, scholars and teachers formed vast potential market for educational tourism.

Table 2. Expected expenditure of different groups on educational tour.

Variables	Items	Price (RMB)	Variables	Items	Price (RMB)
Age	<12	213.2		Students	392.5
	13–18	439.5		Scholars	425.8
	19–25	552.2		Teachers	543.9
	26–40	674		Government officials	294.4
	41–55	703		Corporation managers	281.9
	>56	663.8	Occupation	Enterprise owners	220.8
				Soldiers	118.7
Education	Primary	344.5		Workers	50.8
	Secondary	426.4		Mechanics	114.3
	College	698		Sales clerks	91.7
	Postgraduate	675		Pensioners	169.3

Traveling Motivations on Education Tour

Generally speaking, people take education tours for knowledge gaining and skills improving. However we can divide them into small categories, like scenic sites seeing, historical sites seeing, scientific exploration, language learning, folk arts and crafts making, seminar attending, culture exchange, custom learning, and prospective school touring. As a form of cultural tourism, people's main purposes (seen from Table 3) on an education tour include visiting historical sites, attending seminars, visiting prospective schools, and experiencing local custom, which demonstrate people have diversified motivations when making educational tours.

Table 3. Residents' motivations for educational tour.

Traveling motivations	Natural sites	Historical sites	Scientific exploration	Language learning	Arts & crafts	Seminar & symposium	Custom learning	Culture exchange	Schools touring
percentage%	8	30	9	3	1	17	12	5	15

Besides, education tourists cannot be content with mere one purpose or monotonous itinerary of an education tour. They prefer an education tour meeting their requirements that they may increase knowledge as well as get themselves relaxed. So an innovative education tour with other supplementary activities is significantly welcomed. In today's high-pace lifestyle, people need this multi-functional education tours. And among all the interviewees, 14% prefer to combine education tours with visiting friends and relative (VFR) tours; 46% prefer to have education tours combined with sightseeing tours; 27% prefer to combine it with vacation tours; 7% prefer to have it combined with shopping tours.

Accommodations Choices

According to the survey, students prefer to stay at friends' places or budget hotels; scholars and teachers would like to stay at economical hotels or star hotels; as for government officials, corporation managers and owners, and professionals, their first choices are star hotels possibly due to their high income or coverage of expenditure by government or their employers; one surprise is that pensioners would choose to stay at star hotels considering their economical living style back home; service clerks, workers, and soldiers intend to stay at budget accommodations mainly because of their limited income or simple living style.

Tourism Commodities Preferences

Souvenirs and local commodities reminiscent of the traveling experiences are highly welcomed by education tourists. For those who have strong desire for education tour, their favorite tourism commodities include souvenirs with locality such as t-shirts and back bags bearing local logos or features (92% interviewees like such commodities), relish cuisine (78%), crafts and arts (62%), books (47%), local products (43%), stationary (wool pens, drawing paper, ink and stones for grinding ink powders, 36%), paintings (31%), and relics (29%). Anyway, commodities with local characteristics are among the most favorites.

Information Source for Education Tourists

For a travel agency, it is crucial to have a good command over the education tourists' information source, and that is where they got their knowledge about education tour routes and price, so that they may later intentionally give publicity to their own travel experiences. According to the investigation, 33% of the information comes from travelers' friends and relatives; 27% is from magazines and newspapers; 21% is from schools or universities; 11% is from the Internet; 6% is from other kinds of books and materials; 2% is from the travel agencies promotion activities. Therefore, it is importation to cultivate a good image and reputation among travelers for a travel service. In addition, travel agencies should take advantage of advertisements put up on magazines and newspapers, which are another imperative information sources for potential tourists.

Destination Choices for Education Tour

Destinations are where education tour are conducted. Generally, a destination suitable for education tour may features rich historical relics, or cultural heritages, or ancient culture centers, or places which cultural celebrities born or once lived or studied, or cities having many prestigious research institutions or universities (Li, 2006, pp. 78). When interviewed about their most desirable destinations for education tour, the respondents gave highly scattering answers, which means China abounds in educational resources and have huge potential for developing education tourism. The following 12 cities are the most favorites, including Beijing, Shanghai, Wuhan, Kunming, Shenzhen, Xi'an, Chengdu, Nanjing, Dalian, Hangzhou, Chongqing, Guilin, and Hong Kong. Table 4 is the final ranking in the popularity of education tourists.

Table 4. Rankings of cities in terms of attractiveness for educational tour.

City	H.K.	S.H.	B.J.	N.J.	X.A.	C.D.	W.H.	K.M.	D.L.	H.Z.	S.Z.	G.L.
Ranking	1	2	3	4	5	6	7	8	9	10	11	12
Percentage	14.8	13.9	13.4	10.8	10.5	9.8	8.1	8.0	7.2	6.9	6.8	6.6

We can divide 12 cities into three subcategories, namely cosmopolitans, ancient cities and famous tourist cities. The first category is composed of Hong Kong, Beijing, and Shanghai, and all of them are international municipalities enjoying complete infrastructures, many universities and academic conferences and a developed tourism, which are perfect combinations for education tourists. The second category consists of Chinese most ancient cities which have long history and highly developed civilization, many universities and fast-developing tourism. Owing to their relatively remote location from the developed areas in China or smaller in size, they ranked behind the first category. Cities in the third category are among Chinese best tourists destination for their appealing environment, beautiful scenery or unique custom. We can conclude from this assessment that the common features of destination for education tour are culture oriented and that education tourism is closely related to local culture and development stage of local tourism industry.

CONCLUSION AND MARKETING IMPLICATIONS

In China, both inbound and outbound education tourism markets are proliferating, while domestic market is just taking off. However, the supply of education tourism still lags far behind demands. Current efforts are primarily made to attract and organize students to participate in education tours, this study finds that people at all ages and with different occupations show a common preference of education tours and intend to take such tours in near future. Basically, people aged from 18 to 40, students, teachers, and scholars, people with high education are the major body of education tourists. Education tourists prefer combine education with other activities in the collective form such as package tour. They like cosmopolitans, ancient cities and famous tourism cities with culture environment and developed tourism industry and economy. On their trip, they prefer to buy souvenirs with local personality and stay at economical accommodations such as budget hotels or friends' places. Though they have a strong intention to make education tour, their prospective expenditure on it is not high.

In general, we should develop education tours with varieties of activities. Products should no longer be confined into the mere purpose of "knowledge gaining." Travel services should place some of its emphasis on the innovation of education tours. It is preferable to develop the multi-functional education tours, like the combination of education tour and vacation tours, education tour with shopping tours, education tours with resort holiday tours. As for its destination, we should base our decision on the city popularity table. So travel agencies are supposed to set their education tour in cities like Hong Kong, Beijing, and Shanghai. What is more, the design of the product should cater more for teachers, scholars, and students, because of their overwhelming purchasing power in education tours.

Education tourism in China is still in its initial stage. No travel agency has a stable income from this market (Wang, 2002, pp. 21–24). So it is important for each travel service to cultivate a good image and reputation. First of all, we should control the current quality of education tour so that they can be thought highly of among education tourists; Besides, travel agencies should take advantages of magazines, newspapers, and the Internet to throw their names into each far-fling corner of China, because according to the previous survey advertisements on magazines and newspapers are the education tourists' crucial information source.

In today's epoch of mass tourism, education tourism has become indispensable. Though it has substantial progress in Dalian City, there is still a significant discrepancy between the market demand and supply. If travel agencies want to clinch this big chance and potential, they need to improve their products in aspects such as price, functions, and promotions so that they may catch up with the constantly renewable demands from the prospective tourists.

KEYWORDS

- **China**
- **Dalian**
- **Demands**
- **Educational tour**
- **Residents**

Chapter 17

Traveling Patterns of Arab Tourists in Malaysian Hotels

Zulkifli Ibrahim, Mohd Salehuddin Zahari, Maimunah Sulaiman, Zulhan Othman, and Kamaruzaman Jusoff

INTRODUCTION

This study examined the traveling pattern of the Arab tourists in relation to their purpose and frequency of visit, duration of stay, traveling companions and activities engaged in during the vacation. The preferences of these tourists for hotel restaurant food and front office attributes while staying in selected five star hotels were also investigated. The result demonstrated that Arab tourists came to Malaysia mostly for a vacation with their spouse and children, and the majority of them were visiting for the first time. The major activities engaged in were sightseeing and visiting interesting places plus other activities such as shopping, visiting theme parks and beaches. The average length of stay was from 3 to 10 nights. The findings also revealed that besides other type of cuisines, home cooking (Arab cuisine) was preferred by the Arab tourists. Similarly, the Arab tourists preferred to have a fast check in, friendly and personalized service and courtesy by front office personnel upon arrival at the hotel. The ability to communicate in and understand the Arabic language among the front office personnel also had a profound effect on their fondness. In turn, a strong relationship among government, local authorities, private agencies and hotel operators should be fostered to capture a larger share of this market segment

The global impact from the September 11 terrorist attacks on the US in 2001 and the subsequent unforeseen terrorism has affected the world tourism industry (Hamarneh and Steiner, 2004). These unexpected events have had a significant impact on the traveling mood of international tourists particularly the Arabs from the Gulf region and Muslim communities. The Arabs and the Muslim communities have been blamed for being responsible for terrorism. Consequently, the feeling by Arabs of being misunderstood and unwelcome in non-Muslim countries has increased. The traveling policy against the Arab tourists has become more rigid in many countries especially in the US, UK, Australia, and European nations. Over-reactions, ignorance and chauvinism in those countries have forced many Arabs tourists to look for new frontiers and change their traditional holiday destinations to other countries (Hamarneh and Steiner, 2004). As a result, Malaysia as well as other Asian countries was found to be one of the favorite alternative vacation destinations for the Arabs. Malaysia as a Muslim country shares a common Islamic culture and tradition and the Muslim Arabs feel safer in terms of security, food, shopping, and religious obligation.

Lately, the number of tourist from the Gulf region has risen over the last few years. As reported, the influx of Arab tourists to Malaysia reached a total of 126,000 in 2004; 150,000 in 2005, and 200,000 in 2006 (New Straits Time, 2007). This is further strengthened as the West Asian market is considered as high yield expenditure with an average expenditure of RM3, 397.4 per capita and an average stay of 13.7 nights compared to tourists from other countries. In fact, the Middle Eastern markets turned out to be in the top for per capita expenditure in the year 2003, despite a slight reduction in the Arab tourists' arrivals. However, the decline was expected due to the SARS outbreak and the haze. The income from the influx, outstanding expenditure and spending power among the Arabs tourists have contributed to a significant impact on the Malaysian economy. Such contributions have made the Middle East one of the most important market segments for the Malaysian tourism industry. In line with this new pattern, Tourism Malaysia, tour operators as well as hotel operators should take this opportunity to promote tourism products such as attractions, cultural events, shopping facilities, hotels and services to capture a larger share of this market segment. In other words, understanding the traveling patterns enables the hotel operators in particular to comply with the needs of these tourists, which in turn enhances their satisfaction and leads to repeat visits to this country.

To date, most of the studies pertaining to Arab tourists were undertaken in developed countries (Din, 1989; Graburn, 1997; Houellebecq, 2001; Ritter, 1989). Ritter (1989) investigated the differences between the travel behavioral pattern of Muslims and Arabs and those of their European counterparts. Din (1989) looked on the Islamic concept of tourism while Graburn (1997) discussed the Islamic concept of travel related to the sacred goal of submission to the ways of God as opposed the commercial goals of mass travel that stresses profit maximization and customer satisfaction. Houellebecq (2001) examined the traveling pattern of pilgrims during the hajj season. However, very limited analysis on the behavioral patterns and preferences among these Arab tourists related to Malaysia has been undertaken. This study therefore aimed to identify the traveling patterns of the Arab tourists in relation to their purpose and frequency of visit, duration of stay, traveling companions and activities engaged in. In addition, their preferences regarding hotel restaurant food and front office attributes while staying in Malaysian hotels were also investigated.

METHODOLOGY

As this study looked at the traveling patterns of the Arab tourists to Malaysia, the triangulation approach (quantitative and qualitative) was used as it gives in depth information on issues investigated (Cavana and Dalahaye, 2001). In the quantitative approach, the target population was the Arab tourists who were staying in five star hotels. The reason for choosing five star hotels was based on the information obtained from the Malaysia Hotel Association (2004) and Tourism Malaysia (2004) that the majority of the Arab tourists were staying in these star rated hotels. Nevertheless, despite many hotels falling into this category in Malaysia, the researcher found difficulties in collecting data from the whole country. A report gathered from Tourism Malaysia indicated that most of the Arabs tourists mainly visited Kuala Lumpur compared to other cities in Malaysia (Tourism Malaysia, 2003). Based on this information plus the other mentioned constraints, it was decided to collect the data from the hotels situated in the Kuala Lumpur Golden Triangle. This area is one of the most famous areas for business, commerce and shopping in the heart of Kuala Lumpur, and most importantly, this area is famous for international chain hotels. Most of the five star hotels like Shangri-la, Parkroyal, Mutiara, Sheraton, Ritz Carlton, Renaissance, and many more are located within the vicinity of 4 km. According to Tourism Malaysia (2006), most of the international hotels in this area are very popular among the Arab tourists compared to other hotels in other parts of Kuala Lumpur.

With regard to the instrument, a few factors were taken into consideration prior to its development. The first relates to the language in the instrument. So as to facilitate a better understanding among Arab tourists, it was decided to develop the questionnaires both in English and the Arabic language. The reasons for this were that some of the Arab tourists were believed to understand the English language and some may have a poor understanding of English. The English version was first edited and then translated and written in Arabic by an Arab language lecturer from the Language Centre of Universiti Teknologi MARA (UiTM) who is fluent in both English and Arabic. The questionnaire comprised three sections. The first section was developed to gather demographic information from the respondents. Questions were designed using nominal scales and focused on respondents' age, gender, marital status, profession, and country of origin. The second section was created to record information concerning the traveling pattern of the Arab tourists. Questions such as purpose of visit, frequency of visit, duration of stay were included in this section. It was felt that the inclusion of these attributes would provide significant results about the traveling pattern among these tourists to Malaysia. The third section comprised questions relating to the preferences of the respondents towards hotel restaurant food and front office attributes. This section required respondents to rank the answers.

On the data collection process, letters seeking approval to undertake the study were sent to the human resource managers at each hotel located in the Kuala Lumpur Golden Triangle. Out of 14 hotels, only five hotels granted permission. The five hotels were Berjaya Time Square Hotel and Convention Centre, The Ritz-Carlton, Mandarin Oriental Hotel, JW Marriott Hotel, and Renaissance Hotel. Subsequent to that, meetings with human resource managers at the participating hotels were held as well to explain in detail the instructions, procedure and how the questionnaires were to be administered by the front office personnel. All the respective human resource managers were given a time of around 1 month (August, 2005) to disseminate the questionnaire. Subsequently, the researcher personally collected the filled questionnaires from the respective hotels. Out of 321 questionnaires disseminated, 130 useable questionnaires were collected. The questionnaires were then coded using the Statistical Package for Social Science (SPSS for Window V.16.).

For qualitative information, short structured interviews with selected Arab embassies were undertaken. This is one of the best ways to obtain insights into and clarification of the information of the overall traveling pattern of the peoples from the Arab regions. The selected Embassies were Saudi Arabia, Kuwait, Syria, and United

Arab Emirates. These embassies were chosen because most of the Arab tourists visiting Malaysia are from those countries as reported by Tourism Malaysia (2006). After permission was granted from all attachés, interview sessions were conducted from 3rd September to 17th September 2005 at each respective embassy. The information gathered was then transcribed.

RESULTS AND DISCUSSION

Demographic Profile

Frequencies related to demographic profile of the respondents were computed. Results revealed that the majority of the Arab tourists who visited Malaysia in this study were married with families which made up 77.7% (n = 101) of the sample against 22.3% (n = 29) who were single. The ages ranged from 20 to above 60 years. The highest proportion was between the ages of 30 and 59 years which represents 65.4% (n = 85) of the total respondents followed by those aged 20 to 29 years or 30% (n= 39) and 4.6% (n = 6) respondents over 60 years of age. It could be said from this finding that most of the Arabs tourists visiting Malaysia were among the youth to the middle aged groups compared to older groups

More than 40% (43.8%, n =57) of the respondents were in the occupations classified as administrative, 40.0% (n = 52) were in professional and technical occupations, and 5.4% (n = 7) were students of higher institutions. The rest of the respondents were retirees (4.6%, n = 6), sales and clerical, 3.8% (n = 5), and others (2.3%, n = 3). All in all, the highest proportion of respondents came from among the professional/technical and administrative (83.8%, n = 109). This result fitted with the result of the previous studies (Basala and Klenosky, 2001; Crompton, 1979; Yuan and McDonald, 1990) which indicated that the pattern and frequencies of traveling are among those with high disposable income.

In regard to country of origin, the highest percentage of respondents were from Saudi Arabia (46.9%, n = 61) followed by United Arab Emirates (13.1%, n = 17) and Kuwait (9.2%, n = 12) compared with other neighboring countries such as Syria, Lebanon, Egypt, Iraq, Qatar, Oman, and Yemen. This result was in line with the Tourism Malaysia Report (2006) that the majority of Arabs coming to this country were from the oil producing countries in the Middle East region. In other words, the disposable income of people from these rich oil nations is higher as compared to other Arab nations. The small percentage of the Arab tourists (around 2%) from Iraq and Lebanon was probably due to the internal conflict and political instability in these countries.

Traveling Pattern

Some significantly meaningful results were obtained related to the traveling pattern of the Arab tourists to Malaysia. It appeared that the main purpose of traveling was for a holiday (83.8%, n − 109) compared to business purposes (8.5%, n =11), visiting friends and relatives (2.3%, n = 3), and other purposes (5.4%, n = 7). The majority of them (88.5%, n = 115) were visiting this country for the first time, followed by 7.8% (n = 10) visiting for the second time and 3.3% (n = 5) had visited more than three times.

In view of the fact that the majority of Arab tourists visited Malaysia for the purpose of a holiday, it is not surprising to see 40.8% (n= 53) of respondents in this study staying more than 10 nights over represented those who stayed between 7 and 9 nights (15.4%, n = 20), 4–6 nights (32.3%, n = 42), and fewer than 3 nights (11.5%, n= 15). Therefore, on average the length of stay among the Arabs tourists in Malaysia was 6 nights. This period is considered by the economists to be good enough to generate a substantial amount of revenue to the country through various tourist activities (Pearce, 1983). On traveling companion, 56.9% (n= 74) of the Arab tourists in this study traveled with their spouse and children, 23.1%, n = 30 traveled with their spouse and relatives, 10.0%, (n=13) traveled with business associates, 5.4% (n = 7) traveled with friends, 3.1% (n = 4) traveled alone and 1.5% (n = 2) with other traveling companions. It could be contended that significant proportions of Arab tourists prefer to travel with companions as it probably provides them with security and eases some of the communication problems. This notion supports Polunin, (1989) who noted that traveling within a group provides security. It is also in line with Islamic teaching that encourages individuals especially women and children to travel with muhrim or blood relations. On the other hand, the major activities engaged in were sightseeing and visiting interesting places (80.8%, n = 105), visiting theme parks (10.0%, n = 13), shopping (6.9%, n=9), and other activities (2.3%, n = 3).

Preferences in Hotel Restaurant Food

In the context of this study, food preferences were simply defined as the selection of the type of food preferred by the respondents from choices available to them. In relation to this, the Western food was ranked as the most popular choice among the Arab tourists (rank 1). This was not surprising as Western food is internationally acceptable and served in most of the hotels. This was followed by Indian food (rank 2). The Indian food was favored probably because it had a slight similarity with some of the Arab food. Surprisingly, in this analysis the Middle Eastern food was ranked third in the echelon (rank 3). However, when checking the number of hotels offering Middle Eastern food, only two hotels were found to be offering such food. Malay, Chinese and other food (rank 4) were also found to be slightly acceptable to the Arabs tourists though not as popular as Western, Indian, and Middle Eastern food.

On other food attributes, factors related to quality of food (rank 1) were ranked first by the respondents followed by variety and choices of Arabic food (rank 2), menu for diet-conscious (rank 3), and provision for children in the menu (rank 4). What could be said of this result is that the Arab tourists were willing to spend as long as the quality of food met their expectations. In addition, they also expected to see some of the Arab delicacies including children's delicacies on the hotel restaurant menu.

Preferences in Front Office Attributes

A few questions were posed to measure Arab tourists' preferences in front office attributes upon arrival at the hotel. Fast check-in (rank 1) was recognized as the most important attribute by the Arab tourists followed by friendly and personalized services (rank 2), courtesy displayed by bellmen and receptionists (rank 3), and ability of staff to communicate in Arabic (rank 4). From these ratings it could be said that the majority of Arabs tourists preferred to have fast check-in and to be allocated to their rooms, especially after an extensive and long-haul journey. Politeness and courtesy by the front office personnel were also expected by the Arabs tourists. Besides that they also preferred to have front office staff that could communicate or know a little bit of Arabic. All in all, these findings indicated that efficiency, fast service and friendlier staff are expected by most of the Arab tourists upon arrival at the hotel.

Qualitative Data Attributes

As previously mentioned, a small structured interview with the key informants of se-lected Arab attachés in Kuala Lumpur were undertaken to validate and strengthen quantitative results. The selected Arab attachés were the Royal Embassy of Saudi Arabia, the Royal Embassy of the United Arab Emirates, the Embassy of the State of Kuwait, and the Embassy of the Syrian Arab Republic. Results showed that the four key infor-mants from each embassy generally shared the same views with regard to the overall traveling pattern of the Arabs to Malaysia. Each of them mentioned that most of the Arab tourists frequently travel with family and the majority them are those from the middle aged groups as compared to the older groups. For instance, the key informant, the Saudi Embassy revealed that tourists from the Arab nation were generally middle-aged parents who preferred to bring their children along when traveling. He added that the older Arabs, especially among the Muslims were more likely to devote their life to God and probably were not really interested in traveling abroad except for pilgrimage purposes.

The key informant from UAE embassy emphasized that the majority of Arab women normally traveled with husband or families. Quoted verbatim he said that: "Through my observation, most women in Arab nations always travel with husbands or male relatives. Women are seldom allowed to travel alone. This is especially in the countries near to the Arab Peninsula." This information corresponded well with the quantitative result that there were only 10% of women respondents in this study compared to 90% of male respondents. In regard to occupations, the key informant of the Saudi Arabian embassy noted that the majority of Arab tourists were among those working for the private or government sector, and businessmen. The same view was given by the key informant of the Syrian and Kuwait embassies. This information again supports the quantitative results which revealed that the highest responses were for occupations of administration, professional, and technical work.

On the reasons for visiting Malaysia, the key informants of the Saudi Arabian Embassy claimed that most of the Arabs travel for a holiday. He noted that the Arabs knew that Malaysia has beautiful scenery and a natural environment. For the newly married, they chose Malaysia as their honeymoon destination. He stated that before September 11, the UK and the US had long been popular among the Saudis. However, since the incident, Malaysia has become popular among the Arab nations as this coun-try shares the same religion. On the same note, the key informant of the Syrian Embas-sy commented that; "Since the Syrian government has actively promoted tourism in the past 10 years, the mood of travelling and visiting overseas countries has increased among the Syrian and the Arab nations. Malaysia offers a lot of opportunity concern-ing the culture diversity, multiracial society, the ethnic minority and tourists can find the whole of Asia in one country and that is what they are looking for. They know that Malaysia is the Truly Asia thing. They can eat Chinese food, Indian food and Malay food in this country. The travelling pattern of the Arab peoples has changed. The Arabs or the Muslim peoples find difficulty in getting visas for vacations in America, United Kingdom and Europe. The Syrians do not need visas to come to Malaysia and this is one of the most encouraging things"

With regard to the duration of stay, the majority of the Arab tourists were found to be staying in Malaysia for at least 5 days. This statement was given by most of the key informants. For example, the key informants of Saudi Arabia embassy noted that: "......as far as I know most Saudi tourists were here on holiday and they stayed in this country for at least five days." In terms of the activities engaged in, the information gathered from the informants supported the quantitative results which indicated that shopping is not a priority among the Arabs who are more concerned with exploring the country. For instance, key informant of the Syrian Embassy quoted: "From the information I gathered, most of the Arabs want to see Kuala Lumpur and surrounding areas. It is nice to discover this Muslim country." The key informant of the UAE Embassy commented that: "Arabs from UAE do not put shopping as their priority because they can find cheaper products of the same quality in their country. They go abroad for vacation and seeing the country. Of course, in the vacation they will bring back some souvenirs for the family and relatives."

All in all, the information gathered from interviews validated and strengthened the results given by the respondents in the closed ended questions. On the basis on these research findings, it appears that the pattern of Arab tourists coming to Malaysia is mostly for a vacation with spouse and children and the majority of them are visiting this country for the first time. As is the normal practice for every first time vacation, tourists are expecting the get the best experiences over their entire period of their vacation. In response to this, the government, local authorities, related agencies and the public should collectively portray a good image of Malaysia to the tourists. As such, all frequently visited areas by international tourists (historical places, national mosque, national monuments, and museums) and other popular spots (airport, railway stations, public eating areas, theme parks, beaches, and shopping complexes) should be well maintained and always in a pleasant condition.

As sightseeing is one of the major activities revealed in this study, the cleanliness of the city and surrounding areas therefore should be maintained all time. This is not to say that our local authorities are not concerned with cleanliness, but comments received from the international tourists indicate that they are not satisfied with the level of cleanliness in most of the major cities in Malaysia, especially Kuala Lumpur. Thus, the authorities need to make a greater effort than before to ensure the cleanliness of those places. Another issue of concern is related to public transportation. Although the government and local authorities have provided good public transportation, complaints about the inefficiency of the overall services, dissatisfaction with the dishonest taxi drivers and the reckless bus drivers, and the unfriendliness of public transport personnel still occur and have often been reported by the tourists. The information gathered from interviews with key informants in this study probably supports this notion.

This issue is always being brought up in the local media, even by the politicians. Taking one example, Arab tourists complained that taxi fares sometimes were overcharged in Kuala Lumpur and were not equivalent to the distance. With this, the local authorities should take the necessary steps to provide a more efficient service by the local transport and enhance some of the human aspects such as courtesy, honesty, friendliness, knowledge and information through training and courses. Again, this is not to bluntly accuse the local authorities of never taking action on this issue, but it must be done continually. All in all, it could be said that if the matters raised were not being taken care of promptly and always, sooner or later the image of Malaysia in the eyes of Arabs and other international tourists will be tarnished and subsequently hinder the arrival of new tourists and reduce repeat vacations.

The result of this study also shows that the majority of Arab tourists visiting Malaysia are from Saudi Arabia, Kuwait, United Arab Emirates, and Syria. With that pattern, the government through the Malaysian Tourism Boards needs to increase what they have done up until now to promote Malaysia to all those countries and make known to them what our country can offer them in relation to tourism products as well as business opportunities. Besides that, the needs, traveling pattern, culture, language, and food of these countries need to be further studied so that we will understand what they expect when they visit Malaysia. In addition, other countries such as Iraq, Lebanon, Afghanistan, Turkey, Libya, Yemen, and others cannot be ignored as they are also considered as potential markets for Malaysia despite the internal conflicts a number of these countries are still facing. Besides promoting Malaysia as a new tourist destination among the Arab nation countries, the government is also striving to establish this country as the educational hub for the Middle East region. It is interesting to note that there were a number of university students who responded to this study. It is argued that university students besides having a holiday are probably coming with the intention of gaining a better understanding of our educational system before pursuing their study here. The interviews with a few Arab students in the International Islamic University presumably strengthened this notion. As evidence the Consul General of Saudi Arabia stated that more than 2,000 students from this country are pursuing various fields of study now in Malaysia. In line with this, the government through the Ministry of Education put tremendous effort into organizing the educational expo in Dubai to introduce and promote undergraduate and postgraduate programs in Malaysia.

With regard to food choices, one of the significant findings revealed that besides other types of cuisine, home (Arab) cuisine was preferred by the Arab tourists. Nevertheless, most of the hotels in this study were found not to be offering Arab food in their restaurants. Based on this evidence, hotel operators need to understand in depth, or be more alert to the needs and demands of these groups of tourists pertaining to food. Besides Western and local food, the hotel operators should offer at least three or four of the most popular items of Arab cuisine such as Shawarma, Kebab, falafel, Shish Biryani on the menu, or have an Arab food promotion especially in the peak season when most of these tourists are visiting Malaysia. In line with this notion, some hotels in Kuala Lumpur have taken the initiative in incorporating a few Arab food items in the menu. They in fact hire cooks and chefs from the Middle East during the peak season just to cater to the Arab markets. This smart move has directly encouraged in-house Arab guests to patronize the restaurant and thus increase hotel revenue. In addition, since most of the traveling companions among the Arab tourists were family and children, it would better to include some children's food in the menu.

In relation to Arab tourists' preferences on front office attributes upon arrival at the hotel, the findings indicate that the majority of Arab tourists preferred to have fast check in, friendly and personalized services and courtesy from bellmen and receptionists. This requirement is, in fact in line with what has been obtained by many researchers in this field. Nevertheless, the issue that needs to be addressed is related to language, and from this study it is believed that most of the Arab tourists lack proficiency and understanding of the English language. This has created communication barriers especially in dealing with hotel employees and the public. Owing to these barriers, the Arabs might perceive those hotel employees and other personnel with whom they come in contact as not friendly enough, or less attentive towards them. If these matters are taken lightly by the hotel operators, in the long term it will eventually reduce room occupancy in those particular hotels. In relation to this, since Malaysia is starting to receive a majority of Arabs tourists it is suggested that the hotel operators need to make their premises known by providing personnel who are able to speak Arabic, particularly in the customer contact areas such as the front office and the restaurant. For instance, one or two personnel could be sufficient, or they could hire someone during the peak period. In fact, travel agencies and tour operators should also consider having such services in their operations. The ability to communicate in and to understand their language can have a profound effect on the hotel image and sustain the market. In sum, providing better service could mean return visits to that particular hotel in the near future could be assured.

Although, this study has made a significant contribution to the understanding of the Arab traveling pattern and preferences in hotel restaurant food and front office attributes, there are some flaws or limitations which could lead to further research. First and foremost, a limitation relates to samples used in this study. As only five hotels in the area of Kuala Lumpur's Golden Triangle participated in this study, the overall findings certainly cannot be generalized and represent the whole country. This restriction was due to budget constraints and limited time. Therefore, if more time and a larger budget were allocated, the replication of such research could be carried out in a broader scope with more hotels throughout Malaysia involved. Further research could also be carried out in various categories of hotels throughout the country. The second limitation relates to data analysis. The descriptive analysis undertaken by the researcher has given less statistical evidence to collaborate with the findings. The result would be stronger if a scientific approach to statistics, either a parametric or non parametric procedure, were employed in the data analysis section. We suggest that future research should move towards a more statistical analysis rather just a descriptive analysis. Finally, limitations pertain to the instrument. There were only a few items used to measure tourists' preferences in hotel restaurant food and front office attributes. More attributes pertaining to these variables could be used in future research.

CONCLUSION

From the overall implications of this study, it could be concluded that a strong relationship between government, local authorities, private agencies, and hotel operators should be fostered to ensure that tourists' needs, especially in potential markets in this case Arab tourists, can be fulfilled. In other words, all the above-mentioned bodies should support one other to improve all types of services provided to the tourists. Failure to develop such a unity of approach would mean that the intention of the central government to see Malaysia as a world famous tourist destination, as well as other missions cannot be achieved.

KEYWORDS

- **Arab tourists**
- **Food and beverages**
- **Front office**
- **Hotel management**
- **Preferences**
- **Traveling pattern**

Chapter 18

Problems in Developing Bun Festival Tourism in Hong Kong

Matthew M. Chew

INTRODUCTION

The objective of this study is to discuss on tourism and local development via evaluating an ambivalent case of traditional festival revival and tourism development in Hong Kong: Bun Festival tourism in Cheung Chau Island. The importance of this study is to put into relief the impact of "cultural sustainability"-an evaluative factor that is very insufficiently emphasized and theorized in present critical studies of tourism development. I will show although the most often mobilized critiques against heritage tourism development, as well as cultural inauthenticity, commercialization, deficient in local economic development, and local disempowerment, which can be applied to the case of the Bun Festival tourism, particular social circumstances weaken the force of these critiques in the Hong Kong case. In Hong Kong critical commentators are not entirely against it. Many inhabitants of the Cheung Chau Island grant the neoliberal direction of current tourist development and derive economic benefits from it. Neoliberal exploitation of heritage tourism resources threatens the cultural sustainability of historically rooted local practices of the Bun Festival and in turn threatens the viability of Bun Festival tourism in the long run. This revise will also point to facts and opinion that bare a serious and neglected problem in Bun Festival tourism.

The relationship between tourism and local development is one of the most debated issues in tourism studies. Some implicitly assume that when tourism generates wealth, that wealth will gradually promote development of local places and trickle down to local residents. Critical scholars of tourism, however, doubt that tourism development, especially in its current neoliberal forms, can bring about genuine and sustainable development for localities. Through numerous case studies and analyses of empirical data, they have shown that tourism often hurt localities in economic, environmental, socio-political, and cultural ways, and that the only real benefactors are often the national state and global capital (e.g., Harrison, 2001).

This study contributes to the ongoing debate on tourism and local development through evaluating an ambivalent case of tourism development based on a traditional festival revival in Hong Kong: Bun Festival tourism in Cheung Chau Island of Hong Kong (Note 1). The significance of this case is that it will put into relief the significance of "cultural sustainability"—an evaluative factor that is very insufficiently emphasized and theorized in current critical studies of tourism development (Throsby, 2007). I will illustrate that although the most often mobilized critiques against heritage tourism development—including cultural inauthenticity, commercialization, lack of local economic development, and local disempowerment—are applicable to the case of Bun Festival tourism, particular social circumstances weaken their force in the Hong Kong case. Many local residents of the Cheung Chau Island approve the neoliberal direction of tourist development and derive substantial economic benefits from it. Even critical commentators in Hong Kong are not entirely against it. This study will reveal a serious and neglected problem in Bun Festival tourism: that neoliberal exploitation of heritage tourism resources threatens the cultural sustainability of historically rooted local practices of the Bun Festival and in turn threatens the viability of Bun Festival tourism in the long run.

SOCIAL HISTORICAL CONTEXT OF BUN FESTIVAL'S REVIVAL

Since there are not yet any English language studies of the Bun Festival, I provide here a brief historical context of it as a background for analysis in the substantive parts of this essay. What is currently called in the English language as the "Bun Festival" is the "Taiping Qingjiao" (sacrificial ceremony of peace and purity) ceremony organized by the local residents of Cheung Chau Island in Hong Kong (Choi 2002, 2007). There are similar "Dajiao" (Daoist sacrificial ceremony) festivals in other parts of Southern China and Taiwan, but that of Cheung Chau is currently one of the most well-known one because it features exotic and spectacular elements such as the Bun Scramble event. The mythic origins of Bun Festival of Cheung Chau Island was that it started over 200 years ago when the gods helped local people to survive either a plague or a group of vicious pirates. The Bun Festival currently takes place in early May each year and lasts for 5 consecutive days. A long list of activities take place in the 5 days. Aside from the two biggest tourist attractions—the Bun Scramble and the Floating Children Parade—there are also other parades, street cleansing, burning of paper effigies, lion and dragon dances, vegetarian meals, Cantonese opera, and other activities that tourists can watch.

The term "Bun Festival" was inspired by the steamed buns used in the Bun Scramble event. The Bun Scramble features competitors (who used to be exclusively local residents of Cheung Chau Island) racing upward along 60-feet bamboo tower covered with thousands of steamed buns in order to snatch the bun on the very top of the tower. In 1978, more than 100 people were injured when one of the bun towers collapsed during the race. The government banned the Bun Scramble event after that incident. In the late 1990s, the Island's local tourist revenue dwindled sharply under a confluence of factors including the Asian Financial Crisis and the Island's turning into a notorious suicide spot for Hong Kongers. In 2003, Taiping Qingjiao happened to become the first local festival to occur immediately after the SARS epidemic subsided in Hong Kong. It gained great success as citizens visited the Festival to relax after experiencing the threat of the lethal epidemic for months. Because of the Festival's success in 2003, local leaders of Cheung Chau Island negotiated with the government to revive the Bun Scramble event. The Hong Kong government, which completely embraces neoliberal discourses regarding tourism development, promptly accepted the proposal and subsequently tried to construct the Festival into one of Hong Kong's cultural tourist attractions. In 2005, the Bun Scramble was revived and the tourism discourses on Hong Kong started to market it as the centerpiece of the Festival (Chiu and Tang, 2005). The Festival has been attracting between 40,000 and 50,000 of domestic and international tourist visits to the Cheung Chau Island each year since 2004 (Hui, 2004).

CULTURAL AUTHENTICITY

Cultural and heritage tourism in developing localities tends to be plagued by the problem of inauthenticity. In the commercialized marketing of a local place, its cultural tradition, artifacts, architecture, people, and commodities, the imperative of cultural authenticity often is de-emphasized for the purposes of expedience and cost-effectiveness. Additionally, inauthentic cultural products are manufactured in order to attract the largest number of tourists to consume a locality's culture. This inauthenticity can undermine a locality's heritage directly and indirectly; it displaces the authentic heritage tradition, misinforms tourists, and trivializes cultural differences.

Similar to other cases of heritage tourism, Bun Festival tourism reproduces numerous components of its heritage in distorted and inauthentic ways. A controversial example of its inauthentic cultural reproduction involves the buns used in the Bun Scramble. In the past, edible steamed buns made of flour were stacked on bamboo poles to constitute bun towers. Since 2007, the government and local elites agreed to use plastic buns instead of real, edible ones. The plastic bun, which was subsequently named "pingan bao" (bun of peace), came to be successfully promoted as the talisman and trademark image of the Bun Festival. The plastic buns used on the bun towers were given as souvenirs to tourists. And a wide range of souvenirs themed with image of bun of peace are designed, manufactured, and sold to tourists. There was a small scale public debate in Hong Kong surrounding the adoption of plastic buns (Choi, 2007; Fung, 2007; Kwan, 2008; Lee, 2007). Critical commentators especially point to the irony and sacrilege in the elevating of a recently invented artifact (the plastic bun) into the trademark of the traditional festival.

Another example of cultural inauthenticity is the sanitization and sportification of the Bun Scramble event. Although less discussed by the public than the issue of plastic buns, this example is no less illustrative. The Bun Scramble, at least during its past few decades of existence, performed a social function beyond its religious ritual role. It constituted an arena of competition among different major clans and secret society groups on Cheung Chau Island. These different groups showed off their bodily strength, which in turn correlates to social power in the semi-underworld environment of the Island. The scramble for the top bun was a test of the muscle power of each group and a struggle for social power among the groups (Choi, 2002; Leung, 2007). This social function of the Bun Scramble is not particular conducive to promoting tourism, however. Moreover, its partial connections to organized crime and underground societies could tarnish the civilized image of Hong Kong and the administrative authority of the Hong Kong government. That is why the Bun Scramble has been increasingly reconceived and re-organized as a sports event after its revival in 2005. Participation of the Scramble is widened to the Hong Kong public and international community of sport lovers. The event is reported and televised in the news. Strict safety standards are implemented in the building of towers. For example, a steel structure substituted the traditional bamboo structure since 2005. The Bun Scramble is being marketed to the international public as a unique, ethnic kind of rock climbing sport. The event is thoroughly sanitized: with global participants and international tourist spectatorship, it can no longer function as a competitive arena among clan factions and local secret societies.

The expedient transformation of steamed buns into plastic buns and the sportification of the Bun Scramble are doubtlessly a manifestation of the general problem of cultural inauthenticity observable in tourism development across the globe. They are different, however, from the worst cases of cultural inauthenticity in that there are tenable arguments that justify them. The use of plastic buns is more environmental friendly, hygienic, and economical (to the local community) than real, edible ones. Using a great deal of food for props is wasteful. Very few participants and tourists would want to eat the buns after the Scramble. This is not simply because steamed buns without fillings are unremarkable staple food that is seldom eaten in contemporary Hong Kong. The buns used in the event have to be made in advance and hence are a few days old when the Bun Scramble activities conclude. Moreover, in rainy and humid weather, the buns can go moldy, decompose, and fall off the bun tower. It happened once and the local festival committee had to spend extra money to purchase new buns to replace them. As the Festival and the Bun Scramble event grew, the number of buns required and the money needed to purchase them also increased. It has already reached a point where getting sufficient funding to purchase buns for the bun towers became a heavy burden on the local festival committee. Government funding for the Bun Festival remain very limited—the amount (100,000 Hong Kong dollars; USD 1 = HKD 7.8) is not even enough for purchasing steamed buns for the three bun towers. Plastic buns provide a solution to many of the problems that edible buns cause. Plastic buns are immune to weather changes. They cost two times more than edible buns but because they can be reused for several years at least, they are more affordable in the long run. That is why many local residents, local businesses, and local festival organizers gladly joined hands with the government to make the switch to plastic buns despite its deviation from traditional practices (Chan, 2007).

The sportification and sanitization of the Bun Scramble was in practice motivated by neoliberal and governance imperatives more than anything else (Sofield and Sivan, 2003). However, there are three reasons that compel local people and critics to tolerate if not support the transformation. The first reason to tolerate the present form of sportification and sanitization is its abandonment of the social exclusionary structure of the previous form. Women were informally excluded from the event. Outsiders, including Hong Kong citizens who were not from the Cheung Chau Island and foreign visitors, were also excluded. Since 2005, the Bun Scramble event has become formally opened to both groups (Editorial, 2005).

The second reason to tolerate sportification and sanitization is that the social competitive function of the original event has already become less meaningful to natives of the Island in the contemporary period. The Island was much more socio-political isolated from Hong Kong a few decades ago than now. Dominant local clans and underground societies indeed enjoy a great deal of socio-political control over the Island's residents. But historical social factors have already undermined the control of clans and underground societies over the Island. They include globalization, advanced communicative technologies, demographic changes of the Island (a small influx of new non-local residents and out-migration of young natives), a post-Handover government that is less tolerant of alternative socio-political organizations, and local business efforts to develop the Island into a domestic tourist spot in the past 2 decades. The contemporary socio-political landscape of the Island renders the local competitive function of the event obsolete and anachronistic. It is likely that even without government imperative and policy intervention, the event would be still be transformed in a direction that is similar to present changes as its original local socio-political function fades.

The third reason to tolerate sportification and sanitization involves the personal safety of participants of the Bun Scramble event. When the event functioned primarily as an arena of local factional competition in the past, injury of participants was not a problem to any parties. Because the Scramble was supposed to be a display of bodily power, masculinity, and kung-fu expertise of the participants, it was against participants' own interest to complain about injuries incurred in the event. It also made no sense to sue the organizers if someone was hurt because most participants were connected to the organizing committee. When the Scramble is opened up to participants other than local residents, liabilities increased and safety precautions had to become stricter. The local community has become the host rather than the sole consumer of the Scramble event. Injured outsider participants—who did not join the event to war against any local factions—have no reason to withhold criticism or lawsuits against the event if their injury was caused by the organizers' neglect.

COMMERCIALIZATION, COMMODIFICATION, AND THEIR LOCAL ECONOMIC IMPACTS

Local tourism development in the contemporary world always involves commercialization and commodification; neoliberal directions of local tourism development that the Hong Kong government pursues encourage rampant commercialization and commodification. Local cultural heritage, services, local spaces, community relations, and anything that can be made to create economic profit become targets of commercialization. In the few years after the Bun Festival was targeted as a focus of tourism development, commercialization has already become very salient and commodifying processes are already powerfully re-shaping the contents of the Festival. I will analyze an example of these processes and then assess local economic impacts of commercialization and commodification.

Apart from the spectacular Bun Scramble event, the most widely reported aspect of the Bun Festival in the domestic news of Hong Kong is it souvenir products. Numerous souvenir products have been designed to take advantage of Bun Festival tourism since 2005. They include cushions, wallets, t-shirts, fans, edible bun gift sets, key holders, mobile phone accessories, and other gadgets themed in the form of the Bun, the talisman of the Festival (Chan, 2008). Some of the products, such as "Bun-Man" dolls and electronic game pens, are innovative in terms of design but glaringly irrelevant to the Festival. But disneyization of the Bun Festival cannot do without the production and consumption of such themed and merchandized goods though

(Bryman, 2004). Similar to Disneyland, Cheung Chou Island during the Bun Festival offer themed events, themed goods, and themed food. To the majority of domestic tourists, shopping for such products constitutes the only concrete experience of participating in—instead of being a simple spectator of—the Bun Festival.

The fact that innovative, lucrative, and themed souvenir products are generated for a local tourist spot is nothing new or unusual. Similar processes can be observed elsewhere in the world. But the speed with which this process took shape and became established in the case of the Bun Festival is noteworthy. In only 3 years of time, a large product range is produced and well known brand names were established on the basis of these goods. The production of these souvenirs is organized by small businessmen, some of whom are natives of the Island. In popular media discourses, emergence of these products are portrayed entirely in neoliberal narratives—small entrepreneurs successfully harnessing creativity and innovative instincts to generate wealth. The earliest and most commercially successful entrant to this market was Studio 8.5 and it is praised in these terms (Wu, 2007). One of Studio 8.5's three owners is a native of Cheung Chau who resided in the Island until he was 19 years old (Anon, 2007a). The company built up its brand by selling cushions and other well-designed souvenirs products in 2006. By 2009, it is selling a larger range of souvenirs, steamed buns, and specialized Cheung Chou food products including shrimp paste. Another successful brandname, "Mr Bun", is founded by a native born artist who sells t-shirts.

The distribution of souvenirs relied on retail shops and flea market stalls opened in the duration of the Festival. Many of the souvenir products are retailed through consignment terms—Hong Kong producers supplying the products and the Island's local retailers providing retail space and service. Powerful players such as Studio 8.5 set up their own flea market stalls to sell their products, however. Most local retail shops and restaurants are run by locals but most flea market stalls are not.

The previous example illustrates that commercialization is progressing at a fast pace in Bun Festival tourism. Commercialization can hurt cultural authenticity. The inundation of tourists' festival experience with bun-themed souvenirs and non-traditional food products clearly undermine cultural authenticity. But because cultural authenticity is different to measure and critique of cultural inauthenticity has its own theoretical problems, critics of commercialization often focus on another important problem brought about by commercialization: whether commercialization is achieving its major positive mission in tourism development—the support of the local economy and enrichment of local residents. In the Bun Festival case as well as others, a central factor to answering this question is whether the profits resulted from commercialization flow largely to corporations outside the locality or to local entrepreneurs and residents.

Currently, most of the retail shops, motels, and restaurants are locally owned. Many motels witness full house or substantial occupancy increases during the period of the Festival (Hao, 2009; Ng, 2008). Additionally, hotel operators outside of the Island cannot easily encroach on this market. Restaurants and food shops greatly benefited from the 50,000-strong tourist traffic. The leading local bakery, Kwok Kam Kee Cake Shop, sell approximately 70,000 buns and gained 420,000 Hong Kong dollars (USD 1 = HKD 7.8) of revenue during the Festival period. Kwok, the owner, thinks that competition from the outside does not pose a challenge to his business (Anon, 2008a). Food businesses from outside the Island are devising different plans to encroach on the Bun Festival food market and share the profits. But they have to compromise with local business elites in order to achieve this. For example, Studio 8.5 (partly owned by a Cheung Chau native) has to made deals with local businesses and back off from the bun market. Instead it will focus on non-traditional foods and promote specialized dried foods produced by local residents (Anon, 2008b). The McDonald's restaurant on the Island also sells vegetarian food in order to theme itself, attract tourist consumption, and pay respect to local practices.

The making and retailing of souvenir goods is the area which businesses from outside the Island can encroach on the market without much local elite interference. A significant part of the merchandize has to be distributed to tourists through local retail shops in the Festival duration. But non-local business can also set up independent flea market stalls—which are permitted and organized by the Hong Kong government—to sell their ware (Anon, 2007b). Studio 8.5 is said to have made over HKD 100,000 of profits this way in 2007's Festival duration (Fat, 2008). Studio 8.5 is also selling Bun Festival souvenirs and themed food products from the Island in retail outlets across Hong Kong (i.e., outside of Cheung Chou Island) all year long. By doing this, it on the one hand drains revenues from the Island's tourist business and on the other hand helps to market the Island's produce and the Island to a broader consumer base. Although businesses from outside Cheung Chau Island are sharing the profits generated by the Festival, they have not been able to suppress local businesses and are not likely to be able to do so in the near future. Local entrepreneurs from the Island are as knowledgeable as others Hong Konger about running small business. Moreover, they are well positioned geographically and politically to capture the economic profits generated by the Festival.

Total expenses required by the Festival amounted to approximately HKD 1,300,000 each year in the past few years (Chan, 2008). Government subsidy was around HKD 100,000 per year. Local residents, businesses, and elites had to spend HKD 1,200,000 each year to cover the difference; gifts from commercial sponsors amounted to around HKD 200,000 in 2008 (Kwan, 2008). This means local businesses have to make at least a million HKD in profits in order to turn the Festival into an independently profitable event. While no detailed and reliable statistics of profit figures of local business are available, the Festival is likely to be independently profitable to locals. Kwok Kam Kee alone is booking over HKD 200,000 of profits and the tiny operation of Mr. Bun made the local artist around HKD 50,000 (Anon, 2007b). Four thousand electronic game pens were sold in 2007, making the local businessman approximately HKD 40,000 in profits (Yeung and Chik, 2008). Each medium sized local restaurant can earn around HKD 6-70,000 of revenue per day in the peak days of the Festival (Yeung and Chik, 2008). Added to these the profits of local motel operators and restaurants, the total profits of the Festival duration are likely to exceed a million Hong Kong dollars.

LOCAL DISEMPOWERMENT OR EMPOWERMENT?

From the perspective of local residents affected by festival and heritage tourism, cultural authenticity, and commercialization may not be the most relevant or urgent problematic (Hampton, 2005). Instead, they may care more about whether tourism development is empowering or disempowering them (Cole, 2007). However, because empowerment involves multiple dimensions including the economic, the social, the political, and the self, it is not often easy to measure the local empowerment impact of tourism development. The case of Bun Festival tourism illustrates this complexity.

Viewed from a political angle, the local residents of Cheung Chau Island were not particularly empowered by Bun Festival's revival and tourism. They may actually have been disempowered by it. In the course of government orchestration of the Festival's revival and subsequent development, the reach of the state is concretely extended. Decisions regarding details of the Bun Festival used to be relatively autonomously decided by the local festival committee, but they can be compromised by government imperatives and considerations in the present. For example, to facilitate and simplify the police's work of keeping order during the Festival duration, historical routes of parades have to change and certain local areas are designated as restricted zones. To minimize the liability of the Floating Children Parade, the government pressured the organizers to spend an exorbitant amount of money on buying insurance for the floating children performers. The sanitization of the Bun Scramble and other aspects of the Festival also reflects the undermining of local self-governance and extension of state power. Of course, the government does not always manage to have its way in its formal and informal negotiations with local residents. For example, when the government wanted to reschedule the Bun Scramble event to the daytime to make it more convenient for governance and more user-friendly to tourists, the local festival committee adamantly refused to deviate from the historical practice of starting the event at midnight. The bureaucrats eventually had to back down. On the whole, however, power being ceded to the state from the local elite seems to be the main trend.

Viewed in social terms, whether there is local empowerment or local disempowerment is also unclear. Social integration and identity forging are two of the major social functions of traditional festivals. The revival of the Bun Festival contributes to achieving these two goals for the local community. The subsequent development of the Festival into a widely participated and news worthy event could have weakened the social integration function to some extent. The presence of too many outsiders, the strong need to put on a good show for tourist-spectators, and rampant commercial activities tend to distract from intra-community social bonding. Yet these new circumstances can also contribute to the identity forging function. Local identities are often strengthened by heightened outsider attention and symbolic boundary construction between locals and outsiders.

Viewed from the economic perspective, however, Bun Festival tourism has unmistakably promoted local empowerment. A significant part of the economic profits of the Bun Festival are reaped by local businessmen, as discussed in the previous section. The economic dimension of local empowerment complicates the overall picture of local empowerment in the Bun Festival case by a great deal. This complexity may be explicated through a stakeholder analysis. The major stakeholders of the Festival include the Hong Kong government, local residents of Cheung Chau Island, citizens of Hong Kong, domestic (Hong Kong) tourists of the Festival, and international tourists. In typical cases of heritage tourism development, each stakeholder has a different set of interests and is differently positioned so that they potentially conflict with each other on a range of issues (Ritchie and Inkari, 2006). We also expect to find such conflicts in Bun Festival tourism. For example, one would expect local residents to disagree with Hong Kong's government and citizens on certain issues regarding the Festival. For example, while local residents traditionally see the Festival as their socio-religious heritage, Hong Kong's government and citizens are gradually seeing the Festival as a profitable cultural property of Hong Kong. One expects antagonism between the host (local residents) and guests (international and domestic tourists) to be present, though it may not be very significant due to the short duration of the Festival. One would also expect casual tourists from Hong Kong to try to shape the Festival in ways that are very different from sophisticated cultural tourists from abroad.

Despite potential conflicts among these stakeholders, there exists an important consensus among the most of them. Because of this consensus, potential conflicts are greatly alleviated and many local residents feel personally empowered by festival tourism rather than disempowered by it. The consensus is the prioritization of neoliberal economic development and generation of profits above all else by Hong Kong's bureaucrats, local residents of Cheung Chau Island, citizens of Hong Kong, and domestic tourists. There are probably members of these four overlapping groups who do not prioritize neoliberal development of the Bun Festival over preserving the local heritage of the Festival, but they are a very small minority. Ranked the freest and most business-friendly economy on Earth for the past 15 consecutive years, Hong Kong is one of the most neoliberal places in the world. Financialization and real estate speculation have since the 1980s been the most common themes in the daily discourses of Hong Kongers and their mass media. Local residents of the Island live under the same discursive environment. They have also been developing their Island into a holiday resort for the young and lower-middle class since the 1980s. While Cheung Chau Island remains a relatively secluded community populated mostly by the native-born, it is also located at 90-minute's ferry ride from the busiest central business district of Hong Kong.

Only a handful of domestic critics, scholars, and journalists raised objections against the neoliberal revival of the Bun Festival. International cultural tourists, who should be disappointed by excessive neoliberal transformation of heritage, have not yet expressed any negative sentiments because Bun Festival tourism is still new. There are older local residents of the Island who view the commercialization of their festival heritage with ambivalence, but most locals do not. Becky Chan (2008), who is a native of the Island, interviewed many local residents in 2008 and found that the young, the socio-political elite, and businessmen among them largely welcomed recent transformations of the Festival and the consequences of heritage tourism. While they may not approve all changes brought about by neoliberal tourism development, they think that the financial gains from Bun Festival tourism are substantial enough to justify the undesirable socio-political changes. Many also think that the financial gains are helping to maintain heritage activities that were slowing dying anyways. These discourses show that locals of the Island, similar to other Hong Kongers and residents of developing localities, tend to strongly equate economic benefits with personal empowerment

(Oviedo-Garcia et al., 2008). Political and social empowerment is not terribly impor-tant in their agenda. That is why local residents have been very proactive in partnering with the Hong Kong government to develop the Festival and no local collective action against Bun Festival tourism has been reported.

CULTURAL SUSTAINABILITY

Environmental and ecological sustainability does not appear to be a serious problem in the case of Bun Festival tourism. The Festival's duration is sufficiently short. The Fes-tival is certainly economically sustainable as most of the major stakeholders focus on it. Social sustainability could be a problem in certain aspects, as previously discussed in association with social empowerment. However, local residents' local identities are not particularly threatened by Bun Festival tourism. The younger generations and the elite of the Island have long been exposed to urbanized, modernized, and cosmopoli-tan influences from the global city of Hong Kong.

But cultural sustainability is a real problem. It is being threatened by current ways of developing Bun Festival tourism. There are three ways that a neoliberal direction of tourism development is undermining cultural sustainability in the Bun Festival case. First, sportification, commodification, and commercialization encroach on and eclipse the heritage dimension of Bun Festival tourism. This problem overlaps to s small extent with that of cultural authenticity, except that the focus here is on the loss of historical elements of heritage rather than the loss of authenticity. This is a subtle difference. Because traditions are indeed constructed and ever-evolving, it is prob-lematic to interpret contemporary transformations of Bun Festival heritage as any less authentic than, say, the Festival's form in the 1970s. The 1970s version of the Festival was likely a greatly modified version of the early 20th century version anyhow. It is doubtful, for example, that steamed buns had been used profusely in the early 20th century when Hong Kong was less prosperous or that social competitive functions had been as prominent when the Island was much less populated. However, the cultural sustainability critique of erosion of historical heritage elements in the Festival's con-temporary form is not predicated on the critique that contemporary transformations of the Festival are inauthentic.

It is an observable and empirical fact that certain historical elements of the Bun Festival are displaced or replaced by contemporary elements. Examples include the turning of Bun Scramble into a rock-climbing sport, the wearing of contemporary cos-tume by floating children, the broad serving of modern Western foods such as cotton candy, or the proliferation of contemporary bun-themed products such as electronic game pens. One can remain entirely agnostic about the authenticity and normative status of these changes, while pointing to the practical problems they create for Bun Festival tourism in the longer run. The Bun Festival is marketed as a cultural heritage tourism event. If tourists find that its contents contain too few historical elements, they may lose interest in the Festival. The contemporary elements may well be as fun or meaningful as historical ones. But they inevitably lack the sense of exoticism, the ef-fect of local cultural immersion, and the intellectuality of historical depth—qualities that centrally appeal to cultural tourists. For example, imagine how the Bun Festival's heritage tourism can be tarnished if suggestions like that offered by the Secretary for Home Affairs, Ho Chi-ping, were implemented. Ho proposed in 2005 to stage the Bun Scramble all year round and place dolls and cakes on the bun towers in order to turn it into a tourist attraction for all seasons and also a new kind of sport (Anon, 2005). If the introduction of contemporary elements to the Festival is left completely unchecked, the status of the Bun Festival as a historical heritage tourist occasion will become culturally unsustainable in the not very distant future.

Second, commercialization, the emphasis on spectacles, and sanitization tend to homogenized tourist products. The tourist products presently offered through Bun Festival tourism are limited and not very distinctive. They include the shopping for bun-themed souvenirs, the eating of vegetarian food and steamed buns, and spectatorship of spectacular performances (the Bun Scramble, floating children, lion dances, parades, Cantonese opera, and traditional acrobatics). The Festival has a potentially much larger repertoire of tourist products to offer. Examples include the watching of religious rituals, tours of historical sites and architecture, interaction with local hosts, and participation of festival activities instead of spectatorship. Instead of developing a variety of products, bureaucratic coordinators, commercial tour organizers, and public relations discourses of the Festival focus almost exclusively on originally marginal (but entertaining) aspects of the Festival for mass tourist consumption. Perhaps the majority of tourists are satisfied with such arrangements at present. But this is only the very beginning of global marketing of the Festival. As time goes on, tourists are likely to get tired of the limited variety of non-distinctive products. This applies to mass tourists who are not highly culturally knowledgeable as well as serious cultural tourists. The refusal to branch out from the most readily profitable, mass-appealing tourist products can therefore render Bun Festival tourism culturally unsustainable in the longer run.

Third, because neoliberal tourism development places little policy weight on cultural heritage preservation and supplies minimal resources to it, the traditional know-how, technology, and historical knowledge that are required to reproduce the Festival year after year are in danger of dying out (Du Cros, 2001). It is reported that very few local residents are motivated to inherit the skill and technology of making floating children platforms and bun towers (Anon, 2006; Chan, 2008). Although a significant share of profits generated by Bun Festival tourism is channeled to local hands, they are captured mainly by the local business elite rather than the cultural producers who directly produce the cultural contents of the Festival. Of course the local business elite is informally forced by the local festival committee to contribute funds to ensure that the Festival take place yearly. However, they have no incentive to pay over the bare minimum of operating expenditures. The cultural work of making floating children platforms and of re-enacting other historical religious aspect of the Festival are supposed to be non-commercial, not-for-profit, and voluntary. But they are absolutely indispensable for the high profit parts of Bun Festival tourism—the selling of souvenirs, food, and tours. The Floating Children tradition of Yakou village in Guangdong province has been recognized as a provincial level intangible cultural heritage item by the Chinese government in 2008, for example (Ji, 2008). Similar recognition is not forthcoming in Hong Kong for Cheung Chau Island's Floating Children parade or Bun

Scramble. If the government and businesses keep the lion share of benefits without even trickling them down to cultural producers, Bun Festival tourism could become culturally unsustainable as the cultural producers and their skills die out in the future.

Cultural sustainability is admittedly difficult to define and measure (Throsby, 2001). Unlike biological or ecological damage, there is not an objective way to determine how badly the cultural basis of a certain instance of heritage tourism has been undermined. Despite that, the cultural basis of heritage tourism is similar to the natural environment of tourism in an important aspect: they are being recklessly exploited as an externality for private profit and personal consumption. In the case of Bun Festival tourism, the unsustainable exploitation of culture is led by three major stakeholders. The government provides contextual support including reductionist global tourism PR discourses and neoliberal coordination of the Festival. Local and domestic businesses supplied homogenous and fast profit oriented products. And domestic tourists supply the economic demand through consuming the Festival in a mass touristic way. The only forces aligned against culturally unsustainable exploitation of the Festival are sophisticated international cultural tourists, critical intellectuals in Hong Kong, and older local residents of the Island. Yet with major stakeholders colluding with one another to push Bun Festival tourism towards a neoliberal direction, it is difficult to envision how the development of Bun Festival tourism could be transposed to a more culturally sustainable path in the near future.

CONCLUSION

The previous analyses show that problems that are common to heritage tourism development in developing localities are present in the case of Bun Festival tourism. They include the undermining of cultural authenticity, rampant commercialization and commodification, and local disempowerment. However, I have also mobilized arguments and documented evidence to show that a critique of Bun Festival tourism based on these problems is not neither adequate nor powerful. Some of the most controversial, cultural inauthentic innovations of the current form of the Festival are found to be historical legitimate and locally orchestrated revisions of tradition, or inevitable results of introducing personal safety or social justice in the Festival. Commercialization and commodification, though rampant, are found to have economically benefited local residents more than corporations from outside the Island. Local residents, generally embracing the neoliberal ideology of Hong Kong society, think the economic benefits they are gaining from the commercialized and commodified Bun Festival largely justify their negative consequences. Local residents also feel sufficiently empowered by economic profits even though they are political and social disempowered in moderate ways.

I suggest that a more convincing critique of the neoliberal orientation of Bun Festival tourism can be launched in term of cultural sustainability. The neoliberal development policies, management, and marketing discourses of the Bun Festival encouraged three serious problems: eclipsing of the heritage dimension of heritage tourism, homogenization of tourist products, and dying out of cultural producers, knowledge, and technologies that physically reproduce the Festival year after year. These are not merely abstract, intellectual problems of legitimacy and authenticity. Their impact is practical—they can greatly lower the profitability of Bun Festival tourism. More culturally sustainable policies and management are crucial for preventing Bun Festival tourism from going into the decline phase of its lifecycle as quickly as other over-exploited heritage tourist destinations do.

KEYWORDS

- **Bun Festival**
- **Cultural authenticity**
- **Cultural commodification**
- **Cultural sustainability**
- **Festival tourism**
- **Heritage tourism**
- **Tourism development**

Chapter 19

Tourism Development in Plateau State, Nigeria

Eugene J. Aniah, E. I. Eja, Judith E. Otu, and M. A. Ushie

INTROODUCTION

The unique climate conditions of Plateau State and the numerous tourism attraction and spots has made Plateau State the home of peace and tourism and also tourist haven of Nigeria. This chapter is centered on five resorts in Plateau State such as National Museum, Jos Wildlife Park, ASSOP Falls, Pandom Wildlife Park, and Solomon Lar Amusement Park. Data for resort patronage were provided only in National Musem, Jos Wildlife Park and ASSOP Falls. The critical issue of concerned was on domestic and international patronage of tourist resort between 1996 and 2008, and the recreational facilities provided in each of the resort centers. Data were collected base on questionnaires, directly field observation and interviews. The data collected were analyzed using ANOVA and the results obtained shows that there is a significance variation in the patronage of the different resorts centers used for this study. However, the viability of tourism potentials can only strive effective in Plateau State if there is full participation of the various stakeholders in decision making process.

Almost all nations are in recent times recognizing the importance of tourism and embracing it. No wonder the world tourism organization/WTO 2000, claimed that tourism is among the fastest growing industry in the world. Tourism development had unquantifiable benefits ranging from social physical to economic gains. Socially, it promotes world peace and exposes people to new "worlds or environments" thus making participant to learn about new environments. In Nigeria, the vast tourism potentials such as table mountains beautiful landscapes, colorful folks, overwhelming serenity wildlife, waterfalls and other rich festivals, architecture, and craft has necessitated towards the existing tourism drive in the country. Today Plateau State is blessed with abundant tourism potentials, such as beaches, spectacular rock formations, hydrological bodies, wildlife and waterfall and other rich festival, architecture, and craft which has necessitated towards the existing tourism drive in the State. However, the rich tourism attractions of the State have earned her the slogan "Home of peace and tourism." Apart from this, most of the tourism potential have been converted into tourism resorts while others are still left to fallow without any conscious effort by the government and private individual towards its development.

Beside numerous factors has hindered patronage of tourist resort in Plateau State. These factors ranged from age, gender, occupation, income, and social class amongst others. Regretfully, most of the tourist resort lacks the basic facilities such as accommodation, catering, entertainment, electricity, water which are of essential to tourist and hence making them less attractive in any given location. In this regard, it should be asked if resort development is of economic important in Plateau State, what role does resort play in Plateau State? Is resort development an appropriate tool for sustainable local socio-economic development? This study addressed some of the critical issues on resort potentials, particularly as it relate to patronage and facilities provided in the various resort centers. However, two hypothesis were stated in this study, thus:

Ho: There is no significant variation in the patronage of the selected resorts.
Hi: There is significant variation in the patronage of the selected resorts.

STUDY AREA

Plateau is one of the 36 States of Nigeria. It is located in the central part of the country. It covers an area of about 3,000 square miles, at a general level of about 4,200 feet above sea level and is surrounded by high plains with altitudes ranging from 2,000 to 3,000 feet above see level. Apart from the southern margin which is both very sleep and rather regular in outline, the Plateau is bordered by an irregular margin with gentle slops. This study only covered some selected tourism resort in Plateau State.

MATERIALS AND METHODS

Five tourist resorts were used in this study. There are, Jos wildlife park, Jos National Museum, Solomon Lar Amusement park, ASSOP waterfalls, and Pandom wildlife park. Data were collected using questionnaires and participatory research method (PRM). Four hundred and seventy one (471) copies of questionnaires were administered to occupants living within the resort center using systematic sampling technique. This was to ascertain the recreational activities undertaken by visitors in each tourist resort. While, PRM was employed to obtained data based on domestic and international patronage in National museum, Jos wildlife park and ASSOP falls and facilities provided to tourist in each resort center. However, three hundred and twenty (320) household were used for this study. While two hundred and fifty (250) respondent were drawn from the (320) household sample for this study. The (250) respondent represent the sample size for this research work. Analysis of variance (ANOVA) was adopted for testing the stated hypothesis. It was used to compare the variation within and variation between groups of the resorts. Data on the level of patronage in Pandom wildlife park and Solomon Lar Amusement park were not made available.

LITERATURE REVIEW

Sustainable Tourism Development

Sustainability is one of the key-words of the 1990s. Sustainability and sustainable development were given impetus and made popular by the Brundland report (world commission on environment and development 1987). It defines sustainable development as "development that meet the needs of the present without compromising the ability of future generations to meet their own needs". Both an equity dimension (intergenerational and interrogational) and a social/psychological dimension are clearly outline by this definition the Brundland report also highlighted the "essential needs of the world's poor, to which overriding priority should be given", and "the idea of limitations imposed by the state of technology and social organization on the environment's ability to meet present and future needs" means that such development must be ecologically bearable in life long term, as well as economically viable, and ethically and socially equitable for local communities.

The principle of sustainable tourism was proposed as early as 1988 by the World Tourism Organization, with sustainable tourism envisaged as leading to management of all resources in such a way that economic, social, and aesthetic needs can he fulfilled while maintaining cultural integrity, essential ecological processes, biological diversity, and life support system. Recalling previous declarations on tourism, such as the Manila Declaration on world tourism, the Hague Declaration and the Tourism Bill of rights and tourist Code, the charter for sustainable tourism approved during the World Conference on sustainable tourism, held in Lanzarote in 1995, underlined the need to develop a kind of tourism that meets both economic expectations and environmental requirements, and respects not only the social and physical structure of its destination, but also the local population.

The concept of sustainability has a twin valence: on one hand there is the ecological aspect, that is the conservation of the natural equilibrium of all the components of the natural environment (flora, fauna, water resources, etc); on the other hand there is the anthropological aspect, which could be expressed by the persistence of enjoyment of this environment in spite of growing tourist flows.

It is obvious, at least for the economist, that there is a strong relationship between the two characteristics (ecological and anthropological) of sustainability in tourist enterprise. In fact, the degradation of weaker components of the natural environment, especially if it is irreversible, provokes, first of all, a slow down in the development of tourist activity, with substantial consequences at a social and economic level. Such a situation of backwardness and impoverishment will subsequently result in a loss of interest in conservation and good use of natural and environmental resources, which are of great interest to tourists. Added to this there is also a substantial loss even in the financial profitability of the different commercial activities concerned. According to him, internet may represent one opportunity for making and selling the product.

The Role of the Private Sector in Tourism Development

Scheyvens (2002) in analyzing the role of private sector in tourism development opines that corporate businesses can assist by providing markets, capacity building, monitoring, and micro-financing support for small, medium, and micro-enterprises. Swarbrooke (1999) agreeing with Scheyvens pointed out that the private sector seems to recognize the issues of sustainability, and to recognize the importance of the community as a stakeholder in the paradigm of successful tourism, with the more aware operators and investors understanding something about the needs and requirements of the community. The private sector is more sensitive to the market than any other stakeholder; this is of course nor surprising as private sector stakeholders are interested in financial stability, remuneration, and economic sustainability (UNWTO, 2005). According to Loannides (2002) smaller enterprises may, naturally, have the ability, interest, and spatial positioning to be more sensitive to community needs and objectives.

Godwin (2001) in assessing the role of private sector in tourism development opines that the private sector can contribute to local economic development and poverty reduction by changing the way it does business and through philanthropic activities.

He further emphasized that there are strong commercial motivations for private sector engagement in local economic development and poverty reduction, principally the creation of an enhanced product range, which adds market advantage and of a better business environment, which fosters of favorable staff attitudes, and morale. Potter (2006) agreeing with the works of Goodwin further stress that private sector can foster local socio-economic development by recruiting and training local people, procuring goods and services local and shaping local infrastructure development to include benefit for the poor. Private sector can also encourage tourists to purchase products that are complementing to the core holiday, such as handicrafts, art, local food and beverages and services such as guide services, music, and dance (UNWTO, 2005).

Singh and Dowling (2003) in their study of private sector involvement in tourism development discovered that private sector is capable to undertake joint marketing and promotion, to liberation trade in travel and tourism, to enhance cooperation in raising the quality and sustainability of tourism in any region and to ensure tourist safety and security and human resources development.

Tourism and Economic Development

Hall (2003) in his study on the socio-economic impact of tourism discovered that tourism has become a significant source of foreign exchange revenue for many countries of the world. According to him tourism activities in Maldives contributed 66.6% of the country's gross domestic product (GDP) and accounted for 65.9% of its exports, Roe and Godwin (2002) supported the works of Hall, according to their analysis, tourism industry in Vanuatu has contributed 47% of the country's GDP and 73.7% of its total export earnings. They went further to emphasize that 13 developed countries in Asia (Cambodia, Leo people's Democratic Republic and Neps), tourism accounted for more than 15% of export earnings.

Hall (1999) opines in his study of economic impact of tourism opinion that this industry has contributed to GDP as seen in the Island states of Fiji, Tonga, and Vanuatu.

He further stress that tourism alone contributed 43.5% of the total export earnings of Fiji and one third of its GDP. Other small Islands such as Tonga and Vanuatu are dependent on tourism for half or more of their export earnings. Prentice (2007) in his study opines that tourism in China has provided a substantial contribution to its GDP amounting to 13.7% in 2006. Taking full advantage of the potential of their natural and culture tourist resources, countries in the greater Mekong sub-region are benefiting from the tourism industry. He went further to stress that in 2006, tourism in Cambodia and the Lao people's Democratic Republic accounted respectively for 22.3 and 21.4% of their total export earnings and contributed 19.6 and 9.3% respectively of their GDP.

According to UNWTO (2004) tourism industry contributes significantly to the creation of employment both directly and indirectly. According to UNWTO the industry in the Asian and pacific region provide jobs for about 140 million people representing an average of 8.9% of total employment. It also emphasized that tourism employment in North-East Asia is estimated at 86 million jobs, or 10.1% of total employment. This situation is attributed main to China, where 1 out of 10 persons works in a tourism-related industry. In support of UNWTO's argument, Sharpley and Stelfer (2002) following empirical findings, indicated as part of his illustration, that in Oceania, the workforce in the tourism sector accounted for 14.5% of total employment, or 1 in every 6.9 jobs. The importance of tourism becomes more significant when the structure of the workforce in selected pacific Island economies is analyzed. For instance in 2003, 1 in every 3.2 persons was employed in the tourism sector, while in Vanuatu the ratio was 1 in every 2.4 jobs.

Richards and Hall (2003) opines that tourism industry has become a significant provider of employment in countries of the Asian and pacific region, thereby improving the economic situation of the people of those countries. In addition, revenue generated from tourism has enable Governments to allocate financial resources for improving education and health countries. They further stress that in Maldives, where tourism activity is the economic mainstay, almost 100% of the population is now literate, while the infant mortality rate has improved from 121 per 1,000 in 1977 to 38 per 1,000 in 2002 and over the same period, the average life expectancy at birth increased from 47 years to 67 years.

Table 1. Recreational activities undertaken by the visitors at the resort.

Activity(S)	No. of Patrons	Percentage
Rock climbing	40	7
Sight seeing	54	9
Swimming	76	13
Game viewing	123	21
Horse riding	52	9
Relaxation/drinking	126	22
Total	**471**	

Field work 2008.

RESEARCH FINDINGS

Table 1 gives the summary of some of the recreational activities which the tourist engaged in at the various resorts sampled.

The Table 1 reveals that majority of the visitors are engage in relaxation/drinking a value 27% compare to other variables with values rock climbing 7% swimming 13% game viewing 21% horse riding 9% and sight seeing 22% respectively.

Table 2 shows the level of domestic and international tourist of the national museum resort between 1996 to 2008. The data obtain indicate a high level of domestic tourist patronized in the National Museum compared with international tourist.

The highest levels of patronage of the resorts were recorded in 2003, while 2001 recorded the lowest patronage. The natural museum resort weakness a drastic fluctuation interms of domestic and international patronage.

Table 2. Levels of patronage of domestic and international tourists in national museum resort (1996–2008).

Year	Tourists		Total
	Domestic	International	
1996	75,323	2,546	77,869
1997	76,767	2,979	79,772
1998	67,000	4,0378	71,038
1999	50,213	3,139	537,551
2000	131,457	6,100	137,551
2001	7,082	7,032	14,114
2002	202,727	5,382	208,109
2003	275,809	5,124	280,933
2004	273,012	3,397	276,409
2005	241,871	3,544	245,415
2006	3,691	417	3,244
2007	3980	551	3,391
2008	4085	653	3,493

Source: Management of the resort (2008).

Furthermore, levels of patronage of domestic and international tourist in Jos wild life park resort were obtained.

Table 3. Levels of patronage of domestic and international tourists to Jos wildlife park resort (1996–2008).

Year	Tourists		Total
	Domestic	International	
1996	22,340	767	23,107
1997	28,701	811	29,512
1998	32,589	672	33,260
1999	101,094	806	101,900
2000	65,242	581	65,823
2001	83,917	737	84,654
2002	58,327	409	58,736
2003	90,371	607	90,978
2004	103,923	1,164	10,5087
2005	104,977	2,204	10,718
2006	3,691	417	3,244
2007	3938	551	3,391
2008	4085	653	3,493

Source: Management of the resort (2008).

Table 3 represents annual increase in the patronage of Jos wild life park. International tourists were fewer than domestic tourist. Table 3 reveals that there is a fluctuation in terms of domestic and international tourist arrival to Jos wildlife between 1998 and 2003. This could be due to the religious crises which almost engulfs the entire Plateau State. With regards to ASSOP fall resort. Table 4 shows the level of patronage of domestic and international tourists to ASSOP falls resort.

Comparatively, ASSOP falls recorded the least patronage over the 13 years period covered in this study. The annual totals are relatively low. The domestic patronage shows steady increases from over 8,000 in 1996 to cover 25,000 in 2003. Conversely, the number of international tourists dwindled over the years, but interesting reached the peak of over 4,000 in 2001 when the domestic tourists dropped to the least (3,407) in the same 2001, due to religious crises. However, in other to verify the data collected in the field, the stated hypothesis which was stated as there is no variation in the patronage of the selected resorts was tested and the calculated value of 99.49 was obtained. This result shows that there is significant variation in the level of patronage of the different resorts: Nevertheless, Table 5 shows the facilities provided by respective resorts in the study area.

Tables 5 shows that patronage of any resort is a function of facilities provided. It also reveals that accommodation is the major facilities provided by the Natural museum and Pandam Wildlife Parks with values 67 and 45 respectively.

Table 4. Levels of patronage of domestic and international tourist to ASSOP falls resort (1996–2008).

Year	Tourists		Total
	Domestic	International	
1996	8,245	1,086	10,417
1997	8,413	1,679	10,092
1998	7,903	2,158	1,006
1999	9,587	1,741	11,328
2000	10,898	1,051	11,949
2001	3,490	4,980	8,470
2002	20,853	216	21,069
2003	23,966	101	24,067
2004	21,982	213	22,191
2005	25,050	315	25,365
2006	3,691	417	3,244
2007	3938	551	3,391
2008	4085	653	3,493

Source: Management of the resort (2008).

Table 5. Facilities provided at the resorts.

Facilities	National	Jos	ASSOP	Pandam	Solomon Lar
Library	1	-	-	-	-
Auditorium/hall	1	-	-	1	1
Parking space	3	1	1	8	1
Restaurant/bar	2	-	1	-	1
Conference room	1	-	-	1	-
Open air theater	1	-	1	-	-
Children playing ground	1	-	1	-	1
Accommodation	67	-	-	45	7
Water supply	7	1	1	-	-
Public convenient	6	-	-	4	-
Picnic area	-	-	1	5	-
Canoe	-	-	1	5	-
Nature museum/museum	1	1	-	1	3
Café	-	-	-	-	-
Shopping mail	-	-	-	-	4
Swimming pool	-	-	-	-	1
Lawn tennis court	-	-	-	-	1
Artificial lake	-	-	-	1	1

Source: Field work (2008).

CONCLUSION

This case study shows that Plateau State is endowed with great tourism potential which can be developed to ensure sustainability and socio-economic empowerment of the local people. Consequently, there is a high percentage of patronage by domestic tourist as compared to international tourist over the years. Therefore, if tourism is to contribute to sustainable economic development in Plateau State, a strategy centered on expansion of local empowerment and self employment, development of partnership amongst public and private sectors, improving social and cultural impacts, increasing local access to infrastructure and services provided for tourist must be advocated.

KEYWORDS

- **Destination**
- **Patronage**
- **Resort**
- **Sustainable**
- **Tourism**

Chapter 20

Recreational Valuation of a Natural Forest Park

Sohrabi Saraj B., Yachkaschi A., Oladi D., Fard Teimouri S., and Latifi H.

INTRODUCTION

One of the most important benefits of a forest, which can be considered over the revenue yielded from timber and other wood based products, is the recreational benefits for visitors. Considering the novelty and necessity of evaluating bio-environmental economics of forest parks in developing countries such as Iran, the present study will focus on the evaluation of the willingness to pay (WTP) for a northern Iranian Forest park (Abbas Abad-Behshahr as a case study) utilizing one of the worldwide common methods of evaluation (travel cost method). Based on the method, the park was considered as the center of the fivefold region as concentric circles. The number of visitors was determined using questionnaires and the park's value was determined by estimation of the visitors access cost using travel cost method (here after called TCM). Furthermore, the economic value extracted timber products of the neighboring forestry plan was reckoned. The calculated factor was then compared to the economic value of the park. As a result, the park's recreational value was judged to be much more than produced timber values. Therefore, it is concluded that the unparalleled natural, historical, and bio-environmental values of the park would be preserved by planning an appropriate and well-programmed management system, considering the unique conditions of the Park. Thus, it can fulfill the recreational requirements of the people in the local/national scale.

Forests feature so many values. They act as good reservoir for both wildlife and forest biodiversity among other benefits (Mugambi et al., 2006). Recreation in natural environments has been extensively increased during recent decades, following the increasing rate of the city residence process. Thus, the recreational activities now play a vital role in the public lifestyle. Therefore, equipping the natural recreational venues together with optimizing their usage has been regarded as one of the important duties of the local management.

The Iranian forest parks, located over a wide range of climatic and natural conditions all across the country, are basically regarded as resources containing unique recreational potentials. The public would have different reactions to the parks since none of the regions in which the parks are located show the same condition. Moreover, people have different characteristics according to the factors such as their age, income rate, favors, and so forth. Ecotourism and recreation have interactive relations with several other fields like psychology, sociology, anthropology, geography, and additionally environmental economy (Oladi, 2005). Nevertheless, the value and inclination of the recreational site's usage would be obtained using some worldwide evaluation methods. Regarding the other applications of the forested sites, it is of a great concern that the concept of forest recreational centers be overcome by the assumption of the land's agricultural or timber productivity, or creation of other alternative land uses. Hence, evaluation of recreational sites is one of the tasks that would lead the managers to the economic value of these regions and is due to persuade them to equip the sites.

By assessment of forest parks and recreational areas which comes up to presenting the exact and accurate information and statistics, the potential land use change of the parks into other land uses can finally be avoided. Existence of several methods of evaluating the recreational values would clarify the importance of performing such a process. One method for estimating some of the non-market benefits is the TCM. This tool estimates ecotourism benefits of a protected area based upon observed travel expenses by visitors to the area (Mankhau and Lober, 1996).

Various methods have been proposed so far to evaluate recreational regions and quantify the WTP. The application of methods depends on the regional condition and the factors each method apply. (Hotelling, 1947) stated that the highest travel cost is considered to be the recreational value. Unlike the prices for private goods in efficient markets, the price of some goods, such as ecotourism, if measured only by direct costs such as entrance fees to parks, may not reflect the degree to which these goods are valued. This inaccurate pricing can result in lost revenue or underestimation of the importance of the good. One solution to this problem is to estimate visitors' WTP for the good by using TCM. This model provides an estimate of the benefit individuals received from visiting a site by observing their travel-related expenses (Clawson and Knetsch, 1966; Dixon and Sherman, 1991; Garrod, and Willis, 1992; Krutilla, and Fisher, 1975).

Clawson's study (1959) was carried out on the estimation of the relationship between the visitors and their residential area's distance from the park. Nowadays, this method is one of the most common ways of evaluating the recreational values, well-known as the TCM, which has been widely used for valuing nature-based recreation (Adamowicz, 1994; Adamowicz et al., 1994; Bell and Leeworthy, 1990; Brown and Mendelsohn, 1984; Caulkins et al., 1986; Englin and Mendelsohn, 1991; Fletcher et al., 1990; Garrod and Willis, 1992; Mankhaus and Lober, 1996; Mugambi, 2006; Offenbach and Goodwin, 1994; Shrestha, 2007; Willis, 1991).

Hanley (1989) used the TCM and contingent valuation method (CVM—a method based on creating a virtual market to evaluate non-market goods and services) in the Queen Elizabeth Park (Scotland). The study showed that the WTP in TCM is less than the one obtained of CVM. However, he did not identify which one is more acceptable. Fix and Loomis (1998) applied TCM and CVM for evaluation of non-market facilities in the American Biking Mountains as the study area. They consequently calculated 235 and 206 USD for each hectare by the use of CVM and TCM, respectively. The results clarified that the amount of WTP has been shown slightly more in CVM, compared to TCM.

Rosenberger (1999) carried out a research in recreational regions of Rocky Mountains (USA) utilizing a set of empirical studies amongst various methods including CVM (where some structural questions would be used for the evaluation), hedonic pricing method (HPM—evaluation of goods, services, or non-marketable services based on a virtual market), and TCM. An extended combination was obtained during the study and recreational travels were taken into account as "the real travels for the first time". It also stated natural sources as "the most important factor for tourist attraction".

However, some studies such as Hanley et al. (1998) reported that methods like Choice experiments have important advantages over other environmental valuation methods, such as CVM and TCM. In addition to this, Common et al. (1999) remark that TCM is not able to evaluate the entire economic value of a region. Nevertheless, it is the best method to study the changes in WTP in a recreational site.

In Iran, Yachkaschi (1975) carried out an evaluation process of recreational sites for the first time. He evaluated Si-Sangan forest Park (located in central Mazandaran, northern Iran) using TCM, applying some evaluation methods. The study led to some suggestions for further extension the forest park. Majnounian (1977) calculated the rate of 369,000 Rials (about 434 USD) as the recreational value of Tehran forest Park (in case of having an additional entrance fee of 5 Rials), based on the former study. Arbab (2003), however, suggested that CVM should not be used in developing countries. According to Cooper (2000), TCM is "the best method of evaluating and determining WTP of recreational regions." The TCM has been widely proposed for evaluating non-market goods and/or services. It has been especially used for evaluating recreational sites in Iran. Hence, the main objective of this study was to use TCM to empirically estimate the value of ecotourism benefits of Abbas Abad forest park, as one of the most potentially—hedonic forest parks across the region.

MATERIALS AND METHODS

Study Area

The study site is Abbas Abad, a 138 ha forest park located near Behshahr town in Mazandaran Province, northern Iran ($36° 39' 50^2$ to $36° 47' 32^2$ N and $53° 36' 00^2$ to $53° 42' 40^2$ E—Figure 1). The temperature averages 15.6°C, the annual precipitation is over 640 mm, and the average altitude is 450–530 m above sea level.

Abbas Abad forest Park is one of the Mazandaran's most significant recreational places which have been a temporal host for numerous visitors coming from all over the country. The area's importance is mainly because of its special historical and natural situation. The park, in which a set of wonderful natural and artificial landscapes including a historical dam and a ruin bathroom (belonging to the first King Abbas of Safavid's dynasty) exist, is situated originally in a portion of old-growth northern forests of Iran, composed mainly of broadleaf species such as *Fagus orientalis* Lipsky., *Carpinus betulus* L., *Quercus castaneifolia* C.A. Mey., *Parrotia persica* C.A. Mey., and some more. The forests have always been considered as a recreational place for the civilians who aim to use the natural features of such venues in the best way. It is remarkable that Abbas Abad management plan has been introduced as one of 10 superior Recreational plans by the Cultural Heritage and Recreation organization (CHRO) of Mazandaran Province (Iran). In the near future, probable development and equipment of the park might lead it to become one of the most important recreational centers in the region.

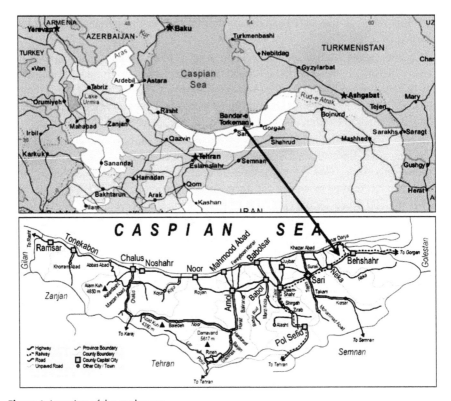

Figure 1. Location of the study area.

There are a number of techniques developed by economists which can be used to assess the economic benefits generated by wilderness recreation. Two prominent methods are the TCM and the CVM.

The TCM, as stated above, has undergone slight modifications from 1947 so far, and has been completed more. This method had already been called "Clawson's Method," but it is now well known as "TCM" worldwide. The TCM is used to estimate the value of recreational benefits generated by ecosystems. It assumes that the value of the site or its recreational services is reflected in how much people are willing to pay to get there. It is referred to as a "revealed preference" method, because it uses actual behavior and choices to infer values. Thus, peoples' preferences are revealed by their choices.

Two variations of the TCM include:

- Simple Zonal TCM, using mostly secondary data, with some simple data collected from visitors.
- Individual TCM, using a more detailed survey of visitors.

The zonal TCM is the simplest and least expensive approach. It will estimate the value for recreational services of the site as a whole. It cannot easily be used to value a change in quality of recreation for a site, and may not consider some of the factors that may be important determinants of value.

The zonal TCM is applied by collecting information on the number of visits to the site from different distances. Because the travel and time costs will increase with distance, this information allows the researcher to calculate the number of visits "purchased" at different "prices." This information is used to construct the demand function for the site, and estimate the consumer surplus, or economic benefits, for the recreational services of the site.

The individual travel cost approach is similar to the zonal approach, but uses survey data from individual visitors in the statistical analysis, rather than data from each zone. This method thus requires more data collection and slightly more complicated analysis, but will give more precise results.

The method selected for data analysis here was a zonal TCM, which was chosen because of two main reasons. First, the existing data included all information needed for estimation of a zonal TCM, whereas the information for other valuation methods would have necessitated an expensive survey. Second, the available CHRO data base does not include observation on individual or household income.

The TCM has straightforward basic principles in which the park (study site) is chosen as the center of concentric circles (Figure 2). Then, by the use of questionnaires, it would be clarified that how many people has visited the park during a specific period. During the study, people were asked to fill the questionnaires only if they visited the park for leisure and with a recreational intention. Using this method, five regions were determined and named as A, B, C, D, and E. The regions had the radius of 20, 40, 60, 80, and 100 km from the park center, respectively. The area of each region was calculated formerly using the dot grid method at 95% accuracy.

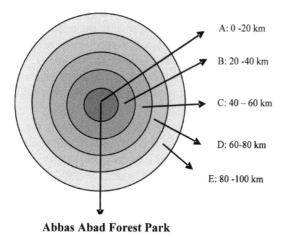

A: 0 -20 km

B: 20 -40 km

C: 40 – 60 km

D: 60-80 km

E: 80 -100 km

Abbas Abad Forest Park

Figure 2. Schematic design of TCM.

The WTP is a portion of the income rate which the consumer is due to pay to improve the welfare condition or prevent its decline. The WTP is used to demonstrate the natural resource's total value for which the consumer will pay to visit. Thus, WTP was calculated using the following formula (eqn. 1):

$$WTP = \sum_{i=1}^{n} n_i \int_{p}^{p} Z(p) \cdot dp \qquad (1)$$

where $Z(p)$ is functions of visitors' ratio (z) subtract the whole visitors divided by the whole population; p is the travel cost average; n is the different regions of main recreational site; n_i is the population of the region I; p_i is the travel cost average of each visitor in region i which rate could be decreased down to zero.

The formula has also been used to evaluate the increase or decrease of the resource value resulted from environmental quality change across the area (Arbab, 2003). The available population census (prepared in 1996 by the National Statistical Centre) was used to calculate the number of people residing inside the zones. The number of the dwellers of the five zones who visited the forest Park was calculated. Besides, the visitors who had no previous decision to visit the park were excluded in the calculation of the park visitors.

The travel cost is equal to the car depreciation rate, in addition to the consumed petrol price per km. The entire value of the Abbas Abad Park region was gained as the sum of the calculated costs belonging to the five regions.

DISCUSSION

Nature-based recreation and tourism is touted as a sustainable means to preserve natural resources while providing a diversity of economic benefits to local communities and national economies (Gossling, 1999; Wood 2002; Wunder, 2000). Usually, many factors affect the economic issues, each having a special degree of importance. Other affecting conditions should be typically considered constant when investigating a specific variable's effects. In the curve related to a recreational site's demand, so many visitors' reactions would be thus ignored to specify the relation between the cost and the amount of uses. The cost doses not solely specify the user's behavior, but it is surely the most effective factor. Clawson (1959), Yachkaschi (1975), Cooper (2000), Kavianpour and Esmaeili (2002) have already studied this topics, observing a direct relation between the cost and the number of visitors. The relation also holds true for Abbas Abad forest park.

The results of the present study showed that improving the eco-environmental sources and/or ecotourism services can have a valuable effect on the increase of the visitor's demands and the WTP in such a forest park, though other effective factors like costs, users characteristics, distance to access the park, time needed to reach the park, time needed to pass through the area, people's leisure time, amount of working hours per week, the visitor's job, the population residing in the park's region, available installations and facilities, and the landscape features actually act a role in the demand. Nevertheless, the improvement of eco-environmental resources/services can be the most significant factor which could be effective in visiting the park, in addition to the costs and users income. Accessibility of enough public transportation facilities (e.g., tele-cabin, hostels/residential venues offering required facilities) can persuade many more visitors to visit the area. This would furthermore be beneficial in improving the economic condition of the local people (residing in Behshahr and surrounding areas) as Oladi (2005) stated that main aim of the recreation is preserving natural sources and creating income sources for local societies.

RESULTS

Characteristics of Visitors

Most visitors who filled the questionnaires were male, married, and 21–30 years old. They averagely had a high school diploma degree, non-governmental careers, and average monthly income around 1,200,000–2,000,000 Rials (≈140–200 USD).

The Number of the Visitors

Some of the socio-economic characteristics of visitors are summarized in Figure 3.

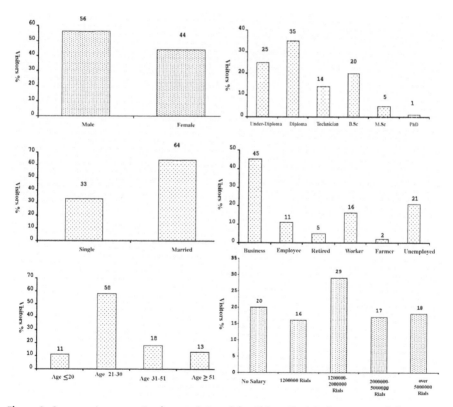

Figure 3. Some socio-economic characteristics of the Abbas Abad Park visitors. Left (from top to bottom): gender, marriage status, and age of visitors. Right (from top to bottom): educational level, main carrier categories, and level of income.

According to the results obtained from the study, 14% of the visitors have visited the park without any previous recreational intention and thus have been eliminated from the calculations. It was formerly specified that almost 908 people have visited the park during the work days and 2,146 during the weekend. Providing that totally 294 work days and 72 holidays existed in the period between summer 2004 to the end of spring 2005, the number of visitors of the Park has been around 422,000. According to the total estimated area of the Abbas Abad recreational site (nearly 138 ha), the amount of visitors ha-1 yr-1 was equal to 3,057. Realistically speaking, only 13 ha of the entire 138 ha would be intensively used by the visitors; hence, the amount would be equal to 32,400 people ha-1 yr-1. As it may be realized, the number of visitors per ha is superfluous, which can probably lead to cause potential ecological harms to the site. Yachkaschi (1975) proved that exploiting the capacities of recreational sites have led gradually to plant biodiversity decline and soil compaction in Si-Sangan forest Park. The signals of such a phenomenon have been also seen in the present study area. As a result, it seems that proper distribution of the recreational equipment across the park can decrease the rate of ecological pressure per ha, which makes more visitors able to be hosted in a wider space.

The Number of Incoming Vehicles

Some 96% of the visitors have visited the park using motorized vehicles, mostly (around 65%) using their own private vehicles. Generally speaking, a number of 143,200 vehicles have entered the park, which included 312 vehicles during the working days and 715 during holidays.

The Amount of Visitors and Distance

The relation between the number of visitors and their distance to the park is reported in Table 1. Results illustrated in the table show how many people have visited the park from the pre-determined zones. Almost 95% of visitors inhabit at most 100 km far of the park. Also, people living in region "A" are the major portion of the visitors, residing less than 20 km distant from the park. In contrast, the "E" region's population form the minimum portion the visitors. The decreasing relation between distance and visitors' rate showed a relatively high correlation coefficient (Figure 4).

Table 1. The number of visitors per region.

Region	Number of visitors (× 10000)	Percent of visitors
A	21	49
B	8.5	20
C	7.6	19
D	3	7
E	2.1	5
Total	42.2	100

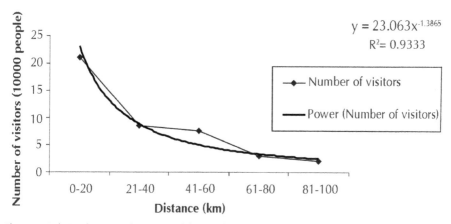

Figure 4. Relation between distance and the number of visitors.

Determining the Cost Value

In order to determine the park's cost value, the visitor's car depreciation cost should be taken into account, in addition to the petrol price. Paykan (as one of the main available family cars used widely across the country) petrol consumption is 12 l\100 km on average. Assuming that the petrol price was fixed at 800 Rials/l in 20042006 (≈0.1 USD), each car's petrol price would be 9,600 Rials (1.2 USD). If petrol and depreciation cost per km would be 224.5 Rials, the mentioned price for an average of three people (averagely carried by each vehicle) would be 75 Rials (≈0.08 USD).

The formulas considering one time visit cost, monetary park value, and final park value are as follows (eqn. 24):

$$OTVC = TCKM \cdot ATWD \qquad (2)$$
$$MPV = OTCV \cdot TV \qquad (3)$$
$$FVP = MPV \cdot NR \qquad (4)$$

where $OTVC$ is the one time visit cost; $TCKM$ is the travel cost per km; $ATWD$ is the average two-way travel distance from the visitor's home area; MPV is the Monetary Park value; TV is the total number of incoming visitors from the region; FPV is the Final Park value; NR is the number of regions.

The populations from A, B, and C regions (up to 60 km distance from the park) form the bulk of visitors, as the others visit the park occasionally passing the region. So, the cost value of the park may be calculated based on these three zone's users. The value would be then 1,266 million Rials for the entire recreational site (138 ha), 9 million per ha, and 97 million for one hectare of the central 13 ha within the site. The relation between costs and the number of visitors, showing a correlation of 0.9, is depicted in Figure 5.

As expected, the larger is the cost, the lower is the number of visitors coming from fivefold regions.

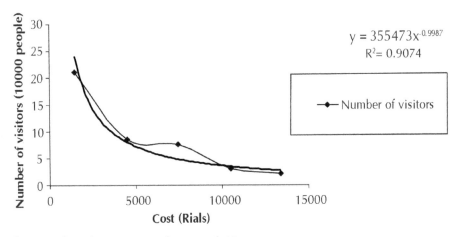

Figure 5. Relation between cost and amount of visitors.

Determining the Cost Value of Timber Production

Khalil Mahalleh-Abbas Abad forestry plan (located in north eastern neighborhood of the Park) has been selected for the assessment of the timber production cost value. The percentage of tree species types, industrial timber and fuel woods were specified independently to determine the cost value. Finally, the pure profit for industrial timber was set to 30% of the average market price and 10% of the fuel wood's market price (according to the information of the forestry plan—Table 2). As a consequence, the recreational value of the park per ha was gained, which was equal to 341,000 Rials (on average 40 USD).

Table 2. Produced timber value of Abbas Abad-Khalil mahalleh Forestry Plan.

Species	Mixture portion %	Industrial Timber %	Fuel wood %	Industrial Timber (m³)	Fuel wood (m³)	Industrial Timber gained profit (Rials)	Fuel wood gained Profit (Rials)	Total value × Mixture portion
Carpinus betulus	60	41	59	1	1.5	300000	52500	211000
Parrotia persica	20	14	86	0.35	2.15	76000	75250	30000
Fagus orientalis	10	49	51	1.22	1.28	717000	44800	76000
Other species	10	37	63	0.9	1.6	189000	56000	24000
Total	100	–	–	–	–	–	–	341000

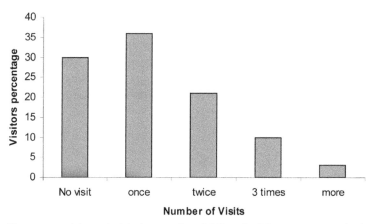

Figure 6. The amount of the park visits in case of availability of public transportation facilities.

Increasing WTP in Case of Availability of Public Vehicles

To achieve the WTP diagram, the following question has been posed: "How many times you would visit the park providing that enough two-way public transportation facilities would be available?" Some 30% asserted that they prefer to travel by personal vehicles, while two-third stated that they are interested in traveling by public vehicles, provided the price is reasonable. The frequency of the park visits is depicted in Figure 6. The visiting trend of the park would raise upwards and rightwards, as reported in Figure 7.

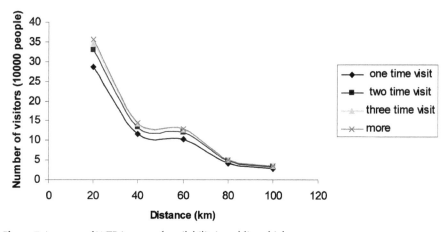

Figure 7. Increase of WTP in case of availabilityin public vehicles.

The raise in the number of visitors for "entire area", "138 ha study site", and "central 13 ha" would be equal to 717,000, 5,000, and 5,500 people per ha respectively. In addition, the cost value of the park will reach 2,152, 15, and 165 million Rials (253,000, 1,764, and 19,400 USD) per ha, respectively.

The Increase of WTP in Case of Creating Residential Places

In order to study the issue, visitors were requested to answer to the following question through the planned questionnaire: "Are you interested in staying in the park over night, if suitable equipments (e.g., tent and/or camping facilities) would be available?". Some 67% of the respondents answered yes. The diagram drawn after the analysis shows an increasing trend upwards and rightwards (just as the case of public vehicles availability—Figure 8).

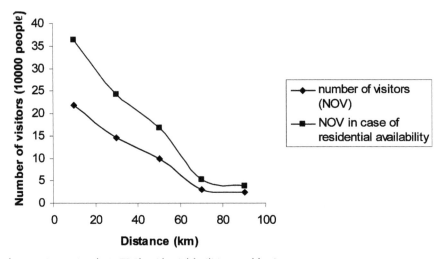

Figure 8. Increasing the WTP if residential facilities would exist.

According to the corresponding figure, the amount of visitors would increase as following in case of residential service improvement: some 675,000 people in the entire general area, 4,800 in the 138 hectare study site, and 51,900 in the central 13 ha. The cost value would thus be 2,025, 14, and 155 million Rials (equivalent to 238,000, 1,600, and 18,200 USD) in the entire area, in the 138 ha study site, and in the inner 13 ha, respectively.

The Decrease in WTP in Case of Entrance Fee Determination

There are a number of effective factors which may cause the visitors to limit (or even give up) their use of the park. Increasing the travel costs, the decline of ecotourism services, and/or decreasing the quality of eco-environmental resources are considered amongst the possible reasons which would cause the decrease in WTP of the park user.

In this study, it was attempted to investigate the tendency of WTP, as a consequence of setting different entrance fees for the five provenance regions. First, people were asked for their WTP an entrance fee to visit the park. If yes, how much would they accept to disburse?

The responses to the above question was up to 1,000, 2,000, and 5,000 Rials (around 1.1, 2.3, 5.8 USD) as for the entrance fee. Hence, it is obvious that fewer visitors would potentially travel to the park from the five provenance region, if an entrance fee would be set, determining a reduction of the cost value of the park. As displayed in Figure 9, 77% of the visitors would accept to pay the entrance fee, of which 66% was willing to pay up to 1,000 Rials, 19% up to 2,000 Rials, and 15% up to 5,000 Rials to enter the park.

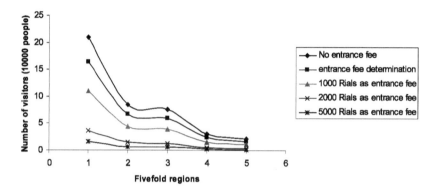

Figure 9. Decreasing WTP in the case of enacting entrance fee.

As a consequence of setting an entrance fee (supposed that no improvement would be done in the recreational condition), the cost value of Abbas Abad Park would be decreased down to 974,000,000 Rials (almost 114,588 USD) in the total area, 7,000,000 Rials (around 823 USD) in 138 ha and 74,000,000 Rials (about 8,705 USD) in the inner 13 ha of the park (Table 3 and Figure 9).

Table 3. Decrease of WTP in case of entrance fee determination.

Conducted Entrance fee	Number of Visitors (x 1000)	Value per ha (1000 Rials)	
		In the inner 13 ha	In 138 ha study site
No fee	32.9	169300	15950
1000 Rials	22	113400	10600
2000 Rials	6.5	37250	3500
5000 Rials	4.4	17100	1600

CONCLUSION

According to the achieved results, the recreational value of the Abbas Abad (1,266 million Rials for the entire recreational site 138 ha, 9 million/ha, and 97 million/ha for the central 13 ha area within the site) is much higher if compared to timber production value (341,000 Rials per ha, on average 40 USD). In other words, the timber value is just 4% of the total park value. Therefore, activities should be carried out in order to preserve, expand, and equip the site for recreation. This would be rewarding also to the local management units and related organizations (e.g., forest, rangeland, and watershed organization of I.R. Iran) which would improve their economic condition, together with supporting the economical conditions of local people. The Abbas Abad Park management should thus be enriched by conducting chain work plans, optimizing eco-tourism services, and removing factors discouraging Park visits.

Some suggestions may be eventually recommended as follows:

- Training the eco-environmental issues inside the forest Park can be done applying different tools and equipments to improve the eco-environmental culture of the visiting people.

- Eco-environmental evaluation using the worldwide-accepted methods can be done for other Iranian forest parks to prevent their further demolition and limitation.

- Interested institutions (e.g., Agriculture and Natural Resources Research Institute of Mazandaran Province) are supposed to act more efficiently on promoting this recreational/ecologically unique region.

- Interested organizations (those involved in preserving and improving forest parks) could create forest parks in other suitable areas across the province to reduce the tourist pressure on the Abbas Abad Park.

- The WTP of other ecotourism facilities can be calculated by the use of TCM.

- Factors involved in increasing/decreasing WTP in the Park may be recognized and applied/avoided to improve and optimize the park performance (e.g., vehicles access into the park should be restricted to certain limits to prevent acoustic pollution, or restaurants and dining facilities should be prevented to be gathered just in a certain part of the park because of possible ecological troubles they can cause).

- The expansion and improvement of the park is strongly recommended by creating ecotourism equipments.

- According to the official definition of a forest park (expanding and equipping the park up to 60% of its area), it is proposed to expand the park's area up to 83 ha, together with installing the necessary facilities based on the visitors' requirements. These can include installing rubbish buckets, tables and benches, pavements, health service, traditional tea shops, children's specific areas, optimizing the use of Abbas Abad dam, establishing theatre halls, cinema, suitable sport fields, and other welfare activities to make the park more pleasant for the visitors. Such a statement has also been emphasized by Shrestha et al. (2007), who stated that "managers can enhance the value of nature-based recreation in the Apalachicola River region if they increase the opportunities for visitors to experience more pristine recreation areas".

- Setting an entrance fee to access the Park at 2,000 Rials (almost 2.3 USD) and doubling it for each entering car (this fee has been formerly received by the management only in summer time). According to the available statistics of 2004 and 2005, a number of 143,200 cars visited the park. Assuming a costant trend for the year 2006, 572,800,000 Rials (nearly 67,300 USD) would be gained by the management. Provided that this money could be spent for expanding and equipping the park, this would consequently affect and improve the socio-economical condition of the local people as well.

The results of this study provide useful information for natural resources management in the region and a rationale to preserve a part of the Northern Iran's unique forest ecosystems #160.

KEYWORDS

- **Abbas Abad Forest Park**
- **Recreational evaluation**
- **Travel cost method**
- **Willingness to pay**

Chapter 21

Estimating Arrival Numbers for Informal Recreation

Andy Jones, Jan Wright, Ian Bateman, and Marije Schaafsma

INTRODUCTION

This chapter describes a novel methodology for generating models of demand for informal outdoor recreation. We analyze visitor data from multiple forest sites across Great Britain. We introduce a wide range of variables typically omitted from most economic demand models of recreation. These include on-site characteristics, and off-site locational drivers of visitation including substitute and complement availability. A Poisson multilevel model is used to model visitor counts, and the methodology is applied to a dataset of more than 10,000 visits to open-access woodland sites. Results confirm it identifies a broader range of demand drivers than previously observed. The use of nationally available explanatory variables enhances the transferability and hence general applicability of the methodology.

Day visits constitute one of the most significant of all leisure activities. Just within England the latest estimates suggested that there are currently around 900 million tourism day visits made each year generating over £37 billion of tourism spending (2005 England Leisure Visits Survey, 2007). This clearly reflects a substantial demand for the recreational services of the countryside which is second only to towns and cities as a day visit destination. However, while there is considerable attention paid to the overall level of such demand, research into the drivers of the precise pattern of visits and why some resources attract greater numbers of visits than others is, we argue, less complete. In particular we highlight the failure of previous studies to fully incorporate the spatial context of recreational resources within demand modeling. This chapter sets out to extend existing methodologies so as to address these deficiencies.

In modeling demand for outdoor recreation the key methodology is the travel cost approach (Champ et al., 2003). This proposes that the number and value of visits made to any given recreational site should be a function of the travel time and associated costs which an individual faces in visiting it; their income and other socio-economic and demographic factors; the facilities and their quality offered at the site; and location factors including the substitute sites available to the individual. Given this then, ceteris paribus, demand for outdoor recreation sites should be linked to the costs of visiting those sites which, under certain assumptions (Mäler, 1974), allows us to infer the value of those visits. While this method was first suggested over 60 years ago (Hotelling, 1949) and has been growing in use since the seminal work of Clawson and Knetsch (1966), it has been dominated by studies which focus upon variables describing on-site facilities and the characteristics of those interviewed via on-site surveys. For instance, Scarpa et al. show that both subjective and objective forest attributes, such as recreational facilities, type of coverage, and size of trees, are important drivers of individuals' willingness to pay (WTP) for forests (Scarpa et al., 2007). The WTP is the maximum amount a person would be willing to pay, sacrifice or exchange for a good, and the value can be estimated using several methodologies. Scarpa et al.'s estimation of the mean WTP for single forests is based on a value function that only includes forest and individual characteristics, but fails to account, however, for off-site characteristics. As in most other Contingent Valuation studies, the effect of the availability, distribution, and accessibility of substitute sites is completely ignored. This causes two problems: (i) studies have generally failed to include objective measures of substitute availability thus risking the biasing of demand and valuation estimates and (ii) reliance upon on-site and survey derived respondent characteristics limits the transferability for which generally available secondary source data is preferable. A lack of transferability necessitates that new surveys be undertaken for each policy decision.

The issue of transferability has become of central academic and policy interest in recent years (Bateman et al., 1999; Brouwer, 2000; Environmental Value Transfer, 2007; Moeltner et al., 2007; Muthke and Holm-Mueller, 2004; Scarpa et al., 2007) with the realization that resource constraints limit decision makers' ability to commission new studies. However, most of the benefits transfer literature has focused almost exclusively upon the estimation of marginal (per visit) values at the expense of assessing the number of visits to which such values should be applied. As we have shown within another context (single site contingent valuation studies Bateman et al., 2006), this strategy raises the prospect of major error as it is the number of visits rather than their marginal value which is liable to be the principal driver of the aggregate value of site creation or improvement.

The present chapter focuses upon three issues vital to the successful transfer of recreation studies:

(i)   We switch the research focus from the estimation of marginal values to the assessment of the quantity demand for visits, thus addressing a major driver of error in assessments of aggregate recreation value;

(ii) Although we use survey data to develop our models of recreation demand, we only use predictor variables which are readily available as national coverages of secondary data (e.g., digital map and census derived measures). This substantially enhances the transferability of findings to previously un-surveyed locations;

(iii) We use a geographical information system (GIS) to derive further explanatory variables, parameterizing the influence of the location of recreational sites upon demand by introducing new measures of demand drivers such as the spatial distribution of substitutes.

These study aims are addressed through a case study of a typical day-visit recreational resource; multi-purposes, open-access woodland in the UK. We use what is, to our knowledge, the largest survey ever employed for recreational demand modeling, comprising more than 10,000 interviews with day visitors to Forestry Commission woodlands all over Great Britain. Furthermore we employ multilevel modeling techniques to address the inherently clustered nature of data collected from surveys at multiple sites. We also make novel use of detailed GIS environmental characterizations to determine travel costs, the characteristics of outset areas, and the availability and type of substitutes. The practical and theoretical benefits of the approach adopted are discussed.

METHODOLOGY

The empirical focus of this research concerns the estimation of recreational visitor numbers at a sample of Forestry Commission woodlands across Great Britain. The Forestry Commission is the largest land manager in Britain and the biggest provider of outdoor recreation, being the government agency responsible for the protection and expansion of more than 750,000 ha of Britain's forests and woodlands (Forestry Facts and Figures, 2009). Recreational use is a significant aspect of woodland management; 77% of all adults reported visiting woodlands in 2009 (Forestry Facts and Figures, 2009). In addition, woodlands facilitate a wide range of recreational pursuits including walking, cycling, horse riding, orienteering, camping, fishing, and bird watching. Public forests also provide a range of key facilities including picnic sites, camping sites, holiday cabins, marked trails, cycle ways, horse riding routes, and information centers. Development of our empirical demand model draws upon responses from the 1996 to 1998 Forestry Commission visitor surveys conducted at 40 forest sites across Great Britain. Each site had one interviewer, who interviewed on a continuous survey basis such that when one interview was completed the next individual passing was then interviewed. For groups of two or more people, one person was selected to be interviewed. A count of individuals or groups not interviewed during the survey period was recorded by the interviewer. Table 1 lists the sites for which survey information was provided and the number of interviews conducted at each. This number is subdivided into day-trippers and holidaymakers, based upon individuals' responses. The survey effort expended at each site as measured by survey hours is an important determinant of the number of interviews completed. Therefore, the number of interviews at a site was divided by the amount of survey effort at the site and standardized to a period of a 24 hr day.

Table 1. Site names, Forest District, numbers of visitors surveyed by type, and survey effort.

| Site Number | Site Name | Forest District | Numbers of Visitor Surveyed | | | Survey |
			Total Visitors	Day Visitors	Holiday Visitors	Effort (Hours)
3	Afan Argoed	Coed y Cymoed, Wales	458	381	76	157.0
6	Alice Holt	South East England	217	209	6	82.0
8	Back O Bennachie	Buchan, Scotland	100	92	8	69.0
9	Beechenhurst	Forest of Dean, England	128	84	43	34.0
14	Black Rocks	Sherwood and Lincolnshire, England	161	123	38	72.0
15	Blackwater	New Forest, England	179	82	93	35.0
17	Blidworth Woods	Sherwood and Kincolnshire, England	216	211	2	106.0
18	Bolderwood	New Forest, England	343	148	194	58.0
20	Bourne Wood	Northants, England	211	200	11	59.5
33	Chopwell	Kielder, England	125	123	2	31.0
34	Christchurch	Forest of Dean, England	132	26	104	24.0

Table 1. *(Continued)*

Site Number	Site Name	Forest District	Numbers of Visitor Surveyed			Survey Effort (Hours)
			Total Visitors	Day Visitors	Holiday Visitors	
40	Countesswells	Kincardine, Scotland	212	209	3	64.0
43	Cycle Centre	Forest of Dean, England	222	154	67	88.0
44	Dalby	North York Moors, England	305	157	148	72.0
46	Delamere	West Midlands, England	684	264	6	153.0
49	Dibden	New Forest, England	215	206	9	89.0
51	Donview	Buchan, Scotland	144	126	18	66.0
61	Garwnant	Coed y Cymoed, Wales	358	274	83	80.5
66	Glentrool	Newton Steward, Scotland	321	114	205	100.0
68	Grizedale	Lakes, England	265	68	197	51.0
72	Hamsterley	Kielder, England	160	119	40	52.0
80	Kielder	Kielder, England	104	38	64	26.5
83	Kings Wood	South East England	102	95	7	72.0
84	Kirkhill	Kincardine, Scotland	207	197	10	107.0
86	Kylerhea	Fort Augustus, Scotland	210	9	200	95.0
95	Mabie	AE, Scotland	686	355	315	108.0
111	Queens View	Tay, Scotland	270	41	228	96.0
117	Salcey	Northants, England	196	185	9	54.0
119	Sherwood Pines	Sherwood and Lincolnshire, England	680	517	163	208.5
121	Simonside Hills	Kielder, England	136	98	37	45.5
126	Symonds Yat	Forest of Dean, England	255	103	152	66.0
128	Thetford High Lodge	East Anglia, England	687	535	149	148.0
129	Thieves Wood	Sherwood, England	307	304	2	108.0
130	Thrunton Woods	Kielder, England	142	89	52	48.0
134	Tyrebagger	Kincardine, Scotland	149	139	9	71.0
137	Waters Copse	New Forest, England	172	75	97	86.5
141	Wendover	South East England	117	112	5	42.0
143	Westonbirt Ab	Westonburt Arboretum, England	440	349	86	44.5
147	Willingham Woods	Sherwood and Lincolnshire, England	176	163	12	124.0
153	Wyre	West Midlands, England	670	567	101	130.5

Although the sample of visitors included both day visitors and holiday makers, unfortunately there was no information available for holidaymakers on their place of stay during their holiday. Hence it was necessary to define outset locations as the home location rather than any temporary address (e.g., a holiday residence). Nevertheless, tests were made to determine if any significant bias was associated with this assignation by stratifying the sample into holidaymakers and day-trippers and undertaking separate analyses for each (results not shown here for brevity). The results obtained were generally comparable; unsurprisingly travel time to substitutes was somewhat more important for day visitors as were the demographic characteristics of the outset location. However, the models did not fundamentally differ in either the type of variables included or the strength of effect, and hence we conclude that the models developed here have general applicability regardless of visitor type.

Environmental and Socio-demographic Characterization

Accurate determination of the visitors' home outset locations is a key piece of information as this provides the reference point for identification of the spatial drivers of visit demand. Postcodes of visitors' home address locations were supplied and used to obtain an outset grid reference from the UK Central Postcode Directory (CPD). A total of 10,862 visitor interview records with usable postcodes were obtained, with corresponding residential locations being mapped in Figure 1. So that geographical variations in visit rates could be examined, visitors were then assigned to outset zones based on their location. Outset zones were delineated based on the boundaries of Local Authority Districts, of which there were 451 in Great Britain at the time of analysis. Districts were chosen because they are large enough to each provide an adequate number of visitor arrivals from each, yet small enough to preserve an acceptable amount of homogeneity of population characteristics within their boundaries. The calculation of travel times from the outset zone of residents to the site at which they were surveyed was undertaken using the ArcGIS package. The population weighted centroid of each outset zone was identified, and a route was developed to estimate the road based travel time from these centroids to all sites. Following the methodology of Brainard et al. each section of the road network was accorded an average speed which reflected data from the Department of Transport which accounted for road designation, and urban/rural status (Brainard et al., 1997). Travel times were then calculated between origins and destinations based on the assumption that visitors would choose the route which minimized time. Bateman et al. show a very strong correspondence between such GIS generated travel times and those reported by woodland visitors interviewed in an on-site survey (Bateman et al., 1996).

Figure 1. Visitor outset locations.

As far as reasonable we sought to allow the analysis to identify potential substitute and complementary attractions by including data on a wide array of sites and facilities ranging from highly similar alternative forests and woodlands, through other outdoor open access sites (including heathland, sandy beaches, other coastline, rivers, inland waterways and canals, scenic areas, and national parks) and built amenities (zoos and wildlife parks, theme parks, National Trust properties, and historic houses). Towns and cities were identified so as to provide a surrogate indicator for some of the attractions not directly measured (e.g., cinemas, shopping centers, sports centers, etc.). A variety of data sources were employed in this undertaking (including the remote-sensed CEH UK Land Cover Database for 1990, Bartholomew's 1:250,000 Digital Database for Great Britain, the Scottish Council for National Parks, the (former) Countryside Commission for Scotland, internet sources (e.g., www.daysoutuk.com), the International Zoo Yearbook (Olney and Fisken, 1998) and the Good Zoo Guide (Ironmonger, 1992).

Travel time values for substitutes were calculated using the same methodology as for the forest sites. However, the size of a substitute feature (e.g., an area of lakeland) may affect its accessibility as small sites can be treated as single point locations, but larger ones are likely to have a greater number of access points, with some closer and some further from outset locations. To account for this, accessibility scores were weighted according to the area covered by each substitute location so that scores were higher for smaller than larger features. Next, to place proportionally greater weight upon substitute features that were more proximal to visitor outset zone locations, these scores were further divided by the square of travel time from each outset origin. Previous research suggests that a squared power produced a good fit to observed visitor patterns (Bateman et al., 2003), so this was used. In addition to the measure of weighted accessibility described above, a further indicator of substitute accessibility was computed as the percentage of each outset zone and surroundings covered by each substitute considered. To account for edge effects that may exist for residents living very close to district boundaries, the availability of substitute facilities in neighboring zones was considered by a procedure whereby each outset zone was amalgamated with its contiguous (boundary sharing) neighbors. The area of each substitute was then calculated for each of these amalgamated zones, and assigned to the principal outset zone. For linear features such as rivers and canals, a buffering technique was first applied to give the features a 20-m width, which was assumed to be a reasonable approximation of real world widths.

As the propensity to seek generalized outdoor recreation experiences such as those provided by forestry may be associated with factors such as wealth, ethnicity, or household structure, a range of population socio-demographic characteristics for each outset zone were calculated from the UK Census of Population. In total 27 indicators were generated, covering transport availability, affluence and deprivation, education, ethnicity, age, and family size. These indicators were also weighted by population density to compute the geographical distribution of population demographic characteristics that may influence visitor numbers.

Generation of Travel Cost Values

The transferable demand function is principally derived from regression models that predict visitation rates from outset zones. Typically, the dependent variable has a skewed distribution, reflecting that the majority of outset zones will provide no visitors to any given site, and hence a Poisson regression model (Lovett and Flowerdew, 1989) suitable for count data analysis is employed, as was the case here. For this study, the desired response variable yi would ideally be set as the total number of visitors to a site. However, observed visitor numbers will of course be conditioned by the degree of interview time on-site. To account for variations in survey effort, the number of interviews recorded at each site from each outset zone was divided by the amount of survey effort expended at that site. Survey effort was initially measured in hours, but this figure was divided by 24 so that the variable became a measure of effort in 24 hr periods. To further allow for variations in population across outset zones, the natural logarithm of the outset zone population was modeled as an offset. This means that our dependent variable is in effect a visitor rate.

One of the most fundamental problems of applying such models arises when the factors influencing the probability of visitors attending any individual site are seen to be operating at a variety of scales. For example, some sites may be either more or less attractive to visitors than others due to factors not captured in those site characteristics that are measured. This means such sites generate more or less visitors than would be predicted from the values of the predictor variables used to describe them. If this is the case the assumption of independence in the residuals from the regression model is violated. Due to such intra-unit correlation, the standard errors may be underestimated and the parameter estimates may be unreliable. Hence, to account for intra-unit correlation and produce efficient parameter estimates and standard errors, this study applied a multilevel (random coefficient) modeling approach using the MLWin software package (Rasbash et al., 2009). A two level structure was used of outset zones (level 1) nested within sites (level 2). Model building followed a staged approach which screened for multicollinearity within estimated models.

The model detailed above provides a prediction of the number of visitors interviewed at each site adjusted for survey effort. However, estimates of total visitation numbers within a specified period (here taken to be 1 year) are clearly of greater policy use. As we have discussed in other contexts, the conversion processes entailed in such translations can be a major source of error (Bateman et al., 2006). This is typically a result of sparse aggregation data, in this case concerning the relationship between the numbers interviewed and actual annual arrivals. The only available data here were annual arrival estimates provided by the Forestry Commission for a subset of five sites included in the preceding analysis.

First, the predictions for each site were multiplied by a ratio of surveyed to unsurveyed (noted as being present but not interviewed) groups, based on information supplied by the Forestry Commission. Next, the temporal distribution of survey effort was directly incorporated in the regression model; variables were created detailing, for each site, the proportion of total effort undertaken in each month of the year. As there were too few surveys (and too little corresponding variation) within the months from

October to April to justify their separate inclusion, only separate variables for each of the months May to September were included within these models. Thus their coefficients, measured as the proportion of total survey effect in each of the months, reflect departures from the base case of interviews outside this period. Estimated values for these coefficients conformed to expectations, with the greatest survey effort being expended in the summer period when visits are highest. Their control for seasonality effects upon survey effort meant that the inclusion of these variables within the model was justified on the grounds that it is likely to provide a superior basis for aggregation to annual visitor predications. The aggregation to annual visits was then achieved by multiplying the derived 24 hr predictions of arrivals (now adjusted for the seasonality in survey effort) by 365.25.

The models estimated here are amenable to calculations of travel cost values incurred by visitors for trips to woodlands, as the travel time variable can readily be related to travel cost estimates. In calculating travel cost, allowance was made for both travel expenditure and travel time values. The procedure used was as follows and is provided in Equation 1. The travel time T (min) of each party interviewed from outset location j was multiplied by one-third (Cesario, 1976; Mackie et al., 2003) of the regional hourly wage rate W (£) (Regional Trends, 1998) of outset location j to calculate travel cost. Travel expenditure from outset location j was calculated as the product of travel time from j and an assumed average speed of 40 mph (specified as 0.67 miles per min) at average costs C per mile. Summing the travel time value and travel expenditure resulted in the travel cost per group from j, and this was multiplied by the total number of party visits Pj from outset zone j to calculate j's travel cost. To obtain the total value of travel costs per site i, the travel costs per outset location were summed on a per site basis. Finally, resulting value was divided by the number of party visits S_i to the site to calculate the average value v_i of a group visit to each site as shown in Equation (1):

$$v_i = \left\{ \sum_{j=1-j} \left[\left(T_j * \tfrac{1}{3} w_j + T_j * 40 * C \right) * P_j \right] \right\} \div S_i \qquad (1)$$

Note that the value, v_i, does not include any element of the consumer surplus. The consumer surplus is the amount that forest visitors would have been willing to pay for their visits but were not required to do so. This value would be higher than our own estimate, which was based only on observed costs from travel. Thus our travel cost estimates may underestimate the true value of forest resources.

RESULTS

The Best Fit Model for Day Visitors and Holidaymakers Combined

Table 2 shows the best fit model obtained to predict arrivals at survey sites. All prior expectations were satisfied. Controlling for population in each outset zone, by far the dominant factor determining visits is the negative influence of higher travel times. In many respects this is not surprising, however the strength and significance of this relationship has an important policy message, that it is the location of a site which primarily determines its level of use.

Table 2. Best-fit model predicting recreational demand for a sample of Forestry Commission woodland sites across Britain. Dependent variable: rates of all visitor types (day-trip and holidaymaker) interviewed from each outset zone, adjusted for survey effort.

Variable	Coefficient	s.e.	t	p
Constant	−11.730	1.775	−6.608	***
Travel time to site	−2.563	0.026	−98.615	***
Travel time to nearest inland water	0.226	0.044	5.199	***
Travel time to nearest heathland	0.170	0.023	7.274	***
Travel time to nearest coast	0.153	0.022	6.888	***
Travel time to nearest National Trust Site	0.105	0.040	2.642	**
Travel time to nearest large urban area	0.044	0.014	3.095	**
Percentage of outset district and surrounding districts classified as woodland	−0.048	0.012	−4.105	***
Percented of outset district and surrounding districts classified as British Waterways canals	−0.018	0.002	−9.588	***
Percentage of outset district households with children	1.157	0.293	3.952	***
Percentage of outset district households with retired head	0.668	0.234	2.854	**
Percentage of outset district population classified as Social Class 1 or 2 (affluent)	0.703	0.086	8.173	***
Percentage of outset district population classified as non-white ethnicity	−0.109	0.029	−3.710	***
Presence of visitor information centre at site	0.640	0.273	2.341	*
Early interviewing effort (7am to 10am)	−0.093	0.030	−3.082	**
'Scottish Tour' site indicator	1.485	0.299	4.967	***
Between site variance parameter	0.581	0.133	4.368	***

One of the key contributions of our analysis is the intensive treatment of substitution effects upon visits. We assessed these effects through two sets of variables. A first set calculates substitute availability in terms of the proximity to potential arrival destinations. A second set of substitute indicators considered the intensity of recreational opportunities in and around outset zones.

Table 2 shows that the signs on the variables measuring the availability of both types of substitute are in the direction expected; those measuring travel time to substitutes are positive, illustrating that outset locations far from alternative substitutes will generate more woodland visits. The negative signs on those variables measuring the area of each substitute around the outset locations show that visitors will be less likely to visit woodlands if there are more alternative destinations around their home. Again this has a clear policy message that providing additional recreational facilities in an area which is already well endowed with such opportunities will generate lower levels of visitation than the provision of new sites in areas which are currently poorly provided for. While commonsense, to our knowledge this is the first time such relationships have been quantified.

Table 2 continues by providing evidence of the extent to which the socio-economic and demographic characteristics of outset zones influence the rate of visitation from those zones. Areas which have higher levels of young children, retired, or higher social classes are all associated with elevated numbers of visitors. This result suggests that families with young children may well be more disposed to outdoor activities and that the retired have less time constraints than others. Similarly higher income groups enjoying greater mobility are more likely to engage in woodland recreation. This latter relation is likely to substantially reflect the present spatial distribution of woodlands which are generally not located within low income areas. A policy of locating woodlands nearer to low income households should go some way to allowing for this effect. In Great Britain the increasing importance of agri-environmental schemes as a source of income for farmers means that the conversion of land from arable to woodland use is a more feasible proposition than has been the case in the past, and Government funding has also been made available for the creation of "Community Woodlands," although the benefits of such initiatives take many years to be fully realized. Hence in the shorter term other possibilities, such as enhancing recreational opportunities in existing woodlands for low income groups, may also be important (Newsome et al., 2004). Even controlling for socio-economics, the model shows that areas with more ethnic populations yield fewer visitors, a result that may reflect tastes or imperfect control for the lower accessibility of woodlands to the primarily urban ethnic community.

Out of the numerous site facility and quality variables gathered, only the presence of information boards at a site proved to exert a significant impact upon the numbers interviewed. Even this may well be acting as a proxy for other facilities or site characteristics or a problem of endogeneity as the decision to install a notice board may well depend on there being sufficient visitors to warrant its construction. What this does show is that, in comparison to the strength of the travel time variable for example, it is the location of recreational woodland rather than its specific facilities (above the common facilities of woodland walks and car parking) which determines visitation.

Two final control variables were significant. Least interesting of these is the negative coefficient of the "Early interviewing effort (7 am–10 am)" variable which allows for variation in the distribution of survey effort across the day, here reflecting the lower interview rate achieved when interviewers had higher proportions of their survey effort focused upon very early hours of the day when visitor numbers were low. More interesting is the fact that sites located in Scotland (labeled as "Scottish tour" sites in Table 2) have a higher number of visitors interviewed than might be expected from their characteristics. Discussions with Forestry Commission staff suggests that this may reflect the influence of touring holidaymakers increasing the number of visitors above that which would otherwise be expected for sites with such small local populations. Examination of the between-site (level 2) residual variance showed no particular trend across sites. We believe the best-fit model is richer than models provided by most previous research and consistently in accordance with prior expectations derived from theory and previously observed empirical regularities. Given this, it appears that the model should be suitable for predicting visitor trends across all sites, which we now consider.

Transferring the Best-fit Model

The main question after estimating a transferable visitation rate function is if the model can provide useful input to the real world planning and decision-making process. Table 3 details predicted arrivals for each site, based on the coefficients obtained in the best-fit regression model when that site was omitted (i.e., adhering to best-practice, out-of-sample prediction methods). Sites marked with an asterisk in the table are those located in Scotland. This provides an assessment of the likely performance of the model in a policy situation where no survey based information is known about a given target site. Inspection of Table 3 shows that while the overall trend of results is encouraging, there is substantial error at certain sites with both under- and over predicted numbers.

Table 3. Transferred predictions of interview numbers for all visitor types from the best-fit model.

Site Number	Site Name	Observed Visitor Number Surveyed	Predicted Visitor Numbers Surveyed	Difference Observed-Predicted	Ratio Observed-Predicted
3	Afan Argoed	458	1086.61	−628.61	2.37
6	Alice Holt	217	701.55	−484.55	3.23
8	Back O Bennachie*	100	71.95	28.05	0.72
9	Beechenhurst	128	111.33	16.67	0.87
14	Black Rocks	161	303.21	−142.21	1.88
15	Blackwater	179	305.06	−126.06	1.70
17	Blidworth Woods	216	906.70	−690.70	4.20
18	Bolderwood	343	668.10	−325.10	1.95
20	Bourne Wood	211	132.35	78.65	0.63
33	Chopwell	125	94.50	30.50	0.76
34	Christchurch	132	50.38	81.62	0.38
40	Countesswells*	212	121.69	90.31	0.57
43	Dean Cycle Centre	222	180.60	41.40	0.81
44	Dalby	305	225.60	79.40	0.74
46	Delamere	684	1086.18	−402.18	1.59
49	Dibden	215	57.71	157.29	0.27
51	Donview*	144	128.88	15.12	0.90
61	Garwnant	358	286.10	71.90	0.80
66	Glentrool*	321	167.45	153.55	0.52
68	Grizedale	265	107.09	157.91	0.40
72	Hamsterley	160	134.23	25.77	0.84
80	Kielder	104	28.08	75.92	0.27
83	Kings Wood	102	137.84	−32.84	1.32
84	Kirkhill*	207	935.21	−728.21	4.52
86	Kylerhea*	210	59.65	150.35	0.28
95	Mabie*	686	618.66	67.34	0.90
111	Queens View*	270	307.90	−37.90	1.14
117	Salcey	196	550.64	−354.64	2.81
119	Sherwood Pines	680	2317.93	−1637.93	3.41
121	Simonside Hills	136	25.42	110.58	0.19
126	Symonds Yat	255	112.73	142.27	0.44

Table 3. (Continued)

Site Number	Site Name	Observed Visitor Number Surveyed	Predicted Visitor Numbers Surveyed	Difference Observed- Predicted	Ratio Observed- Predicted
128	Thetford High Lodge	687	650.38	36.62	0.95
129	Thieves Wood	307	801.27	−494.27	2.61
130	Thrunton Woods	142	49.94	92.06	0.35
134	Tyrebagger*	149	612.53	−463.53	4.11
137	Waters Copse	172	97.09	74.91	0.56
141	Wendover	117	211.98	−94.98	1.81
143	Westonbirt Ab	440	174.80	265.20	0.40
147	Willingham Woods	176	158.90	17.10	0.90
153	Wyre	670	1749.85	−1079.85	2.61

In order to further inspect the relationship between observed and predicted interview numbers, Figure 2 provides a measure of observed versus predicted visits (using our model from Table 2). The included regression line indicates the expected positive relation between observed and predicted values. According to a simple correlation test ($\rho = 0.709$; $p < 0.001$) and a χ^2-test examining the ability of the model to predict visits ($\chi^2 = 11.00$; $p < 0.001$), the model performs well overall. However, inspection of Figure 2 suggests some degree of systematic deviation between predicted and observed visit (interview) rates. In particular observed visit rates appeared to be truncated at roughly 700 interviews. It may be that interviewers were instructed to finish interviewing, or decided to do so of their own accord, once this level was reached. Accepting that this will militate against a clean test of our model it is nevertheless clear that this best-fit model differentiates well between sites with high and low visitor interview numbers.

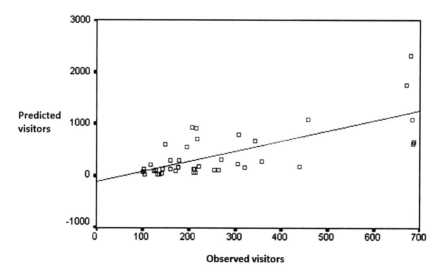

Figure 2. Plot of observed and predicted visitor interview numbers.

Estimates of Annual Arrivals

The output from the regression model was then used to predict annual arrivals at the subset of sites at which actual arrival data was available as a comparator. Unfortunately the Forestry Commission was only able to supply estimates of total visitor numbers for five of the sites in their survey dataset. Even these were supplied with strong caveats regarding their likely accuracy; hence we have no perfect criterion measure of actual visits and have to accept these rather imperfect estimates at this restricted number of locations. Given these caveats, comparisons at these sites are given in Table 4.

Table 4. Comparison of Forestry Commission and model estimates of annual visits to five woodlands.

Site Name	Forestry Commission Estimate of the Number of Party Visits p.a.	Model Prediction of Number of Party Visits p.a.
Beechenhurst	72,845	79,504
Blidworth Woods	63,849	116,553
Chopwell	33,708	71,334
Mabie	51,704	56,561
Symonds Yat	77,525	108,154
Total	299,631	432,106

The overall correspondence between Forestry Commission and model-derived estimates of arrivals has a ratio of 1.44. Given the prior caveats, the comparative ranking of sites is perhaps more important. The top three sites and lower two sites are consistent across the two sets of estimates suggesting that the model can robustly distinguish between high and low visitation sites. Given the uncertainty with regard to the Forestry Commission estimates of overall annual totals, we feel this is a satisfactory finding.

Estimation of Travel Cost Values

Using our previously described methodology, travel cost values were generated separately for all visitors, day-trippers, and holidaymakers to yield the values detailed in Table 5. As expected, travel costs are higher for holidaymaker than day-trip visitors. It is important to recall that the values detailed in Table 5 are travel costs rather than consumer surplus values which would require further information than was available in the Forestry Commission data (see (Champ et al., 2003) for details). Combined with the predicted annual visitor numbers from the five sites for which Forestry Commission estimates were available, the travel cost values placed by visitors on each site can be estimated and are presented in Table 6. A comparison of the values in Table 6 with the regression model coefficients used to generate them (Table 2), shows the predominant driver of differences in site value is population accessibility (specified from travel time), with the accessibility of substitute sites being of secondary importance, and site characteristics having the smallest influence.

Table 5. Travel cost value for all visitors, day-tripper, and holidaymakers for each site.

Site Number	Site Name	All Visitors	Day Visitors	Holiday Visitors
3	Afan Argoed	8.62	4.02	31.76
6	Alice Holt	4.30	4.09	11.10
8	Back O Bennachie	12.24	6.61	77.01
9	Beechenhurst	14.00	8.79	24.26
14	Black Rocks	9.32	5.17	22.78
15	Blackwater	19.62	8.16	29.85
17	Blidworth Woods	2.95	2.74	26.46
18	Bolderwood	18.71	6.58	27.97
20	Bourne Wood	5.73	4.88	21.10
33	Chopwell	4.02	4.00	5.25
34	Christchurch	18.15	14.72	18.79
40	Countesswells	3.63	2.79	62.24
43	Cycle Centre	13.13	7.93	25.21
44	Dalby	20.54	12.06	29.54
46	Delamere	4.53	4.44	6.62
49	Dibden	3.85	3.48	12.25
51	Donview	15.48	8.13	66.92
61	Garwnant	11.12	5.22	30.72
66	Glentrool	35.77	13.84	47.78
68	Grizedale	25.59	10.38	30.83
72	Hamsterley	16.49	11.14	32.65
80	Kielder	35.79	19.50	45.00
83	Kings Wood	17.38	15.62	41.27
84	Kirkhill	5.11	3.26	41.53
86	Kylerhea	85.83	58.30	87.13
95	Mabie	20.28	6.43	36.47
111	Queens View	57.25	27.19	62.84
117	Salcey	3.78	3.14	17.22
119	Sherwood Pines	8.95	3.85	25.13
121	Simonside Hills	17.66	8.74	41.57
126	Symonds Yat	19.76	11.76	25.19
128	Thetford High Lodge	11.64	7.74	25.74
129	Theives Wood	2.58	2.52	12.78
130	Thrunton Woods	19.34	6.01	42.45
134	Tyrebagger	4.56	3.39	22.93
137	Waters Copse	18.98	8.24	27.28
141	Wendover	4.96	4.61	12.78
143	Westonbirt Ab	11.75	8.59	24.91
147	Willingham Woods	8.28	7.18	22.92
153	Wyre	6.81	4.65	18.95

Table 6. Estimated travel cost values to five woodlands for converted model predictions of annual visitor numbers.

Site Name	Travel Cost Value
Beechenhurst	£990,619
Blidworth Woods	£564,116
Chopwell	£374,503
Mabie	£1,417,418
Symonds Yat	£1,211,324
Total	£4,557,980

DISCUSSION AND CONCLUSION

The main objective of the study was to develop a model to predict visitation rates at recreational sites, taking account of the accessibility and facilities of the resource, the availability of substitutes and variation in population characteristics. A GIS-based methodology was developed to analyze the spatial distribution of these various determinants which were then modeled within a hierarchical (multilevel) zonal travel cost framework. Allowance was made for survey effort and the resulting model performs well against all prior expectations. The strongest predictor of visitor arrivals is accessibility (travel time) but strongly significant substitution effects were identified for competing natural and man-made resources. Household characteristics also affect visitation rates in expected ways.

The methodology developed through this chapter allows the policy analyst to parameterize a wide set of visit demand determinants. As such we refine a highly flexible policy formulation and analysis tool which sits well with the drive of governments internationally towards evidence-based policy making.

The research is presented with some caveats. The travel cost methodology adopted assumes that the woodland at which each survey was undertaken was the sole destination on the trip, and also that no pleasure, or utility, was obtained from the journey. In situations where this was not the case, for example where enjoyment was derived from scenic driving or sight-seeing along the way, the value attached to the recreational site may be overestimated. In this respect, WTP values from the analysis may overestimate true figures. We also benefitted here from Great Britain being an island state, meaning we did not have the problem of "edge effects" (e.g., the proximal availability of substitutes that we did not have information on across a border) that would occur if our analysis had been based on a jurisdiction surrounded by others. Although information was available that allowed day visitors and holidaymakers to be differentiated, no details were recorded on the holiday location of holidaymakers, and hence our analysis was based upon the measurement of travel times from home for this group. This restricted the ability of our analysis to differentiate between the motivations for visiting a particular region for a holiday, and the choice the specific forest site. There was also evidence of truncation of interview numbers at heavily visited locations, suggesting that there were survey capacity limitations that may have prevented us differentiating some sites with very high visitor numbers. A further restriction lies in the fact that the Forestry Commission were unable to supply large numbers of annual visitor numbers for calibration purposes and even those that were provided came with strong caveats regarding their likely accuracy. This is not an unusual state of affairs. While the UK has good survey data concerning the outdoor activities of households, this is not spatially explicit and there is a clear need for such data to inform both research and planning.

The methodology developed here is deliberately designed for general applicability and transfer. A notable feature is the utilization of generally available national coverage databases for generating the predictors of visits. Key data sources were the Ordnance Survey and UK Census; data that are available to researchers and policy makers alike. Furthermore, while the initial processing of data takes some time, once generated the data surfaces should be valid for some considerable time and require only occasional updating. Road networks, the availability of substitutes and the socioeconomic and demographic profiles of regions only change gradually with time and we estimate than updating would only be needed at most every 5 years with longer periods (such as the 10 years gap between Census dates) probably being acceptable for most analyzes. Of course, one disadvantage of this focus on infrastructure and physical features is that matters of culture and perception are not encompassed. For example, authors such as Stedman (Stedman, 2003) have shown that physical features do contribute to feelings of sense of place in forest environments, yet cultural components such as constructed meanings and place attachment can also important. These undoubtedly also contribute to the value of forest resources, yet we were not able to incorporate such considerations in our work. One implication of this is that our models may be more appropriate for strategic-level planning where population-wide decisions are being made. However, our failure to incorporate the more experiential characteristics of sites into our transfer functions might mean that further surveys would be required for operational considerations, such as those associated with woodland design.

Individual analyzes can of course readily posit policy induced changes such as the creation of new recreational opportunities, although it should be noted that different resource types may have differing transition profiles; the creation of a new lake may result in a rapid transition to maximum visitation levels but this may be less true for woodlands where the impact upon visitation of the naturally slow rate of forest establishment needs to be allowed for.

Whilst a number of limitations of the work have been highlighted, the function transfer model developed here explicitly addresses one of the major empirical problems facing successful function transfer; spatial complexity between sites. Previous work has faced severe problems in addressing this issue. The issue is important because even the most fundamental predictor of visit numbers, travel time, has strong spatial heterogeneity. The GISs coupled with high quality digital map databases provide novel opportunities to produce measures of the underlying determinants of recreational visits. Furthermore, these measures can be obtained in a consistent manner for both surveyed study sites and un-surveyed target sites. It is this consistency, compatibility, availability, and richness of measures which provides the quantitative measurements vital for successful function transfer. Although we find that the location characteristics are still the main drivers of site visits, we argue that for increased reliability future recreation and valuation studies, using both revealed and stated preference methods, should attempt to include indicators that reflect the availability of different type of substitutes in their value functions. It is likely that the demand from decision makers for benefit transfer applications will continue to increase in the future, primarily due to the increasing emphasis being placed on outdoor recreation and the expense and time-consuming nature of survey data collection. Inexpensive benefit transfer estimates are frequently required as organizations now have to be more commercially accountable. Consequently improving the robustness of benefit transfer techniques is likely to remain a topic for significant research in the future.

KEYWORDS

- **Arrival modeling**
- **Forests**
- **Sustainable tourism**
- **Transferrable demand**

ACKNOWLEDGMENTS

We thank the Forestry Commission for the provision of data and funding for this research.

Chapter 22

Local Residents' Attitudes Toward Tourism

Maureen Y. Bender, Jinyang Deng, Steve Selin, Doug Arbogast, and R. A. Hobbs

INTRODUCTION

The purpose of this study was to understand residents' attitudes toward tourism development in the town of Ansted, WV, using self-administered surveys. The attitude assessment in this study was part of a tourism planning process conducted for the town. The results indicate that perceptions of tourism development among Ansted's residents are generally homogeneous and highly positive. They do not believe that issues normally resulting from increased tourism, such as crowding, increased prices, or pollution would be a problem for the community. Rather, they are inclined to support tourism development for its potential to spur local economic development and provide related benefits. This finding is consistent with the social exchange theory that the more dependent a community is on economic benefits, the more likely it is that the community will support tourism development. The findings of this research will be an important contribution to a plan for sustainable tourism development in Ansted.

West Virginia is the second most rural state in the United States (West Virginia Department of Health and Human Resources, 2007). Rural communities in the state have been struggling to improve residents' quality of life without compromising the appealing features that are associated with rural places. In many parts of the world, tourism has been regarded as an effective means of promoting rural economic development and diversification. However, tourism can also destroy the resources on which its development depends. Community-based tourism planning has been used to solve this dilemma by considering local residents' attitudes toward tourism development during the tourism planning process. The purpose of this study is to understand residents' attitudes toward tourism development and its impacts in rural Ansted, WV. The attitude assessment in this study is part of a tourism planning process being conducted in the town.

Established in 1873, the Town of Ansted, WV, is located along US Highway 60 on a portion of the Midland Trail National Scenic Byway overlooking the New River. The town is rich in Civil War and coal mining history. It has many historic attractions, including Civil War-era buildings, museums, and African-American cemeteries. There are also abundant natural attractions in and around the community, including Hawk's Nest State Park, the Midland Trail National Scenic Byway, and the New and Gauley National Rivers.

West Virginia is one of the most economically depressed states in the country, with a state average per-capita annual income of $16,477, lower than the national average of $21,587 (Ansted Blueprint Community, 2007). The town of Ansted had a 1999 per-capita annual income of $15,671 (as reported in 2000 U.S. Census data), which is lower than the state average and much lower than the national average (Ansted Blueprint Community, 2007).

LITERATURE REVIEW

Residents' attitudes toward tourism development have been extensively examined from social, economics, and environmental perspectives. The literature review for this study focuses on the importance of uncovering residents' attitudes toward tourism development during community-based tourism planning and a discussion of previous studies concerning resident attitudes.

Tourism is often characterized by haphazard development that generates unevenly distributed benefits. Such circumstances apply especially to rural communities, in which few residents stand to benefit directly from tourism. Many communities experience economic leakages, in which most of the profits from tourism leave the community. This outflow occurs mainly because those who have decision-making authority over tourism development reside outside the community. This situation can lead to the eventual deterioration and abandonment of tourism destination sites, leaving the local people worse off than before tourism development began (Mitchell and Reid, 2000). There is also increasing interest in the social and environmental impacts—both positive and negative—that tourism can bring, especially with respect to environmental and economic sustainability (Allen et al., 1988). Many tourism practitioners and researchers have begun to favor "community-based tourism", in which communities are placed at the center of tourism planning and management (Mitchell and Reid, 2000). Proponents argue that community participation in tourism planning and development is necessary to ensure that the benefits of tourism reach community residents (Simmons, 1994). In addition, this type of planning encourages local employment and small business development, which in turn promote higher economic multipliers. A community approach to decision-making also helps to ensure that traditional lifestyles and community values are respected. Community participation also may generate environmental benefits; where local natural resources are essential to tourism, community members would ideally act as stewards in environmental conservation (Campbell, 1999).

As discussed above, it is important to understand local residents' attitudes toward tourism development in order to plan and develop tourism in a sustainable manner. Accordingly, local residents' attitudes toward tourism have been widely examined in the literature. Harrill (2004) outlined three types of factors that influence attitudes toward tourism development: socioeconomic factors, spatial factors, and economic dependency.

Previous studies have examined the relationship between residents' attitudes and socioeconomic variables such as gender, income, and length of residence. Findings in these studies are not always consistent. For example, Allen et al. (1993) found that length of residence did not significantly influence attitudes toward tourism development in 10 rural Colorado communities. In contrast, Girard and Gartner's (1993) Wisconsin study, McCool and Martin's (1994) Montana study, and a Virginia study by

Williams et al. (1995, cited in Harrill, 2004) all found that long-term residents were more supportive of tourism development than short-term residents. In other research, gender has been found to be a more consistent predictor of residents' attitudes toward tourism development. For example, Mason and Cheyne (2000) found that women were less supportive of tourism development than men due to perceived negative impacts like increases in traffic, noise, and crime. Similar findings were also reported by Harrill and Potts (2003) in their study of Charleston, SC.

Several studies have investigated the relationship between locations/activities of tourism development and residents' attitudes, based on the hypothesis that "the closer a resident lives to concentrations of tourism activity, the more negative his or her perception will be of tourism development" (Harrill 2004, p. 253). Tyrell and Spaulding (1984) found that Rhode Island residents had less favorable attitudes toward the tourism facilities close to their homes because of trash and litter. Gursoy and Jurowski (2002, cited in Harrill, 2004) found that residents who used a nearby national recreation area frequently were more strongly opposed to tourism development than residents who visited less frequently. In addition, Harrill and Potts (2003) found that residents of a neighborhood in a tourism core of Charleston received the brunt of the negative impacts from tourism and were less supportive of tourism development than residents of other communities farther away from the core. Raymond and Brown (2007) used spatial analysis to study Victoria, Australia, residents' attitudes toward tourism development based on their proximity to the development. They found that on surveys most residents offered conditional support for tourism development regardless of how far they lived from the center of the development. However, spatial analysis identified place-specific differences in residents' opinions about what types of tourism development would be acceptable or inappropriate.

Finally, according to social exchange theory, residents' attitudes toward tourism depend largely on how many tourism dollars can be generated and kept in the community (Harrill, 2004). In addition, those who think they can benefit from tourism development are more likely to support it. Tyrell and Spaulding (1984) found that Rhode Island business owners and town officials showed stronger support for tourism development than other residents. In a study of the gambling community of Deadwood, SD, Caneday and Zeiger (1991) reported that the more money residents made in tourism-dependent jobs, the less likely they were to identify negative impacts. A study by Husbands (1989) in the Victoria Falls area of Zambia also found that white-collar workers had more positive attitudes toward tourism development than workers in the lower-tier managerial class. However, not all studies support this theory, especially if factors such as tourism-induced environmental deterioration come into play. For example, Liu et al. (1987) found that residents of Hawaii, North Wales, and Istanbul were more concerned about tourism's environmental impacts on their communities than its economic benefits.

METHODOLOGY

Findings from the literature, including the Tourism Impact Attitude Scale developed by Lankford and Howard (1994), were used to design a questionnaire to administer to Ansted residents. The questionnaire consisted of three sections: (1) perceptions of Ansted as a tourism destination or gateway community; (2) attitudes toward tourism development impacts (economic, environmental, and social); and (3) background information. Participants were asked to answer questions in Sections 1 and 2 using a 5-point Likert scale (1 = strongly disagree to 5 = strongly agree). In addition, a blank space was provided for open-ended comments about tourism in Ansted.

One hundred and sixty-one copies of the questionnaire were distributed at a community meeting, at town hall, and at the high school (in order to get the input of the younger community members) in October 2007 and during tourism planning activities in November 2007. Eighty-five questionnaires were completed and returned for a 52.8% response rate. Data were analyzed by descriptive statistics and t-tests using SPSS 11.5 for Windows.

RESULTS

Socio-demographic Information
The survey respondents consisted of an almost equal number of males (50.6%) and females (49.4%). More than half (53.6%) of the participants were over the age of 55. The most common occupation was retirement (35.3%), followed by various professions, none of which stood out above the rest. Professional occupations were the most common at 10.3%. Most of the respondents (61.4%) had a household income between $20,000 and $60,000/year (the majority of whom earned less than $40,000/year). All of the respondents had at least a high school education and 40.4% had either an undergraduate or graduate degree. Finally, more than half of the respondents (59.8%) had lived in Ansted for at least 15 years and more than a quarter had lived in the town for 35 years or more.

Perceptions of Ansted as a Tourism Destination/Gateway Community
Figure 1 presents participants' perceptions of Ansted as a tourism destination and/or a gateway community. Responses to all 14 statements concerning the town as a tourism destination and/or a gateway community were highly positive. For instance, the majority of respondents believed communities in the region should attract more visitors (91.8%). They also favored tourism development in and around Ansted (89.3%) and believed that Ansted could serve as a gateway to surrounding parks and attractions (86.6%).

T-tests indicated that there were no significant differences between males and females, between the more and less educated, or between the affluent and the less affluent in their responses to the 14 statements about Ansted as a tourism destination with the following exceptions. Females (M = 3.68) were more likely (p < 0.003) than males (M = 3.02) to believe that Ansted is already a tourism destination. Respondents who had attended college (M = 4.52) were more supportive of Ansted forming partnerships with surrounding communities (p < 0.010) than those who had less education (M = 3.92). Those with an annual income of less than $60,000 (M = 3.22) were more likely to believe that Ansted is competitive with surrounding communities in tourism development (p < 0.031) than those who made over $60,000 per year (M = 2.47).

There were, however, some significant differences between age groups (See Table 1). Respondents age 55 and above were generally more positive in their perceptions of Ansted as a tourism destination than respondents under 55. This observation was especially true in their perceptions of tourism development in and around Ansted (p < 0.000), Ansted's competitiveness with the surrounding communities in tourism development (p < 0.001), and Ansted's potential to become more of a tourism destination (p < 0.002). Despite these differences, both groups were not significantly different from each other in the other five statements: Ansted is already a tourism destination; is visited by a large number of visitors; should be in partnership with surrounding communities in tourism development; should be a political advocate for Hawks Nest State Park; and needs beautification.

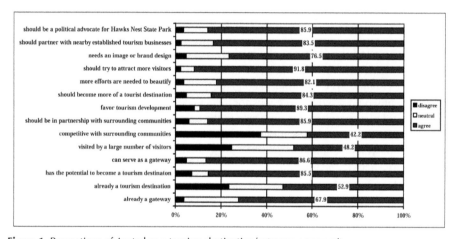

Figure 1. Perceptions of Ansted as a tourism destination/gateway community.

Table 1. Differences between age groups concerning perceptions of Ansted as a tourism destination.

	Age	Mean	Mean Difference	t	Sig. (2-tailed)
1. Ansted is already a gateway to surrounding parks/ attractions	< 55 ≥ 55	3.50 4.18	−0.68	−3.174	.002**
2. Ansted is already a tourism destination	< 55 ≥ 55	3.15 3.49	−0.34	−1.476	.144
3. Ansted has the potential to become a tourism destination	< 55 ≥ 55	4.05 4.67	−0.62	−2.984	.004**
4. Ansted can serve as a gateway to surrounding parks/ attractions	< 55 ≥ 55	4.05 4.64	−0.58	−2.945	.004*
5. Ansted is visited by a large number of visitors	< 55 ≥ 55	3.03 3.38	−0.35	−1.614	.110
6. Ansted is competitive with surrounding communities in tourism development	< 55 ≥ 55	2.50 2.41	−0.91	−3.531	.001**
7. Ansted should be in partnership with surrounding communities in tourism development	< 55 ≥ 55	4.15 4.49	−0.34	−1.567	.121
8. I favor tourism development in and around Ansted	< 55 ≥ 55	4.13 4.91	−0.78	−3.934	.000**

Table 1. (Continued)

	Age	Mean	Mean Difference	t	Sig. (2-tailed)
9. My community should become more of a tourism destination	< 55 ≥ 55	4.05 4.68	−0.63	−3.141	.002**
10. More efforts are needed to beautify my community	< 55 ≥ 55	4.13 4.48	−0.35	−1.887	.063
11. Communities in this region should try to attract more visitors	< 55 ≥ 55	4.33 4.73	−0.40	−2.635	.010**
12. Ansted needs an image or brand design for tourism development	< 55 ≥ 55	3.95 4.42	−0.47	−2.328	.022*
13. Ansted should partner with nearby established tourism businesses	< 55 ≥ 55	4.10 4.58	−0.48	−2.487	.015*
14. Ansted should be a political advocate for Hawks Nest State Park	< 55 ≥ 55	4.41 4.44	−0.03	−0.164	.870

Note: *p<.05; **p<.01.

Attitudes Toward the Impacts of Tourism Development

The respondents generally had positive attitudes towards the impacts of tourism development (Figure 2). Concerning economic impacts, 90.6% believed that tourism development would provide more jobs for local people, 87.1% felt that the tourism industry would play a major economic role in the community, and 82.4% supported the development of new tourism facilities. However, only 36.9% would support tax levies for tourism development and most of the respondents (73.8%) did not want gambling to be a tourist activity near the town.

Regarding social impacts, most of the respondents believed that tourism would produce more cultural events (89.3%) and an increase in the quality of public services (58.8%). Only 15.7% believed that crime would increase as a result of tourism. Similarly, only 27.1% thought that tourism would cause crowding problems.

The participants were equally optimistic when responding to statements about tourism's potential environmental impacts on their community. Most (87.1%) believed that long-term planning by the town and region could control the negative impacts of tourism on the environment and 60% believed tourists would contribute to conservation efforts in the region. In addition, they did not think that tourism development would lead to increased litter (61.2%) or air pollution (82.4%). Overall, 77.4% of the respondents believed that the benefits of tourism outweigh the negative consequences of tourism development. In addition, 89.3% felt that tourists are valuable.

Results of t-tests concerning perceptions of tourism development's impacts are presented in Table 2. There were no significant differences between males and females in their attitudes toward the impacts of tourism development. Moreover, education did not affect participants' responses except for one statement; those residents who had attended college (M = 4.40) were more likely than those who had not attended college (M = 4.04) to think that tourism would produce more cultural events in the community (p < 0.024). In terms of income, those with higher incomes ($60,000 or more per year, M = 1.84) were significantly less likely than those with lower incomes (M = 2.51) to believe crime would increase in the community due to tourism (p < 0.029). In addition, the affluent (M = 1.80) were also less likely to feel that there would be more litter in the community as a result of tourism (p < 0.019).

The differences between age groups, however, were again quite prevalent with those ages 55 and over being more positive in their attitudes toward tourism development than those under 55. For example, concerning economic impacts and benefits, respondents 55 and over were more likely than their under-55 counterparts to believe that: tourism in the community will play a major economic role (M = 4.58 for 55 and over and M = 4.08 for under 55, p < 0.014); the community should encourage more intensive development of tourism facilities (M = 1.60 for 55 and over and M = 2.18 for under 55, p < 0.034); and the benefits of tourism outweigh the negative consequences of tourism development (M = 4.51 for 55 and over and M = 3.76 for under 55, p < 0.001). In the case of social impacts, those over 55 (M = 4.44) believed more strongly than those under 55 (M = 4.11) that tourism would produce more cultural events for the community (p < 0.025) and that tourists are valuable (M = 4.73 for the former and M = 4.34 for the latter, p < 0.026). Regarding environmental impacts, those 55 and over more strongly agreed than those under 55 that long-term planning by the town and region can control negative impacts (M = 4.53 for the former and M = 4.10 for the latter, p < 0.023) and that tourists will contribute to conservation efforts in the region (M = 3.91 for the former and M = 3.21 for the latter, p < 0.002).

Finally, many open-ended comments were written on the surveys. The two main topics were a desire to maintain Ansted's small-town atmosphere and concerns about the negative impacts of nearby strip mining on tourism development and the environment.

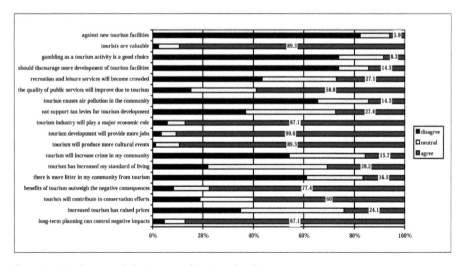

Figure 2. Attitudes toward the impacts of tourism development.

Table 2. Difference between age groups in their attitudes toward the impacts of tourism development.

	Age	Mean	Mean Difference	t	Sig. (2-tailed)
1. Long-term planning by my town and region can control the negative impacts of tourism on the environment	< 55	4.10	−0.43	−2.325	.032*
	≥ 55	4.53			
2. Increased tourism has raised prices in general	< 55	2.77	−0.02	−0.098	.922
	≥ 55	2.79			
3. Tourists will contribute to conservation efforts in the region	< 55	3.21	−0.71	−3.188	.002**
	≥ 55	3.91			
4. The benefits of tourism outweigh the negative consequences of tourism development	< 55	3.76	−0.75	−3.332	.001**
	≥ 55	4.51			
5. There is more litter in my community from tourism	< 55	2.46	0.26	1.019	.311
	≥ 55	2.20			
6. Tourism in my community has increased my standard of living	< 55	2.85	−0.24	−0.946	.347
	≥ 55	3.09			
7. Tourism will increase crime in my community	< 55	2.46	0.24	0.924	.358
	≥ 55	2.22			
8. An increase in tourism will produce more cultural events	< 55	4.11	−0.34	−2.287	.025*
	≥ 55	4.44			
9. Tourism development in my community will provide more jobs for local people	< 55	4.23	−0.32	−1.864	.066
	≥ 55	4.56			
10. The tourism industry will play a major economic role in this community	< 55	4.08	−0.50	−2.519	.014*
	≥ 55	4.58			
11. I would not support local tax levies for tourism development	< 55	2.90	0.24	0.832	.408
	≥ 55	2.66			
12. Tourism causes air pollution in the community	< 55	2.26	0.42	1.621	.109
	≥ 55	1.84			
13. The quality of public services will improve due to tourism in my community	< 55	3.46	−0.27	−1.134	.260
	≥ 55	3.73			
14. Many recreation and leisure facilities will become crowded by tourists	< 55	2.72	0.14	0.583	.561
	≥ 55	2.58			
15. The community should discourage more intensive development of tourism facilities	< 55	2.18	0.58	2.156	.034*
	≥ 55	1.60			
16. Gambling as a tourism activity is a good choice for Ansted	< 55	1.68	−0.05	−0.200	.842
	≥ 55	1.73			
17. Tourists are valuable	< 55	4.34	−0.39	−2.275	.026*
	≥ 55	4.73			
18. I am against new tourism facilities, which will attract more tourists to my community.	< 55	1.72	0.38	1.852	.068
	≥ 55	1.33			

Note: *p<.05; **p<.01

DISCUSSION AND CONCLUSION

Residents of the town of Ansted generally held positive views toward initial tourism development in their community. They were more focused on tourism's positive impacts than its negative impacts. In addition, residents' awareness of plans to develop tourism in their community will help them prevent decision-making with which they disagree. In this way, they will be able to maintain ownership over tourism development.

There was a discrepancy between the optimism of respondents age 55 and over and the less positive attitudes of those under the age of 55. This difference may be due to the low representation of respondents in the age 18–25-year-old group (3.6%) and the 26–39-year-old group (7.1%). It could also be attributed to nostalgia that the older generation feels for the town but which the younger generation may lack. Younger people also seem to feel that the town does not have much of an ability to improve and revitalize. Whatever the reasons, it is important that the younger generation, especially those aged 18–25, become more involved with town development planning. If these young people do not feel strongly about Ansted's restoration, it is unlikely that young adults will carry out any tourism planning and implementation. Perhaps a participatory model targeting the 18- to 25-year-old age group could be useful in motivating the younger generation to become more involved in tourism development planning in the community.

As mentioned previously, there is no major concern among respondents about the environmental impacts of tourism development. For example, respondents did not feel tourism would bring more litter or air pollution to the community. This result could be explained by the social exchange theory as discussed above. Similar findings were also reported in Andressen and Murphy's (1986) study of two Canadian communities, where local residents focused on the potential economic benefits of increased tourism and did not think that tourism had created social or environmental problems.

Although the respondents to the Ansted survey believe that the benefits of tourism will outweigh the negative impacts, this response does not mean that negative impacts will not occur. It is important that the community residents recognize these consequences so that they will be able to monitor and attempt to control negative environmental impacts and to plan accordingly if negative impacts are escalating. On a more positive note, the respondents did recognize the importance of long-term planning to control the potential negative environmental impacts of tourism. They also believed that tourists would contribute to environmental conservation efforts in the region.

An interesting finding from this study is that gambling was not regarded as an attractive or appropriate tourism activity. Previous studies have found that casino gambling can be an effective driver of rural economic development in the United States (Reeder and Brown 2005) and that gambling is not strongly opposed in some communities (e.g., Long 1996). This strong contrast suggests that Ansted residents hope to maintain their town's rural atmosphere.

Residents also expressed their wish to maintain their small-town atmosphere in the comments. Small towns are becoming scarce due to urban sprawl and rampant development. The acknowledgement of the value of their small town will greatly benefit the residents of Ansted. They can promote their small town as a unique destination that tourists will want to visit.

This hope was also evident in their comments about outside influences, especially strip mining for coal. If tourists want to come to a small town bordered by beautiful, green hills, they will be sorely disappointed if they come to a small town surrounded by unsightly strip mines. Therefore, the community will need to plan accordingly. Residents may need to engage in dialogue with the coal companies as well as their state representatives in order to stop strip mining or to work out some sort of compromise. If strip mining continues as planned, the community will need to develop a tourism plan that takes the strip mines into consideration. During a conversation with the researcher, one study participant suggested building a platform for tourists to view the strip mines in order to promote conservation and a grassroots movement against strip mining.

In conclusion, this survey was conducted in conjunction with a tourism planning process and its findings contribute to the understanding of how the community of Ansted, WV, perceives tourism development and its potential impacts.

KEYWORDS

- **Ansted's residents**
- **Respondents**
- **Tourism**
- **T-tests**

Permissions

Chapter 1: Tourism was originally published as "Tourism" by *U.S National Park Service*. Reprinted with permission under the Creative Commons Attribution License or equivalent.

Chapter 2: Tourism Development in Local Communities was originally published as "Community Capacity Building in Tourism Development in Local Communities" in *Journal of Sustainable Development Vol.3, No.1, 2010 at CCSE*. Reprinted with permission under the Creative Commons Attribution License or equivalent.

Chapter 3: Local Communities and Tourism Development was originally published as "Barriers to Community Leadership Toward Tourism Development in Shiraz, Iran" in *European Journal of Social Sciences – Volume 7, Number 2 (2008)* Reprinted with permission under the Creative Commons Attribution License or equivalent.

Chapter 4: Rebuilding After Catastrophe was originally published as "The Value and Effect of the Tourism Industry's Priority to Restoration and Rebuilding after Catastrophe" in *International Journal of Business and Management Vol.4, No.8, 2009 at CCSE*. Reprinted with permission under the Creative Commons Attribution License or equivalent.

Chapter 5: Tourist Preferences Study Using Conjoint Analysis was originally published as "An empirical study of tourist preferences using conjoint analysis" in *International Journal of Business Science and Applied Management, ISSN 17530296, Vol.5, No.2, 2010*. Reprinted with permission under the Creative Commons Attribution License or equivalent.

Chapter 6: Tourist Satisfaction and Destination Loyalty Intention was originally published as "The tourist experience: Exploring the relationship between tourist satisfaction and destination loyalty" in *ORIGINAL SCIENTIFIC PAPER Vol. 58 No 2/ 2010/ 111-126*. Reprinted with permission under the Creative Commons Attribution License or equivalent.

Chapter 7: Recreation, Tourism, and Rural Well-being was originally published as "Recreation, Tourism, and Rural Well-being" by *United States Department of Agriculture*. Reprinted with permission under the Creative Commons Attribution License or equivalent.

Chapter 8: Rural Tourism was originally published as "Rural Tourism: An Annotated Bibliography" by *United States Department of Agriculture*. Reprinted with permission under the Creative Commons Attribution License or equivalent.

Chapter 9: Development and Research of Rural Tourism was originally published as "The Development and Research of Rural Tourism Based on Leisure Experience" in *International Journal of Business and Management ISSN 18333850, Vol.2, Issue 6, 2009*. Reprinted with permission under the Creative Commons Attribution License or equivalent.

Chapter 10: Cultural Tourism: Gold Mine or Land Mine was originally published as "Cultural Tourism: Gold Mine or Land Mine" by *United States Department of the Interior Park Service/ Cultural Resources*. Reprinted with permission under the Creative Commons Attribution License or equivalent.

Chapter 11: Heritage Tourism was originally published as "Heritage Tourism" in *CRM, Cultural Resource Management, Vol.25, No.1, 02*. Reprinted with permission under the Creative Commons Attribution License or equivalent.

Chapter 12: Position Paper on Cultural and Heritage Tourism was originally published as "Position Paper on Cultural and Heritage Tourism" by *United States Department of Commerce*. Reprinted with permission under the Creative Commons Attribution License or equivalent.

Chapter 13: Historical Authenticity in Heritage Tourism Development was originally published as "Consideration of historical authenticity in heritage tourism planning and development" in *Wiles, Craig; Vander Stoep, Gail 2008. Consideration of historical authenticity in heritage tourism planning and development. In: LeBlanc, Cherie; Vogt, Christine, comps. Proceedings of the 2007 northeastern recreation research symposium; 2007 April 15-17; Bolton Landing, NY. Gen. Tech. Rep. NRS-P-23. Newtown Square, PA: U.S. Department of Agriculture, Forest Service, Northern Research Station: 292-298.* Reprinted with permission under the Creative Commons Attribution License or equivalent.

Chapter 14: Tourism Image Orientation Study of Tianjin was originally published as "A Study on Tourism Image Orientation of Tianjin" in *International Journal of Business and Management ISSN 18333850, Vol.1, No.6, 2009.* Reprinted with permission under the Creative Commons Attribution License or equivalent.

Chapter 15: Management Strategy for China Group Hotel was originally published as "Discuss on the Improvement of Management Strategy for China Group Hotel" in *International Journal of Business and Management ISSN 18333850, Vol.1, No.3, 2009.* Reprinted with permission under the Creative Commons Attribution License or equivalent.

Chapter 16: Education Tourism Market in China was originally published as "Education Tourism Market in China An Explorative Study in Dalian" in *International Journal of Business and Management ISSN 1833-3850 by Canadian Center of Science and Education.* Reprinted with permission under the Creative Commons Attribution License or equivalent.

Chapter 17: Traveling Patterns of Arab Tourists in Malaysian Hotels was originally published as "Travelling Pattern and Preferences of the Arab Tourists in Malaysian Hotels" in *International Journal of Business and Management ISSN 1833-3850 by Canadian Center of Science and Education.* Reprinted with permission under the Creative Commons Attribution License or equivalent.

Chapter 18: Problems in Developing Bun Festival Tourism in Hong Kong was originally published as "Cultural Sustainability and Heritage Tourism Development: Problems in Developing Bun Festival Tourism in Hong Kong" in *Journal of Sustainable Development ISSN 1913-9063 by Canadian Center of Science and Education.* Reprinted with permission under the Creative Commons Attribution License or equivalent.

Chapter 19: Tourism Development in Plateau State, Nigeria was originally published as "Resort Potentials as a Strategy for Sustainable Tourism Development in Plateau State, Nigeria" in *Journal of Sustainable Development ISSN 1913-9063 by Canadian Center of Science and Education.* Reprinted with permission under the Creative Commons Attribution License or equivalent.

Chapter 20: Recreational Valuation of a Natural Forest Park was originally published as "The recreational valuation of a natural forest park using travel cost method in Iran" in *Sohrabi Saraj B, Yachkaschi A, Oladi D, Fard Teimouri S, Latifi H (2009). The recreational valuation of a natural forest park using travel cost method in Iran. iForest 2: 85-92. [Online 2009-06-10] URL: http://www.sisef.it/iforest/contents/? Ifor0497-002.* Reprinted with permission under the Creative Commons Attribution License or equivalent.

Chapter 21: Estimating Arrival Numbers for Informal Recreation was originally published as "Estimating Arrival Numbers for Informal Recreation: A Geographical Approach and Case Study of British" in *Sustainability 2010, 2, 684-701; doi: 10.3390/su2020684.* Reprinted with permission under the Creative Commons Attribution License or equivalent.

Chapter 22: Local Residents' Attitudes Toward Tourism was originally published as "Local Residents' attitudes Toward Potential Tourism development: The Case of Ansted, West Virginia" in *Proceedings of the 2008 Northeastern Recreation Research Symposium GTR-NRS-P-42.* Reprinted with permission under the Creative Commons Attribution License or equivalent.

References

1

Bangs, R. (1992). The ethos of ecotourism. *Men's Fitness Magazine.*

Bergstrom, J. C., et al. (February 1990). Economic impacts of recreation spending on rural areas: A case study. *Economic Development Quarterly* 4(1).

Bonds, J. and Buchanan, T. Dr. (1988). *State Parks and Wyoming's Economy, Summary Statistics of the 1988 Visitor Survey.* Wyoming Recreation Commission and University of Wyoming, Laramie, WY.

Bureau of Land Management (1987). *Recreation 2000.* US. Department of the Interior, Bureau of Land Management, Washington, DC.

California Department of Commerce (March, 1988). *Regional Economic Impacts of California Travel 1985 and 1986.* Prepared by Dean Runyan Associates, California Department of Commerce, Office of Economic Research, Sacramento, CA.

California Department of Commerce (1989). *Number and Characteristics of Travelers to California in 1988.* Prepared by Shulman Research. California Department of Commerce, Office of Economic Research, Sacramento, CA.

Colorado River Outfitters Association (November, 1992). *River Use in the State of Colorado.* Buena Vista, CO.

Cooper, R. B., Sadowske, P. S., and Kantor, M. D. (1979). *Winter Recreation Visitor Study, Wisconsin.* University of Wisconsin-Extension, Recreation Resources Center, Madison, WI.

Cordell, H. K. and Bergstrom, J. C. (March 15, 1989). *Economic Effects of Rivers on Local and State Economies: National Park Service River System.* USDA Forest Service, Southeastern Forest Experiment Station, Outdoor Recreation and Wilderness Assessment Group, and University of Georgia, Department of Agricultural Economics, Athens, GA.

Crandall, K. Leones, J., and Colby, B. G. (October, 1992). *Nature-Based Tourism and the Economy of Southeastern Arizona.* University of Arizona, Department of Agricultural and Resource Economics, Tucson, AZ.

Feasey, B. (December 5, 1989). Executive Director, Yakima Greenway. Telephone communication.

Governor's Committee on the Environment (June 14, 1988). *Report of the Committee on the Environment.* New England Governors Conference, Inc.

Gray, J., Sue H., and Mistele, M. (December, 1987). *Wisconsin's Northwoods Area—A Study of Daily Visitors.* University of Wisconsin Extension, Recreation Resources Center, Madison, WI.

Hershel Sarbvin Associates (1986). *Proceedings of the Governor's Conference on the Economic Significance of Recreation in Illinois.* Office of the Governor, Springfield, IL.

Hill, P. J. Dr. and Noble, S. T. (1991). *The Economic Impact of Amateur Sports in Alaska.* University of Alaska Anchorage, Institute of Social and Economic Research, Anchorage, Alaska.

Logar, C. M. and Rose, A. Z. (August, 1984). *Economic Impacts of Whitewater Boating on the Gauley River.* Prepared for Corps of Engineers—Huntington District. West Virginia University, College of Business and Economics, and College of Mineral and Energy Resources, Morgantown, WV.

Miles, L. B. (December, 1987). *The Economic Impact of Recreational Use of the St. Croix River.* Masters Thesis. University of Maine, Department of Agriculture and Resource Economics, Orono, ME.

Mittleider, J. F. and Leitch, J. A. (October, 1984). *Economic Contribution of State Parks to the North Dakota Economy.* North Dakota Agricultural Experiment Station, North Dakota University, Fargo, ND.

Moran, C., Wilkinson, W., and Fremont, J. (1986). Literature review paper for PCAO.

Office of Planning and Research, State of California. (1978). *Economic Practioner's Manual.*

Oregon Tourism Division (March, 1994). *1992 Economic Impacts and Visitor Volume in Oregon.* Prepared by Dean Runyan Associates, Oregon Tourism Division, Economic Development Department, Portland, OR.

Phillips, J. (March 1994). Eco-tours by Kayak on the Bay. *Sunset Magazine,* Western Edition.

Povey, D., Kiellor, S., Pruett, M., and Whyte, S. (July, 1988). *Columbia River Gorge Sailboard Economics—The 1987 Season.* Prepared for: The Columbia River Ports of Cascade Locks, Skamania, Klickitat, Hood River, The Dalles; The Columbia River Commission; and the Oregon State Tourism Division. Eugene, OR: University of Oregon, Community Planning Workshop Report.

Scenic America (November/December, 1987). Fact Sheet: Sign Control and Economic Development. *Sign Control News.*

Schwecke, T., Sprehn, D., Hamilton, S., and Gray, J. (January, 1989). *A Look at Visitors on Wisconsin's Elroy-Sparta Bike Trail.* University of Wisconsin-Extension, Recreation Research Center, Madison, WI.

Stout, D. (1986). Testimony at Orlando PCAO hearing.

Swain County Board of Commissioners (April, 1982). *An Economic Impact Study of the Whitewater Resource of the Nantahala River Gorge on Swain County and the Region.* Technical assistance provided by North Carolina Department of Natural Resources and Community Development. Swain County Board of Commissioners, NC.

U.S. Department of Commerce (Revised 1986). *Tourism USA.* Prepared by the University of Missouri, Department of Recreation and Tourism, University Extension. US Department of Commerce, Travel and Tourism Administration and Office of Travel Development, Washington, DC.

U.S. Travel Data Center (1989). *1988 Domestic Travel in Review.* U.S. Travel Data Center, Washington, DC.

U.S. Travel Data Center (1990). The Economic Impact Model (TEIM)—A Brief Description of the Products Available from the Model Developed and Operated by the U.S. Travel Data Center. U.S. Travel Data Center, Washington, DC.

University of Arizona Water Resources Center (April, 1994). Heritage Funds Riparian Area. *Arizona Water Resource.* University of Arizona, Tucson, AZ.

2

Andereck, K. and Vogt, C. (2000). The relationship between residents' attitudes toward tourism and tourism development options. *Journal of Travel Research* 39(1), 27–36.

Andriotis, K. (2005). Community Groups' Perceptions of and Preferences for Tourism Development: Evidence from Crete. *Journal of Hospitality and Tourism Research* 29(1), 67–90.

Andriotis, K. and Vaughan, R. D. (2003). Urban residents' attitudes toward tourism development: The case of Crete. *Journal of Travel Research* 42, 172–185.

Ap, J. (1992). Residents' perceptions on tourism impacts. *Annals of Tourism Research* 19(4), 665–690.

Appelrouth, S. and Edles, L. D. (2007). Sociological Theory in the Contemporary Era. California State University, Pine Forge Press, Northridge.

Aref, F. and Ma'rof, R. (2008). Barriers to Community Participation toward Tourism Development in Shiraz, Iran. *Pakistan Journal of Social Sciences* 5(9), 936–940.

Aref, F. and Ma'rof, R. (2009a). Community Leaders' Characteristics and their Effort in Building Community Capacity for Tourism Development in Local Communities. *International Journal of Business and Management* 4(10).

Aref, F. and Ma'rof, R. (2009b). Community Leaders' Perceptions toward Tourism Impacts and Level of Building Community Capacity in Tourism Development. *Journal of Sustainable Development* 2(3, Nov).

Aref, F. and Ma'rof, R. (2009c). Level of Community Capacity Building for Tourism Development According to Types of Tourism

Activities. *American Journal of Scientific Research* **5**.

Aref, F., Ma'rof, R., and Sarjit, S. G. (2009d). Community Perceptions toward Economic and Environmental Impacts of Tourism on Local Communities. *Asian Social Science* **5**(7), 130–137.

Aref, F., Ma'rof, R., Zahid, E., and Sarjit, S. G. (2009e). Barriers of Tourism Industry through Community Capacity Building. *International Review of Business Research Papers* **5**(4), 399–408.

Austen, P. (2003). Community Capacity Building and Mobilization in Youth Mental Health Promotion. Retrieved September, 5, 2008, from [http://www.phac-aspc.gc.ca/mh-sm/mhp-psm/pub/community-communautaires/pdf/comm-cap-build-mobil-youth.pdf].

Balint, J. (2006). Improving community-based conservation near protected areas: The importance of development variables. *Environment Management* **38**(1), 137–148.

Beeton, S. (2006). Community development through tourism. In: Landlink Press, Australia.

Chapman, M. and Kirk, K. (2001). Lessons for Community Capacity Building: A summary of the research evidence. Retrieved October 2, 2007, from [http://www.scot-homes.gov.uk/pdfs/pubs/260.pdf].

Chaskin, R. (2001). Building community capacity: a definitional framework and case studies from a comprehensive community initiative. *Urban Affairs Review* **36**(3), 291–323.

Chen, J. S. (2000). An investigation of urban residents' loyalty to tourism. *Journal of Hospitality and Tourism Research* **24**, 5–19.

Chen, J. S. (2001). Assessing and visualizing tourism impacts from urban residents' perspectives. *Journal of Hospitality and Tourism Research* **25**, 235–250.

Clinch, R. (2004). The Community Capacity Building Impacts of the Baltimore Empowerment Zone. The Jacob France Institute, Baltimore, USA.

Cole, S. (2007). Tourism, culture and development: hopes, dreams and realities in East Indonesia. Channel View Publications, Clevedon, UK.

Cultural Heritage News Agency. (2006). Shiraz to be registered in UNESCO's city of literature. Retrieved April 1, 2008, from [http://www.chnpress.com/news/?section=2&id=6162CHN (Cultural].

Cupples, J. (2005). What is community capacity building? Retrieved March 3, 2008, from [https://www.ccwa.org.uk/v2/downloads/cms/1121303664.pdf].

Dollahite, S., Nelson, A., Frongillo, A., and Griffin, R. (2005). Building community capacity through enhanced collaboration in the farmers market nutrition program. *Agriculture and Human Values* **22**, 339–354.

Ebbesen, L. S., Heath, S., Naylor, P., and Anderson, D. (2004). Issues in Measuring Health Promotion Capacity in Canada: a multi-province perspective. *Health Promotion International* **19**(1), 85–94.

Eyler, A., Mayer, J., Rafi, R., Housemann, R., Brownson, C., and King, C. (1999). Key informant surveys as a tool to implement and evaluate physical activity interventions in the community. *Health Education Research* **14**(2), 289.

Fiona, V. (2007). Community Capacity Building—A review of the literature. Retrieved July 12, 2008, from [http://www.health.sa.gov.au/PEHS/branches/health-promotion/0711-capacity-building-review-lit.pdf].

Fisher, D. K. (2005). Characteristics of Effective Leaders in Economic Development: An Exploratory Study. Retrieved June 5, 2009, from http://www.allbusiness.com/human-resources/employee-development-leadership/1052513-1.html

George, L. S., Fulop, M., and Wickham, L. (2007). Building capacity of environmental health services at the local and national levels with the 10-essential-services framework. *Journal of Environtal Health* **70**(1), 17–20, 63.

Gibbon, M., Labonte, R., and Laverack, G. (2002). Evaluating community capacity. *Health and Social Care in the Community* **10**(6), 485–491.

Godfrey, K. and Clarke, J. (2000). The tourism development handbook: A practical approach to planning and marketing. London, Continuum.

Goodman, R., Speers, M., Mcleroy, K., Fawcett, S., Kegler, M., Parker, E., et al. (1998). Identifying and defining the dimensions of community capacity to provide a base for measurement. *Health Education and Behavior* **25**(3), 258–278.

Green, G. P., Marcouiller, D., Deller, S., Erkkila, D., and Sumathi, N. R. (1986). Local dependency, land use attitudes, and economic development: Comparisons between seasonal and permanent residents. *Rural Sociology* **61**, 427–445.

Grover, R. and Vriens, M. (2006). The handbook of marketing research: uses, misuses, and future advances: Sage Publications.

Gursoy, D. and Rutherford, D. G. (2004). Host attitudes toward tourism: An Improved Structural Model. *Annals of Tourism Research* **31**(3), 495–516.

Hackett, H. (2004). Community capacity building. Paper presented at the conference of social assistance professionals in the provincial and municipal sectors. Retrieved May 29, 2009, from [http://www.ranaprocess.com/Articles/Articles/Community%20Capacity%20Building.pdf]

Hafeznia, M. R., Eftekhari, A., and Ramazani, I. (2007). A Comparative Study on the Tourism Policies in Pre and Post Islamic Revolution of Iran, Case Study: Babolsar in the Coast of Caspian Sea. *Journal of Applied Sciences* **7**(24), 3836–3874.

Harris, A. (2001). Building the capacity for school improvement. *School Leadership and Management* **21**(3), 261–270.

Israel, D. and Beaulieu, J. (1990). Community Leadership. A. Luloff and L. Swanson (Eds.), *American rural communities*. Westview Press, San Francisco, CA.

Ivanovic, M. (2009). Cultural Tourism. USA: Juta and Company Limited.

Kayat, K. (2002). Power, social exchanges and tourism in Langkawi: Rethinking resident perceptions. *The International Journal of Tourism Research* **4**(3), 171–191.

Labonte, R., and Laverack, G. (2001a). Capacity building in health promotion, Part 1: for whom ? and for what purpose ?' *Critical Public Health* **11**(2), 111–127.

Labonte, R. and Laverack, G. (2001b). Capacity building in health promotion, part 2:whose use?

And with what measurement? *Critical Public Health* **11**(2), 129–138.

Labonte, R., Woodard, G. B., Chad, K., and Laverack, G. (2002). Community capacity building: A parallel track for health promotion programs. *Canadian Journal of Public Health* **93**(3), 181–182.

Laverack, G. (2001). An Identification and Interpretation of the Organizational Aspects of Community Empowerment. *Community Development Journal* **36**, 40–52.

Lawler, E. J. (2001). An affect theory of social exchange. *The American Journal of Sociology* **107**(2), 321–325.

Lawton, L. J. (2005). Resident perceptions of tourist attractions on the Gold Coast of Australia. *Journal of Travel Research* **44**, 188–200.

Limbert, J. W. (2004). Shiraz in the age of Hafez: the glory of a medieval Persian city. Seattle: University of Washington Press. Littrell, D. W. and Hobbs, D. (1989). "The self help approach." J. A. Christenson and J. Robinson (Eds.), Community Development in Perspective.

Luloff, E., Bridger, C., Graefe, R., Saylor, M., Martin, K., and Gitelson, R. (1994). Assessing rural tourism efforts in the United States. *Annals of Tourism Research* **21**(46–64).

Maclellan-Wright, F., Anderson, D., Barber, S., Smith, N., Cantin, B., Felix, R., et al. (2007). The development of measures of community capacity for community-based funding programs in Canada. Health Promotion International **22**(4), 299–306.

Marre, A., and Weber, B. (2007). Assessing Community Capacity in Rural America: Some Lessons from Two Rural Observatories. Corvallis: Rural Studies Program, Oregon State University.

Martin, B., McGuire, F., and Allen, L. (1998). Retirees' attitudes toward tourism: Implications for sustainable development. *Tourism Analysis* **3**, 43–51.

Mason, P. (2003). Tourism impacts, planning and management. Jordan Hill, Oxford: Butterworth–Heinemann.

Moscardo, G. (Ed.). (2008). Building community capacity for tourism development. Australia.

Moutinho, L. (Ed.). (2000). Strategic management in tourism. University of Glasgow Business School, CABI Publishing, UK.

Murphy, P. (1985). *Tourism: A Community Approach*. Methuen, New York.

Perdue, R. R., Long, P. T., and Allen, L. (1990). Resident support for tourism development. *Annals of Tourism Research* **17**(4), 586–599.

Raeburn, J., Akerman, M., Chuengsatiansup, K., Mejia, F., and Oladepo, O. (2007). Capacity building: Community capacity building and health promotion in a globalized world. *Health Promotion International* **21**(1), 84–90.

Reid, M. and Gibb, K. (2004). 'Capacity building' in the third sector and the use of independent consultants: evidence from Scotland. Paper presented at the International Society for Third Sector Research 6th International Conference, Ryerson University, Toronto, July 11–14, 2004.

Richards, G. and Hall, D. (Eds.). (2000). Tourism and sustainable community development. USA: Routledge. Rural Voices for Conservation Coalition. (2007). Building Community Capacity Issue Paper. Retrieved June 10, 2009, from [http://www.sustainablenorthwest.org/quick-links/resources/rvcc-issue-papers/Capacity%20Building%202007.pdf]

Schultz, J. (2004). Boomtown USA: The 7 keys to big success in small towns: Hemdon, VA: National Association of Industrial and Office Properties.

Seremba, F. and Moore, J. (2005). Building community capacity for healthy eating through the use of tailored resources. *Journal of the American Dietetic Association* **105**(8, Suppl. 1), 56–56.

Smyth, J. (2009). Critically engaged community capacity building and the 'community organizing' approach in disadvantaged contexts. *Critical Studies in Education* **50**(1), 9–22.

Taylor, R. (2003). Indigenous Community Capacity Building and the relationship to sound governance and leadership. Paper presented at the National Native Title Conference. Retrieved April 3, 2009, from [http://ntru.aiatsis.gov.au/conf2003/papers/russell.pdf].

Thompson, B., Lichtenstein, E., Corbett, K., Nettekoven, L., and Feng, Z. (2000). Durability of tobacco control efforts in the 22 community Intervention trial for smoking cessation (COMMIT) communities 2 years after the end of intervention. *Health Education Research* **15**(3), 353–366.

Travel Industry Association of America. (2005). Executive summaries—The historic/cultural traveller 2003 edition. Retrieved December 20, 2008, from [http://www.tia.org].

Victurine, R. (2000). Building tourism excellence at the community level: Capacity building for community-based entrepreneurs in Uganda. *Journal of Travel Research* **38**(3), 221–229.

Von Kroff, M., Wickizer, T., Maeser, J., O'Leary, P., Pearson, D., and Beery, W. (1992). Community activation and health promotion: Identification of key organizations. American *Journal of Health Promotion* **7**, 110–117.

Wickramage, K. (2006). Building the capacity for health promotion in resource poor, tsunami devastated and conflict ravaged zones. *Promotion Education* **13**(3), 208–210.

Yoon, Y., Gursoy, D., and Chen, J. (2001). Validating a tourism development theory with structural equation modelling. *Tourism Management*, **22**(4), 363–372.

3

Andereck, K. and Vogt, C. (2000). The relationship between residents' attitudes toward tourism and tourism development options. *Journal of Travel Research* **39**(1), 27–36.

Andriotis, K. (2005). Community groups' perceptions of and preferences for tourism development: Evidence from Crete. *Journal of Hospitality and Tourism Research* **29**(1), 67–90.

Andriotis, K. and Vaughan, R. D. (2003). Urban residents' attitudes toward tourism development: The case of Crete. *Journal of Travel Research* **42**, 172–185.

Ap, J. (1992). Residents' perceptions on tourism impacts. *Annals of Tourism Research* **19**(4), 665–690.

Aref, F. and Ma'rof, R. (2009). Community leaders' characteristics and their effort in building community capacity for tourism development in local communities. *International Journal of Business Management* **4**(10).

Aref, F., Ma'rof, R., and Sarjit, S. G. (2009). Community perceptions toward economic and environmental impacts of tourism on local communities. *Asian Social Science* **5**(7), 130–137.

Ary, D., Jacobs, C., and Rezavieh, A. (1996). *Introduction to Research in Education* (5 edition). Harcourt Brace College Publishers, New York.

Chaudhary, M., Kamra, K. K., Boora, S. S., Kumar, R. B., Chand, M., and Taxak, R. H. (Eds.) (2007). *Tourism Development: Impacts and Strategies*. Vedams eBooks (P) Ltd, New Delhi.

Chen, J. S. (2000). An investigation of urban residents' loyalty to tourism. *Journal of Hospitality and Tourism Research* **24**, 5–19.

Chen, J. S. (2001). Assessing and visualizing tourism impacts from urban residents' perspectives. *Journal of Hospitality and Tourism Research* **25**, 235–250.

Chon, K. S. (2000). Tourism in Southeast Asia: A new direction. Haworth Hospitality Press, New York.

Cultural Heritage News Agency (2006). Shiraz to be registered in UNESCO's city of literature. Retrieved April 1, 2008, from [http://www.chnpress.com/news/?section=2&id=6162CHN(Cultural]].

Eyler, A., Mayer, J., Rafi, R., Housemann, R., Brownson, C., and King, C. (1999). Key informant surveys as a tool to implement and evaluate physical activity interventions in the community. *Health Education Research* **14**(2), 289.

Grover, R. and Vriens, M. (2006). The handbook of marketing research: Uses, misuses, and future advances, Sage Publications.

Gursoy, D., Jurowski, C., and Uysal, M. (2002). Resident attitudes: A structural modelling approach. *Annals of Tourism Research* **29**(1), 79–105.

Gursoy, D. and Rutherford, D. G. (2004). Host attitudes toward tourism: An improved structural model. *Annals of Tourism Research* **31**(3), 495–516.

Harrill, R. (2004). Residents' attitudes toward tourism development: A literature review with implications for tourism planning. *Journal of Planning Literature* **18**(3), 251–266.

Jurowski, C., Uysal, M., and Williams, R. (1997). A theoretical analysis of host community resident reactions to tourism. *Journal of Travel Research* **36**(2), 3.

Kayat, K. (2002). Power, social exchanges and tourism in Langkawi: Rethinking resident perceptions. *The International Journal of Tourism Research* **4**(3), 171–191.

Lawler, E. J. (2001). An affect theory of social exchange. *American Journal of Sociology* **107**(2), 321–325.

Limbert, J. W. (2004). Shiraz in the age of Hafez: The glory of a medieval Persian city. University of Washington Press, Seattle.

Martin, B., McGuire, F., and Allen, L. (1998). Retirees' attitudes toward tourism: Implications for sustainable development. *Tourism Analysis* **3**, 43–51.

Mason, P. (2003). Tourism impacts, planning and management. Butterworth–Heinemann, Jordan Hill, Oxford.

Ming, G. A. and Wong, P. P. (2006). Residents' perception of tourism impacts: A case study of Homestay Operators in Dachangshan Dao, North-East China. *Tourism Geographies* **8**(3), 253–273.

Moscardo, G. (Ed.) (2008). *Building Community Capacity for Tourism Development*. Australia.

Moutinho, L. (Ed.) (2000). *Strategic Management in Tourism*. University of Glasgow Business School, CABI Publishing, UK.

Nyaupane, G. P. and Thapa, B. (2006). Perceptions of environmental impacts of tourism: A case study at ACAP, Nepal. *The International Journal of Sustainable Development and World Ecology* **13**(1), 51–61.

Perdue, R. R., Long, P. T., and Allen, L. (1990). Resident support for tourism development. *Annals of Tourism Research* **17**(4), 586–599.

Sharma, K. K. (2004). *Tourism and Socio-cultural Development*. Sarup and Sons, New Delhi.

Singh, S., Timothy, D. J., and Dowling, R. K. (Eds.) (2003). Tourism in destination communities. CABI publishing, Cambridge, USA.

Thompson, B., Lichtenstein, E., Corbett, K., Nettekoven, L., and Feng, Z. (2000). Durability of tobacco control efforts in the 22 community Intervention trial for smoking cessation (COM-MIT) communities 2 years after the end of intervention. *Health Education Research* **15**(3), 353–366.

Vogt, C. A. and Jun, S. H. (2004). *Residents' Attitudes Toward Tourist Market Segments and Tourism Development in Valdez, Alaska: A Comparison of Residents' Perceptions of Tourist Impact on the Economy and Quality of Life.* Paper presented at the Proceedings from the 2004 Northwest Recreation Research Symposium.

Von K. M., Wickizer, T., Maeser, J., O'Leary, P., Pearson, D., and Beery, W. (1992). Community activation and health promotion: Identification of key organizations. *American Journal of Health Promotion* 7, 110–117.

Wang, Y. and Pfister, R. E. (2008). Residents' attitudes toward tourism and perceived personal benefits in a rural community. *Journal of Travel Research* 47, 84–93.

Yoon, Y., Gursoy, D., and Chen, J. (2001). Validating a tourism development theory with structural equation modelling. *Tourism Management* **22**(4), 363–372.

4

Shen, H. and Chen, S. (2006). A comprehensive study of management of tourism industry crisis. *Journal of Hebei Normal University* (6).

Tourism (2008). The Preponderant Industry in After-Catastrophe Rebuilding—Sichuan Daily's Exclusive Interview on Shao Qiwei. *Sichuan Daily* 6, 5.

Zhang, G. and Wei, X. (2003). *China's Tourism Effect of "SARS" and All-sided Reviving.* Social and Scientific Document Press, (8).

Zhang, H. (2002). *Tour Economics.* Tour and Education Press, (9).

5

Boyd, S. W. and Timothy, D. J. (2001). Developing partnerships: Tools for interpretation and management of World Heritage Sites. *Tourism Recreation Research* **26**(1), 47–53.

Bramwell, B. and Lane, B. (1999). Collaboration and partnerships for sustainable tourism. *Journal of Sustainable Tourism* **7**(1), 1–5.

Butler, R. W. (1991). Tourism, environment and sustainable tourism development. *Environmental Conservation* **18**(3), 201–209.

Carroll, J. D. and Green, P. E. (1995). Psychometric methods in marketing research: Part I, conjoint analysis. *Journal of Marketing Research* **32**, 385–391.

Clow, K. E., James, K. E., Kranenburg, K. E, and Berry, C. T. (2006). The relationship of the visual element of an advertisement to service quality expectations and source credibility. *Journal of Services Marketing* **20**(6), 404–411.

D'Amore, L. J. (1992). Promoting sustainable tourism—The Canadian approach. *Tourism Management* **13**(3), 258–262.

Dewhurst, H. and Thomas, R. (2003). Encouraging sustainable business practices in a non-regulatory environment: A case study of small tourism firms in a UK National Park. *Journal of Sustainable Tourism* **11**(5), 383–406.

File, K. M. and Prince, R. A. (1992). Positive word of mouth: Customer satisfaction and buyer behaviour. *The International Journal of Bank Marketing (UK)* **10**, 25–39.

Font, X. and Ahjem, T. E. (1999). Searching for a balance in tourism development strategies. *International Journal of Contemporary Hospitality Management* **11**(2/3), 73–77.

Fox, J. (1997). *Applied Regression Analysis, Linear Models, and Related Methods.* Sage, Thousand Oaks, CA.

Gilmore, A., Carson, D., and Ascencao, M. (2007). Sustainable tourism marketing at a World Heritage site. *Journal of Strategic Marketing* **15**(May–July), 253–264.

Go, F. M., Milne, D., and Whittles, L. J. R. (1992). Communities as destinations: A marketing taxonomy for the effective implementation of the tourism action plan. *Journal of Travel Research* (Spring), 31–37.

Green, P. E. and Krieger, A. M. (1993). Conjoint analysis with product-positioning applications. In *Marketing.* J. Eliashberg and G. L.

Lilien (Eds.). North-Holland, Amsterdam, pp. 467–515.

Green, P. E. and Krieger, A. M. (1997). Using conjoint analysis to view competitive interaction through the customer's eyes. In *Wharton Dynamic Competitive Strategy*. G. S. Day, D. J. Reibstein, and R. E. Gunther (Eds.). John Wiley & Sons, New York, NY, pp. 343–66.

Green, P. E., Krieger, A. M., and Wind, Y. (2001). Thirty years of conjoint analysis: Reflections and prospects. *Interfaces* **31**(Suppl. 3), S56–73.

Green, P. E. and Rao, V. R. (1969). Non-metric Approaches to Multi Variate analysis in Marketing, working paper, Wharton School, University of Pennsylvania, U.S.A. (Original not seen), cited by P. E. Green and V. Srinivasan (1978). Conjoint Analysis in Consumer Research: Issues and Outlook. *Journal of Consumer Research* **5**(2), 103–123.

Green, P. E. and Rao, V. R. (1971). Conjoint measurement for quantifying judgemental data. *Journal of Marketing Research* **8**(3), 355–363.

Green, P. E. and Srinivasan, V. (1978). Conjoint analysis in consumer research: Issues and outlook. *Journal of Consumer Research* **5**(2), 103–123.

Green, P. E. and Srinivasan, V. (1990). Conjoint analysis in marketing: New developments with implications for research and practice. *Journal of Marketing* **54**(4), 3–19.

Haaijer, R., Kamakura, W., and Wedel, M. (2000). Response latencies in the analysis of conjoint choice experiment. *Journal of Marketing Research* **37**(3), 376–382.

Hoffman, K. and Turley, L. W. (2002). Atmospherics, service encounters and consumer decision making: An integrative perspective. *Journal of Marketing Theory and Practice* **10**(33).

Incredible India Campaign. Retrieved from [http://www.incredibleindiatourism.com/].

Kotler, P. (2000). *Marketing Management: The Millennium Edition,* 10th edition. Prentice-Hall International (UK) Limited, London.

Kuhfeld, W. F., Tobias, R. D., and Garratt, M. (1994). Efficient experimental designs with marketing applications. *Journal of Marketing Research* **31**, 545–557.

Levitt, T. (1981). Marketing intangible products and product intangibles. *Harvard Business Review* (May–June), 95–102.

Malviya, A. K. (2008). Tapping the neglected and hidden potential of tourism in Uttar Pradesh. *Presentation in Conference on Tourism in India-Challenges Ahead*, IIM-Kozhikode, May 15–17, 2008, dspace.iimk.ac.in/bitstream/2259/548/1/129-136+A.K.+Malviya.pdf

McKetcher, B. (1993). Some fundamental truth about tourism: Understanding tourism's social and environmental impacts. *Journal of Tourism Management* **1**(1), 6–16.

Morgan, N. J. and Pritchard, A. (2002). *Tourism, Promotion and Power: Creating Images, Creating Identities*. Wiley, Chichester.

Palmer, A. (2000). *The Principles of Marketing*. Oxford University Press, Oxford.

Pullman, M. E., Moore, W. L., and Wardell, D. G. (2002). A comparison of quality function deployment and conjoint analysis in new product design. *Journal of Product Innovation Management* **19**(5), 354–364.

Tourism Overview in 2005–2006. Retrieved from [http://www.economywatch.com/business-and-economy/tourism-in-2005-06.html].

Tourism Policy. Retrieved from [http://tourism.indiabizclub.com/info/tourism/scheme_of_rural_tourism/scheme_for_integrated_development_of_tourist_circuits].

Tourism Policy for Uttar Pradesh. Retrieved from [planningcommission.nic.in/plans/stateplan/upsdr/vol-2/Chap_b5.pdf].

Tourism Policy for Uttar Pradesh. Retrieved from [www.up-tourism.com/policy/new_policy.htm].

Tourism Policy and Schemes implemented by M/o Tourism, Retrieved from [http://www.tourism.gov.in/policy%5CPolicySchemes.htm].

Tourism Satellite Accounts for India, NCAER. Retrieved from [http://www.tourism.gov.in/survey/TSAI.pdf].

Tourism Statistics for India. *Annual Report on the Status of Tourism in India.* Published by Ministry of Tourism, Government of India, Retrieved from [http://tourism.gov.in/AnnualReport07-08.pdf].

UP Tourism Statistics. Retrieved from [http://www.tourism.gov.in/survey/up.pdf].

Williams, A. (2006). Tourism and hospitality marketing: Fantasy, feeling and fun. *International Journal of Contemporary Hospitality Management* **18**, 482–495.

WTO (1993). *Sustainable Tourism Development: A Guide for Local Planners.* World Tourism Planners, Madrid.

WTTC Travel and Tourism Economy Research. Retrieved from [http://www.indiandata.com/travel/travel_demand.html].

Zhou, Z. (2004). *E-Commerce and Information Technology in Hospitality and Tourism.* Thomson Delmar Learning, New York.

6

AHETA (2005). Balanço do ano turístico 2004. Perspectivas 2005. Retrieved October 15, 2005, from [http://www.aheta.pt/Bal2004.htm].

Alexandros A. and Shabbar, J. (2005). Stated preferences for two Cretan heritage attractions. *Annals of Tourism Research* **32**(4), 985–1005.

Arbuckle, J. L. and Wothke W. (1999). AMOS 4.0 user's guide. Chicago: Small Waters Corporation, USA.

Baker, D. A. and Crompton, J. L. (2000). Quality, satisfaction and behavioural intentions. *Annals of Tourism Research* **27**(3), 785–804.

Bauer, H., Mark, G., and Leach, M. (2002). Building customer relations over the internet. *Industrial Marketing Management* **31**(2), 155–163.

Beerli, A. and Martín, J. D. (2004). Tourists' characteristics and the perceived image of tourist destinations: A quantitative analysis—a case study of Lanzarote, Spain. *Tourism Management* **25**(5), 623–636.

Bentler, P. M. (1990). Comparative fit indexes in structural models. *Psychological Bulletin* **107**, 238–246.

Bentler, P. M. and Bonnet, D. G. (1980). Significance tests and goodness of fit in the analysis of covariances structures. *Psychological Bulletin* **88**, 588–606.

Bigné, J. E. and Andreu, L. (2004). Emotions in segmentation: an empirical study. *Annals of Tourism Research* **31**(3), 682–696.

Bigné, J. E., Andreu, L., and Gnoth, J. (2005). The theme park experience: An analysis of pleasure, arousal and satisfaction. *Tourism Management* **26**(6), 833–844.

Bigné, J. E., Sánchez, M. I., and Sánchez, J. (2001). Tourism image, evaluation variables and after purchase behaviour: Inter-relationship. *Tourism Management* **22**(6), 607–616.

Bitner, M. J. (1990). Evaluating service encounter: The effects of physical surroundings and employee responses. *Journal of Marketing* **54**, 69–82.

Bollen, K. A. (1988). A new incremental fit index for general structural equation models. *Paper presented at 1988 Southern Sociological Society Meetings*, Nashville, Tennessee.

Bollen, K. A. (1989). Structural equations with latent variables. New York: John Wiley and Sons, Inc. Bowen, D. (2001). Antecedents of consumer satisfaction and dis-satisfaction (CS/D) on Long-Haul inclusive tours: A reality check on theoretical considerations. *Tourism Management* **22**, 49–61.

Bramwell, B. (1998). User satisfaction and product development in urban tourism. *Tourism Management* **19**(1), 35–47.

Brodie, R. J., Coviello, N. E., Brookes, R. W., and Victoria, L. (1997). Towards a paradigm shift in marketing: an examination of current marketing practices. *Journal of Marketing Management* **13**(5), 383–406.

Cai, L. A., Wu, B., and Bai, B. (2003). Destination image and loyalty, *Cognizant Communication Corporation* **7**, 153–162.

Chen, J. and Gursoy, D. (2001). An investigation of tourists' destination loyalty and preferences, *International Journal of Contemporary Hospitality Management* **13**, 79–86.

Chon, K, (1989). Understanding recreational travellers' motivation, attitude and satisfaction. *The Tourist Review* **44**(1), 3–7.

Cossens, J. (1989). Positioning a tourist destination: Queenstown—a branded destination? Unpublished Ph.D thesis. University of Otago, New Zealand.

Court, B. and Lupton, R. (1997). Customer portfolio development: Modelling destination adopters, inactives, and rejecters. *Journal of Travel Research* **36**(1), 35–43.

Cronin, J. J. and Taylor, S. A. (1992). Measuring service quality: A re-examination and extension. *Journal of Marketing* **56**, 55–68.

Dick, A. S. and Basu, K. (1994). Customer loyalty: toward an integrated conceptual framework. *Journal of the Academy of Marketing Science* **22**(2), 99–113.

Flavian, C., Martinez, E., and Polo, Y. (2001). Loyalty to grocery stores in the Spanish market of the 1990s. *Journal of Retailing and Consumer Services* **8**, 85–93.

Fodness, D. (1994). Measuring tourist motivation. *Annals of Tourism Research* **21**(3), 555–581.

Font, A. R. (2000). Mass tourism and the demand for protected natural areas: a travel cost approach. *Journal of Environmental Economics and Management* **39**(1), 97–116.

Fornell C. (1992). A National Customer Satisfaction Barometer: The Swedish Experience. *Journal of Marketing* **56**(1), 6–21.

Francken, D. A. and Van Raaji, W. F. (1981). Satisfaction with leisure time activities. *Journal of Leisure Research* **13**(4), 337–352.

Gallarza, M. G. and Saura, I. G. (2006). Value dimensions, perceived value, satisfaction and loyalty: An investigation of university students' travel behaviour. *Tourism Management* **27**(3), 437–452.

Gallarza, M. G. and Saura, I. G. (2006). Value dimensions, perceived value, satisfaction and loyalty: An investigation of university students' travel behaviour. *Tourism Management* **27**(3), 437–452.

García, S. D. and Martinez, T. L. (2000). Análisis de ecuaciones estructurales. T. L. Martinez (Ed.), Técnicas de análisis de datos en investigación de mercados (pp. 489–557). Ediciones Pirámide, Madrid.

Hair, J., Anderson, R., Tathan, R., and Black, W. (1995). *Multivariate Data Analysis with Readings* (4th edition). Prentice-Hall, New Jersey.

Hallowell R. (1996). The Relationship of Customer Satisfaction, Customer Loyalty, Profitability: An Empirical Study. *International Journal of Service Industry Management* **7**(4), 27–42.

Homburg, C. and Giering, A. (2001). Personal Characteristics as Moderators of the Relationships between customer satisfaction and loyalty. An empirical analysis,.*Psychology and Marketing* **18**, 43–63.

Iso-Ahola, S. and Mannel, R. C. (1987). Psychological nature of leisure and tourism experience. *Annals of Tourism Research* **14**(3), 314–331.

Joreskog, K. G. (1969). A general approach to confirmatory maximum likelihood factor analysis. *Psychometrika* **34**, 183–202.

Joreskog, K. G. and Sorbom, D. (1986). LISREL VII: Analysis of linear structural relationship by maximum likelihood and least square method. Scientific Software, Mooresville.

Kotler, P. (1994). Marketing Management: Analysis, Planning, Implementation and Control (8th ed.). Prentice-Hall International, Englewood Cliffs, NJ.

Kozak, M. (2001). Repeaters' behaviour at two distinct destinations. *Annals of Tourism Research* **28**, 784–807.

Kozak, M. and Rimmington, M. (2000). Tourism satisfaction with Mallorca, Spain, as an off-season holiday destination. *Journal of Travel Research* **38**(3), 260–269.

La Barbara, P.A. and Mazursky, D. (1983). A Longitudinal Assessment of Consumer Satisfaction/Dissatisfaction: The Dynamic Aspect of the Cognitive Process. *Journal of Marketing Research* **20**, 393–404.

Mai, L. W. and Ness, M. R. (2006). A Structural Equation Model of Customer Satisfaction and Future Purchase of Mail-Order Speciality Food. *International Journal of Business Science and Applied Management* **1**(1), 1–13.

Maroco, J. (2003). Análise estatística com utilização do SPSS. Lisboa: Edições Sílabo.

Mazursky, D. (1989). Past experience and future tourism decisions. *Annals of Tourism Research* **16**, 333–344.

Meulman, J. J. and Heiser, W. J. (2004). SPSS-Categories, 13. Retrieved January 12, 2006, from [http://www.csc.um.edu.mt/courses/spss/manuals/SPSS%20Categories%2013.0.pdf].

Mittal, V. M. and Kamakura, W. (2001). Satisfaction, repurchase intent and repurchase behaviour: Investigating the moderating effect of customer characteristics. *Journal of Marketing Research* 131–142.

Mohsin, A. and Ryan, C. (2003). Backpackers in the northern territory of Australia. *The International Journal of Tourism Research* **5**(2), 113–121.

Niininen O., Szivas, E. and Riley, M. (2004). Destination loyalty and repeat behaviour: An application of optimum stimulation measurement. *International Journal of Tourism Research* **6**, 439–447.

Noe, F. P. and Uysal, M. (1997). Evaluation of outdoor recreational settings. A problem of measuring user satisfaction. *Journal of Retailing and Consumer Services* **4**(4), 223–230.

Oh, H. (1999). Service quality, customer satisfaction, and customer value: A holistic perspective. *International Journal of Hospitality Management* **18**, 67–82.

Oliver, R. L. (1980). A cognitive model of the antecedents and consequences of satisfaction decisions. *Journal of Marketing Research* **17**, 46–49.

Oliver, R. L. (1999). Whence consumer loyalty? *Journal of Marketing* **63**, 33–44.

Oppermann, M. (2000). Tourism destination loyalty. *Journal of Travel Research* **39**, 78–84.

Petrick, J., Morais, D., and Norman, W. (2001). An examination of the determinants of entertainment vacationers' intention to revisit. *Journal of Travel Research* **40**(1), 41–48.

Petrick, J. F. (2004). Are loyal visitors desired visitors? *Tourism Management* **25**(4), 463–470.

Pine, B. J., Peppers, D., and Rogers, M. (1995). Do you want to keep your customers forever? Harvard Business Review, March–April, pp. 103–14.

Ross, R. L. and Iso-Ahola, S. E. (1991). Sightseeing tourists' motivation and satisfaction. *Annals of Tourism Research* **18**(2), 226–237.

Scharma, S. (1996). Applied multivariate analysis. John Wiley and Sons, Inc, New York.

Schofield, P. (2000). Evaluating Castlefield urban heritage park from the consumer perspective: Destination attribute importance, visitor perception, and satisfaction. *Tourism Analysis* **5**(2–4), 183–189.

Schumacker, R. E. and Lomax, R. G. (1996). A beginner's guide to structural equation modeling, Lawrence Erlbaum Associates, Inc, New Jersey.

Shoemaker, S. (1989). Segmentation of the senior pleasure travel market. *Journal of Travel Research* **27**(3), 14–21.

Spreng, R. A. and Mackoy, R. D. (1996). An empirical examination of a model of perceived service quality and satisfaction. *Journal of Retailing* **72**(2), 201–214.

Steiger, J. H. (1990). Structural model evaluation and modification: An interval estimation approach. *Multivariate Behaviour Research* **25**, 173–180.

Tucker, L. R. and Lewis, C. (1973). A reliability coefficient for maximum likelihood factor analysis. *Psychometrika* **38**, 1–10.

Turnbull, P. and Wilson, D. T. (1989). Developing and protecting profitable customer relationships. *Industrial Marketing Management* **18**, 233–238.

Um, S., Chon, K., and Ro, Y. (2006). Antecedents of revisit intention. *Annals of Tourism Research* **33**(4), 1141–1158.

Um, S. and Crompton, J. (1990). Attitude determinants of tourism destination choice. *Annals of Tourism Research* **17**, 432–448.

Uysal, M., Mclellan, R., and Syrakaya, E. (1996). Modelling vacation destination decisions: A behavioural approach. *Recent Advances in Tourism Marketing Research*, 57–75.

Weaver, P. A., McCleary, K. W., Lepisto, L., and Damonte, L. T. (1994). The relationship of destination selection attributes to psychological, behavioural, and demographic variables. *Journal of Hospitality and Leisure Marketing* **2**(2), 93–109.

Woodside, A. and Lysonski, S. (1989). A General model of traveller destination choice. *Journal of Travel Research* **27**(4), 8–14.

Yoon, Y. and Uysal, M. (2005). An examination of the effects of motivation and satisfaction on destination loyalty: A structural model. *Tourism Management* **26**(1), 45–56.

Zimmer, Z., Brayley, R. E., and Searle, M. S. (1995). Whether to go and where to go: Identification of important influences on seniors' decisions to travel. *Journal of Travel Research* **33**(3), 3–10.

7

Basker, E. (September, 2002). *Education, Job Search and Migration*. Working Paper No. WP 02-16, Department of Economics, University of Missouri-Columbia.

Beale, C. L. and Johnson, K. M. (1998). The identification of recreational counties in nonmetropolitan areas of the USA. *Population Research and Policy Review* **17**, 37–53.

Brown, D. M. (2002). *Rural Tourism: An Annotated Bibliography*. Unpublished manuscript, available electronically at [www.nal.usda.gov/ric/ricpubs/rural_tourism.html].

Cook, P. J. and Mizer, K. L. (1994). *The Revised ERS County Typology*. RDRR-89, U.S. Department of Agriculture, Economic Research Service.

Deller, S. C., Tsung-Hsiu, (Sue) T., Marcouiller, D. W., and English, D. B. K. (May, 2001). The role of amenities and quality of life in rural economic growth. *American Journal of Agricultural Economics* **83**(2), 352–365.

English, D. B. K., Marcouiller, D. W., and Cordell, H. K. (2000). Tourism dependence in rural America: Estimates and effects. *Society and Natural Resources* **13**, 185–202.

Galston, W. A. and Baehler, K. J. (1995). *Rural Development in the United States: Connecting Theory, Practice, and Possibilities*. Island Press, Washington, DC.

Gibson, L. J. (1993). The potential for tourism development in nonmetropolitan areas. In *Economic Adaptation: Alternatives for Nonmetropolitan*

Areas. D. L. Barkley (Ed.). West-view Press, Boulder, CO, pp. 145–164.

Greenwood, M. J. (1975). Research on Internal Migration in the United States: A Survey. *Journal of Economic Literature* **13**(2), 397–433.

Greenwood, M. J. (1993). Migration: A review. *Regional Studies* **27**(4), 295–383.

Hakim, S. and Buck, A. J. (1989). Do casinos enhance crime? *Journal of Criminal Justice* **17**, 409–416.

John, D., Batie, S. S., and Norris, K. (1988). *A Brighter Future for Rural America?* National Governors' Association, Center for Policy Research, Washington, DC.

Johnson, K. M. and Beale, C. L. (2002). Nonmetro recreation counties: Their identification and rapid growth. *Rural America* **17**(4), 12–19.

Marcouiller, D. W. and Green, G. P. (2000). Outdoor recreation and rural development. In *National Parks and Rural Development: Practice and Policy in the United States*. G. E. Machlis and D. R. Field (Eds.). Island Press, Washington, DC, pp. 33–49.

McGranahan, D. (2000). *Boon or Bust? New Technology Manufacturing in Low-Skill Rural Areas*. U.S. Department of Agriculture, Economic Research Service, Rural Industry briefing room. Retrieved from [www.ers.usda.gov/Briefing/Industry/boonorbust/ch1.htm].

McPheters, L. R. and Stronge, W. B. (1974). Crime as an environmental externality of tourism: Miami, Florida. *Land Economics* **50**, 288–292.

Page, S. J., Brunt, P., Busby, G., and Connell, J. (2001). *Tourism: A Modern Synthesis. London*. Thomson Learning, UK.

Patton, S. G. (1985). Tourism and local economic development: Factory outlets and the reading SMSA. *Growth and Change* **16**(3), 64–73.

Reeder, R. J. and Brown, D. M. (2004). *Economic and Fiscal Conditions in Rural Recreation Counties*. Paper presented before the Southern Regional Science Association's annual meeting in New Orleans, LA, March 11–13.

Rephann, T., Dalton, M., Stair, A., and Isserman, A. (1997). Casino Gambling as an economic development strategy. *Tourism Economics* **3**, 161–183.

Rephann, T. J. (1999). Links between rural development and crime. *Papers in Regional Science* **78**, 365–386.

Rosenfeld, S. A., Berman, E. M., and Rubin, S. (1989). *Making Connections: 'After the Factories' Revisited*. Southern Growth Policies Board, Research Triangle Park, NC.

Smith, M. (1989). *Behind the Glitter: The Impact of Tourism on Rural Women in the Southeast*. Southeast Women's Employment Coalition, Lexington, KY.

8

Baldwin, F. (1994). Once upon a time, happily ever after. Appalachia 27(4), 38–44.

Bontron, J. -C. and Lasnier. N. (1997). Tourism: A potential source of rural employment. In Rural Employment: An International Perspective, R. D. Bollman and J. M. Bryden (Eds.). CAB International, New York, pp. 427–446.

Bourke, L, and Luloff, A. E. (1995). Leaders' perspectives on rural tourism: Case studies in Pennsylvania. J. Comm. Devel. Soc. 26(2), 224–39.

Brass, J. L. (Ed.) (1996). Community Tourism Assessment Handbook. Western Rural Development Center, Oregon State University, Corvallis, Oregon. Retrieved from [http://extension.usu.edu/files/publications/publication/pub__5885350.pdf 7.10 MB(.pdf)].

Brown, T. L. and Decker, D. J. (1993). Economic and Social Significance of Recreational Access for the Rural Community. Extension Service, West Virginia University, Morgantown, West Virginia, R.D. No. 759.

Burr, S. W. (1995). The Rural Action Class's Perceptions of Tourism and its Potential for Economic Development: Case Studies from Four Rural Pennsylvania Counties. General Technical Report, Report No. INT-323, pp. 82–89.

Chang, W. -H. (2000). Bibliography of Economic Impacts of Parks, Recreation and Tourism. Retrieved from [http://www.msu.edu/user/changwe4/bibli.htm/].

Culbertson, K., Turner, D., and Kolberg, J. (1993). Toward a definition of sustainable development in the Yampa Valley of Colorado. Mount. Res. Devel. 13(4), 359–369.

Dane, S., Webb, A. J., and Whiteman, J. (2001). Stories across America: Opportunities for Rural Tourism. National Trust for Historic Preservation, Washington, DC. Retrieved from [http://www.nal.usda.gov/ric/ricpubs/stories.htm].

DeLyser, D. (1995). Preservation with a grain of salt: The fantasy heritage of California's Ghost Town. Small Town 25(5), 4–13.

Frederick, M. (1992). Tourism as a Rural Economic Development Tool: An Exploration of the Literature. Bibliographies and Literature of Agriculture. Number 122. U.S. Department of Agriculture, Economic Research Service, August.

Goldman, G. and Nakazawa, A. (1994). Impact of Visitor Expenditures on Local Revenues. Western Rural Development Center, Oregon State University, Corvallis, Oregon. Report No. 145. Retrieved from [http://extension.usu.edu/files/publications/publication/pub__4238108.pdf (.pdf)].

Guglielmino, J. E. (1998). Touring to economic health. American Forests 103(4), 31.

Henning, S. A. (1996). Developing a rural tourism marketing strategy based on visitor profiles. Louisiana Agri. 39(1), 8–9.

Hilchey, D. (1993a). Agritourism in New York State: Opportunities and Challenges in Farm-based Recreation and Hospitality. Farming Alternatives Program, Department of Rural Sociology, Cornell University, Ithaca, New York.

Hilchey, D. (1993b). Leisure Trends Create Opportunities for Farmers. AgFocus, November, p. 10.

Johnson, P. and Thomas, B. (1990a). Employment in Tourism: A Review. Indus. Rel. J. 21(1), 36–48.

Johnson, P. and Thomas, B. (1990b). Measuring the local employment impact of a tourist attraction: An empirical study. Reg. Stud. 24(5), 395–403.

Jurowski, C. (1996). Tourism means more than money to the host community. Parks and Recrea. 31(9), 110–118.

King, D. A. and Stewart, W. P. (1996). Ecotourism and commodification: Protecting people and places. Biodiv. Conserv. 5(3), 293–305.

Lash, G. Y. B. (1998). Blending Development with Nature through Ecotourism. Proceedings of the Society of American Foresters, National Convention, pp. 178–182.

Lobo, R. (2001). Helpful Agricultural Tourism (Agri-tourism) Definitions. Retrieved from [http://www.sfc.ucdavis.edu/agritourism/definition.html].

Long, P. T. and Nuckolls, J. S. (1994). Organizing resources for rural tourism development: The importance of leadership, planning and technical assistance. Tour. Recrea. Res. 19(2), 19–34.

Marcouiller, D. W. (1997). Toward integrative tourism planning in Rural America. J. Planning Liter. 11(3), 337–357.

Rátz, T. and Puczkó, L. (1998). Rural tourism and sustainable development. Paper presented at the September 1998 Rural Tourism Management: Sustainable Options conference, Auchincruive, Scotland. Part 1. Retrieved from [http://www.ratztamara.com/rural.html].

Sadowske, S. and Alexander, P. (1992). Strategic initiatives in tourism and travel established for cooperative extension. Rural Devel. News 16(5), 7.

Shields, P. O. and Schibik, T. J. (1995). Regional tourism marketing: An analogical approach to organizational framework development. J. Trav. Tour. Mark. 4(1), 105–113.

Stabler, M. J. (Ed.). (1997). Tourism and Sustainability: Principles to Practice. CAB International, New York.

Stynes, D. J. (2000). Economic Impacts of Tourism. Retrieved from [http://www.msu.edu/course/prr/840/econimpact/].

Travel Industry Association of America. (2001a). Rural Tourism: Small Towns and Villages Appeal to U.S. Travelers. Retrieved from [http://www.tia.org/Press/pressrec.asp?Item=111].

Travel Industry Association of America. (2001b). Economic Impact of Travel in the U.S., 2000.

Weaver, G. (1986). Tourism Development: A Potential for Economic Growth. In New Dimensions in Rural Policy: Building Upon our Heritage, Subcommittee on Agriculture and Transportation of the Joint Economic Committee, U.S. Congress, pp. 440–444.

Weaver, G. (1991). TTRA annual conference focuses on rural tourism development issues. Rural Devel. News 15(1), 8–9.

Woods, M. D. (1992). The tourism/rural economic development link. Blueprints for Economic Development, Cooperative Extension Service. Oklahoma State University 2(2), p. 2.

9

China National Tourism Administration (1997). *The Sustainable Development Tourism–Local Traveling Plan Guide*. Traveling Education Publishing House. (9), Beijing.

Dai, B. (2005). The Comparison Research to the Development Pattern of Rural Tourism in China and Overseas, Online Retrieved from [http://www.lotour.com/zhuanti/xiangcunlvyou], pp.11–8.

Fei, X. (1986). *Peasant Life in China*. Jiangsu People's Publishing Agency, NanJing (10), 6.

Gilmore, J. H. and Pine, B. J. (2002). *The Experience Economy*. Mechanical industry publishing house, Beijing, (5).

Kaili, J. R. (2000). Freedom to be—A new sociology of leisure. Kunming: Yunnan People's Publishing Agency, 24. *International Journal of Business and Management* (December, 2007)

Leng, Z. (2005). On tourism experience in experience economy era. *The Economy and Culture of Frontier Area*. (10), 16.

Liu, D. (2006). About Rural Tourism. *Agricultural Tourism and Folk-custom Tourism*. Online Retrieved from [http://travel.people.com.cn/GB/index.html], pp. 4–18.

Liu, H. (2005). Ponder about the Connotation of Rural Tourism. X*ihua Normal University Journal* (the Version of Philosophy and Sociology) (2), 16.

Mcinttosh, R. W. and Goeldner, C. R. (1984). *Tourism*. Grid Publishing Inc. Columbus, Ohio, pp. 171–172.

Shao, Q. (2006). The director general of National Travel Agency. *The Function of Rural Tourism in Constructing New Countryside*. Online Retrieved from [http://www.cnta.gov.cn], pp. 4–30.

Xie, Y. (2005). Getting experience in tourism—The core in traveling world. *Guilin Institute of Tourism Journal* **12**(6), 5.

Yang, M. (1980). *The Evolution of Modern Countryside Society*. Juliu books company, Taipei, pp. 49–58.

Yuan, Y. (1990). *Rural sociology*. Sichuan University publishing house, Chengdu, (5), pp. 47–49.

10

Canada (1987). Department of Industry, Science and Technology. Tourism Canada. *A Profile of Canada's Attractions from a Tourism Perspective*. Ottawa, pp. 7–8.

Canada (1991). Department of Industry, Science and Technology. Tourism Canada. *Canadian Tourism Facts*. Ottawa, p. 1.

Canada (1991). Department of Industry, Science and Technology. Tourism Canada. *Enquete sur le secteur du tourisme culturel*. Ottawa, p. 21.

Canada (April, 1992). Department of the Environment. Canadian Parks Service, "An Economic Statement and Visit Profile of Atlantic Region National Parks and National Historic Sites," manuscript on file, Socio-Economic Analysis Section, Atlantic Regional Office, Halifax.

Conference Board of Canada. (March, 1993). Canadian Tourism Research Institute, "Flat Performance Forecast." *CTRI Exclusive*. Ottawa, p. 10.

Ekos Research Associates. (1988). *Culture, Multiculturalism and Tourism Pilot Projects and Related Studies: A Synthesis*. Communications Canada, Ottawa, p. iv.

Great Britain (1991). Tourist Board and Employment Department. *Tourism and the Environment: Maintaining the Balance*. London, p. 15.

MacDonald, G. (1992). Cultural Tourism in the Museum Community. In *Joining Hands for Quality Tourism*. R. S. Tabata et al., (Eds.). University of Hawaii, Honolulu, pp. 243–245.

13

Ashworth, G. J. (1994). From history to heritage: From heritage to identity: In search of concepts and models. In *Building a New Heritage: Tourism, Culture and Identity in the New Europe*. G. J. Ashworth and P. J. Larkham (Eds.). Routledge, London.

Barthel-Bouchier, D. (2001). Authenticity and identity: Theme-parking the Amanas. *International Sociology* **16**(2), 221–239.

Cohen, E. (1988). Authenticity and commoditization in tourism. *Annals of Tourism Research* **15**(3), 371–386.

Crabtree, B. and Miller, W. (1992). *Doing Qualitative Research*. Sage, London.

Garrod, B. and Fyall, A. (2000). Managing heritage tourism. *Annals of Tourism Research* **27**(3), 682–708.

Green, J. (1993). *Getting Started: How to Succeed in Heritage Tourism*. National Trust for Historic Preservation, Washington, DC.

Hargrove, C. (1999). Authenticity: The essential ingredient for heritage tourism. *Forum Journal* **13**(4), 38–46.

Hargrove, C. (2002). Heritage tourism. *Cultural Resource Management* **25**(1), 10–11.

Herbert, D. (1995). Heritage places, leisure and tourism. In *Heritage, Tourism and Society*. D. Herbert (Ed.). Mansell, New York.

Iggers, G. (1997). *Historiography in the Twentieth Century: From Scientific Objectivity to the Post-modern Challenge*. Wesleyan University Press, Middletown, CT.

Loewen, J. (1999). *Lies Across America: What our Historic Sites get Wrong*. The New Press, New York.

Lowenthal, D. (1998). *The Heritage Crusade and the Spoils of History*. Free Press, New York.

McKercher, B. and duCros, H. (2002). *Cultural Tourism: The Partnership Between Tourism and Cultural Heritage Management*. The Haworth Hospitality Press, New York.

Tilley, C. (1997). Performing culture in the global village. *Critique of Anthropology* **17**(1), 67–89.

Waitt, G. (2000). Consuming heritage: Perceived historical authenticity. *Annals of Tourism Research* **27**(4), 835–862.

Wang, N. (1999). Rethinking authenticity in tourism experience. *Annals of Tourism Research* **26**(2), 349–370.

15

Dai, B. (1993). Research on the creative development in China hotel managing company. *Journal of Guilin Institute of Tourism* 3.

Qin, Y. (2004). Discuss on several mistaken fields in the China hotel group development process. *Tourism Tribune* 2.

Xu, Q. and Li, X. (2006). Analysis on the reasons of hotel group growing based on RBT. *Tourism Tribune* 3.

Yu, C. (2005). Research on hotel enterprise's growing model. *Journal of Shandong University*.

Zou, T. (1993). Group strategy of China hotel enterprise: Development model and policy guidance. *Tourism Tribune* 3.

16

Dong, N. (2004). A preliminary analysis of education tourism market. *Liaoning Economy* (10), 12–15.

Guo, Y. (2000). *Vocation Economy.* Guangzhou Economics Press, Guangzhou, Chapter 1.

Li, T. (2006). *Introduction to Tourism* (Revised Edition) Higher Education Press, [M].Beijing, Chapter 4.

Wang, B. and Zhao, R. (2002). A research into traveling behavior of Xi'an residents. *Human Geography* (5), 21–24.

Wang, L. (June 16, 2005) Campus touring heat. *Beijing Morning* (10).

Wen, Q. (2005) Advice for developing education tourism. *Journal of Huaihua Normal University* (3), 25–29.

Yuan, Y. (November 10, 2003). Analysis of Japanese Education Tour to China. *Chinese Tourism Post.*

17

Basala, L. S. and Klenosky, D. B. (2001). Travel style preferences for visiting a novel destination: A conjoint investigation across the novelty familiarity continuum. *Journal of Travel Research* **40**, 172–182.

Cavana, B. and Dalahaye, B. (2001). *Applied Business Research: Qualitative and Quantitative Methods.* John Wiley, Brisbane.

Crompton, J. L. (1979). Motivation of pleasure vacation. *Annals of Tourism Research* **6**(4), 408–424.

Din, K. H. (1989). Islam and tourism—Patterns, issues, and options. *Annals of Tourism Research* **16**, 542–563.

Graburn, N. H. (1977). Tourism: The sacred journey in host and guests. In *The Anthropology of Tourism.* V. Smith (Ed.). University of Pennsylvania Press, Philadelphia, pp. 17–31.

Hamarneh, A. A. and Steiner, C. (2004). *Rethinking the Strategies of Tourism Development in The Arab World After September 11, 2001.* Online Retrieved from [http://www.islamictourism.com], (Accessed on June, 2005).

Houellebecq, M. (2001). Platform. *Original French title: Plateforme.* Flammarion, Paris, pp. 306–321.

Malaysia Hotel Association. (2004). Malaysian Association of Hotels: Annual Report.

New Straits Time, Malaysia. (March 8, 2007). *Malaysia an Ideal Tourist's Destination.*

Pearce, P. L. and Caltabiano, M. L. (1983). Inferring travel motivation from travellers' experience. *Journal of Travel Research* **22**(Fall), 16–20.

Polunin, I. (1989). Japanese travel boom. *Tourism Management* **10**(1), 4–8.

Ritter, W. (1989). On desert and beaches: Recreational tourism in the Muslim world. *Tourism Recreation Research* **14**(2), 3–10.

Tourism Malaysia. (2003). Annual report on profile of tourists by selected market. *Planning and Research Division.*

Tourism Malaysia. (2004). Annual report on profile of tourists by selected market. *Planning and Research Division.*

Tourism Malaysia. (2006). Annual report on profile of tourists by selected market. *Planning and Research Division.*

Yuan, S. and Mcdonald, C. (1990). Motivational determinants of international pleasure time. *Journal of Travel Research* **4**(Fall), 42–44.

18

Anon (2005). Wenhua buyinggai bei geli baoshan qike qiangdangao (Culture should not be severed from the festival; bun towers should not be replaced by cake towers). May 10.

Anon (2006). Changzhou lao shifu tan houji wuren piaoshi tongnan tongnu nanzhou. (Old master of floating children performance in Cheung Chau laments the lack of a heir and difficulty of finding kids to perform). *Takungpao*, May 4.

Anon (2007a). Taiping Qingjiao ping'anbao 4 ri zhuan 10 wan (Selling Taiping Qingjiao peace buns and making a hundred thousand dollar in four days). *Easyfinder*, May 16.

Anon (2007b). 'Ping'an' shiwu remai shengyi'e baiwan. ('Pingan' accessories sell well with a million dollars of revenue). *Hong Kong Daily News*, May 25.

Anon (2008a). Ping'anbao remai jingpin shouhuanying (Peace buns sell and souvenirs greatly welcomed). *Hong Kong Daily News*, May 13.

Anon (2008b). Ping'anbao jingpin guanming Zhang Baochai (A peace bun-themed souvenir named after Cheung Bochai). *Singtao Daily*, May 11.

Broadcasting Unit of RTHK. (2007). Wutu Wuqing, Vol 3: Changjiao Changyou (My land and my love, volume 3: Jiao ritual lives on in Cheung Chau). *Radio and Television Hong Kong*. August 2.

Bryman, Alan. (2004). *The Disneyization of Society*. Sage Publishers.

Chan, B. (2008). You chang baoshan dao chang 'jiao' shan: luyou fazhan dui changzhou dajiao chuantong de yiyi yu defang chongquan (From bun scramble to plastic bun scramble: The meaning for tourism development to Cheung Chau's tradition and local empowerment). Undergraduate Thesis, Hong Kong Baptist University.

Chiu, Y. M. and Tang, K. P. (2005). Ping'anbao vs sugubao quwenhua de lüyou wenhua tuiguang zaidihua de linghuo kuaguo jingying (Peace buns versus vegetarian mushroom burgers: De-cultured cultural tourism marleting and localized, flexible cross-national management). *Mingpao Daily*, May 30.

Choi, C. C. (2002) Zuqun ningjü de qianghua: Cheung Chau Jiaohui. (Reinforcement of clan integration: Cheung Chau Island's Dajiao ritual). In *Zhushen Jianianhua: Xianggang Zongjiao Yanjiu* (Carnival of the gods: Studies of Hong Kong religions). C. H. Chan (Ed.). Oxford University Press, Hong Kong.

Choi, C. C. (2007). Xisu bianbuting (Tradition is ever-evolving). *Mingpao Daily*, Jul 27.

Cole, S. (2007). Beyond authenticity and commodification. *Annals of Tourism Research* **34**(4), 943–960.

Cultural Studies@Lingnan 8 (Nov) Online Retrieved from [http://www.ln.edu.hk/mcsln/8th_issue/feature_03.shtml], (Jun 20, 2008).

Du Cros, H. (2001). A new model to assist in planning for sustainable cultural heritage tourism. *The International Journal of Tourism Research* **3**(2), 165–170.

Editorial. (2005). Don't spoil festival with year-round bun scramble. *South China Morning Post*, May 14.

EFat, C. H. (2008). Taiping qingjiao chanpin sharu shiqu qiangke (Taiping Qingjiao products into encroaching on the city's market). *FACE Weekly*, May 7.

Fung, M. Y. (2007). Zhenjiabao zhi mi (The puzzle of real versus fake buns). *Apple Daily*, May 23.

Hampton, M. P. (2005). Heritage, local communities and economic development. *Annals of Tourism Research* **32**(3), 735–759.

Hao, J. (2009). Xintui pingan qizibing ji xi nianqingke (New promotion of qizi biscuits to attract youthful customers). *Wenweipo*, Apr 12.

Harrison, D. (Ed.) (2001). *Tourism and the Less Developed World: Issues and Case Studies*. CABI Publishers, Oxon; New York.

Hui, P. (2007). Plastic buns strip festival of heritage, says baker. *South China Morning Post*, February 15.

Hui, S. H. (2006). Taiping qingjiao de zaiyanjiu (Re-investigating Taiping Qingjiao). In-Media Hong Kong. Online Retrieved from [http://www.inmediahk.net/public/article?item_id=117408&group_id=122], (Jun 20, 2008).

Ji, B. (2008). Zhongshan guancha renwu diaocha jianshe wenhua mingcheng renwu zhuanfang xilie zhi er. (Zhongshan observation; people and investigation: interviews of figures who contributed to the construction of great cultural cities, interview 2) *Nanfang Daily*, Jun 26.

Kwan, Y. Y. (2008). Qiangbao tuibian huanlai shangji yu… (Bun Scramble transformed into business opportunities and…). *Mingpao Daily*, May 8.

Lee, S. M. (2007). Qiang 'jiaobao' tan wenhua chengchuan (A discussion of cultural inheritance from the perspective of 'plastic bun' scramble). *Hong Kong Economic Journal*, May 23.

Leung, P. S. (2007). Chuantong zaizao: 'Changzhou Taiping Qingjiao' yu 'Zhonghuan Miaohui' (Remaking tradition: Cheung Chau's Taiping Qingjiao and The Central's Temple fair).

Ng, C. Y. (2008). Shengyi wangguo xinnian shanghu xiaohuo baiwan. (Better business than the Chinese New Years; businesses sold more than a million dollar worth of goods). *Singtao Daily*, May 13.

Oviedo-Garcia, M. A., Castellanos-Verdugo, M., and Martin-Ruiz, D. (2008). Gaining residents' support for tourism and planning. *International Journal of Tourism Research* **10**(2), 95–109.

Ritchie, B. W. and Inkari, M. (2006). Host community attitudes toward tourism and cultural tourism development: The case of the Lewes District, southern England. *International Journal of Tourism Research* **8**(1), 27–44.

Sofield, T. H. B. and Sivan, A. (2003). From cultural festival to international sport: The Hong Kong Dragon Boat Races. *Journal of Sport Tourism* **8**(1), 9–12.

Throsby, D. (2001). *Economics and Culture.* Cambridge University Press, Cambridge.

Throsby, D. (2007). Tourism, heritage and cultural sustainability: Three golden rules. In *Cultural Heritage, Local Resources and Sustainable Tourism*. L. F. Girard and P. Nijkamp (Eds.). Routledge.

Wu, K. W. (2007). Zhengbao dananhai chenggong kao zou xiaxi (Bun bakery boy relying on business niche to gain success). *Mingpao Daily*, Jun 22.

Yeung, Y. T. and Chik, W. H. (2008). Dafa ping'anbao cai shengyi jinsheng sancheng 4wan ren yongwang xiaofei Changzhou wangbao (Getting rich from peace buns; business went up 30 percent; 40 thousand people go visit Cheung Chau Island for consumption). *Hong Kong Commercial Daily*, May 13.

19

Aniah, E. J. (2005). Tourism Development in Cross River State, Nigeria: A Compendium of Tourist Sites and Potential Tourism Areas. *Calabar Journal of Liberal Studies, (CAJOLIS)* **8**(2), 57–78.

Aniah, E. J. and Iwara, E. E. (2005). Tourism Development in Cross River State, Nigeria: A compendum of tourist sites and potential tourism areas. *Calabar Journal of Liberal Studies* **8**(2), 51–78.

Aniah, E. J. and Iwara, E. E. (2005). An Exposition and Analysis of Tourist Sites in Nigeria. *Calabar Journal of Literary Studies* **1**, 139–157.

Aniah, E. J., Iwara, E. E., and Edu, E. (2007). Tinapa Tourism and Business Resort, a model for the socio-economic development of Cross River State: Constraint and Temporal Perspectives. *Tropical Focus* **3**, 131.

Burkart, A. J. and Medlile, S. (1981). Tourism: Post, present and future Heinemann, London, pp. 45–47.

Cooper, C. (1992). *Tourism: Principle and Practice,* Pitman publishing, London.

Davidson, 12 (1993). Tourism, Pitman Publishing, London: A Division of London Longman Group UKS Ltd. Dowling, R. K. (2003). Tourism in destruction communities, CABI Publishing, Oxford, English and Cambridge, USA.

Ejom, F. (2004, January), Editorial special edition on project Tinapa. *Mofinews* **3**(4), 15–21.

Falade, O. (2001). Economic implication of developing tourism Nigeria is the three tier Government of Nigeria. In D. Aremu, (Ed.). Cultural and eco-tourism development in Nigeria: The role of three tiers government and the private sector (pp.18–21). Hope Publishers, Ibadan.

Forster, E. B. (2004). DLS 20 billion Dubai land amusement. Retrieved on August 20, 2005, from [http://www.ameinfor.com], E. Gideon, (Ed.) (1994). An introduction to regional planning. Hutchinson, London.

Glali, B. E. (2004). Positive impact of tourism. Retrieved on August 20, 2005, from [http://www.gavegherstravels.com]

Goodwin, H. (2002). The tourism industry and poverty reduction: A business primary. Pro-poor tourism brief No.2 URL [http://www. Proportionism. Org. uk/final % 20 business 20 brief. Pdf]

Grolier, M. I. (1978). Tourism. *American encyclopedia* **19**, 877–879.

Hall, C. (2003). Politics and Place: An analysis of Power in Tourism Communities, Oxford, English 99–114.

Hall, C. M. (1999). Rethinking collaboration and partnership: A public policy perspective. *Journal of Sustainable Tourism* **7**(3), 274–289.

Hutsman, W. (1995). Recognizing patterns of leisure constraints. *Journal of Leisure Research*, 335.

Jumbo, C. (1983, August 30). Public-private partnership. *Daily Time* pp. 8–9.

Kessei, F. (1994). The role of tourism in South Africa. (White Paper on the Development and Promotion of Tourism in South Africa). Retrieved on August 20, 2005, from [http://www. admini.com.html].

Kigoth, W. (2000). Sustainable tourism: A regional perspective. *Tourism Management* **18**, 433–440.

Leonard, J. L. (2005). The future of tourism: An introductory forum. Spectrum Press, Aba.

Mason, P. J. L. (2005). Tourism, Environment and development. Manor Park Press, East Bourn.

Money, R. (2001). Popular Participation, employment and the fulfillment of basic needs. *International Labour Review* **118**(1), 27–38.

Mosely, D. (1974). Growth centres in spatial planning. Pergamon Press, London.

Potter, D. (2006). Enhancing community involvement in tourism development issues and challenges, international institute for the environment and development (UED), London, English.

Prentice, R. (2007). Strategic management for tourism communities: Bridging the gaps. *Tourism Management* **28**(3), 940–946.

Richard, G. and Hall, D. (2003). Tourism and sustainable Community Development, Routledge, London, UK.

Rilley, M. L. (2002). Tourism Employment: Analysis and Planning. Channel view, Clevedon.

Robinson, H. (1979). *A Geography of Tourism. Macdonald and Evans especially Ecotourism.* Paper presented at the tourism awareness seminar held at State Library Complex, Calabar.

Scheyvens, R. (2000). Tourism for development: Empowering Communities, Pearson Education Limited, Harlow, England.

Swarbrooke, J. (1999). *Sustainable Tourism Management.* CAB Publishing, Oxford, England.

United Nation World Tourism Organization (2004). United Nation World Tourism Organization, National and Regional Tourism Planning. Methodologies and Case Studies. UNWTO, Madrid, Spain.

United Nation World Tourism Organization (2005). United National Tourism Organization, Market, Tourism more sustainable. A guide for policy makers, UNWTO, Madrid, Spain.

20

Adamowicz, W. (1994). Habit formation and variety seeking in a discrete choice model of recreation demand. *Journal of Agricultural and Resource Economics* **19**(1), 1931.

Adamowicz, W., Louviere, J., and Williams, M. (1994). Combining revealed and stated preference methods for valuing environmental amenities. *Journal of Environmental Economics and Management* **26**, 271292. doi:10.1006/jeem.1994.1017.

Arbab, H. (2003). *Environmental and natural resources economics*. Nei Publications, p. 73.

Bell, F. W. and Leeworthy, V. R. (1990). Recreational demand by tourists for saltwater beach days. *Journal of Environmental Economics and Management* **18**(3), 189205. doi:10.1016/0095-0696(90)90001-F.

Brown, G. and Mendelsohn, R. (1984). The hedonic travel cost method. *The Review of Economics and Statistics* **66**, 427433. doi:10.2307/1924998.

Caulkins, P., Bishop, R. C., and Bouwes, N. W. (1986). The travel cost model for lake recreation: A comparison of two methods for incorporating site quality and substitution effects. *American Agriculture Economics Association* 291297.

Clawson, M. (1959). Methods of measuring the demand for and value of outdoor recreation. *Resources for the Future*, Reprint Number 10. Brookings Institutions, Washington, DC, USA.

Clawson, M. and Knetsch, J. L. (1966). *Economics of outdoor recreation*. The Johns Hopkins Press, Baltimore, ML, USA.

Common, M., Sen, A., and Selden, T. (1999). The travel cost method. *Australian journal of Agricultural and Resource Economics* **43**(4), 457477. doi:10.1111/1467-8489.00090.

Cooper, J. C. (2000). Nonparametric and semi-nonparametric recreational demand analysis. *American Journal of Agricultural Economics* **82**(2), 451462. doi:10.1111/0002-9092.00038.

Dixon, J. A. and Sherman, P. B. (1991). Economics of protected areas. *Ambio* **20**, 6874.

Englin, J. and Mendelsohn, R. (1991). A hedonic travel cost analysis for valuation of multiple components of site quality: The recreation value of forest management. *Journal of Environmental Economics and Management* **21**(3), 275290. doi:10.1016/0095-0696(91)90031-D.

Fix, P. and Loomis, J. (1998). Comparing the economic value of mountain biking estimated using revealed. *Journal of Environmental Planning and Management* **41**(2), 227236. doi:10.1080/09640569811731.

Fletcher, J. J., Adamowicz, W., and Graham-Tomasi, T. (1990). The travel cost model of recreation demand: Theoretical and empirical issues. *Leisure Sciences* **12**, 119147.

Freeman, A. M. (1993). The measurement of environmental and resource values: Theory and methods. *Resources for the Future*. Washington, DC, USA.

Garrod, G. and Willis, K. (1992). The amenity value of woodland in Great Britain: A comparison of economic estimates. *Environmental and Resource Economics* **2**(4), 415434. doi:10.1007/BF00304970.

Gossling, S. (1999). Ecotourism: A means to safeguard biodiversity and ecosystem functions. *Ecological Economics* **29**, 303320. doi:10.1016/S0921-8009(99)00012-9.

Hanley, N. (1989). Valuing rural recreatin benefits. *Journal of Agricultural Economics* **40**(3), 361374. doi:10.1111/j.1477-9552.1989.tb01117.x.

Hanley, N., Wright, R. E., and Adamovicz, V. (1998). Using choice experiments to value the environment. *Environmental and Resource Economics* **11**(3–4), 413428. doi:10.1023/A:1008287310583.

Hotelling, H. (1947). The economics of exhaustible resources. *Journal of Political Economy* **39**, 137175. doi: 10.1086/254195.

Kavianpour, K. and Esmaeili, A. (2002). Recreational-economical evaluation of Si Sangan forest park. *Pajouhesh and Sazandegi* **55**, 9295.

Krutilla, J. V. and Fisher, A. C. (1975). *The Economics of Natural Environments: Studies in Valuation of Commodity and Amenity Resources*. The Johns Hopkins University Press for Resources for the Future, Baltimore, ML, USA.

Majnounian, H. (1977). *Economic evaluation of Khazaneh forest park*. University of Tehran Press, Tehran, Iran, p. 105.

Mankhaus, S. and Lober, D. J. (1996). International ecotourism and the valuation of tropical rainforests in Costa Rica. *Journal of Environmental Management* **47**, 1–10. doi:10.1006/jema.1996.0031.

Mugambi, D., Mugendi, D., Wambugu, A., and Mburu, J. (2006). Estimating recreational benefits of Kakamega forest in Kenya using the travel cost method. In *Proceedings of the Symposium: "Prosperity and Poverty in a Globalised World-Challenges for Agricultural Research"*. Tropentag, Bonn, Germany.

Offenbach, L. A. and Goodwin, B. K. (1994). A travel-cost analysis of the demand for hunting trips in Kansas. *Review of Agricultural Economics* **16**(1), 5561. doi: 10.2307/1349520.

Oladi, D. J. (2005). *An Introduction to Ecotourism (translation)*. University of Mazandaran Press, Mazandaran, Iran, p. 384.

Rosenberger, R. (1999). The value of ranch open space to tourists. *Growth and change* **30**(3), 6673.

Shrestha, R. K., Stein, T. V., and Clark, J. (2007). Valuing nature-based recreation in public natural areas of the Apalachicola River region, Florida. *Journal of Environmental Management* (in press). doi: 10.1016/j.jenvman.2006.11.014.

Willis, K. G. (1991). The recreational value of the forestry commission estate in Great Britain: A Clawson-Snetsch travel cost analysis. *Scottish Journal of Political Economy* **38**(1), 5875. doi:10.1111/j.1467-9485.1991.tb00301.x.

Wood, M. E. (2002). *Ecotourism: Principles, Practices, and Policies for Sustainability*. United Nations Environmental Program, Tour Mirabeau, France and the International ecotourism society, Burlington, VA, USA.

Wunder, S. (2000). Ecotourism and economic incentives—An empirical approach. *Ecological Economics* **32**, 465479. doi:10.1016/S0921-8009(99)00119-6.

Yachkaschi, A. (1975). *An Introduction to the Iranian National and Forest Parks*. University of Tehran Press, Tehran, Iran, p. 135.

Zobeiri, M. (2000). *Forest measurement*. University of Tehran Press, Tehran, Iran, p. 401.

21

2005 England Leisure Visits Survey (2007). Natural England: Sheffield, UK, 2007.

Bateman, I. J., Day, B. H., Georgiou, S, and Lake, I. (2006). The aggregation of environmental benefit values: Welfare measures, distance decay and total WTP. *Ecological Economics* **60**, 450460.

Bateman, I. J., Garrod, G. D., Brainard, J. S., and Lovett, A. (1996). A. Measurement, valuation and estimation issues in the travel cost method: A geographical information systems approach. *Journal of Agricultural Economics* **47**(2), 191205.

Bateman, I. J., Lovett, A. A., and Brainard, J. S. (1999). Developing a methodology for benefit transfers using geographical information systems: Modelling demand for woodland recreation. *Regional Studies* **33**, 191205.

Bateman, I. J., Lovett, A. A., and Brainard, J. S. (2003). *Applied Environmental Economics: A GIS Approach to Cost-Benefit Analysis*. Cambridge University Press, Cambridge, UK.

Brainard, J. S., Lovett, A. A., and Bateman, I. A. (1997). Using isochrone surfaces in travel-cost models. *Journal of Transport Geography* **5**, 117126.

Brouwer, R. (2000). Environmental value transfer: State of the art and future prospects. *Ecological Economics* **32**, 137152.

Cesario, F. J. (1976). Value of time in recreation benefit studies. *Land Economics* **52**, 3241.

Champ, P. A., Boyle, K., and Brown, T. C. (2003). *The Economics of Non-Market Goods and Services*, Volume 3. A Primer on Non-Market, Kluwer Academic Press, Dordrecht, The Netherlands.

Clawson, M. and Knetsch, J. L. (1966). *Economics of Outdoor Recreation*. Johns Hopkins Press, Baltimore, MD, USA.

Environmental Value Transfer: Issues and Methods (2007). S. Navrud and R. Ready (Eds.). Springer, Dordrecht, The Netherlands.

Forestry Facts and Figures (2009). The Forestry Commission. Edinburgh, UK.

Hotelling, H. (1949). *An Economic Study of the Monetary Evaluation of Recreation in the National Parks*. National Park Service, Washington, DC, USA.

Ironmonger, J. (1992). *The Good Zoo Guide*. Harper Collins Publishers, London, UK.

Lovett, A. A and Flowerdew, R. (1989). Analysis of count data using Poisson Regression. Professional Geographer **41**, 190198.

Mackie, P. J., Fowkes, A. S., Wardman, M., Whelan, G., Nellthorp, J., and Bates, J. (2003). *Value of Travel Time Savings in the UK.* Institute for Transport Studies, University of Leeds, Leeds, UK.

Mäler, K. G. (1974). *Environmental Economics: A Theoretical Inquiry.* Johns Hopkins University Press, Baltimore, MD, USA.

Moeltner, K., Boyle, K. J., and Paterson, R. W. (2007). Meta-analysis and benefit transfer for resource valuation—Addressing classical challenges with Bayesian modeling. *Journal of Environmental Economics and Management* **53**, 250269.

Muthke, T. and Holm-Mueller, K. (2004). National and international benefit transfer testing with a rigorous test procedure. Environ. *Resource Economics* **29**, 323336.

Newsome, D., Moore, S. A., and Dowling, R. K. (2004). *Natural Area Tourism: Ecology, Impacts and Management.* Channel View Publications, Clevedon, UK.

Olney, P. J. S. and Fisken, F. A. (1998). *International Zoo Yearbook, Volume 36.* The Zoological Society of London, London, UK.

Rasbash, J., Steele, F., Browne, W. J., and Goldstein, H. (2009). *A User's Guide to MLwiN, v2.10.* Centre for Multilevel Modelling, University of Bristol, Bristol, UK.

Regional Trends (1998). *Office for National Statistics.* London, UK.

Scarpa, R., Hutchinson, W. G., Chilton, S. M., and Buongiorno, J. (2007). Benefit value transfers conditional on site attributes: Some evidence of reliability from forest recreation in Ireland. In *Environmental Value Transfer: Issues and Methods, the Economics of Non-Market Goods and Services.* S. Navrud and R. Ready (Eds.). Springer, Dordrecht, The Netherlands, pp. 170205.

Stedman, R. C. (2003). Is it really just a social construction? The contribution of the physical environment to sense of place. *Society and Natural Resources* **16**, 671685.

22

Allen, L. R., Hafer, H. R., Long, P. T., and Perdue, R. R. (1993). Rural residents' attitudes toward recreation and tourism development. *Journal of Travel Research* **31**(4), 27–33.

Allen, L. R., Long, P. T., Perdue, R. R., and Kieselbach, S. (1988). The impact of tourism development on residents' perceptions of community life. *Journal of Travel Research* **26**, 16–21.

Andressen, B., and Murphy, P. E. (1986). Tourism development in Canadian travel corridors: Two surveys of resident attitudes. *World Leisure and Recreation* **28**(5), 17–22.

Ansted Blueprint Community. (2007). Ansted: A community profile of current conditions and capacity. Retrieved December 2, 2007 from [http://www.blueprintcommunities.com/wv/locations/communityprofiles/Ansted%20Community%20Profile.pdf.]

Campbell, L. M. (1999). Ecotourism in rural developing communities. *Annals of Tourism Research* **26**(3), 534–553.

Caneday, L. and Zeiger, J. (1991). The social, economic, and environmental costs of tourism to a gambling community as perceived by its residents. *Journal of Travel Research* **30**(2), 45–49.

Girard, T. C. and Gartner, W. C. (1993). Second home second view: Host community perceptions. *Annals of Tourism Research* **20**(4), 685–700.

Harrill, R. (2004). Residents' attitudes toward tourism development: A literature review with implications for tourism planning. *Journal of Planning Literature* **18**(3), 251–266.

Harrill, R. and Potts, T. D. (2003). Tourism planning in historic districts: Attitudes toward tourism development in Charleston. *Journal of the American Planning Association* **69**(3), 233–244.

Husbands, W. (1989). Social status and perception of tourism in Zambia. *Annals of Tourism Research* **16**(2), 237–253.

Lankford, S. V. and Howard, D. R. (1994). Developing a tourism impact attitude scale. *Annals of Tourism Research* **21**(1), 121–139.

Liu, J. C., Sheldon, P. J., and Var, T. (1987). Resident perception of the environmental impacts of tourism. *Annals of Tourism Research* **14**(1), 17–34.

Long, P. T. (1996). Early impacts of limited stakes casino gambling on rural community life. *Tourism Management* **17**(5), 341–353.

Mason, P. and Cheyne, J. (2000). Residents' attitudes to proposed tourism development. *Annals of Tourism Research* **27**(2), 391–411.

McCool, S. F. and Martin, S. R. (1994). Community attachment and attitudes toward tourism development. *Journal of Travel Research* **32**(2), 29–34.

Mitchell, R. E. and Reid, D. G. (2000). Community integration: Island tourism in Peru. *Annals of Tourism Research* **28**(1), 113–139.

Raymond, B. and Brown, C. (2007). A spatial method for assessing resident and visitor attitudes towards tourism growth and development. *Journal of Sustainable Tourism* **15**(5), 520–540.

Reeder, R. J. and Brown, D. M. (2005). Recreation, tourism, and rural well-being. United States Department of Agriculture, Economic Research Service, Economic Research Report Number 7.

Simmons, D. G. (1994). Community participation in tourism planning. *Tourism Management* **15** (2), 98–108.

Tyrell, T. J. and Spaulding, I. A. (1984). A survey of attitudes toward tourism growth in Rhode Island. *Hospitality Education and Research Journal* **8**(2), 22–33.

U.S. Department of Commerce, U.S. Census Bureau. (2000).

.West Virginia Department of Health and Human Resources. (2007). A Healthier Future for West Virginia—Healthy People 2010. Retrieved November 1, 2007 from [http://www.wvdhhr.org/bph/hp2010/objective/1.htm]

Index

For Product Safety Concerns and Information please contact our EU
representative GPSR@taylorandfrancis.com
Taylor & Francis Verlag GmbH, Kaufingerstraße 24, 80331 München, Germany